POPULOUS PLACES

For my mother and father who worked so hard to achieve their dream, a home in the suburbs – the home where I grew up and was happy.

'It's an excess of virtue that has produced suburbia, the desire of man not to be a wanderer on the face of the earth, but to have a kingdom of his own.' Bruce Dawe

POPULOUS PLACES
AUSTRALIA'S CITIES AND TOWNS

edited by
Anna Rutherford

ACKNOWLEDGEMENTS

I would like to thank Aarhus University Research Foundation for its support towards this volume.

I would also like to thank Henrik Bødker, Lars Jensen and Mette Jørgensen for their help towards the preparation of this book and Kirsten Holst Petersen for organising the *Populous Places* conference.

COVER: 67 Scholey Street, Mayfield, NSW.
Painting by Audrey White.

First published in 1992 by Dangaroo Press
Australia: G.P.O. Box 1209, Sydney, New South Wales, 2001
Denmark: Geding Søvej 21, 8381 Mundelstrup
UK: 80 Kensington Road, Earlsdon, Coventry

ISBN 1 - 871049 - 77 - 6

CONTENTS

Introduction: Changing the Lens of Attention

> 'The history of the establishment of a British Colony in Australia is inextricably bound up with the foundations of towns'.
>
> Helen Proudfoot.

In writing this introduction, I was reminded of Dr Johnson's comment about the metaphysical poets. In their work he said 'the most heterogenous ideas are yoked by violence together'. The ideas may not be heterogenous but I assure you that the yoking, though perhaps not violent, took some ingenuity. This was because the papers covered so many disciplines and periods.

All the papers in the volume were given at a conference held at the University of Aarhus in 1988. As joint conference organizers both Kirsten Holst Petersen and I were determined to move away from the Bush legend. We believed that if we deliberately chose an urban theme and made the conference an interdisciplinary one we would have more chance of achieving our aim. By placing emphasis on Australia's cities and towns, their beginnings, their growth and their present state, we hoped that another image of Australia might emerge. As Jenny Strauss rightly surmised, our aim was to change the lens of attention. In doing so we hoped that we could more easily examine the validity of Russel Ward's Australian Legend, the myth of Australia that remains the most dominant and domineering, epitomised by Paul Hogan and *Crocodile Dundee*, and promoted relentlessly throughout the Bicentennial Year by the majority of the people and Hawke's government alike. For example John Williamson's song, 'True Blue', was taken up by the government and given a multi-media exposure. When the aboriginal Country and Western singer, Roger Knox, was asked what his attitude to 'True Blue' was he replied, 'Shit, I don't go along with that. Who's blue? I'm black. We don't want to be blue. I'm true but they can't accept that fact, that I'm true. 'True Blue', that doesn't do anything for me. *Dundee* and all that shit. We've been here for thousands and thousands of years.'

John Rickards remarks in his paper that Nationalism is a mixed blessing if a blessing at all, for it seeks to simplify, to compel, and it easily lends itself to slogans like 'Australia First' or 'One Australia'. The massive demonstration that took place in Sydney on January 26th, 1988 against the official celebration was an indication that there are many like Roger Knox, not only the aboriginal people but white Australians as well, who reject the simplification of the Paul Hogan image and demand recognition of Aboriginal land rights, as the rock group 'Midnight Oil' did in their song 'Beds are Burning'.

> the time has come
> to say fair's fair

to pay the rent
to pay our share

the time has come
a fact's a fact
it belongs to them
let's give it back

Yet in spite of the fact that Australia is an increasingly urban, cosmopolitan, heterogenous society the bush myth remains (see Gareth Griffiths's paper).

Australians, we are told, are one of the most highly urbanised societies in the world. But both Peter Quartermaine and Peter Fitzpatrick talk about the empty city. Now if we don't live in the bush and the city is empty, where do we live? Do I dare suggest it. We live in that most maligned place in Australia – Suburbia.

Robin Gerster in his paper takes as his touchstone Louis Esson's much quoted statement:

> Nothing in our present society is wildly desirable, but if one had the choice, it would be better to live in a slum area than in a bourgeois suburb. The slums have more character, perhaps base character, and decidedly more potentialities. Life is more vivid and picturesque there. People dance, and have passions, and live, in a sense, dangerously. In the suburbs all is repression, stagnation, a moral morgue.

The attitude of most of our writers to suburbia is much the same as Esson's and I must admit that it is one that has not only irritated me but also angered me.

How many of the satirists of suburbia would be willing to live in the rat-infested, unhygienic conditions of the inner city slums, slums that were remarkably similar to their counterparts in the old world? It's all right to live in Paddington (if you can afford it) now that it's trendy 'Paddo' and featured in *Vogue* etc. But how about that earlier period?

The writer's attitude to these slum dwellers has always caused me concern, for I feel that it smacks very much of 'perving' on the 'picturesque' poor, like the 'picturesque' native. And I ask myself what makes a wine and cheese party to raise money for Musica Viva superior to a beer and barbecue party to raise money to buy a new ball for the local basketball team. In the suburbs in which I grew up all the houses had been recently built – it was a new sub-division of Mayfield. I can remember that as soon as all the families moved in they got together to form the Mayfield South Progress Association. No, the aim of the association was not to raise money for a concert hall. Its aim was to persuade the local council to provide a bus route into the city centre via the heavy industries, where most of the men worked. No one in the area owned cars. The campaign was eventually successful and I can remember very clearly the first day the 104 bus route came into existence. The bus itself was decked with flags and everyone from the association had one free ride. I might add I had mixed feelings about the success of the project as I had been trying to persuade my father to buy a car. After the 104 started I knew I had no chance for, as he said, 'why do I want a car when I've got a 72 seater, chauffeur driven, stopping almost outside my door?' I can only agree with Peter Fitzpatrick when he says that by restricting suburbia's representation to satire and ridicule, we have 'disenfranchised its "constituency" and that is most of us'.

The question of public transport and its importance for the development of Australian cities is explored by Lionel Frost, whilst Renate Howe in her paper gives a vivid and realistic picture of the slum 'exotics' so much celebrated by the intellectuals. Most of the residents of those inner slum suburbs stayed there, not because life there was more 'vivid and picturesque' but because they couldn't attain the material conditions for the suburban life style. She quotes from Shirley Fitzgerald's book, *Rising Damp*

> ... it cannot be denied that the idea of the detached house, with garden, in the suburbs, was the goal of many people, and important in the imagery of what constituted the good life in Sydney... The ubiquitous terrace house, was both symbolic of the rift between dream and reality, and in real terms generated health problems associated with close living.

What applied to Sydney also applied to Melbourne. 'Melbournians', Howe said 'may have voted with their feet for life in the suburbs but their steps were directed by social laws where a sizable proportion were left marching on the spot'. Lionel Frost also points out that Australia's early immigrants, almost solely of British origin, brought with them an overwhelming preference for living in suburbia – it would appear that they were quite happy to forgo the dancing and the passions – and this preference has continued. Peter Proudfoot in his paper on Canberra tells how the early Town Planning Movement in Australia was concerned with social welfare, with many of the policies related to housing, health and recreation that could contribute to a more egalitarian society, and that Australia's suburbanization has been conditioned by this town planning ideology and Howard's Utopian Garden City Theory. Canberra has been referred to as seven suburbs in search of a city but, Peter Proudfoot says, public opinion seems quite happy with a landscape dominated capital.

Renate Howe (and several other papers) raised the question of class and questioned another of the myths clung to by many Australians, that we are a classless, egalitarian society. Stephen Alomes shows that the egalitarian myth is a fallacy and that Australia has in fact been run by a small Protestant (Jews and Catholics were excluded) elite. These elites were drawn from wealthy families, attached principally to certain professions (law, medicine, church), educated at private schools and universities based on the Oxbridge system and staffed by graduates from that system. This explains in many ways the development of what A.A. Phillips called the 'cultural cringe', and why it took so long for Australian literature, history etc. to be introduced into our education system.

Stephen Alomes argues that the power of the establishment continued until the 1960s when it began to be challenged by the rise of new national and international interests, and to a certain extent I believe that to be true. But with the overall swing to the right, the increase and flourishing of private schools which receive financial support from the government, all to the detriment of the state schools, I see the old elite still in power. It may, and has been, forced to widen its admission criteria but it is still very much in control. For a further discussion of culture and elites see in particular Frank Davidson's paper on the Boyds and

Carl Bridge's on 'Gentlemen and Mechanics'. The mention of mechanics leads on to John Barnes's paper on Joseph Furphy and John Longstaff. Barnes shows that the attitude of the local population of Shepparton differed very little from the elite when it came to a recognition of their local artists. They failed to understand and appreciate the radical nature of Furphy's great work but were more than willing to claim Longstaff, who had painted portraits of both King Edward and Queen Alexandra, as 'Our Shepparton Artist'. Furphy was never 'Our Shepparton writer'.

One point raised by Stephen Alomes was the power of the Protestant elite and their exclusion of both Catholics and Jews. Shurlee Swain examines the sectarian issue. It so often amuses me today when I find the Anglo Saxon and Celt grouped together by other ethnic groups with the inference that the former two groups, i.e. Anglo Saxon, Celt were one big happy family. They may be *now* but there could be no fiercer battles fought in Australia's early history and right up to the 1960s than between Catholic and Protestant. Shurlee Swain quotes the surgeon to the Port Phillip Association who claimed that the Irish were 'utterly useless ... intellectually inferior even to the aborigines', whilst the new colony of South Australia was promoted to settlers as being free from 'papists and pagans'. It is good that such a situation no longer exists but it is well to remember that it did. To ignore its existence is to ignore an important aspect of Australia's social history. For example, the balls held in cities and bush towns alike were usually held on Fridays, a day when Catholics (at that time) didn't eat meat. There would always be two sittings of supper, one before midnight, one after, and careful attention was paid to the fact that there would be Catholic helpers on the Committee as well as Protestant to make sure all the best food wasn't served at the first sitting.

It seemed fitting to conclude the volume with essays that argue that the traditional city/bush, urban/rural distinctions represent a false dichotomy. Judith Kapferer agrees that the bush legend and all that goes with it is an incontestable fact. But, she points out, the qualities attached to it, egalitarian, physical endurance, mateship, resistance to opposition etc. are *not* particularly rural. Anyone who has grown up in an industrial town, or a suburb for that matter, will confirm that. The rural worker, Kapferer argues, is as much at the mercy of urban capital circulating in an international arena, as is the urban worker; the division between economic and political terms are not only fake (the Labor Party must still be reeling from the shock of Cessnock electing a Liberal member and Newcastle an independent in the election before last), but, Kapferer argues, these divisions are constantly utilized in a divide and rule strategy. The false opposition of the interests of rural and urban workers is promoted by the mass media, an apparatus of the ruling group which can be relied upon to further that group's interests. For example soap operas such as *The Flying Doctors* and *A Country Practice* present an essentially urban fantasy of life in the country and are a tremendous success both in Australia and abroad. I read recently that one reason given for their success was that they were not 'impure' like American soaps and in fact they could be regarded as modern versions of the medieval morality plays!

By using certain rural industrial disputes, e.g. the Mudginberri dispute, Judith Kapferer shows that urban and rural workers can be shown to have more in common, socially and culturally, politically and economically, *as* workers, than they are different by their place of residence.

By the 1970s over 80% of Australia's population lived in its cities and towns. 'Academic' recognition of Australian mythology, the Bush myth, was rejected and replaced by the Urban myth. But, argues Colin Patrick, this simple and strict division of urban and rural is not so simple, nor is it correct. His paper examines the basic postulates of the Urban myth:

- that the character of the city owes nothing to the environment,
- that the essential functions of urban life are independent of natural processes, and
- that the city is isolated from the surrounding Bush.

and goes on to show the naivete behind all these postulates and the consequences of that naivety. The environment determined the situation of the cities, the misuse of it caused whole scale pollution, including the pollution of that most sacred and beloved of all of Australia's natural attractions, the beach. The shame of it when Sydney councils were forced to place signs (in Japanese as well as English) on their beaches, even Bondi Beach – 'This beach is polluted'.

Australia, like every other continent, is subject to natural disasters, more so than most 'Said Hanrahan'. Bushfires, floods, cyclones and even earthquakes have been and continue to remain threats. The environment, Colin Patrick argues, intrudes as much into modern Australian life as it ever did. The urban Myth must recognize this and act accordingly. If it does so it will become more than a fashionable way of rejecting an apparently outdated concept. Two papers that support Colin Patrick's view are those by Arnis Siksna and Roderick J. Lawrence. Siksna discusses how we have created spaces and townscapes that have distinctly Australian traits and how one of the major determinants was the physical nature of the continent. We had a need for shade in the summer, and one answer was our verandahs. Roderick Lawrence, discussing Colonial Housing, comes up with exactly the same argument, namely that external and indigenous influences have been embodied in the domestic architecture in Australia.

'The best laid schemes o' mice an' men/ Gang aft a-gley'. Robert Burns's words are apt ones I believe when considering the ideals and reality presented by so many of these papers: Dawes's plan for Sydney, Furphy's idealism, Catherine Helen Spence's dream of Utopia, the visions of a fairer, egalitarian society in the new world.

Focusing on the reality and not on the myth may lead to a degree of pessimism. But this should not to be the case. For I believe that it is only when we face the reality, ugly as at times it may be, that we can understand where we have gone wrong, and this I believe is the first step towards righting these wrongs. Like Mr Polly, I would say, 'If the world does not please you, *you can change it*'. A return to innocence is impossible. But my answer to the question posed by Bruce Bennett at the conclusion of his paper, 'Can the river and stray butterflies, still cast their old spell?' is yes. I remain, like Mr Polly, an optimist.

HELEN PROUDFOOT

The Puzzle of Governor Phillip's Two Plans

> 'When the time shall arrive that the European settlers on Sydney Cove demand their historian, these authentic anecdotes of their pristine legislator will be sought for as curious, and considered as important.'
>
> 'Anecdotes of Governor Phillip', John Stockdale, 1789.

The history of the establishment of a British Colony in Australia is inextricably bound up with the foundation of towns. The first landfall in 1788, at Botany Bay, and the decision to move the nucleus of the settlement to Sydney Cove in Port Jackson, a few kilometres to the north, is well known. This first urban settlement then grew to become the largest city on the continent.

The siting and foundation of this town of Sydney was therefore of crucial significance to the development of the Australia we know two hundred years later. One would expect that its planning and initial development would have been closely followed by historians. And so it has been, in many ways. But there have been many voices from the past telling us about the various aspects of this important event, and many voices in our own time overlaying them. It has become difficult to distinguish the several voices and to weigh their relative importance.

We might start with Phillip's voice, writing about the process of settlement in the book he arranged to be published in London in 1789, even before he left Sydney to return back to England, *The Voyage of Governor Phillip to Botany Bay, with an Account of the Establishment of the Colonies of Port Jackson and Norfolk Island*, printed by John Stockdale of Picadilly in a handsome large volume. Or rather, it is assumed it is Phillip's voice; for the papers sent back to be assembled in this very rapidly-produced volume are a heterogeneous lot, a veritable rag-bag of official and non-official writings, much more so than, say, a government report of today would be.

When we read it again, indeed, the voice which starts to emerge is not that of Phillip at all. It is John Stockdale's voice. It is Stockdale who emerges as the first historian of the colony; in fact, Phillip himself may not have arranged to have his despatches from Sydney, which were the primary sources of many parts of the book, to be published at all. In the 'Advertisement', which serves as a prologue to the volume, Stockdale tells us that 'The official papers of Governor Phillip, which were liberally supplied by Government, formed at first our principal source of intelligence.' He went on to say that his own efforts to give the public more information 'produced a gradual influx of materials', and with more vessels arriving back home from New South Wales he had been able to gain additional communications. He apologises for the delay in the publication of the book occasioned by these circumstances, but confidently hopes that 'nothing material has been omitted that is connected with its principal object, the formation of a settlement promising both glory and advantage to this country.'

The volume he produced, large in size, and heavy with engravings and appendices, is indeed informative. It traces the voyage of the eleven ships of the First Fleet from Portsmouth to the Canary Islands; then the next leg of the voyage to Rio de Janeiro and its 'prosperous' passage to the Cape of Good Hope, and then its longest and most perilous passage to the great southern continent. There, in January 1788, they made landfall, exactly at Botany Bay.

In the next section Stockdale discusses the first weeks after arrival, the English impressions of the new country and its natives, the difficulties encounted in making provision for the settlers, both convict and military, and their interest in the strange birds and animals of the country. He gives details about the people involved.

In Chapter XIII Stockdale writes specifically about 'the settlement at the head of the harbour' of Sydney Cove and the buildings actually erected, and of 'the intended town'. In this chapter the first considered 'plan' of Sydney Cove is appended. It is titled 'Sketch of Sydney Cove, Port Jackson in the County of Cumberland, New South Wales'. This plan has been known as the Dawes Plan, though its attribution is ambiguous; the original manuscript plan is held in the Public Record Office, London, and the version printed in the book has only the acknowledgements, 'The Coast Line by W. Dawes, the Soundings by Capt Hunter', along with the inscription of the engraver's name, T. Medland, and 'Published July 7, 1789 by J. Stockdale'. Nevertheless, it is this plan which has been taken as the first official Town Plan of Sydney.

Elsewhere, I have compared this plan with several others which pre-dated it, so I will not go into detail here again about these.[1] In this paper, I want to consider the salient features of this published plan, and compare them with those of the plan drawn three years later when Phillip left the colony in December 1792. The manuscript of this second plan has survived; two versions of it on both sides of a single sheet of paper, and is held in the State Archives Office of New South Wales.

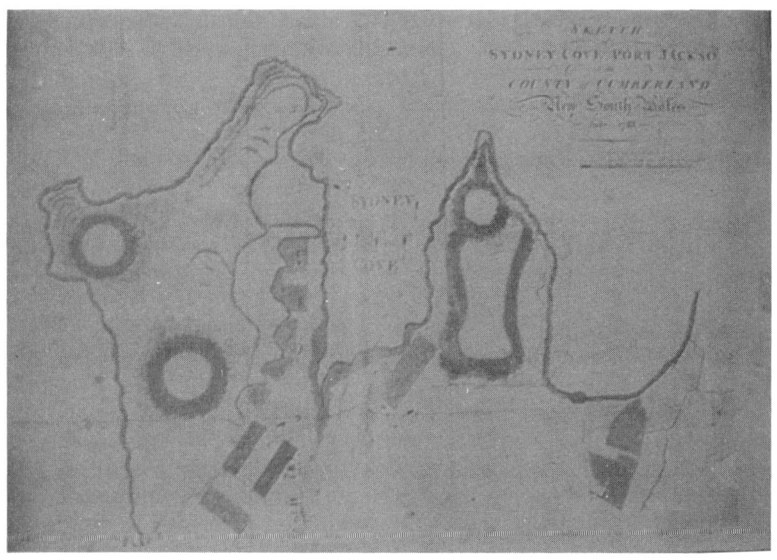

Fig.1. 'Sketch of Sydney Cove, Port Jackson, July 1788.' Printed by John Stockdale in his book *The Voyage of Governor Phillip to Botany Bay* (London, 1789).

The Dawes Plan of July 1788 is really two plans in one. The puzzle is to discern who were the authors of (a) the base map, which shows the coast-line, the major topographical features, the estuary of the Tank Stream, and the buildings existing at that time; and (b) the overlaid plan, drawn in precise straight lines, without benefit of topographical detail, which suggests Phillip's future intentions for the town.

We have three sources of information as clues; firstly, the acknowledgement on the map itself of Lieutenant William Dawes as the author of the 'coastline'; secondly, the remarks made by Phillip in his despatch of 9 July 1788, which reached London with Lieutenant Shortland of the 'Alexander' after a long voyage back via the China Seas; and thirdly, the comments in the letters written by Dawes to the Rev Nevil Maskelyne, the Astronomer Royal at Greenwich, who Dawes had trained under as an astronomer and who was the man who he reported to about his astronomical work.

Phillip's remarks are echoed in part by Stockdale in his chapter and embellished with some philosophical reflections about the process of settlement. They are also endorsed by Captain Watkin Tench later in his account of the colony.

I will start with Phillip's despatch of 9 July 1788. This was his second major despatch from the colony, the first having been written on 15 May previously. The engraving was made in London a year later, in July 1789. Phillip wrote clearly about what he intended, but it must be acknowledged that it was more an idea than a carefully considered plan at this stage, and we do not know exactly how closely Dawes was involved. Nevertheless, as we will see, Dawes was involved in a major way generally in the 'surveys' carried out in the fledgling colony.

Phillip writes: 'I have the honour to enclose [for] your Lordship the intended plan for the town.' He goes on to talk about the positions of his own Government House and the house of the Lieutenant-Governor, the huts of the convicts, and the Observatory being built under Lieutenant Dawes; he says the temporary buildings are marked in black, and the intended ones in red. The stores were to be commenced in the next few months.

He writes that 'Some regular plan for the town was necessary, and in laying out of which I have endeavoured to place all public buildings in situations which will eligible hereafter, and to give a sufficient share of ground for the stores, hospitals, &c., to be enlarged, as may be necessary in the future. The principal streets are placed so as to admit a free circulation of air, and are two hundred feet wide. The ground marked out for Government House is intended to include the main guard, Civil and Criminal Courts, and as the ground that runs to the southward is nearly level, and a good situation for buildings, streets will be laid out in such a manner as to afford a free air, and when the houses are to be built, if it meets with your Lordship's approbation, the land will granted with a clause that will ever prevent more than one house being built on the allotment, which will be sixty feet in front and 150 feet in depth.'[2]

Phillip adds that these arrangements would 'preserve uniformity in the buildings', 'prevent narrow streets', and the 'many inconveniences' which the increase of inhabitants would otherwise find afterwards. There was some discussion about the name of the town and according to Daniel Southwell in a letter home, and John White in his Journal, there seems to have been a proposal to name it 'Albion'; but the name adopted at first for the cove in Port Jackson, Sydney Cove, named after Lord Sydney, continued to be used.[3]

When we go to the *Voyage*, however, we find some added reflections, presumably written by Stockdale, about the process of settlement, which colour Phillip's plain account of his intentions. The chapter opens with a marvellous paragraph which distills for his readers the impressions gleaned from the letters and accounts he had access to, His skill as a writer enables him to convey an authentic atmosphere to the report sent to the Government. It is worth quoting in full:

> There are few things more pleasing than the contemplation of order and useful arrangement, arising gradually out of tumult and confusion; and perhaps this satisfaction cannot any where be more fully enjoyed than when a settlement of civilized people is fixing itself upon a newly discovered or savage coast. The wild appearance of land entirely untouched by cultivation, the close and perplexed growing of trees, interrupted now and then by barren spots, bare rocks, or spaces over-grown with weeds, flowers, flowering shrubs, or under-wood, scattered and intermingled in the most promiscuous manner, are the first objects that present themselves; afterwards, the irregular placing of the first tents which are pitched, or huts which are erected for immediate accommodation, wherever chance presents a spot tolerably free from obstacles, or more easily cleared than the rest, with the bustle of various hands busily employed in a number of the most incongruous works, increases rather than diminishes the disorder, and produces a confusion of effect, which for a time appears inextricable, and seems to threaten an endless continuance of perplexity. But by degrees large spaces are opened, lines marked, and a prospect at least of future regularity is clearly discerned, and is made the more striking by the recollection of former confusion.

So Stockdale is acting as Phillip's historian, commenting on his report, heightening its effect, drawing out its significance. In fact, this chapter of the book is the climax of the voyage of the fleet; the colonists had arrived, and were starting the process of settlement. They had created 'a prospect at least of future regularity' which could be clearly discerned; the town of Sydney had been founded. Stockdale further paraphrases the rest of Phillip's despatch, and then concludes his chapter with another distilled commentary, optimistic in tone: 'On the whole,' he writes, 'nothwithstanding the difficulties and disadvantages at first experienced... and the sicknesses which prevailed... the settlement at Sydney Cove wore a very promising aspect ... and there can be no doubt that it will be found

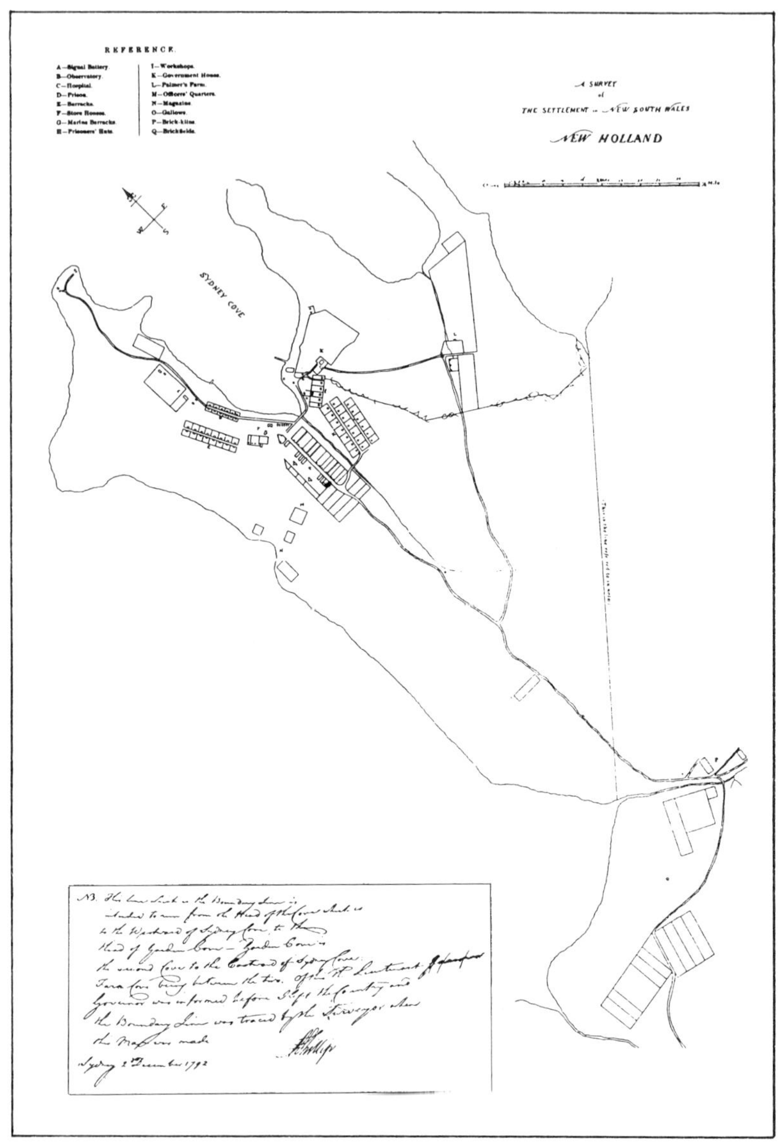

Fig.2. 'A Survey of the Settlement in New South Wales, New Holland', signed by Governor Phillip on 2 December 1792, just before he left the colony. (Archives Office of NSW, Map SZ430).

hereafter fully to answer every expectation which was formed when the design was projected.'

Captain Watkin Tench, however, was also adding his interpretation of the plan in his *Narrative of the Expedition to Botany Bay,* which was published in some haste in London in the same year, 1789, by J. Debrett, a rival publisher to John Stockdale, located almost opposite him in Piccadilly. Tench wrote; 'The plan of the town was drawn, and the ground on which it is hereafter to stand surveyed, and marked out.' He comments that 'To proceed on a narrow, confining scale, in a country of the extensive limits we possess, would be unpardonable: extent of empire demands grandeur of design.' But he goes on to have doubts about their ability to execute such a plan: 'How far this will be accompanied with adequate dispatch, is another question, as the incredulous among us are sometimes hardy enough to declare, that ten times our strength would not be able to finish it in as many years.'

Phillip's despatch was carried by Lieutenant Shortland in the Transport 'Alexander' to Batavia, and then back to England; Stockdale particularly acknowledges Shortland's account of his voyage back, and those of Lieutenants Ball, Watts, and Captain Marshall, and thanks the public officials by name, and the collectors Mr Latham and Sir Joseph Banks.

The third source of information is found in the letters written by William Dawes to the Rev. Nevil Maskelyne. The originals are held at Herstmonceaux Castle, Sussex, a branch of Greenwich Observatory. In these letters, at last, we hear a personal identifiable voice, describing the conditions in the colony with clear, unprejudiced eyes. The involvement of Lieutenant Dawes with the town plan of 1788 is confirmed also by Daniel Southwell in his correspondence where he says he believes the 'ingenious Mr Dawes is particularly engaged' in the plan of the town.

Writing on 30 April 1788, Dawes says: 'The extreme aeconomy of Government, not allowing them to give salaries to proper persons to perform the necessary business of settlement has obliged the Govenor to appoint me to do the Duty of Engineer and Officer of Artillery, and the inability of the Surveyor to perform his business has also thrown a great part of that on my hands;'[4]

Dawes wrote again on 10 July 1788 about his activities in the colony, in part apologising for not writing more frequently because he had been kept very busy since the landing: ... 'my time has been so much taken up with the business the Governor has desired me to do and with the building of the observatory that I had no opportunity to write, ... besides, our situation being in a thick wood, which after rain becomes an entire swamp, will partly account for the impossibility of sitting down much to writing.' In October 1788 he wrote again with details of his astronomical observations, with the comment that he 'would willingly have declined doing the duty of Engineer and Officer of Artillery' because this work had prevented him making more observations.

The next surviving letter was not written until 26 October 1790, and by this time Dawes was becoming exasperated with his extra duties and says that he had been obliged to tell the Governor 'very plainly and respectfully' that he could not do all the additional surveying work. He writes that, 'The greatest hindrance to Astronomy has been the unfortunate want of abilities in the Surveyor of Lands, who being totally ignorant of his business, it has of course been necessary to employ some other person on it, it has followed that everything in that way, of any consequence, has passed through my hands.'

These letters from Dawes firmly establish the role that he played in laying out the plans of both Sydney and Parramatta, which was founded at the head of the harbour near the most promising farming land some 20 km inland in 1790. They discount any major input by Augustus Alt, the officer officially appointed as Surveyor of Lands.[5]

This then is the context of the Dawes' Plan of Sydney. It is constantly cited and reproduced, and its arrangement of one very wide street with the projection of two more at the same width is uncritically praised in town planning literature as 'far-sighted'. The warning of Captain Tench, however, proved all too true. When Phillip took his leave of the colony after nearly five anxious and harrassing years, the over-lay of imagined regularity had vanished. It was replaced by a much more pragmatic and less grandly conceived plan, where the 'extent of empire' was only an idea in Whitehall, and the colony made what it could of its close and straightened circumstances.[6] (See p. 6 for this plan).

The major but narrow street runs along the western side of the Tank Stream between some plots marked out and the military barracks, and wanders northwards past the convicts huts and the hospital towards the observatory; it is crossed by a road up to the Governor's house on the eastern side of the Cove; a tentative division between 20 marked out plots, also on the eastern side, later became another street; and another between 16 plots on the western side is regularly drawn. Random plots unrelated to any overall scheme start to appear. There is no attempt at planning a 'prospect of future regularity'. The plan was one of expediency rather than regularity.

This second plan, entitled 'A Survey of the Settlement in New South Wales, New Holland', was distinguished by a 'Boundary Line' marked as a straight line on the map between the head of Woolloomoo Bay and the head of Darling Harbour (then called Cockle Bay), and an appended note in Phillip's handwriting gives an instruction that 'It is the Orders of Government that no ground within the Boundary Line is ever granted or let on Lease and all houses built within the Boundary line are and are to remain the property of the Crown.'; signed A. Phillip, Dec. 2, 1792.

Phillip's instruction was to cause headaches for his successors, Governors Hunter and King. To freeze ownership of land on such a wide scale in the very nucleus of the settlement was, at the least, simplistic; the best construction is that it was merely a holding measure, to be revised at a later time, but Phillip's use of the word 'ever' seems to make his intention clear.

The ownership or leasehold of the land was a key factor in the relationship of the government to the governed; it had to be defined in order to give a permanent, settled character to the form of the town; it had to allow the people, who were, after all, British citizens even if they had been convicted for a crime for a period, some rights and expectations. It was something that neither Phillip nor his superiors in the Colonial Office had thought about very clearly, but these rights had been long debated by the political philosophers in England after the upheavals of the civil wars of the seventeenth century, and had surfaced again after the American Revolution and the chaos of Revolutionary France.[7] They formed an integral part of the dialogue between the supporters of the monarchy and the concept of 'sovereignty', and the supporters of the idea of the wider distribution of power between the landholding classes in England.

We do not know if questions of political theory were debated at Sydney Cove: we do know that the more pressing exigencies of the moment claimed attention. Phillip's Boundary Line for the town of Sydney seems to raise the question of the balance of public versus private land in the urban context. Both Phillip's successors, Governors Hunter and King, had to struggle with bottled-up pressures connected with the distribution of town lands. Historians have studied the spread of settlement in New South Wales mainly in terms of rural land occupation and tenure. Urban land tenure needs also to be recognised as a most powerful factor.

The balance of property rights between public and private ownership was to become a key issue when Governor Bligh assumed office in 1806, and was to prove a major factor in the rejection of his governorship in the so-called 'Rum Rebellion'.[8] Even under Macquarie after 1810 the question of urban land tenure had still to be worked out. The connection of the ownership of property with political rights was not merely one of upper-class or lower-class rivalry; it was fundamental to the political and social organisation of a new, transplanted society.

So the 'Sketch' prepared for Stockdale's Voyage reveals more than a simple town plan. The puzzle it presents us with is worth unravelling. It sheds light on three main players: John Stockdale, William Dawes, and Governor Phillip himself.

A further enigma is to be found in the character of Phillip himself. Despite the many words written about him, he refuses to reveal himself as a rounded character. He kept no diaries, wrote few personal letters, and published no later recollections about his time in New South Wales. Contrasted with Captain James Cook, Phillip remains a shadowy figure. Cook, of course, died a martyr's death, and became a legendary figure whose lustre still colours the finding and founding of Australia. He was eulogised immediately after his violent death in popular legend, in paintings and etchings, in plays and pantomimes, and in the travel and scientific literature of the day. Phillip seems to be a much more enigmatic figure; he seems to elude our grasp, much to our subsequent loss when we search to find a legendary founder of our beloved Sydney.

Cook, in a contemporary pantomime performed in London, was depicted by the artist ascending to heaven in trails of glory, a scenic effect which was later translated to a printed engraving entitled 'The Apotheosis of Captain Cook'. Bernard Smith has described the process whereby Cook was made into a national hero after his death, borne up aloft by the allegorical figures of Britannia and Fame, the agent of triumphant but benign British expansion into the Pacific.[9] Phillip, however, received no such attention; it took a hundred years before he was commemorated by a statue in the city he founded.

Fig.3. 'The Apotheosis of Captain Cook', engraving, 1785, (see footnote 9).

NOTES

1. See Helen Proudfoot, Anne Bickford, Brian Egloff, Robin Stocks, *Australia's First Government House*, Allen & Unwin for the Department of Planning, Sydney, 1991.
2. *Historical Records of New South Wales*, Vol.I, Part 2, Government Printer, Sydney, 1893, pp.145-148; Phillip to Lord Sydney, 9 July, 1789.
3. Cited by Alan Atkinson, 'Taking possession: Sydney's First Householders', chapter in Graeme Aplin (ed.), *A Difficult Infant : Sydney before Macquarie* (Sydney: New South University Press, 1988), p. 74.
4. Letters written by Lieutenant William Dawes to Rev Nevil Maskelyne, Astronomer Royal, Greenwich, between 1788 and 1792; manuscripts held at Herstmonceaux Castle, Sussex. Copies kindly sent to the author in 1985 after my visit there to read them.
5. A case has been made in favour of Augustus Alt being the author of the plan by John-Paul Johnson of the University of NSW in his thesis 'The Phillip Towns', 1985; Alan Frost in his *Arthur Phillip* (Melbourne: Oxford University Press, 1987), merely attributes this plan to the Governor.
6. See H. Proudfoot et al., *op. cit.*
7. See David Neal, *The Rule of Law in a Penal Colony* (Cambridge: Cambridge University Press, 1991). In his Introduction, Neal makes this point about the recognised 'rights' of British subjects.
8. Alan Atkinson, *op. cit.*
9. The engraving is after Philippe Jacques de Loutherbourg and John Webber, 1785; a copy is in the Dixson Library, Sydney; Bernard Smith, 'Cook's Postumous Reputation', in Robin Fisher and Hugh Johnstone (eds.), *Captain James Cook and His Times* (Vancouver, 1979), pp.159-183, cited in William Eisler and Bernard Smith, *Terra Australis*, published catalogue to an exhibition at the Art Gallery of New South Wales, 1988.

PETER QUARTERMAINE

City Limits

> Cities, unless one can live in sheltered luxury, disturb me. Walking along those crowded pavements, into those pushing shops. The noise of the gutters and horns, the smell of petrol and people, the anxiety on every face ... But not Sidney, who is a city man, stimulated, as one should be I'm sure, by all the sights and sounds, longing to get in, to compete, to give it a go.

So wrote Cynthia Nolan from a Greek island to an Australian friend in March 1956, at a time when her husband Sidney was already – though not yet a 'Sir' – making a name for himself as a painter of 'outback' Australian scenery.[1] Her comments capture many of the dominant images that recur in cultural discussion of the city, both positive and negative. On the negative side there is the recoil from crowds, noise, smell and stress; on the positive a recognition that the city offers social stimulation, competition and opportunity. Nolan himself was to settle eventually in London, insofar as he settled anywhere, but in the pleasant Thameside area of Putney.

The cities of Australia differ strongly in history, climate and culture - and in their very populations. Yet they all have more in common with each other, and with almost any British city, than I might be thanked for pointing out. As D.H. Lawrence observed in 1929:

> The English character has failed to develop the real urban side of man, the civic side. Siena is a bit of a place, but it is a real city, with citizens intimately concerned with the city. Nottingham is a vast place sprawling towards a million, and it is nothing more than a vast amorphous conglomeration. There is no Nottingham, in the sense that there is Siena.[2]

Australia has inherited that British inability to use a city centre as that natural focus for markets, meetings (and, in the case of Siena, the world-famous Palio) which every Italian piazza thrives on. A shopping mall is a poor substitute, deck it as you will. I was struck in 1988 by how deserted the centre of Sydney was at evenings and weekends, the silence broken only by the eerie crash of piledrivers sinking the foundations of new glass towers for banks and insurance companies. Life flows to the harbour and to the suburbs; the city centre as such is abandoned.

'God made the country, and man made the town', wrote the eighteenth-century English poet William Cowper, and we have paid a high price for such dismissal of that supremely important artefact in which most of us live. It is rare to find creative artists sharing the sentiments of the poet Bruce Dawe, who wrote in 1969: 'it's an excess of virtue that has produced suburbia, the desire of man not to be a wanderer on the face of the earth, but to have a kingdom of his own'.[3]

The city we 'see', no matter which, depends upon a viewpoint itself conditioned by (for example) race, gender, education, health and wealth. My own image of Sydney is hopelessly wonderfully - conditioned by the three summer months we spent in the waterside flat of friends in Neutral Bay during our first visit to Australia in 1973. The friends are divorced and remarried, the flat sold, but those harbour views, commuter trips by ferry to the Mitchell Library, and the metal tinkle of rigging against masts are part of my Sydney still.

The Tasmanian writer Christopher Koch explores this sharp sense of the coterminous past and present of his home city of Hobart:

> One can walk all over Hobart in a few hours: this town of grandfathers. I am moving today through two earlier Hobarts, their ghostly after-images appearing all the time: the Hobart of the 1940s and my childhood, and the Hobart of the 1840s, and Captain Hurbugh [Koch's great-great-grandfather]: a sailor's town; a convict town.[4]

An important aspect of Australia's populous places traced by Koch is that the most important city for Australians at the period when he grew up (he was born in 1932) was not in Australia at all, but London. Many Commonwealth writers have written of the draw – and often, on arrival, of the disappointments – that this metropolitan heart of darkness held for them. Here is Koch, named as he tells us 'like many another child of the Empire in the thirties', after A.A. Milne's Christopher Robin – recapturing his vision of London from Hobart in the 1940s:

> The fires of London, smug or apocalyptic, glowed at the centre of our universe, since London was the City: the capital of the world. There was no other city that mattered; Melbourne and Sydney were mere towns, and New York was rumoured to be a monstrosity. London was both the city of cities, and the all-wise, half-forbidding friend.[5]

Such recognition of the formative role played by imaginative apprehensions of the city suggests that concern over the 'distortions' or 'inaccuracies' in images of the city held in earlier periods, while understandable, is misplaced. T.S. Eliot's influential view of twentieth-century London in *The Wasteland* as an 'unreal city', a description which fused his own first-hand knowledge of London with his reading of Dante's *Inferno*, blurred any easy distinction between the real and the false.

Differing needs and expectations bring different views of the same city, as Koch realises very clearly, but to accept that a particular vision has faded does not entail denying the truth it once embodied:

> These are archaic emotions, now ...But those who dismiss them as a sentimental absurdity have no conception of their intensity, and fail to understand the central convictions and fantasies that history can brew up, shaking whole generations with their poignancy; making them willing to die for such fantasies. Afterwards, as a joke, they are made to be merely quaint.[6]

In a passage which closely mirrors accounts by the Trinidadian writer V.S. Naipaul of his own colonial education, Koch testifies to the formative power of literature although, again like Naipaul, Koch haunted his local cinema whenever possible. The Britain he so admired was as much fiction as fact, hut no less real for being derived from what he terms 'shadows on the wall of Plato's cave' in distant Tasmania:

> We were subjects of no mortal country; hidden in our unconscious was a kingdom of Faery: a Britain that could never exist outside the pages of Hardy, Kenneth Grahame, Dickens and Beatrix Potter; and yet it was this country we confidently set out to discover. We sailed, as soon as we reached our twenties, for isles of the Hesperides we never doubted were real.[7]

Today things are rather different, but casts of mind still play their part in determining how we respond to terms such as 'city', 'town' and, crucially in Australia, 'suburb'. A recent commentator offers some useful thoughts on both the Australian environment and the Australian psyche; useful since the real suburbs exist on a rapid transit route somewhere between the two:

> Contemporary Australia is significant neither for its empty outback, nor for the concentration of its population in capital cities, nor for suburban living. More distinctive is the importance that suburbia occupies in the national mentality, where it is at once enshrined as the ideal way of life and mocked as the enemy of culture and innovation. If city life seemed dull, the suburbs were perceived as irredeemably flat so that 'suburban' defined not just a place to live, but also a refusal to think, or to feel.[8]

If cultural attitudes to suburbia are complex, the relation between a work of art and its creator is no less so. My opening quotation places Sidney Nolan, seen by London in the postwar period as such a 'typically Australian' artist, in a fresh light, and there is similar evidence for Russell Drysdale. Notwithstanding his youthful passion for long-distance outback cycling (some early reviews of his work refer to him as 'the former racing cyclist') Nolan seems always to have been a city person, in lifestyle if not in subject matter. This is no more surprising than that the contemporary Australian artist Jeffrey Smart, who has lived in rural Tuscany for almost twenty years now, should paint mostly man-made or urban scenes. Neither artist chose to live in suburbia, though Smart claimed mischievously in a recent letter that the new rail link to Florence makes his Tuscan village 'suburban'. In any case, oppositions between natural and man-made landscapes are not as sharp as they seem, since many 'natural' landscapes in Australia are as man-made as any suburb.

Since European settlement Australia has always been a land of populous places; although boasting suburbs far more spacious than Europe's, Australia's cities still contain a disproportionately high percentage of the country's overall population. Early Australian paintings emphasise the tight focus of initial settlement, looking as they do from the unpopulated landscape towards tangible evidence, mostly that furnished by the architect and the engineer, of 'progress'. Australian illustrated journals in the latter half of the nineteenth century recorded with pride the destruction of buildings which evoked an earlier, and what was seen as a more 'primitive', settler era. Not until the Centennial year of 1988 was there much interest in what we would term 'heritage', an interest which was sharpened by that alertness to history which came with the turning of the century and the approach of federation. It was Henry Lawson who pointed out tartly, amid the celebrations of 1888, that his country's schoolchildren still knew more British history than Australian.

Settlement and population growth in Australia was defined as much by technology as by terrain: the gun, the steam engine and the jump-stump plough – more recently the internal combustion engine in the air and on tarmacadam – have all played different but crucial roles. Moreover, populous places abroad – traditionally London, but increasingly New York, Tokyo, Singapore, Djakarta and Beijing – have defined the motives and methodologies both of Australia's population growth and of its being recorded (or not) for posterity.

Darwinian theory and the pressure of real estate, what today would be termed 'market forces', combined to ensure that the Aboriginal peoples of Australia had no place in such 'development'. In the world of commerce and industry, that supposed 'real world' so beloved by economic commentators, Aborigines were useful only as cheap labour in the very system that dispossessed them. In art they featured as 'primitive' spectators on the margins of an all-white pastoral arcadia, convenient yardsticks against which the viewer was invited to measure the progress of settler civilisation.[9]

Attitudes to environment reveal the pasts we choose for ourselves, a choice in which 'national fictions' play an influential role. In Australia, as in Britain, such fictions mostly eschew populous places in favour of terrain less representative but unique – peculiar even – to the continent. In Australia this is usually that assemblage of landscape icons that runs from Arthur Streeton's woodsplitters to Paul Hogan's outback hero. Australian fiction's general preference for the rural over the urban has been taken too literally by many critics, and emphasised by their own preference for examining the representation of the land – with its greater metaphysical possibilities – rather than urban society.[10]

The extent to which Australian experience has mirrored that of city-dwellers elsewhere has often been downplayed both within the country and overseas, whether for crudely commercial ends, as with *Crocodile Dundee*, or more subtly, as in much writing on painting and in literature. In the decades following the Second World War especially, there was intense interest in London critical circles in 'discovering' Australian culture, an attitude of British critics which recurred in the 1970s with Australian film. Many of the writers and artists so 'discovered' were treated almost as noble savages untouched by the supposedly all-important Renaissance, let alone by more recent history.

Troubled by their own recent history, British critics turned with relief and condescension to the supposedly innocent painters of the Australian outback whose work still depicted mankind in what could be interpreted as an epic struggling with the elements. Reviews of Russell Drysdale's early paintings of drought scenes in the 1940s praised his recording of settler culture's destruction of a fragile environment by over-grazing. A few years later, though, with his reputation already growing, the tone of critical comment shifted significantly and granted him a more heroic status: critics now saw his paintings as depicting doughty survivors in a 'timeless' and hostile environment.

Such a shift from settler as vandal to settler as victor exaggerates differences between city and hush. Agriculture worldwide is discovering late in the day that its technology can be just as damaging as that of urban-centred industry. In Britain, too, the need to reduce agricultural production means that the future of many farms may lie in recycling their past to tourists as part of the heritage industry. The real danger, though, of the shift from culture (society's interaction with the environment) to nature (society posed heroically against a 'land beyond time') is that 'it converts the contingent and interested actions of history into the inevitable and disinterested processes of the natural order of things.' Such a move 'pre-empts calls for change by removing it from the agenda – one cannot change nature.'[11]

Undue Australian focus on the bush rather than the city is to be attributed more to cultural commentators than to writers or artists; images have been incorporated into the canon which fit with existing preconceptions. In the case of cities one effect of this has been to exclude from much critical discourse that place where most Australians actually live, the suburb:

> From the 1860s to the 1960s the history of the Australian city is one of vigorous, continuous growth; a growth the beneficence of which was rarely questioned. But it was also a century in which landscape painting was the dominant artistic genre.[12]

In the 1974 UNESCO Conference paper in which he advanced this analysis, Bernard Smith went on to draw disturbing conclusions from such selective vision and concluded that, even though landscape artists had done much to awaken interest in the natural environment, this preoccupation with landscape 'had been largely responsible for the creation of a false consciousness of what it is to be an Australian'. As Smith noted in discussing his involvement in the (ultimately successful) battle to save his Sydney suburb of Glebe from the planners: 'That which cannot be readily accommodated to a preconceived pattern, an existing mental set, is usually not seen, much less enjoyed.'[13]

Australian culture, like that of many other Commonwealth countries, was for long totally dependent upon metropolitan which meant overseas – structures and contacts for cultural production and assessment: publishing, finance, exhibitions, dealers and reviews. To some extent this is still true. It is rarely recognized, though, that overseas interest in Australian culture is often largely shaped by the local preconceptions of the overseas centre itself. Typically, too, such preoccupations are neatly transferred to the country or culture under 'objective' scrutiny. In his Introduction to the 1961 Whitechapel Exhibition of Australian painting, Kenneth Clark refers to the 'sudden appearance of an Australian school of painting'; it would have been more honest to have cited his own 'sudden' acquaintance with Australian painting in 1947, on his first visit to that country.[14]

There is now lively scholarly interest in the complex pattern of Australia's cities. Certainly until the national mythology incorporates more aspects of the urban environment it will remain inadequate. As long ago as 1856 the Australian literary critic Frederick Sinnett claimed that 'true art makes keenly pleasurable the contemplation of what, in its absolute shape, we tire of every day of our lives.'[15] In their postwar, postmodern and multicultural phase, Australia's populous places suggest that whoever is tired of them is indeed tired of life itself.

NOTES

1. The letter was to Pat Flower, Drysdale Correspondence, Mitchell Library, Sydney. ML MSSS 386/4.
2. 'Nottingham and the Mining Country' in *Selected Essays* (Harmondsworth: Penguin, 1968), pp. ll4-122. Reference on p. 121.
3. Craig McGreyor (ed), *In the Making* (Melbourne: Thomas Nelson, 1969), n.p.
4. Christopher Koch, 'Return to Hobart Town' in *Crossing the Gap: A Novelist's Essays* (London: the Hogarth Press, 1987), pp. 84-90. Reference on p. 88.
5. 'Maybe It's Because I'm a Londoner' in *Kunapipi*, Vol VIII, No 1, 1986, p. 4.
6. *Ibid.*, p. 7.
7. *Ibid.*, p. 7.
8. Humphrey McQueen, *Suburbs of the Sacred* (Ringwood: Penguin, 1988), p. 36.
9. See, for example, Bernard Smith's *Australian Painting 1788-1970* (Melbourne: Oxford University Press, 1970) and Tim Bonyhady's *Images in Opposition: Australian Landscape Painting 1801-1890* (Melbourne: Oxford University Press, 1985) especially chapters 2 and 3.
10. Graeme Turner, *National Fictions: Literature, Film and the Construction of Australian Narrative* (Sydney: Allen & Unwin, 1986), p. 36.
11. *Ibid.*, p.35.
12. Bernard Smith, 'On Perceiving the Australian Suburb', in George Seddon's and Mari Davis's (eds) *Man and Landscape in Australia: Towards an Ecological Vision* (Canberra: Government Publishing Service, 1976), pp. 289-304. Reference on p. 292. The essay is also included (minus the useful plates) in Smith's collection of writings *The Antipodean Manifesto: Essays in Art and History* (Melbourne: Oxford University Press, 1976).
13. Bernard Smith, 'The Myth of Isolation' in *The Antipodean Manifesto*, pp. 57-59, Reference on p. 61.
14. *Recent Australian Painting* (London: Whitechapel Gallery, 1961), p. 4.
15. Frederick Sinnett, 'The Fiction Fields of Australia' first published in *The Journal of Australasia* in September and November 1856), reprinted in John Barnes (ed) *The Writer in Australia: A Collection of Literary Documents 1856 to 1954* (Melbourne: Oxford University Press, 1969), pp. 8-32. Reference on p. 12.

ROBIN GERSTER

GERRYMANDER: The Place of Suburbia in Australian Fiction

Cultural debate in Australia has traditionally satisfied its fetish for national self-definition by asserting a simple opposition of contexts. The conventional dichotomy of the rural and the urban – the sanctioned 'Bush' and the despised 'City' – may still hold some attraction for vestigially nationalistic commentators who hold the view that, given the relative similarity of metropolitan centres, the essence of a country is to be found out in the land.[1] But its relevance to contemporary Australia is minimal. Australia has always been predominantly urban, of course; these days, however, the metropolitan culture is much more entrenched than it was around the turn of the century, when the *Bulletin* writers, lampooned by Thomas Keneally as 'safe city dwellers', were constructing the bush legends from their base in inner Sydney.[2]

A more compelling and culturally revealing duality in the representation of the Australian context is the split in perceptions of the inner-urban and suburban environments: a split which is especially evident in Australian fiction, on which I will concentrate here, but which is perhaps also evident in both poetry and drama. In *Social Patterns in Australian Literature* (1971) T. Inglis Moore argued that Australian writers have indulged in 'literary gerrymandering' by privileging the country over the city. But by the abundance of urban-centred texts his own study addresses – and on the evidence produced and examined by critics such as Ian Reid – it is clear that the hold of the city on the Australian imagination has been severely underrated.[3] The real 'gerrymander' has not been exerted against the city itself, but against the suburbs and in effect against the majority of Australians who live there: an anomaly in a literature with, it is customarily claimed, an egalitarian, democratic ethos. The denigration of the suburbs by Australian writers, artists, and historians is inveterate. In fiction, suburbia is not only attacked by the pedlars of the bush mythology, it is habitually dismissed with cosmopolitan contempt by urban-oriented writers as a place fit solely for satire, if indeed it is a place worth writing about at all. The critics have done their work well. In an essay on the urban context of the contemporary Australian novel, a third-year student at my university rails against the suburbs as 'a breeding ground' of 'juvenile delinquents and old ladies with blue hair', and attacks their 'conservative conformism' and the 'simple-minded parochialism' that 'typifies their inhabitants'. Herself a product of leafy eastern Melbourne, she launches her discussion with a remark which inadvertently constructs an image of suburbia suggestive of the very opposite of the convention. 'The suburbs', she sententiously intones, 'have a bad name'.

Whereas the intellectual enclaves and working-class slums of the inner city are celebrated for their ideological attraction and aesthetic potential, for their cultural energy and diversity, for their LIFE, suburbia is used as a metonym for living death. Its geographical and metaphysical connotation is that of a middle-class limbo located somewhere between the blessed bush and the fascinatingly infernal inner city. A comment about the two milieux made in 1911 by Louis Esson posits a dichotomy which appears again and again in Australian fiction:

> Nothing in our present society is wildly desirable, but if one had the choice, it would be better to live in a slum area than in a bourgeois suburb. The slums have more character, perhaps base character, and decidedly more potentialities. Life is more vivid and picturesque there. People dance, and have passions, and live, in a sense, dangerously. In the suburbs all is repression, stagnation, a moral morgue.[4]

Suburbia constitutes one of Australia's richest semiotic fields. Its cultural meanings, however, constellate around the central image of the barren wasteland, a place of stifling conformity, crass materialism, and spiritual *accidie*. Even more negatively, for Australian writers, it is understood to be inimical to the independent, artistic, or broadly 'bohemian' sensibility. Driving along Melbourne's Dandenong Road toward the 'endless red brick', Morley, the Carlton-based writer who narrates Barry Oakley's *Let's Hear it for Prendergast* (1970), wonders where he can land his 'module' on the 'barren suburban surface'.[5] The historical reference is to the recent Moon Landing: Morley has entered the orbit of another world. His estrangement derives from the combination of fear and contempt that afflicts many Australian novelists in dealing with suburbia. They are unwilling to explore beyond the 'surface'; they shrink from close encounters with the suburbanites, perhaps because they are afraid of seeing an image of themselves. The sense of difference from the mainstream culture that is cultivated by many Australian artists and intellectuals prohibits close communication, even empathy. Satire and blank neglect become convenient refuges.

The great icons of suburbia – the brick veneers, garages, family cars and so on *ad nauseam* – are consistently invoked in order to put the suburbanites in their place. The ornamental emblazoning of the family home with fanciful names is a particularly flexible ironic focus. In *My Brother Jack* (1964) George Johnston renames his childhood home 'Avalon' not merely because of its comical pretentiousness, but also because the romantic allusion highlights the frustration of his alter ego, David Meredith, a cultural outsider who craves escape from the 'shabby suburban squalor' into which he was born. More directly, the appearance of 'Avalon' on the first page of the novel alerts its readers to the central theme of suburban Australia as a land of the living dead. D.H. Lawrence in *Kangaroo* (1923) similarly exploits Australian suburban house names for their bathetic nuances – most notably when it is pointed out to Richard Somers that the name of the villa he has leased in Sydney is not, as he had read it, the exotic-looking 'Torestin', but the rather less exciting 'To Rest In'.[6] The so-called 'nature strip' is also commonly targeted for its suburban symbolism. Characteristically, the shorn strip of lawn by the footpath is used as an emblem of the suburbanite's vicarious relationship with nature. 'The motor mower rampant. Over grass vert. Should be part of the national coat of arms', mocks the iconoclastic hero of *Let's Hear it for Prendergast*.[7] The implication here is that average suburban man, dubbed 'Norm Dullsville' in Oakley's novel, falls pathetically short of the rugged male stereotype lionized by nationalist legend. This, admittedly, is effective antidotal satire, though of the legend itself rather than poor old Norm.

The line dividing satire and gratuitous insult in the treatment of suburbia in Australian fiction, however, is often fine to the point of invisibility. Patrick White's imagined outer Sydney wasteland – the spiritual Sahara of Sarsaparilla, Barranugli and Paradise East – is a microcosm of contemporary suburban Australia. Most of White's suburbanites are caricatures, or to be more precise grotesques, than fully realized characters. His particular fondness is for creating inane, spiritually-shrivelled suburban women – Mrs Jolley and Mrs Flack (who lives in a brick veneer called 'Karma') in *Riders in the Chariot*, for example, or Mrs Dun in *The Solid Mandala* ('dun' being White's favoured pejorative colour), or the vile Mrs Hogpen in the story 'Down in the Dump', who obsessively swabs her telephone with disinfectant. Interestingly, White invoked these stereotypes during a period, the 1960s, when the suburban housewife was exploited satirically as a cultural object, Barry Humphries' Edna Everedge (a more gormless creature then than the worldly sophisticate she has become) being the popular example. The unspoken assumption, in White and more generally, is that suburbia is an essentially *female* domain. It's no place for a man: look at 'Norm Dullsville'. Theoretically opposed to the nationalist tradition, White lends tacit support to the bushman myth by turning suburbia into a geographic hell ruled by female demons. Sniggering contempt for suburban (usually female) philistinism sometimes has the effect of corrupting White's fictional discourse. Describing in *Riders in the Chariot* Shirl Rosetree's pride in her 'texture-brick home' at 15 Persimmon Street, Paradise East, he tediously lists her 'streamlined, glass car', her 'advanced shrubs', her grandfather clock 'with the Westminster chimes', her 'walnut-veneer radiogram', her 'mix-master' and even her washing machine.[8] What emerges from a reading of this catalogue of possessions is not so much suburban materialism – anyone, after all, is entitled to own a washing-machine, or even a grandfather clock – but White's own waspish preoccupation with it. He employs the Shirl Rosetrees of this world as the most common of denominators against which the few spiritually rich suburbanites are celebrated for their difference.

Suburbia's most culpable quality, to many Australian writers, is its antagonism to art and to artistic production. In one of several moments of unintended comedy in *The Solid Mandala,* Mrs Dun actually 'hisses' at the very mention of books and libraries.[9] Louis Esson's wildly romantic rhetoric again supplies a representative attitude: the suburban home, he says, 'stifles the devil-may-care spirit, the Dionysian, the creative spirit. It denounces Art, enthusiasm, heroic virtue. The Muses are immolated on its altar of respectability'.[10] This equation of the creative impulse with the heroic spirit is especially revealing, as it signals a central issue in Australian autobiographical narrative – the conflict between the artistic consciousness and an incompatible suburban environment. David Meredith's adolescent anguish as a bookish misfit in the stifling atmosphere of 'Avalon' is exacerbated, when he finally marries, by a move to the 'sterile desolation' of Beverley Park Gardens, a new housing estate in Melbourne. On the roof of his 'double-fronted, ultra-modern, red brick three-bedroom villa' installing an aerial for a new 'console-radio', he surveys the 'red and arid desert' of the subdivision and suffers a terrible vision of the tedium and complacency of suburban life and ritual, a vision crucial in instigating those 'proceedings of divorcement' from both his enthusiastically suburban wife and his country that eventually send him into a long period of expatriation.[11] Meredith, always eager to blame his environment for his emotional and creative frustrations, jealously compares the aspiring 'House and Garden' desolation of his new home in Beverley Grove with 'Bangalore', the significantly 'old' and 'dilapidated' Toorak mansion of Gavin Turley, a fellow journalist. For the Turley residence's decaying nineteenth-century splendour, inside and out, and its 'dense', 'dark', 'damp' garden, read 'PROPER ENVIRONMENT FOR THE REAL ARTIST'; for the Beverley Grove brick veneer 'tastefully' decorated by Meredith's wife, with its levelled, treeless sixty-foot frontage, read 'HOW COULD ANYONE WRITE HERE?' It really is that simple: Meredith even juxtaposes descriptions of Turley's chaotic, littered study with the 'burgundy coloured square of feltex' and kitsch bric-a-brac of his own. There's no crumpled paper in Meredith's suburban waste-paper basket: Turley has three overflowing ones under his trestle work-table; from the window of *his* study Turley could dwell on the rank vegetation and broken statuary of his 'splendid' old garden: all Meredith can see from his small window is the top of a paling fence, part of a brick wall, and the plumbing outlets from his neighbour's bathroom...[12]

In *My Brother Jack,* the shift from an older, inner-urban to a newer, suburban location is often described as stultifying to the artist. Even the abysmally shabby and mediocre 'Avalon' has 'more things of true value' than the hideously middle-class, and significantly nameless, 'home' in Beverley Grove.[13] For adolescents with artistic aspirations, such a shift can be highly damaging. Barbara Hanrahan's narrator in *Kewpie Doll* (1984) remembers the family move to one of Adelaide's new suburbs, away from the stimulating working-class milieu in which she had happily spent her childhood, with something approaching horror. Her description of the new house calls on several familiar suburban signifiers – the rotary clothes hoist, the laminex table, household gadgetry, and (a nice touch) the plastic Mexican on the front porch. In this sterile environment, asserts the narrator, 'There wasn't any mystery'. But the biggest obstacle of all was the presence of an indoor, press-button toilet. She had been fond of the outdoor lavatory (with chain) at the former house, thinking of it as a 'bower, its old brick walls cocooned with bridesmaid's fern and creeper', and, even more suggestively, as a 'dark and mysterious...private place'.[14] The romantic associations here oddly ascribed the 'dunny' may have a cultural explanation. The reading of the old-fashioned Australian backyard in a semiotic study of Australian popular culture, *Myths of Oz* (1987), suggests that the outdoor privy, usually surrounded by vegetation, formed an urban link with the indigenous Australian rural tradition, a tradition to which the elaborately-designed 'outdoor living areas' of modern domestic landscaping do not defer.[15] In *Monkey Grip* (1977) Helen Garner tacitly recognises the connection by having her narrator, Nora, gaze 'bucolically' at the rank vegetation and mechanical debris of her tiny Fitzroy backyard as she sits meditatively on the 'dunny'. The outdoor toilet, furthermore, is often invested with rich imaginative potential in Australian fiction. To Hurtle Duffield, the artist-hero of White's *The Vivisector* (1970), the vine-hooded lavatory in the yard of his ramshackle Paddington house is a 'secret shrine' of aesthetic contemplation and inspiration. Flooded by sunlight and garlanded with flowers, it is a place in touch with nature, unlike the antiseptic indoor WC, which is a kind of denial of it.[16]

The dunny motif is an aspect of the proposition that, while the inner-city paradoxically retains traces of the Bush, suburbia is intrinsically 'anti-Nature' and, by extension, anti-Art. In *Kewpie Doll* the narrator pointedly remarks that the new suburb to which she has been transported was once covered with orchards and vineyards; now all that sprouted were dismal 'houses like boxes'.[17] A similar dialectic is at work in another autobiographical novel structured around an expatriation theme, David Malouf's *Johnno* (1975). Remembering his enforced adolescent move to 'one of the best suburbs' of Brisbane, 'Dante' pines for the old wide-verandahed inner-urban house (located in South Brisbane) in which he grew up, with its 'damp mysterious storerooms', its verdant backyard and its nearby disreputable park populated by metho drinkers and swarms of insects. By contrast, everything in the large flashy house at 'Arran Avenue,

Hamilton, Brisbane, Queensland, Australia' is 'glossy' and 'modern', disparaging adjectives in a national genre which privileges the essentially European quality of age, a quality only, if at all, to be found in the cosmopolitan inner city. Like Hanrahan, Malouf asserts that the 'old' environment holds more 'mystery' for the autobiographical subject than the new, 'mystery' providing a special stimulus to the developing artistic talent.[18] (Hence the inevitable voyage to the Old World by the narrators of both *Kewpie Doll* and *Johnno*.) Again and again in Australian retrospective fiction, the childhood relocation from 'old' to 'new' is registered as an aesthetic as well as geographic shift. This can produce curious modifications of narrative perspective, as for example in 'The Great Wall of China', the opening story of Laurie Clancy's collection *City to City* (1989). The story is a post-war childhood reminiscence, recalling the family move from a 'decrepit old' weatherboard house (with a 'rambling', arboreal backyard) in the established inner Melbourne suburb Elwood to a 'brand new house in a brand new street' in the then outer suburb of Hampton. Though the dominant voice in the story is that of the narrator as a pre-adolescent, in remembering his anticlimactic first sighting of the new house in a dauntingly standardized housing development, he falls into the judgmental language of the sophisticated aesthete. 'It was the newness and rawness that appalled the observer,' he remarks. The project 'appeared to have been designed without the least regard for aesthetics'.[19]

Just as a shift *to* the suburbs shocks the aesthetic system, a move to the inner city *from* the suburbs provides nourishment to starving sensibilities. Hal Porter in *The Watcher on the Cast-Iron Balcony* (1963) reminisces that as a young man teaching in suburban Melbourne in the late 1920s, he often took the train to the city to savour 'Life' – a capitalized word he repeats a dozen times within two pages. Disdaining suburbia, the young Porter's construction of inner Melbourne is that of a 'magic place' of potential danger and depravity, its nineteenth-century lanes and cul de sacs harbouring eccentrics, prostitutes, markets, bookshops, bars and foreign cafés, the latter of which were religiously avoided by the 'general Australian' but frequented by the 'intelligentsia and decadentsia'. This heady milieu for a budding artist offered sanctuary from suburbia and from suburban values. In the sequel to *The Watcher*, *The Paper Chase* (1966), Porter describes the area around Collins and Bourke Streets during the thirties as a hive of 'studios, love-nests, and *pieds-à-terre* away from mum and dad...'.[20] As Richard Haese has written of the creative life of the period, the migration of young writers and artists from suburbia to inner Melbourne during the 1930s, along with a counter-movement to the bush outside the metropolis altogether, represented the 'desire for a flexible, permissive and creative sense of community' unobtainable in the suburbs that 'girdled' (note the use of a *female* image of constriction) the city. To both urban and rural artistic colonies, suburbia posed a threat to 'freedom, creativity and progress'.[21]

The counter-cultures of the 1960s and early 1970s were similarly motivated by a hankering after an environment in which individual freedoms could be pursued and artistic energies catalysed. Generational rebellion against the 'suburban values' embodied by the middle-class parental domain created attitudes akin to those expressed by Porter in the thirties. A social worker in a classic Australian 60s text, Peter Mathers' *Trap* (1966), for example, swears that among the 'old houses' and the 'back lanes and alleys' of Fitzroy and Collingwood, 'there's more life – real, squirming, dancing life – than to the square mile of suburban Ringwood or Highett or Preston'.[22] Helen Garner's stories of chaotic communal life in Fitzroy and Carlton capture this historical ambience. Commitment to, in Esson's Nietzschean terms, the ideal of 'living dangerously' proves personally costly for Garner's young radicals – as is most clearly implied in the mutually destructive relationship between Nora and the junkie Javo in *Monkey Grip*. But there are few regrets. Nora's exhilarating ride back to the crumbling buildings and narrow roads of Collingwood after a stupefyingly suburban Christmas lunch in capitalist Kew conveys not only escape but a defiant rejection of an entire way of life and mode of thinking.[23] As in a more overtly political novel with a similar Collingwood/Kew urban axis, Frank Hardy's *Power Without Glory* (1950), cartographical detail in *Monkey Grip* not only promotes 'realism', but signifies a carefully designed map of cultural values and moral attitudes. Frank Moorhouse's fictionalization of late sixties inner Sydney counter-cultural life, though spiced with satire, likewise celebrates city life at the expense of the middle-class suburbs. Moorhouse's 'modern urban tribe' contains many martyrs to the rebellious cause, especially women, for whom the new heterosexual freedoms and feminist ideology are often incompatible. Confused by the complications of their lives, many of his intellectual, political and sexual activists look back longingly to the safe suburban womb from whence they had sprung; but though they cannot escape that world they cannot return to it. The pull of what Moorhouse calls 'the city's emotional magnetic field' is too powerful. Like Cindy, a young student in *The Americans, Baby* (1972) who 'was not of the suburbs any more', they have spent too long discovering themselves in the city to cash in their individuality for the perceived anonymity of the suburbs.[24]

Garner, Mathers and Moorhouse tap into an Australian tradition of urban writing that extends back at least as far as the 'larrikin' novels and narratives that were in vogue early this century. As in contemporary urban fiction, the inner city is prized, in a work such as Louis Stone's *Jonah* (1911), for its Dickensian human diversity and vitality. The intellectual 'pushes' of Moorhouse's Sydney of the 60s and 70s and the larrikin pushes of the pre-First World War slums are culturally connected by a mutual preference for anti-social, anti-authoritarian postures and practices. In *Jonah*, the mindless violence of the street gangs is stridently deplored, but the larrikin's quaint vulgarity and contempt for authority are sympathetically handled. More broadly, their inner-urban stamping ground – such sites as Paddy's Market, that 'debauch of sound and colour and sound' – is privileged as an arena in which the most fundamental human drives are played out.[25] *Jonah* fictionalizes an attitude which is endemic in Australian fiction, particularly in texts, like *My Brother Jack*, which are the products of a comfortably *bourgeois* sensibility. Slum-dwellers, the argument runs, are quintessentially interesting because their poverty makes them so. To David Meredith, fatuously commending 'the grim adventure of true poverty' to his readers, the 'dangerous' slums of Fitzroy and Collingwood provide the opportunity for 'audacities' in an increasingly docile middle-class society; the suburbanites, by pitiful contrast, have the temerity to accept their 'mediocrity'.[26] But what Meredith would really like, of course, is enough money to live in dishevelled bohemian grandeur like this friend, Turley of Toorak. That's *real* class.

As is evidenced by the equivocal attitude toward the slums in the social realist fiction that developed in Australia from the time of the Depression, the charms of the inner city create problems for the novelist who wishes to use it as a locale for the raising of political issues. The 'slum fiction' of a novelist such as Kylie Tennant is highly ambivalent, trying to combine documentation of the poverty of an exploited proletariat with a lyrical celebration of working-class humanity, communal values and humour. The slum becomes the tragic product of corrupt capitalism, a focus for political outrage, and, irresistibly, a place of enormous attraction. The attitude of Bramley Cornish, the hero of Tennant's *Foveaux* (1939), toward the slum-dwellers draws attention to these ambiguities. Cornish 'liked the dirty, tragic cheery people, their bravery and their horrible patience, contented in Hell. He liked the streets and the muddle of factories and houses and lanes where everything was unexpected. He liked the funny little squares where cats sat amid staghorns on the curious pillars outside houses nearly a hundred years old.'[27]

Less formally realist novelists such as Christina Stead and Patrick White are also ambivalent toward the city. In *Seven Poor Men of Sydney* (1934) and *For Love Alone* (1944), Stead documents the human misery and corruption created by social inequality and environmental hegemony, but she also plays up the picturesque aspects of slum-life for all they are worth. Her description, in *Seven Poor Men of Sydney*, of a sensuous summer evening among the tenements of Wooloomooloo, with its images of warm pavements, heaving bosoms, hairy chests, gas-jets illuminating bedrooms of stockings and corsets, children's revelry, even the 'rancid' breeze blowing in from the wharves where the workers are singing,[28] is so wonderfully sordid that the political thrust of the novel is effectively negated. Who, one might ask, would want to do away with the poverty that makes such appealing squalor possible? In White's essentially apolitical fiction, the city is alternately depicted as an apocalyptic underworld, as in *The Tree of Man* (1956), and as a place of spiritual and creative renewal. Degradation and rebirth are closely linked in *The Vivisector*, the most metropolitan of White's novels. Perhaps this ambivalence, in a novel about a painter much inspired by physical sensation, comes from White's own sense of 'wet, boiling', 'beautiful, ugly' Sydney as a city of contrasts and contradictions.[29] Much of *The Vivisector*'s narrative vitality stems from its detailed pictures of the sleazy inner city. Recovering from a stroke, Hurtle Duffield – son of a bottle-o and a washerwoman: son of the slums – takes to the streets, which he sees as 'rivers of life'. Walking the pavements of his squalid neighbourhood constantly revivifies him: 'The smell of the streets made him feel alive: warm pockets of female flesh; lamp-posts where dogs had pissed; fumes of buses going places.'[30]

Occasionally, in White, artistic creation to match the procreative capacity dramatized in *The Season at Sarsaparilla* (1965) does occur out in the suburbs, as the dying efforts of the Aboriginal painter Alf Dubbo in *Riders in the Chariot* indicate. But at both aesthetic and metaphysical levels White regards the suburbs as, 'barren-ugly'. More than that, they represent the failure of Australian civilization. Brian Kiernan has pointed out in a discussion of *The Vivisector* that the fate of Grandpa Duffield, who borrowed a mule in order to fulfil his 'dream' of riding to the centre of the continent but died of a seizure on the Parramatta Road, suggests a 'mock-heroic' Australian allegory.[31] The bogging down of national aspirations in the wilds of suburbia is implied; the limitations of national vision circumscribed; and the pioneering Bushman figure debunked.

Who, then, among Australian writers is prepared to give suburbia a voice? Certainly, it has its champions, cultural commentators such as Donald Horne, Craig McGregor and Hugh Stretton, but these are writers of social analyses rather than imaginative constructs. And often their conclusions are decidedly dodgy: Craig McGregor, for instance, has argued that the relatively high birthrate of Canberra ('described once as seven suburbs in search of a city') is proof-positive of its seething vitality.[32] Paradoxically, perhaps, expatriate fiction is more effective in arguing suburbia's case because it commonly allows for some final acceptance of its limitations and recognition of its potentialities. Malouf's *Johnno*, with its narrative movement from the suburbs, to overseas, then return and qualified reconciliation with the rejected home environment, provides a model, as to some extent does the story of Nora Porteous in Jessica Anderson's *Tirra Lirra by the River* (1979). It may be suggestive of a welcome shift in attitudes that a few members of the generation of Australian writers who have risen to prominence in the past ten years – one thinks of Marion Halligan, Peter Goldsworthy, Gerald Murnane – use the suburban site as more than a convenient focus of cultural criticism, while Helen Garner's more mature work shows signs of a rapprochement with the middle-class milieu she rejected in her youth. Alan Wearne's verse-novel set in post-sixties Melbourne, *The Nightmarkets* (1985), is a contemporary text which explodes the myth of suburban deadness. In one scene, Sue Dobson, cynical veteran of the urban counter-culture, takes a friend to the family home deep in the suburbs as part of a tour of the city. 'Take any normal street of average length and just/ consider all that fucking!', she advises her companion. 'Simply concentrate on/ a street of a suburb: *that's* mindblowing!'[33] Bolstered by the verb so favoured by Garner's urban gypsies, this observation neatly rebukes those who mechanically dismiss the suburbs as passionless and sterile.

I have not wanted to argue here that the suburbs should be celebrated, and I acknowledge that a negative treatment of suburbia and suburban 'ideology' has produced some of the more profound cultural critiques and technically innovative fictions of recent years: witness David Ireland's apocalyptic western Sydney in *The Chantic Bird* (1968) and *The Glass Canoe* (1976), the riotous burlesque of Canberra in David Foster's *Plumbum* (1983), the migrant fictions of writers such as Ania Walwicz, which register the disorienting impact of the Australian domestic terrain on the European mind, and most notably, the psycho-cartographic characterizations of Adelaide and Canberra in Murray Bail's *Holden's Performance* (1987). I do say, however, that the virtual restriction of suburbia's representation to satire and ridicule has disfranchised its 'constituency' (that is, most of us), and that this has led to a compensatory and gratuitous glamorization of the inner city which has had the effect of depoliticising ostensibly political fictions. Bruce Dawe's words in the poem 'Homo Suburbiensis', if we can forgive him the exclusive use of the male noun, are relevant here. Suburban man – whom Dawe significantly places in a luxuriant, productive backyard – doesn't offer all that much, 'but as much as any man can offer – time, pain, love, hate, age, war, death, laughter, fever'.[34] It is time the full range of these neglected qualities was represented in Australian fiction.

NOTES

1. See John Docker, *In a Critical Condition: Reading Australian Literature* (Ringwood: Penguin, 1984), p.36; also Graeme Turner, *National Fictions* (Sydney: Allen & Unwin, 1986), pp.25-6.
2. See *The Chant of Jimmie Blacksmith* (Sydney: Fontana, 1978), p. 174.
3. T. Inglis Moore, *Social Patterns in Australian Literature* (Sydney: Angus & Robertson, 1971), p. 18; Ian Reid, *Fiction and the Great Depression* (Melbourne: Edward Arnold, 1979), esp. pp. 28-36.
4. Louis Esson, 'The Suburban Home', in *The Time Is Not Yet Ripe*, ed. Philip Parsons (Sydney: Currency Press, 1973), p. 73.
5. Barry Oakley, *Let's Hear it for Prendergast* (Ringwood: Penguin, 1971), p. 102.
6. D.H. Lawrence, *Kangaroo* (Harmondsworth: Penguin, 1950), pp. 15-16.
7. *Let's Hear it for Prendergast*, pp. 150-51. See also Allan Ashbolt, 'Myth and Reality: Godzone Part 3', *Meanjin*, 25 (Dec. 1966), pp. 373-74. Ashbolt bemoans how far 'the Australian man of today' ('A block of land, a brick veneer, and the motor mower nbeside him in the wilderness') has slipped from the masculine paragon established by his forebears.
8. Patrick White, *Riders in the Chariot* (London: Eyre & Spottiswoode, 1961), p. 231.
9. Patrick White, *The Solid Mandala* (Harmondsworth: Penguin, 1969), p. 17.
10. *The Time Is Not Yet Ripe*, p. 73.
11. George Johnston, *My Brother Jack* (London-Sydney: Collins, 1964), pp. 284-86.
12. *Ibid.*, see pp. 264-75, 276-77.
13. *Ibid.*, p. 286.
14. Barbara Hanrahan, *Kewpie Doll* (London: Chatto & Windus, 1984), pp. 82-3.
15. John Fiske, Bob Hodge and Graeme Turner, *Myths of Oz: Reading Australian Popular Culture* (Sydney: Allen & Unwin, 1987), pp. 46-7.
16. Patrick White, *The Vivisector* (Harmondsworth: Penguin, 1973), pp. 396-97, 306-7; see Helen Garner, *Monkey Grip* (Melbourne: McPhee Gribble, 1977), p. 226.
17. *Kewpie Doll*, pp. 82-3.
18. David Malouf, *Johnno* (Ringwood: Penguin, 1976), pp. 4, 49-50.
19. Laurie Clancy, *City to City* (St Lucia: University of Queensland Press, 1989), p. 8. See also pp. 5-6.
20. Hal Porter, *The Watcher on the Cast-Iron Balcony* (London: Faber & Faber, 1963), pp. 217-19; *The Paper Chase* (Sydney: Angus & Robertson, 1966), pp. 71, 98.
21. Richard Haese, *Rebels and Precursors: The Revolutionary Years of Australian Art* (London: Allen Lane, 1981), pp. 28-9.
22. Peter Mathers, *Trap* (Melbourne: Sphere Books, 1978), p. 17.
23. *Monkey Grip*, p. 189.
24. Frank Moorhouse, *Futility and Other Animals* (Sydney: Angus & Robertson, 1969). p. 145; *The Americans, Baby* (Sydney: Angus & Robertson, 1972), p. 46.
25. Louis Stone, *Jonah* (Sydney: Angus & Robertson, 1979), p. 69.
26. *My Brother Jack*, pp. 41, 285.
27. Kylie Tennant, *Foveaux* (Sydney: Sirius, 1946), p. 310.
28. Christina Stead, *Seven Poor Men of Sydney* (Sydney: Angus & Robertson, 1965), p. 139.
29. Patrick White, *Flaws in the Glass* (London: Jonathan Cape, 1981), p. 151.
30. *The Vivisector*, pp. 520, 557.
31. Brian Kiernan, *Images of Society and Nature* (Melbourne: OUP, 1971), p. 137; see *The Vivisector*, p. 11.
32. Craig McGregor, *People, Politics and Pop* (Sydney: Ure Smith, 1968), p. 52.

33. Alan Wearne, *The Nightmarkets* (Ringwood: Penguin, 1986), p. 64.
34. Bruce Dawe, 'Homo Suburbiensis', in *Condolences of the Season: Selected Poems* (Melbourne: Cheshire, 1971), p. 96.

GARETH GRIFFITHS

City and Bush in the Australian Theatre 1922-1988

Despite the awesome sweep of my title I do not intend to attempt a full survey of the presentation of urban life on the Australian stage over the last sixty years or more. The title is intended to indicate that some significant factors affecting the presentation of urban life, and the formation of the image of the City and its significance in Australian theatre since at least the 1920s seem to me to be consistent, and persistent. In fact it would have been just as easy and meaningful to have selected an earlier or later date, rather than 1922, which many of you will recognise is a reference to the opening production of the Pioneer Players in Melbourne; since, as Margaret Williams has rightly noted, the history of Australian plays on the commercial stage for eighty years or so before Louis Esson had already gone a long way to establishing that popular and distinctive Australian theatre which Esson sought to create in the 1920s. Indeed, as more recent critics like John McCallum have argued part at least of Esson's problem might have been that his view of a national theatre ignored this popular, native tradition and was too self-consciously conceived in terms of foreign models, especially the Irish and Russian models, models which were largely irrelevant to Australian conditions. Vivian Smith too had the same perception, as he phrased it, that 'The Pioneer Players failed to live past a few productions mainly because of public indifference, but also because there was no genuine equivalence between the Irish and the Australian situation.'[1]

The major difference between Australia and Ireland as between Australia and other countries, such as nineteenth century Russia, to which Esson looked for models, was that Australia had no original, 'primitive' culture to which the new European descended settlers could lay simple claim. As John Dunmore Lang had realised as early as the 1830s although the emerging consciousness of identity on the part of the new settlers of their difference from their originating centre of colonial power might lead them to reject its names (and culture) as 'badges of oppression' and dispose them in preference to 'like the native names', a long and difficult process of appropriation needed to be undergone before these names and the culture of the original inhabitants they signified might be available for use as signs of Australianness at large. That such appropriations are still fraught with unresolved issues was made perfectly clear in the Bicentennial year of European invasion/settlement.

For invader/settler colonies such as Australia then there was no ur-volkisch tradition to revive, as in the Irish and Russian models that so exercised Esson's imagination. Those 'shepherds going mad in lonely huts' which Vance Palmer noted[2], Synge saw as appropriate material for Esson's purpose were not and never could be the original 'type' of Australian national character, the essence of Australianness on the model of the proto-Irishness which Synge felt he had recorded in the life of the Irish peasant or Tolstoy in that of the Russian. In fact, of course, they couldn't be for Synge or Tolstoy either since the enterprise of such primitivist, Herderian projects is vitiated at base by its essentialist assumptions about culture. Founded in Romantic, essentialist and representationist views of culture, and also, of course, constructed in terms of a model which imposes a fixed chronological (diachronic) model of development on the historically dynamic and continuous social and class complexities (synchronic complexities) it hides, it functions, in practice, to obscure such differences under a consensual national or racial model which replaces the idea of historical change with that of essential national character and characteristics. Synge, significantly, began his observations of the 'essential' rhythms of Irish speech, as he himself records, by 'listening to the servants through the crack' in the floor of his lodgings in County Wicklow. Such middle-class, urban romanticisms are endemic in the construction of these stereotyping models of the rural origins of essential, national life. Esson's retreats to the bush-camp at Mallacoota in Victoria set up by E.J. Brady to allow Melbourne's urban bohemians to experience the 'real' Australia is flavoured by the same limitations, as indeed were Tolstoy's idealisations of the peasants and Russian country life, as Chekhov (a writer committed to social change, despite his reputation in the English-speaking world) was later to note with some irony.

The problem was even more complex in a post-colonial settler culture, such as Australia. It was so from the beginning, but became even more so after the first great rush of foreign migration in the gold fever of the eighteen forties and fifties. Ironically, the 'shepherds' in the Australian bush were, by the second half of the nineteenth century, as Joseph Furphy (Tom Collins) was to record so successfully in *Such is Life*, as likely to be speaking with a Chinese, German or Irish accent as with an Australian bushman's drawl. The features of the 'authentic' Australian bushman were constructed then, as now, by the artists of the city, though it must be said, with less commercial success than now, as *Crocodile Dundee* bears witness.[3]

What Furphy perceived and recorded was the essential post-coloniality of the society he sought to record. The fact that its distinctive feature consisted in, indeed had to consist in, not in some discoverable or recoverable essential national characteristic but in a historically constructed hybridised complexity, a complexity which persists into the present and hybridised complexity, a complexity which persists into the present and which is likely to be a feature of its foreseeable future. In the fact, that is, that it existed and came into being within and through a series of evolving cultural intersections, intersections which involved displacement and dislocation as their dominant characteristic. This was reflected in the novel's very structure with its continual digressive pattern, and in the kaleidoscopic variety of dialect Furphy perceived as constituting the reality of Australian speech in bush, as in city environments.

Paradoxically Esson was able to see and record this in his brief early studies of urban life in a way which his mythologising of the 'bush' prevented him from doing in the later plays with a bush setting. For example, in the setting of Spiro's cafe for the play *The Bride of Gospel Place* produced by the Pioneer Players in 1926, where much of the by-play of Act 1 revolves around the interaction between the Melbourne street characters and Spiro, the Greek owner

> Milky: Eh, Spiro!
> Spiro: What-a you want?
> Milky: Two cup-a da coff'! (They all laugh)
> Spiro comes from behind the counter, excited and gesticulating.
> Spiro: Listen to me, young fellow. (Tapping Milky on shoulder.) You go somewhere else.
> Milky: Eh!
> Spiro: (impressively) I don't serve thief.
> Milky: (rising) Hear the Dago talking to me.
> Spiro: (excitedly) I ain't no Dago. I'm Greek.
> Milky: Shut the gate, he's bolted!
> Spiro: I'm Greek-Greek!
> Milky: What's stung Spiro?
> Master: If you call him a Dago he goes off like a packet of crackers.[4]

The sense of Australia as a complex society, more justly and accurately represented by images of social and cultural intersection and conflict as by homogenous shared essential and characteristic values is even more marked in Esson's much earlier short play (adapted from his own story) *The Sacred Place* (1911) which deals with a disputed debt between an Indian street hawker and an Indian moneylender in Melbourne. The play was produced in 1912[5] by William Moore at one of his Drama Nights at the Turn Verein, (significantly, as the name indicates, itself the hall of a German Club.

> Akbar Almad: Jhuta, Jhuta!
> Shah: Your heart is black,, Muhammed.
> Muhammed: Tum kya bola, Shah Shereef!
> Shah: I say you are the son of a dog.
> Akbar Almad - Kutta! Kutta!
> Muhammed: I thrust the insult back in your face.

> (Muhammed rushes at Shah. Constable keeps them apart. The hawkers gather round muttering).
> Muhammed: I summon you. I summon you.
> Constable: That's enough. Keep back there. No disturbance. You can argue the matter out without fighting.

[Forced by Shah to swear to the truth on the Koran in the Sacred Place, the small shrine at the back of the room which constitutes the mosque for the little community of hawkers, Muhammed backs down.]

Once we cease to be bound in our judgements by Esson's own obsession with the project of establishing a national theatre, and cease to accept the nationalist and essentialist views of Australian culture which this embodied we can begin to assess Esson's achievement in terms of his success in mirroring the actual complexities of his contemporary world and not with his success in creating such influential stereotypes of the national mythology as the dying stockman from his most critically acclaimed play, *The Drovers*. Instead we can reevaluate the neglected urban plays and see how these are much more significant and symptomatic representations of Australian life then, as now, presenting, as they do, Australia as a place where a national consciousness has been, perforce, constructed out of the intersection of a succession of migrancies, and displacements, all in their various ways in interaction with the experience of a new place and of a sense of dislocation and otherness.

More importantly we can see that similar problems to those faced by Esson continue to haunt the presentation of contemporary urban Australian experience on our stage.

This is not, as I have said, an accidental, nor yet a 'natural' feature but, like the bush myth a construction, or representation which has social and ideological determinants. It is, moreover, a construction which has been a consistent and persistent feature of the presentation of urban life in a neglected group of Australian theatre texts. These urban texts have frequently confronted the theme of difference not in terms of the simple, Romanticised mythology of the formation of a distinctive national character in response to a harsh, physical environment, but in terms of the cultural effects of such determinants as linguistic and cultural alienation and marginalisation as an inescapeable feature of all post-colonial experience. As we have seen in the case of these early Esson texts non-Anglo-Celtic migrant experience is a clear and frequently dramatised instance of this difference. But non-English speaking migrant experience is only a particularly clear and forceful representation of an overarching condition of dislocation endemic to an invader/settler colony. Linguistic and cultural dislocation occurs in some degree even to the free settler of English stock, free, in theory at least, to continue in the exercise of his Englishness, and yet who, as text after text demonstrates, feels constrained within one generation or sometimes less to seek markers of difference which can express his sense of 'otherness' and distinction from the culture of the originating centre. This, is, of course, at the root of Esson's own concern and is the source of the drive to establish the 'bush' myth itself.

Thus, it is within this wider conception of a post-colonial Australian cultural formation of difference that the 'bush myth' finds its distinctive place. Viewed contextually, thus, it becomes one of a number of markers of dislocation (a very important one, and indisputably the most dominant in the culture for most of its existence). But this dominance results from the specific historical and political forces which bring it into prominence, and not because it incorporates some natural and essential Australianness. Read contextually the privileging of the 'bush' over the city is the privileging of one form of the representation of colonial dislocation, from landscape, climate and environment, over others, more particularly over urban dislocations reflecting social inequalities, class and race divisions etc...divisions in which the authority of the centre over the margin, of the empowered over the underprivileged, of the majority over the minority etc...is reflected in ways historically formative to post-colonial discourse, and with strong consequences for the political and cultural models which it inevitably underwrites.

As recent work has shown, this privileging of the 'bush' setting over the 'urban' (working in conjunction with other forces, such as the swing to the right in Australian politics in the early fifties) has had a very distorting effect on Australian theatrical representation, and also on the theatre histories which record and perpetuate this distortion for future generations. The important conference on the period 1920-1955 held at the home of the neglected Campbell-Howard Collection of Australian plays at the University of New England, Armidale in 1986, drew attention to much that had been neglected in our views of the themes and development of Australian drama. Amongst the most important revisionings was the stress on the neglect of the radical writers associated with the left-wing New Theatre Movement in Melbourne and, especially, in Sydney during the period from 1932 to the early sixties. The re-evaluation of the work of the radical playwrights associated with the New Theatre in this period stresses the need to acknowledge a continuity of radical writing, concerned with such issues as race, migration, and class conflict in an urban environment; with the political development of Australia; and with the social movements which have shaped it, from industrial conflicts to two World Wars and their profound effect on social life in Australia. Significantly, as Leslie Rees has noted, this has not been the case in plays regarded as mainstream events in modern Australian theatre. For example, he notes of The Doll that it '...offered its own intimate problems in personal relationships for solution, its domestic battle between illusion and reality unrelated particularly to the Australian evolutionary story, for instance, the war period, which would have been part of The Doll's seventeen years, is not mentioned.'[6]

What this acknowledges is the need to trace an alternative, if largely suppressed, tradition in Australian theatrical self-representations which have given due acknowledgement to these large-scale social and political forces. This alternative tradition, links the early Bohemian portraits of the life of an urban lumpenproletariat (e.g., in plays like Esson's *The Woman Tamer*, 1910) and multiracial community of the slums (*The Sacred Place*, 1911, and *The Brided Gospel Place*, 1926) with the work of the radical (frequently female) writers for the New Theatre in the period before, during and after the Second World War; with the satirical and protest work of the APG in the sixties and of writers such as John Romeril who emerged from this and who continued to work largely in community theatre and in other marginalised theatres; and with later community theatre groups such as migrant theatre groups and multicultural companies such as Sydney's *Sidetrack Theatre*; and finally, perhaps, the work of more recent socially and politically conscious writers such as Dorothy Hewett, Louis Nowra and Stephen Sewell, who have all tackled these themes in their work for theatre, and for television.[7]

The dominance of the bush myth and the theatre forms to which it has given rise has overshadowed this strand in our theatrical history. It is peculiar that the bush myth and the tradition to which it gave rise should have had this suppressive role in twentieth century Australian theatre, since the usual view is that it is the source of the populist egalitarian traditions of 'mateship', the bush socialism of the early pastoral unions, and so on. This is certainly a strand and an important one in its social effects. The radical companies of the forties and fifties reflected the continuation of this in the fact that it was the bush play, *Reedy River*, replete with songs like 'Click Go The Shears', 'The Ballad of 1891', 'My Old Black Billy' etc...which long financed the more aggressively political shows, as did later plays such as Oriel Gray's compilation *Henry Lawson*. What this reflects, of course, is the fact that the 'bush' in itself is as potent a setting for representations of socially conscious art as the city, properly treated. But, after Esson, and in the form constituted by him in *The Drovers*, the template for the serious bush plays of the thirties, forties and fifties[8], its concerns here been largely with the problems of heroic individuals battling a hostile enviroment and facing a tragic and inescapable fate. All plays in this tradition, even those not directly concerned with the bush have reflected this dominant ideological framework. For this representation of the bush ethos Esson's *The Drovers* (written 1919) is the classic source. The dying stockman's 'hymn to the good life of the bush' is, as John McCallum notes, 'in every (male) Australian's kitbag'

> I've lived my life careless and free, looking after my work when I was up to it, and splashing my cheque like a good one when I struck civilisation. I've lived hard, droving and horse-breaking, station work and overlanding, the hard life of the bush, but there's nothing better, and death's come quick, before I'm played out.

Underpinning this myth is an Australianised tragic vision, rooted in stoicism and in an ideology of Providential acceptance of a 'natural' world to which man is willy-nilly subject. As the dying Briglow remarks to the boss of the drive

Briglow: Well, it's been a good life. I'm satisfied.
Boss: That's the way to look at it Briglow.
Briglow: It's fate.
Boss: That's right. It's fate.
Briglow: No man can dodge his fate.

It was this same tradition of bush stoicism which underpinned and supported the heroism and waste of the Diggers dying at Gallipoli or in the trenches of Flanders in the recently finished War to End All Wars. Yet the political lessons to be drawn from this are nowhere present in Esson's piece, nor in the many celebrations of fatalistic bush stoicism as a national trait to which it gave rise. From this we might conclude that, in the theatre at least, after 1920 the myth of the bush is no longer in the service of a tradition of political consciousness and egalitarianism and has been coopted to a much more romantic concern with national myths and legend-making.

The only notable exceptions to this asocial and apolitical strain in the plays of the Bush tradition after the 1920s are the occasional foray into the plight of the new migrant and the Aboriginal and their marginalised roles in the xenophobic and racist world of station and small bush town. George Landon Dann's late thirties play *Fountains Beyond* which deals with the plight of aborigines, especially its part-white protagonist, in the fringe settlement of a northern Queensland coastal town or Oriel Grey's *Sky Without Birds*, 1952, which deals with Jewish migrants, and *Burst of Summer*, 1960, which deals with the return of a Jedda-like Aboriginal actress to a small town and her re-departure when she realises that the only role it has to offer her is as a drunk and a 'tart from the flats'. One of the most powerful treatments of racist attitudes in the Australian bush was by a writer whose work is central to the radical New Theatre tradition discussed above, Mona Brand, who, in 1948, wrote *Here Under Heaven*, which deals with the prejudiced reception accorded the Singaporean refugee wife of a returned AIF soldier when he brings his bride home to his parents' cattle station. That its attack on Australian attitudes was justified received strong confirmation when, as Christine Tilley has pointed out, it was rejected for professional theatre production despite an enthusiastic reception when played by the New Theatre in Melbourne on the grounds that '"there is no colour problem in Australia"', ipso facto it would be irrelevant to Australia's experience and not worthy of a large commercial production.'[9] It is, of course, symptomatic that the bush plays which reflect social issues deal with communities and racial groups who threaten the homogenous, romantic version of the 'bush' which the nationalist, essentialist myth has developed.

Existing theatrical accounts, too, have fostered the idea that the authentic Australian theme is the heroic individual isolated in a hostile bush environment, tragically and inevitably overwhelmed by implacable natural forces of flood, fire and drought. Theatre histories give much more attention to plays which mirror this theme than those which mirror the alternative representation of Australia as a diverse, politically conflictual, multi-cultural urban country with self-determined and politically soluble problems. Leslie Rees, for example, in his major 510 page 1973 account *The Making of Australian Drama* devotes only two pages to the plays of the New Theatre radical women writers Mona Brand and Oriel Gray, whilst the history of the New Theatre is relegated to scattered references and a section of an Appendix. Likewise the great Western Australian writer, Katherine Susannah Pritchard receives only two pages, neither of which makes mention of plays such as *For Instance,* the story of an English girl in an Australian clothing factory, presented to a conference on women's suffrage in London in 1914 or of the powerful political agit-prop work she did in the thirties in plays like *The Great Strike* (an early doco-drama which her son Ric Throssell dates from 1931), *Forward One,* 1935, and *Women of Spain,* 1937, which Throssell recalls seeing performed on the back of a truck at a Perth Spanish War Relief Rally.[10] On the other hand Douglas Stewart and the Verse Drama of the Forties receives a Chapter heading, and no less than nineteen pages devoted to an analysis of Stewart's work particularly *Fire On The Snow,* Stewart's romanticised study of the heroic figure cut by Scott on his last expedition; *Ned Kelly,* in which the theme of a central hero is obvious, and finally *Shipwreck,* that black study of inverted individual power which centres on the Batavia Disaster of 1629 and the Republic of Murderers set up in its aftermath by the mutineer, Cornelius.

Likewise in the section dealing with the new experimental theatre which emerged in the early seventies the stress is on the single mainstream work by Boddy and Ellis *The Legend of King O'Malley.* There is no mention in this or in most extant accounts of the experimental work of writers like Brand at the New Theatre in the late sixties. Christine Tilley again draws attention to this omission in our theatrical record.

> Neither *Going, Going, Gone,* on the sale of Australia to foreign multinationals, nor *On Stage Vietnam,* the history of the Vietnamese people and their struggle for national independence, were greeted as innovative in style by the critics when in fact they preceded *The Legend of King O'Malley,* 1970, by Michael Boddy and Bob Ellis by some three years, which was welcomed into mainstream Australian drama as a breakthrough in style – a style in which the form was the message. This example is one of the most glaring occasions of Brand's exclusion, in that she had been testing new directions in Australian playwriting style in an amateur theatre three years prior to it being hailed as new and innovative by the reviewers of the

> professional production of *The Legend of King O'Malley*, and by some of the people who have contributed to writing the history of Australian drama'.[11]

(Tilley is targeting an article by Margaret Williams which she footnotes, but it is with a sense of contrition that I admit to sharing the limitations of Rees's and Williams's pieces in an article which I published as late as 1980 in which I cited the O'Malley piece as just such a 'breakthrough'.)

In fact, of course, in the work of the community theatres we saw a continuing concern with urban social and political issues and with the non-naturalistic experimentation which frequently accompanied these concerns. For example, the plays of the neglected female, radical playwrights of the period mounted by these companies and, still until recently largely overlooked by theatre historians, seem most clearly and yet with least recognition to prefigure issues still relevant to the Australia of the eighties. For example, Dymphna Cusack's prophetic political piece, *Pacific Paradise* again taken up by the New Theatre, rather than by professional companies after it won attention in the 1955 Trust competition, dealt with the very contemporary issue of the use of a small Pacific island as a site for the military trials of a new weapon and the effects of this callous experimentation on the lives of the inhabitants. Other plays such as Oriel Gray's *Let's Be Offensive*, 1943, Patricia and Cedric Flower's *Pot of Message*, 1949, Mona Brand's send up of the Commission to investigate the ludicrous Petrov Affair, *Out of Commission*, 1955, or the group-devised plays which might have proved direct working models for the APG's attempts at ensemble work, such as *Press the Point*, 1950, *The Follies Bourgeois*, 1951, and *United Notions*, 1953, because of the conditions described above remained largely unknown to the theatreworkers of the next generation radicalised by the Vietnam war and by the theatre experiments which accompanied its protest in America. It was the New York company *Cafe La Mama* and the *San Franciscan Mime Troupe* which were their inspiration not the, in many ways more relevant, but forgotten, work of the Australian New Theatre movement.

It might be worth asking why so many of us interested in the accurate history of Australian theatre got these things wrong for so long? There are a number of reasons for this. First of all, it reflects the tendency of theatre historians to privilege the work and the traditions associated with professional and mainstream theatre over that of even the most influential and experimental amateur, or community theatres; even though it is clear with hindsight that, in Australia at least, such amateur and community theatre pieces have been and continue to be producers of the most powerful and innovative work through the whole of this century.[12] In its turn this reflects the fact that unless successful in a professional venue plays are unlikely to survive as published or even printed texts, and so are unlikely to be brought to the attention of the theatre historian working from the conventional sources. This is clearly the case with the work of

K.S. Pritchard mentioned above, for example. Second, it reflects the specific censorship of this radical theatrework in the cold war climate of the fifties, a censorship which existed literally not just metaphorically, as recent work has demonstrated. The New Theatre received no reviews in the general press, nor had paid advertisements accepted by major newspaper groups, from 1949 until the unofficial ban was lifted in 1963.[13] This crucial gap in Australian theatre history meant that younger, radical playwrights and directors such as John Romeril and Kerry Dwyer at the APG in the sixties were unaware of the earlier models for a politically active, urban theatre provided by the work of the New Theatre in the thirties, forties and fifties. The plays of this period, to which the younger generation had been denied easy access not only reflected a continuing concern with urban, multi-cultural working class issues but also introduced to Australia a non-naturalistic, revue style of performance very different from the naturalistic play which dominated the commercial theatre. The new wave of plays usually dated from the success of *The Summer of the Seventeenth Doll* in 1957 had introduced Australian audiences to plays with a contemporary theme, but remained firmly fixed in a naturalistic mould.

In the absence of a lack of awareness of this tradition the new generation of radical writers who formed the APG out of Betty Burstall's Cafe La Mama in Carlton, Melbourne in the early sixties, notably the group of young University radicals such as John Romeril, Bill Garner, Lindsay and Margo Smith, etc..whom Jack Hibberd has recently and rather sourly, perhaps, characterised[14] as 'the Monash Maoists' were, as John Romeril has said, denied a perception of a native tradition of radical, engaged, non-naturalistic theatre and forced instead to derive their models of post-Brechtian epic theatre, of worker-participation theatre and of street agit-prop companies from the accounts of these forms in the back-issuses of the Tulane Drama Review on the shelves of the University Library. Although, as is now clear, all these forms had had an extensive history of employment in Australia over the previous thirty years. Finally, and not the least, it seems to me to reflect the continuing domination of the ideology which informs the 'bush' play tradition since the 1920s, the tendency to privilege texts which deal with the struggle of an heroic individual over odds. (King O'Malley, for example, constructs itself through this particular myth very strongly). Plays which have a communal or social concern, or which seek to dismantle the idea of the isolated, individual achiever as the Australian archetype were correspondingly neglected. Such plays only succeed in the professional theatre by negotiating a relationship with the expectations of the audience and by offering at least the formal thematic lineaments if not the political and ideological sinews of this particular mythology, e.g. Dorothy Hewett's *The Man from Mukinupin*, the play which restored her work to critical attention by powerfully deconstructing the very elements of the 'bush' myths which it employed to achieve productions by our leading companies; or, more recently, Louis Nowra's brilliant adaptation of Xavier Herbert's *Capricornia*, a production which might well bring earlier treatments of the theme of the mixed race child to mind, such as the George Dann play *Fountains Beyond* mentioned above. Plays which ignore the myth, such as John Romeril's urban musical *Jonah Jones* are neither well produced nor well received, since they fail to meet the expectations dominating both theatre industry and audience in the nineteen eighties.

In fact all those plays which have succeeded in addressing political and social issues successfully in a mainstream venue have done so by working in and through the existing theme of the bush/country-town world as that of archetypal 'authentic' Australia, whilst denying its function as reinforcer of the ideology which has usually sustained this, an ideology reflecting an individualistic, politically conservative and xenophobic world view.

So powerful has the myth of the 'bush' as the essential Australian experience been that only plays which have made this kind of compromise have received widespread recognition and performance. Other theatre has been dismissed as a 'minority' concern, not of interest to Australians at large, the ubiquitous 'man in the street' (or should we say 'man in the bush', though 'man in the suburb' might be the most accurate soubriquet of all in terms of simple demography) who, in a circular way, have been taught by the force of such representation to identify their 'Australianness' only through such circumscribed and historically biased stereotypes.

Fortunately the alternative and more radical tradition which opposes this construction of Australianness has also remained alive, if only in the work of a new generation of theatreworkers outside the mainstream, professional companies. The limited funding of community theatres by the Arts Council in the last few years has allowed a number of groups concerned with reflecting the social and political realities of urban, multicultural Australia to emerge. Yet the same neglect which characterised the treatment of the radical theatres of the post-war period can now be seen to be affecting the work of companies concerned with modern, urban, multicultural Australian issues such as migrant educational deprivation, unemployment and cultural isolation. The newspapers and critics continue to neglect the work of both the migrant language theatres which have sprung up in all the major cities, and the work of such multicultural groups as Sydney's *Sidetrack Theatre*, whose poly-ethnic company led John Romeril to suggest that it was the only group genuinely qualified both by personnel and by interest to be called an Australian 'national theatre'. *Sidetrack* was founded by Don Mamouney and Grahame Pitts in 1979. Their work over the last ten years has consistently represented Australian culture as complex, and as founded in the conflictual social concerns that one might expect in a modern society which has absorbed people from all parts of the world and which has not been isolated from the social and economic divisions which are a characteristic of modern urban societies.

The dominance of the 'bush myth', initiated in the nineteenth century theatre, and developed by such influential figures as Esson and Palmer in the twenties, has privileged the 'bush' ideology of heroic individualism and natural tragedy over the equally powerful possibilities (displayed, as we have seen, even in the earlier work of those writers who constituted the national mythology such as Esson himself) of urban cosmopolitan multicultural life with its possibilities for social dialogue and political self-determination as the characteristic Australian material condition of existence since the late nineteenth century. This was, unconsciously perhaps, but with great consequence, the result of the choice of a consensual, idealising and apolitical mythology of the lone Australian hero (white, male and Anglo-Saxon) battling an environment of natural enemies over a conflictual, but potentially dialogic, material. The emergence of this stereotype suppressed the representation of the complexities of Australian life in the twentieth century, a representation which stressed the constructed nature of social reality and the ability of society to actively order and reorder that reality according to its political and social goals. This choice, which as a result of the powerful role played by media censorship of this alternative tradition in the conservative backlash of the late forties and fifties and by the role of theatre history in perpetuating the privileging of the texts of the canonical 'bush' tradition over that of the radical, marginalised little theatres, remained the dominant one until recently, militated against the modern professional theatre's attempts to represent the complexities of post-war Australian society, to depict its increasingly multi-racial nature, to register its continuing social inequalities, and racial disharmonies, and to assert its increasing dependence on a so-called international economy whose strings are firmly pulled from elsewhere.

Again, it is left to theatre companies existing outside the mainstream, and subject to an erratic attention from the media and from academic criticism to keep the representation of these concerns alive and to reflect the continuity of these issues in the increasingly complex multicultural reality of the modern Australian city. Fortunately, plays like Sidetrack Theatre's *Out From Under* or the more recent and powerful *Kin* demonstrate that this tradition of urban, radical theatre (if almost as neglected by press and funding bodies as the earlier radical work of the New Theatre movement) is very much alive, and as responsive as ever to the ironic gaps which open up between public mythologies, the arts which enshrine them, and the interpretative space they occupy in the consciousness of the actual Australian in the cities of the eighties. Thus, in Sidetrack's play *Out From Under* which examines educational goals and aspirations to betterment in the migrant community the poem 'Australia' by A.D. Hope becomes not an instrument of 'liberatingly ironic' self-definition but an instrument used to impose a new and different kind of 'uniformity' on the working-class migrant youth, Michael, whose natural abilities and skills (as a mechanic and craftsman) are denigrated by a family, and a teacher (himself a migrant's son) who have confused the ability to absorb the 'language' and concerns of middle-class, Anglo-Celtic Australian culture (represented, ironically, via the Hope text which the children are 'studying') and the 'empowerment' it confers with educational achievement and self-definition. As the mother realises at the play's end, the poem like the education system it serves, actually functions not as a tool to liberate and define through the creative use of ironic distance, but as a means of imposing uniformity in the name of the new officially endorsed image of a national culture and so indirectly works to convince working-class, migrant kids like Michael Capoti that they are not 'worth' getting 'out from under'. In a powerful final monologue in which the mother equates the teacher's advice with the stereotyped birthing techniques the doctors had sought to impose on her when she was giving birth to the child, Michael, she exposes the oppressive nature of the discourse within which she and her son continue to be marginalised and suppressed, a discourse in which, as mother, worker and migrant (dare one say producer) she continues to be excluded despite the claims of the poem to be speaking, in some sense, 'for' Australia and forging an identity for its inhabitants.

> I didn't go to university. But I'm a good cook, and I can sew lots of things - don't need a pattern. You're just like your grandfather, Michael. When you were a baby you were just the same as you are now. I knew if I was going to tie you up in blankets you would kick and push until you got them off. Maria was happy to just sit there - not like Michael kicking and throwing things off. And shoes - I could never keep them on you. Thank goodness we were in a warm country. I don't know. People always telling you what to do, trying to tie you up. They don't know you like I do, my friend ...
>
> Like when I was having you in the hospital – so many people telling me what to do! Just as well I didn't understand most of what they were saying. Would only have made me feel worse ...
>
> It was like they were trying to stop you my boy ... But they didn't stop you my boy, you came alright, with your little fat face, all red like ... angry, then I take you straight away on my stomach and then we both cry and laugh all together, like we just won a bloody war. Only you been fightin' ever since. I didn't know it would be like that. I didn't know it would be like that. So many people thinking there's only one way to do things and so many babies being born and not being loved for just what they are.
>
> You don't let them tell you you're stupid, Michael.

The continued existence of such powerful theatrical statements is evidence of the fact that the alternative tradition of radical and critical social awareness is still alive, a tradition whose determinants are the material existence of the majority of Australians, the citizens of a complex, modern, heterogenous and largely urban society with both the conflicts, and divisions this entails and the possibilities for growth and change which this suggests. In practice the predominance of the bush myth and its domination of Australian theatrical representation has been, as I have argued, itself a feature in constructing the view of Australia and Australianness which dominates our institutional practices. Until some more effective narrative of the alternative representations of Australianness which this tradition has deprivileged emerges this will continue to be the case. This paper is designed merely to draw attention to this possibility, and to note that the process is now under way in terms of theatrical history. For example, Tony Mitchell's two-part account of Italian theatre in both the Italian language theatres and in multicultural community theatre since the end of the nineteenth century writes a whole neglected chapter into the account, and draws attention too to the powerful presence of a contemporary Australian theatre whose 'work goes beyond a simple exploration of migrant folklore to an examination of the political and cultural clashes endemic to the migrant experience.' (Mitchell *Australian Drama Studies*, 11 p. 37.) Although this revision of the culture of such a migrant group is to be welcomed in and for itself, it is also symptomatic of the need to revise the history of Australian self-representation in the theatre and in other arts in terms of a more complex model than that imposed on that experience by the romantic simplifications privileged by the 'bush' tradition. Plays like *Essendon Lewis* which is a sort of theatrical extension of BHP's television advertisements for the 'Quiet Achiever' do not properly represent the long and complex history of the Australian working class in such industrial towns as Newcastle, Wollongong and Broken Hill. Yet any effective representation of Australia must surely include an account of the life of these important urban communities, whose inhabitants are no less a part of the Australian reality than Esson's swaggies and lonely shepherds. Important contemporary texts dealing with such communities, for example, John Romeril's *The Dud War* have never received a professional performance, let alone achieved the status of print. Indeed this is true of most of the significant texts discussed in this paper. Is it surprising then that Australian theatre history should be so unrepresentative of the powerful alternative traditions which have been so much a feature of its actual practice, if not of its mainstream and commercial theatres.

It is only when this sense of a unity in and through difference as the inescapable project of any post-colonial society such as Australia, where indigenous peoples, invader-settler people and more recent migrant groups have all been subject to dislocative experience is accepted, and replaces the idea of a single, homogenous 'Australian' essential nature endemic to the ideology of the bush-myth that the kind of persistent marginalisations of groups as diverse as migrants, blacks, women, city dwellers can be achieved, before in the words of a recent Australian play's title song, *Kin*. It is only when this sense of a unity in and through difference is accepted, and replaces the idea of a single, homogenous 'Australian' essential nature endemic to the ideology of the bush-myth that the kind of persistent marginalisations of groups as diverse as migrants, blacks, women, and city dwellers can be overcome. It is only when this sense of a unity in and through difference is accepted that in the words of the final song of *Sidetrack Theatre*'s bi-centennial play, *Kin*, kin-ship can be achieved.

> Celebration won't begin
> Till We Realise We're Kin (Repeat)
>
> The Party's Been and Gone
> With a Jingoistic Song
> They Said Don't Dig Up the Past
> Or the Party Would not Last
> Bring Your Kin Along
> They Can Sing Their Cute Folk Song
> Racial Strain Won't Disappear
> After Celebration Year
>
> (Seems) Too Much to Say
> (So Much) Ignorance in our Way
> (Til' We) Respect Our Different Kin
> The Celebration Won't Begin
>
> Til We Realise We're Kin
> The Celebration Won't Begin (Refrain)

NOTES

1. Vivian Smith, *Vance Palmer* (Melbourne, Australian Writers and their Work, OUP, 1971), pp. 8-9.
2. In fact, this isn't quite what occurred. Esson had been telling Synge about the 'boundary riders, shepherds or swaggies, who sometimes went mad, or half-mad, from the loneliness of their surroundings' and 'Synge apparently replied, 'But when they are going mad, are they not interesting then?' This is recorded in Louis Esson, *Ballads of Old Bohemia* edited by Hugh Anderson (Melbourne: Red Rooster Press, 1980), p.174, and quoted in John McCallum, *Australian Drama 1920-1955*, p. 44.
3. Esson's friend and contemporary, Vance Palmer, has to be credited with one of the earliest perceptions of the significance of Furphy's work in the construction of an Australian consciousness. 'Such is Life', he remarked, at the time of its reissue at his instigation in 1917, 'will become a classic for the next generation'. He 'believed throughout his life', as Vivian Smith has noted, 'that the proper recognition of Joseph Furphy would mark the coming of age of Australian literary culture'. Smith Vance Palmer Australian Writers and their Work OUP 1971 pp. 7-8.
4. Louis Esson, *The Southern Cross and Other Plays* (Melbourne: Robertson and Mullens, 1946).
5. The same year incidentally in which Gregan McMahon produced at the Melbourne Repertory Company Esson's only full-length play of urban, political life, the long undervalued *The Time is Not Yet Ripe* which is enjoying a much deserved revival in critical esteem.
6. Leslie Rees, *The Making of Australian Drama* (Sydney: Angus and Robertson, 1973). In Fact, *The Doll*, was, as critics have noted, in many ways only a modified version of the traditional bush play, both in its characters (bushworkers transplanted to the city) and in its continuing, if uneasy, concern with such classic themes as mateship, the spree mentality, and the fraught relationship of the sexes in Australian society. To be fair to *The Doll* it was new in that it did not uncritically celebrate these elements, and brought a cold eye to bear on some of their assumptions. But it is best viewed, perhaps, as the first of those pieces which succeeded by deconstructing the subject and premises of the bush myth rather than as the first of the new generation of distinctly urban plays. In the mainstream theatre issues such as non-Anglo-Celtic migrancy continued to be represented only by such crudely stereotyping pieces as Beynon's *The Shifting Heart*, and inner city life continued to centre on a petty-criminal world of the Bohemian lumpenproletariat identical with that of Esson's representation in 1910-12 (for example, Peter Kenna's *The Slaughter of St Theresa's Day*). These were the Elizabethan Theatre Trust play-competition winners of 1958 and 1959 respectively.
7. For a discussion of the work of these writers see Mitchell *op. cit.*
8. The other treatment in this period is, of course, the comic bush-life of the adaptation of Steele Rudd's *On Our Selection*, probably the most popular bush representation of the twentieth century in Australian theatre, and notable for the totally apolitical treatment of what is, in possibility at least, a highly significant social theme for twentieth century rural Australia.
9. Tilley p.12.
10. See 'Paths Towards Purpose: The Political Plays of Katherine Susannah Pritchard and Ric Throssell' in *Australian Drama 1920-1955* (Armidale, 1986), pp. 28-39.
11. Tilley, pp. 13-14.
12. As the early Esson pieces cited bear witness, and as the work of companies like Sidetrack cited below still show.

13. Mona Brand, at the 1986 Armidale conference referred to this as '...the first icy breath of he cold war that was to breathe on the Australian New Theatre Movement ... bringing with it a dearth of reviews, a partial advertising boycott, etc...'
14. Hibberd Gillick p. 14.

PETER FITZPATRICK

Views of the Harbour: The Empty City in Contemporary Australian Drama

The exceptionally sleazy Mike McCord, the hustler and film producer on the make in Williamson's play *Emerald City* (1987), has a vision splendid. It is of Australia as a giant movie production house, catering to the American market where the real money is to be made. His sales pitch to Malcolm, the merchant banker, nicely fuses the values of the new monetarism with the new internationalism in art:

MIKE: The world's a global village, Malcolm. A merchant banker in New York has got far more in common with you than a sheep farmer from Walgett, right?
MALCOLM: (*nodding*) It's high time we stopped being so bloody parochial.
MIKE: (*nodding*) Stuff the gumnut clique. Let's start making rational business decisions for a change. The North American market is three hundred million, ours is fifteen. Where does the future lie?

Whatever the dubious relevance of Mike's perceptions to Australian cinema, the exchange is quite suggestive in its application to mainstream Australian theatre in the eighties. The concept of the 'global village' is powerfully evoked in all the plays with which this discussion is concerned, though it is placed within frameworks of critical analysis which are very different from the value-system which enables Mike to embrace it so warmly. In each of these plays, too, its relation to the more familiar preoccupations with cultural definition is much more equivocal than the simple polarity which Mike argues. But the recent emergence of a number of plays which draw on the seemingly universal iconography of the modern city, and which make internationalism a subject if not (as Mike recommends) a shrewd professional practice, is sufficiently remarkable to demand some attention and explanation.

Mike's terms for the prevailing models of parochialism need some adjustment in relation to the theatre. In one sense the 'gumnut clique' was 'stuffed' from the beginning on the stage; the rich evocations of the outback, and the archetypal conflicts of fire, flood and famine which could fill the wide screen, proved resistant to the naturalistic conventions and proscenium stages which constituted the dominant dramatic tradition. There were a number of voices in the late seventies which echoed Malcolm's view that it was time for an end to parochialism in the theatre. But the model to which they were objecting was the mythologizing of suburban culture in which a number of the new playwrights had located their sense of what was distinctively Australian. The mainstream theatre of the seventies took as its primary focus the styles of living which reflected directly the experience of the relatively affluent, relatively sophisticated middle-class that provided the audience for the establishment companies. While the prevailing mode of satiric celebration was rarely more than superficially naturalistic in form, playwrights like Williamson, Buzo, Oakley and De Groen drew mostly on the neatness with which a suburban living-room can fit a proscenium stage.

The interactions occurred in domestic places which were furnished and located in ways which assisted sociological placement; the fact that Don gives his election-night party in his smart split-level in leafy outer-suburban Lower Plenty, while Oakley's marital skirmishes in *Bedfellows* are played out in tastefully renovated Carlton on the edge of the city, distinguishes between sub-species of trendiness in the interests of a sharper social diagnosis. In the great tradition of Ibsenite naturalism, there are clues everywhere in the decor; the prints on the walls, the books left with artful carelessness on the coffee-table, even the choice of a door-bell, constitute a semiotic minefield. As in Ibsen's plays too, the action is customarily confined to that single room which represents the public face of bourgeois privacy; it moves only occasionally to the more developed intimacy of the bedroom, and it never goes into the workplace.

The strength of naturalistic signification runs directly counter to the multiple locations and the impersonal forms of power which the dramatizing of the city entails. In this sense, naturalistic models were as inimical to the depiction of the urban cultures dotted around the fringe of the continent as they were to the depiction of the mythology of its centre. In verse and prose narrative, forms for the reflection of urban experience were well-established. Those concerns in drama, in the work of Louis Esson and others, retained a largely domestic focus which makes it more appropriate to describe them as plays of the inner suburbs, rather than plays of the city. And while the rough vaudevillian mode later provided some lively exceptions to this tendency, in the Hibberd and Romeril extravaganza *Marvellous Melbourne* (1970) and Dorothy Hewett's *Pandora's Cross* (1980), it was a form unsympathetic to the analysis of a complex reality.

The explanation for the absence of dramatic treatments of the fragmentation of urban living does not lie exclusively in terms of dominant dramatic structures, of course. It is also true that living in cities, in the sense in which that might be understood by an American or European, was not until recently part of the Australian experience. The notion of the city as both a commercial centre and a focus for high-rise, high-density accommodation is very new, and very localized; the apartments which compete for views of Sydney Harbour have no significant counterparts in other Australian cities. In *Emerald City*, Williamson defines Sydney's internationalism in precisely those terms, and establishes a mythic contrast with the low-slung suburban sprawl of Melbourne, where the living is gentler, more principled, and more in touch with the gumnuts. In the discussion that follows, I will be dealing in particular with six plays of the city – Patrick White's *Big Toys* (1977), David Williamson's *Sons of Cain* (1985) and *Emerald City*, Stephen Sewell's *The Blind Giant is Dancing* (1983) and *Dreams in an Empty City* (1986), and Michael Gow's *The Kid* (1983). All six locate their actions specifically in Sydney, and establish moral polarities which give a new dimension to the choice of 'Sydney or the bush'. And all six develop the metaphor of 'the view', not only as an index of social hierarchy, but as the central term in an analysis of states of profound moral failure.

The earliest of these plays, *Big Toys*, retains the same set through its three acts; the Bosanquets' penthouse apartment is thoroughly documented as a triumph of 'uncluttered contemporary luxury in Terribly Good Taste'. The sterility of all its stylish surfaces is nicely caught in the one thing that grows there – at the centre of the circular glass coffee table is a bonsai Moreton Bay fig tree. White's form of satiric exposure here depends, like Williamson's in *Don's Party*, on our coming to know the environment very well as a means to understanding the lives it contains. And that process depends in turn, of course, on an identification of the audience as one which can make the appropriate recognitions and judgments; an audience which can, in this instance, distinguish 'Terribly Good Taste' with capital letters from very good taste without them. The seeming solidity of the room is important, too, in setting up the later awareness of its desperate fragility; outside is the precariousness of the balcony, and beyond that the pressure of the void which induces in Mag a kind of existential vertigo as she feels 'the black wind off the harbour'. In *Big Toys* the walls literally dissolve, and the power of that effect relies on our having accepted that this is a theatre of realistic illusion.

The city-plays of the 'eighties insist on a flexibility of staging which is incompatible with naturalistic scenic detail. They rely on token forms of social placement, which are sometimes visible but, in Sewell especially, are more often left simply to inferences from the dialogue. These tendencies in staging and structure may in part be seen as the purely functional shorthand by which the playwright seeks to create the impression of the crowdedness and miscellaneity of city life. But in the physicality of performance, the absence of visual clues in the stage picture can be as suggestive as their presence, in developing images of emptiness, anonymity and disorientation. The Sydney and Adelaide productions of the two Sewell plays, for example, not only omitted all but the most essential of props but employed a revolve stage to facilitate the rapid transitions in both place and time which the action requires. There are fifty-nine scripted sequences in *Blind Giant* and fifty-five in *Dreams*, and a revolve is obviously a practical solution. But in performance the movement of the stage not only fostered a kind of manic intensity in the continuity of the playing which reflected and sustained the emotional pressure, but also suggested powerfully the remorselessness of the processes in which the people were caught up. The system was dramatized as a machine turning at the centre of a dark and indefinable space, going nowhere in a hurry with a degree of self-generated energy that seemed to guarantee catastrophe.

What I have outlined so far is a theatrical response to the modern city which seems merely to illustrate the cliché of urban alienation. Mike McCord would find such a vision hopelessly uncommercial, but he would be cheered at least by the fact that universal commonplaces are safely exportable, and have already been well and truly worked over by the older cultures. In what follows I hope to suggest some perceptions of the city in these plays which give that vision a distinctively Australian emphasis and analysis. The discussion will focus on two areas in particular: the implications of views of the Harbour, and the refinement of the old internationalism-versus-parochialism debate in terms of resistance to a new form of the colonial cringe.

When Mag Bosanquet brings home for the first time the radical Trade Unionist Terry Legge who is to be her new hobby, her first move is to show him the view from the balcony:

MAG: Anyway, Terry, I shan't turn on the light yet, because I want you to see this fantastic view.

(She draws back the curtain from the glass wall. The lights are on above the Harbour. She speaks triumphantly:)

There! Sydney!

(She and Terry go out on to the terrace and stand a few moments by the parapet without speaking.)

The fantastic view of Sydney is a great conversation-starter in several of the plays I am considering. Both the Williamson plays begin with the central male character acknowledging its beauty before he sets about the repudiation of all that it comes to signify. In *Emerald City*, Colin is discovered at a window in the office of his agent, Elaine, asking a question that he perceives as rhetorical – 'What other city in the world could offer a view like this?' Kevin, the crusading ocker journalist in *Sons of Cain*, qualifies his admiration with a note of irony as he stands at the office window of Rex, the editor who is about to employ him:

KEVIN: Commanding view, Rex.
REX: One of the perks of moving up into upper management.
(*Pause*)
I suppose you guessed I didn't ask you here to admire the view.

But in one sense, of course, Rex has asked him there to do just that, and the view from the window provides a permanent trump in the power-games played out before it. The more commanding the view, the more visible the command. The second scene of the play puts Rex on the defensive, as he visits the office of Warren Belconnen, the newspaper baron, where 'the view from the window is even better than Rex's office'. In scene three, Kevin is in the box seat, as he conducts interviews with a string of hopeful women; however, his place in the chain of command is self-evident – the office is small, and has no view.

In this city where the luxury apartment blocks jostle with the office towers for a glimpse of the water, the residential pecking-order is as self-proclaiming as the commercial one. Mike McCord feeds Colin's artistic paranoia with tantalizing suggestions of the way his agent has exploited his talent – 'She's the one living in splendour in Darling Point. You're stuck here in a terrace in Paddington. Why should she have the harbour views?' And in Mike's own career there are tangible signs of his going up in the world. His old high-rise apartment has a view all right, but it consists of a massive billboard for disposable diapers; later his entrepreneurial huckstering wins him a penthouse, where we discover his girlfriend Helen wistfully at the window – 'I don't think I'll ever get tired of this view. Come and have a look. The eighteen-footers have got their spinnakers out today'.

The views are 'fantastic', for some people, in Sewell's Sydney, too. In *Blind Giant*, the Faustean central figure Allen Fitzgerald meets the witch-woman Rose Draper at one of those smart-set cocktail parties which provide regular forums for wheeling, dealing and destroying reputations in *Emerald City*. They are standing on the balcony, overlooking the harbour, in a stillness broken only by the tinkle of a glass windbell, when she makes her opening gambit:

ROSE: It's beautiful, isn't it?
ALLEN: (*startled*) What? The Harbour?
ROSE: The windbell.

Rose signals her unpredictability in this exchange, but she too is sensitive to commanding views; she has one at the office, and another at home, with a balcony where she shoots herself after playing her part in Allen's corruption and thus corroborating her despair.

The view in each of these instances signifies a disconnection from the social realities below, and from the self. Merely to possess a living and working space is not enough; the ownership of a prospect, of all that one surveys, comes to define the hubristic assertion of control. It is more than the exercise of social power, the literal embodiment of being upwardly mobile and a high flier. Within each of these sequences there is a suggestion of the archetype of spiritual temptation, in which the world is on offer in return for the soul. That is what Mag is after in her toying with Terry Legge, and it is the stake in the game between Allen and Rose. Even in the world of Williamson's plays, where the elements of humour and self-reference ensure that the action remains within the thoroughly secular context of interpersonal politics, both Kevin and Colin realise that what they see from those lovely windows represents a fundamental challenge to their integrity.

The most developed of all the temptation scenes is that in *Dreams in an Empty City*, when the millionaire Wilson plays a shamelessly overt Satan to the Christlike Chris, a common man who refuses to despair:

CHRIS: What do you know of man! You, sitting here in the stench of your own moral decay! What could you possibly know?
WILSON: Let me show you what I know!
(He begins to pull the curtain aside)
Let me show you the power of evil! The city, Chris: one of the most beautiful cities in the world. A city sprung from greed and ambition, built from human flesh, every building the grave of a labourer whose life was less important than the profit its construction meant. The city, Chris, thrown up by finance and speculation, conceived in bribery, corruption and murder. A sparkling, empty edifice of dreams and nightmares. Listen to it, Chris, listen to it sigh; listen to its misery, its glory, its hunger. Feel the hum as power flows through it, organizing it, animating it, connecting every part of it from the magnate in his penthouse to the single mother in her room. The city, Chris, the city of death glistening in the light of its own conceit. All this could be yours, nothing stands in your way. Know what men are and the world is yours. Stand here and imagine yourself the ruler of what you see, feel its power inside you and tell me honestly there's anything outside it, anything more real. This is what I know! This is the horror of our life!

Sewell is as unembarrassed about the directness of his invocation of Christian myth as he is about the clarity of his political analysis; the visions of the city which White, Gow and Williamson offer stop well short of apocalypse. But for each of them, too, the city is much more than location. In the debates about the relative values of Melbourne and Sydney which dominate the early scenes of *Emerald City*, Sydney is burdened with a range of adjectives which develop some of Wilson's perceptions. It is 'amazing', 'stunning', 'abundant', 'decadent', 'odd', 'pulsing', 'garish', 'cosmopolitan', 'dreadful' and 'evil'; it is variously 'the most exciting city in the world' and merely 'New York without the intellect'. Elaine will later put the mythography of the cities into a commonsense perspective; no city can be all those things, she argues, and Sydney merely reflects the moral variety of its people more sharply than places like Melbourne, where there are fewer temptations. She calls Sydney 'a playground for the demons within'. Its influence, though, is more active than her metaphor allows.

For all these playwrights, the city is not just a neutral arena for ethical choice; it is an active force in a moral contest, oppressive both physically and metaphysically, with all the power of the super-life which Wilson attributes to it. And the demon, in each of the contests, is more than materialism and the desire for status; the demon can wear those faces, but in these plays his real name is despair.

Sewell's sense of the intricate power-relationships of the capitalist system gives the demon a still more definite shape. His conception of the city includes the subordinate meaning of the word which is customarily denoted by a capital C – the City as financial nexus. *Blind Giant* pulses with disturbing metallic sounds which relate the rushing of the juggernaut to its explicit context in the machinery of production and exchange, while the rattle of computer print-outs generating money for nothing pervades the action of *Dreams in an Empty City*. Sewell's perception of economic interconnectedness requires in both plays a panoramic scope; while most of the action rests with the power-brokers, the pockets of ordinary domesticity and terrible suffering consistently relate the view from the elevated window to the truncated vision in the streets below.

The emptiness of the city in Sewell's plays is wholly metaphorical – it refers to an ethical and emotional sterility which underlies the tumult and the shouting. Like Dickens in his adaptation of the resources of the nineteenth-century novel to the experience of life in the new industrial city, Sewell uses the panoramic plot as a structural analogue of his society. The initial impression with both writers is of vastness and confusion, and a fragmentation which seems to defy orderly resolution. But the process of the plot is a coming to order, as the essential interconnections between the members of the fictive society are exposed and clarified. That they were not evident before is represented as in part a consequence of urban chaos and the shock of the new, and in part a product of the wilful mystification practised by individuals who exploit the system to wholly selfish ends.

Such a process of explanation and coming to order cannot occur in *Big Toys*, where the centre of the conflict lies in the way possessions and pretences at life can be used to repel knowledge of the self and of the reality of annihilation. Nor can it be developed in either of the Williamson plays, which are inclined to run up against the indeterminateness of the 'real life' situations on which their plots are based. Both White and Williamson restrict the perspectives of their plays to the view from the balcony, or its repudiation. Gow's *The Kid* offers an interesting contrast in this respect, since its concern is wholly with the powerless, and with the view from below. The fragmentation of the plot here directly reflects the perception of the mystified victim. Gow's disaffected street-kids are presented as casualties of the modern city; their adult contacts are confined entirely to sundry landladies, employers and exploiters designated merely as Man A, B and C, and Woman A, B and C. When they manage to inveigle themselves into a room in a high-rise Sydney apartment block, Woman B describes their accommodation in glowing terms:

WOMAN B: This is it. This comprises your entire flat. Higher up, of course, they get bigger, they're actually apartments ... View? Yes, there is one. Come here. You really need a chair, but open it up.
(*They lean out*)
See there, between the kiddies' bike factory and the wogs on the corner. That's a bit of the bay, that grey bit, past the smoke stacks. See it. Let me guide your head. Just look straight ahead. See it? ... We have one hundred and sixty units in the block. I believe it's the largest in the Southern Hemisphere. Not counting Housing Commission, of course ...

Sometimes, perhaps, there is something to be said for having no view at all. The turn towards the beauties of the sky and the water is at the same time a turn away from views of the kiddies' bike factory and the wogs on the corner. Certainly Allen in *Blind Giant* prefers to be viewless, as he says when Rose registers her first impressions of his ground-level office at the Rank and File Co-ordinating Centre:

ROSE: Why don't you clean your windows? You might be able to see something.
ALLEN: If you knew what was out there you'd understand why.

Later Allen does have a room with a view, but, far from enabling a wider perception of the relatedness of things, it signifies his alienation from his kind and all he professed to believe in. He goes to the window, but only to shout 'Lies!' to the revolutionaries chanting under his balcony.

The distinctive topography of Sydney in this way offers images of the moral state of urban society which are themselves distinctive. The implicit comparison with other Australian cities which are less blessed, less brilliant, and thereby less recognizably part of the 'global village' of which Mike McCord believes himself a citizen, introduces another distinctively local aspect of the analysis.

Australian theatre, like Australian literature generally, has tended to define its images of cultural distinctiveness against the models of old-world colonialism. Images of the empty centre of the continent, and of the empty suburbs at its edges, have developed their resonance in contrast to European systems of understanding and behaviour. The image of the empty city in these plays is similarly related to forms of American cultural imperialism. In Sewell's plays a number of Americans flit in and out of the action. They are very smooth, very urbane (in the fullest sense of the word). They may be mysterious entrepreneurs, they may be C.I.A operatives – whatever they are, though, they move and speak with the assumption of power. In *Emerald City* the question of American influence is consistently an issue. What Mike McCord means by 'international' is American, whether the subject is art or the city of Sydney. Mike relocates 'Black Rage', written by an Aboriginal woman about her own experience of oppression, in Tennessee; all his projects for film and television are clones of American successes. The sense of an embattled colonialism is implicit in the habits of verbal reference – thus Kate, Colin's wife, remarks that 'Prime time television in America is to art what McDonald's is to cooking'.

In each of the plays, there are pockets of what passes for distinctively Australian experience within or just outside the empty 'international' city. Even in the nightmare world of Sewell's plays there are glimpses of domestic warmth, and reminders of familial connections with suburban and rural Australia. In *Emerald City*, Melbourne becomes the focus for such traditional associations. There is a certain irony, though, in the way the myth that asserts the value of what Melbourne represents is itself a myth drawn from the apparently predatory American culture. The original Emerald City is, of course, located in another Oz; when Dorothy resists the glamour and the potential power which the emerald city offers, and chants the magic words 'there's no place like home' which carry her back to Kansas, she chooses the enduring ties of the traditional community. The yellow brick road led to a palace, but all that it promised proved a fraud. The implication seems to be that even if Melbourne is as boring as Kansas, it is less lonely living there than in a global village.

White's play *Signal Driver*, which suggests through its three acts the insidiousness with which Sydney has devoured its suburbs, offers some telling images of the inexorability of the process. The script calls for the sounds of traffic moving 'more viciously' by the opening of the third act; the trees that were there at the start have gone, and tower blocks are proliferating on the scrim at the rear. Stephen Curtis's design for the Lighthouse Company added 'Two large billboards, advertising Japanese and American cars, which pushed the action to the edge of the road and obliterated our view of the landscape'. Suggestions of that kind could be dismissed as the feeble protests of greenies and luddites, were it not for the pressure generated by the concept of the morally empty city as a tangible and threatening force.

The most striking development among Australian plays of the 'eighties has been the quest for explanatory rather than merely descriptive myths, which is characterized by the attempt to place distinctively Australian experience within a wider moral and political context. The plays which develop the image of the empty city represent the most important form of that quest. They reflect significant shifts in both the dominant theatrical mode and in our forms of cultural self-consciousness. Malcolm, the merchant banker in *Emerald City* whom I quoted at the beginning in his mercenary exchange with Mike McCord, might see their currency as a response to his complaint that 'It's high time we stopped being so bloody parochial'. But the international city on the harbour has in all these plays afforded a view which gives to the concept of urban alienation a distinctively Australian emphasis. They are all concerned with the difficulty, or impossibility, of cultural retrieval. Mike McCord welcomes the prospect of total absorption into the 'global village' with unqualified glee:

MIKE: (*nodding*) Stuff the gumnut clique. Let's start making hardheaded, rational business decisions for a change. The North American market is three hundred million, ours is fifteen. Where does the future lie?

Mike poses the question 'Where does the future lie?' rhetorically, with all the complacency of the profiteer. The contemporary plays of the city implicitly ask it too, but they do so in a moral and cultural framework which makes it a disturbingly urgent and open question.

Note: All of the six plays which are the subject of this paper are published by Currency Press, Sydney and are currently in print.

JENNIFER STRAUSS

Colonial Poet to City Theorist? Michael Dransfield's Incomplete Evolution

Prosperity

monday to friday at the plant
concrete yards are busy with
vehicles and movement altho most of what
moves is machinery
now and then a human figure crosses the open space
looking small & helpless
in the sky above the plant not much is blue
behind the buildings in a grey channel something
oozes past seeming to have been a river

on friday night when the machines are silent
& the watchman finishes his rounds
walking away with gun and torch like some
mistaken supplicant then only the dark
finds it way through wire fences
and sometimes due to atmospheric conditions (for which
the management is not responsible) the wind will rise
or in the wasteland hours of industrial sunday
rain might start falling inadvertently as if
still thinking of a plant as some kind of
flower[1]

Like this for years

In the cold weather
the cold city the cold
heart of something as pitiless as apathy
to be a poet in Australia
is the ultimate commitment.

When y've been thrown out of the last car
for speaking truthfully or mumbling poems
and the emptiness is not these stranded
endless plains but knowing that you are completely
alone in a desert full of strangers

and when the waves cast you up who sought
to dive so deep and come up with
more than water in yr hands
and the water itself is sand is air is something
unholdable

you realize that what you taste now in the mornings
is not so much blood as the failure of language
and no good comes of singing or of silence
the trees wont hold you you reject rejection
and the ultimate commitment is survival (*C.P.*, p. 51)

I have chosen to begin with these two poems because they illustrate the combination, in different proportions, of two strands in Dransfield's poetry – metaphysical vision and social criticism – and it is the intertwining of these, an intertwining not finally sustained, that gives depth to his poetry of the city. But they also illustrate the typically bad press that the city has received in Australian poetry – when, that is, it has had a press at all. By contrast, in fiction, the presence at least of the city (if not its nature) has been unproblematical, and it has figured frequently as an accidental historical setting or as an ideological construct, or as some combination of the two. Certainly though, it is rare, even in fiction, to find that quality of envisionment which Bruce Bennett identifies in Patrick White's *The Vivisector* and *The Eye of the Storm* as the reverberance of a 'created world of contending ugliness and beauty'.[2] Bennett overlooks, I think, the similar quality in Stead's *Seven Poor Men of Sydney*;[3] and it is not accidental that it was for these two novelists that H.M. Green proposed the category of poetic novel. In doing so he was endorsing the notion that it is particularly to poetry that we look for a vision which will illuminate the mundane, and *contain* it illuminated, neither annihilating it by abstraction nor transforming it into the fantastic. We have such poetry in the Australian tradition, but it is much more likely to be concerned with nature than with the city, as indicated by the fact that Hope's distinction of this kind of illumination as metaphysical rather than strictly philosophical is made in relation to the poetry of Judith Wright.[4]

Such illumination does not necessarily call for the grand scale or the heroic subject, and it is often difficult to tell whether it has a distinct boundary with that which has traditionally been called 'imagination'. Is it operative, for instance in Dransfield's 'Rainpoem'?:

three days of rain: indoors

the mind runs over some
eternal mysteries
polishing them lightly: outdoors
even the hugest man seems frail,
gentle, trying to keep dry
a loaf of new bread. (*C.P.*, p. 102)

Or is this merely an engaging example of the 'naturalizing' into poetry of the details of urban living – a process that certainly is becoming more and more commonplace, and which may thereby be doing more than overt argument to subvert essentialist notions that the urban has no proper place in poetry. Certainly, however, when we look at expressions of general values in serious poetry[5] the city seems to be, until very recently, an irrelevant absence or a symbol of negative value, as it is in the two Dransfield poems initially quoted. Why should I think this matters? Because I believe that the value of the special knowledge that poetry offers is that it allows us a distinctive form of entry not only into that which is other (the alien, that which is not ourselves, our time, our place) but also into the familiar, that which *is* our time, our place, our selfhood. If a large part of our social existence is ignored or perceived only negatively, our cultural self-perception is deprived. And as various demographers, cultural historians and journalists are fond of pointing out, Australia is one of the most urbanized nations in the world.[6] This would be difficult to tell, not so much from the actual mass of our literary productions, as from the canon of those productions preserved in literary discussion and scholarship. Perhaps this Conference signals something new: personally I congratulate the conveners for at least changing the lens of attention.

The formulation of the idea of the city in Australian poetry has been determined by features stemming both from our European cultural heritage and from the specifics of Australian historical experience. It has been fundamentally affected by that over-riding tendency in Western European thinking towards dichotomous organization of experience, a tendency which can be strikingly exemplified by the oppositional construction of the urban and the rural and the persistence with which one term or the other has been accorded superior status.

Historically, the valorization of nature as the positive, the good, the real, and its location in the unsocialized or the rurally-socialized landscape, passed from English romanticism into Australia and dominated the way that Australian writers came to terms with their environment, not least in the way that the generic term 'the bush' was used both for the natural physical landscape and for the rural social life established within it. And while much poetic energy beyond that of Dorothea Mackellar's 'I love a sun-burnt country' went into accommodating the sheer otherness of actual physical nature in Australia to poetic experience and diction,[7] the question of the life of man within this environment was even more problematic.

The hardships of bush life may have provoked angry rejection of sentimental idealization in Lawson's 'Up the Country', but it was Barbara Baynton, not Henry Lawson, who took the path of Zola's *Germinal*, and was rewarded with cultural neglect, while Lawson was honoured for providing a route to the valorization of the bush through the location of positive virtue in the shared endurance of hardship. Where, moreover, such hardships could be seen as a consequence of an economic *system*, not merely of natural disasters such as those that continually threatened to ruin Hanrahan, social guilt tended to be allocated to city dwellers and institutions.[8] This identification of the city as the den of self-indulgent capitalism appears in the concluding stanzas of Barcroft Boake's 'Where the Dead Men Lie'. While pastoral workers die, 'Strangled by thirst and fierce privation... Out on Moneygrub's farthest station'

Moneygrub, as he sips his claret,
  Looks with complacent eye
Down at his watch-chain, eighteen-carat –
  There, in his club, hard by:
Recks not that every link is stamped with
Names of the men whose limbs are cramped with
Too long lying in grave mould, camped with
  Death where the dead men lie.[9]

While this acknowledges the existence – and the importance – of the city, the threatening image of that city as both corrupt and powerful may provoke a counter-assertion of the life of cities as artificial, essentially unreal, and this may lead to a facile ignoring of the sufferings of the city's poor and dispossessed. Geoff Page's 'Grit: A doxology'[10] has an easy attractiveness in its praise of 'the country women/ of my mother's generation', but loses sympathy when it gets to 'I praise their scorn/for the city of options, the scholars/in their turning chairs and air-conditioned theories'. There were not too many options for the women struggling to bring up six children in the slums of Melbourne or Sydney at the time that Page speaks of, and even in our enlightened present not too many women know their cities in terms of the soft touch described in these dismissive lines.

Lawson, who was, like many writers, a more complex figure than is allowed for in his canonical status, has over-ridden such easy divisions to leave an outspokenly sympathetic representation of city poverty in 'Faces in the Street',[11] although this is a poem that raises some other points of interest to our topic in its suggestion of the rubbery boundaries between city and suburb, and in its lingering notion that, the corruption of cities being contingent, Australia offered a new historic chance to build 'fair young cities'.

They lie, the men who tell us for reasons of their own

That want is here a stranger, and misery's unknown;
For where the nearest suburb and the city proper meet
My window-sill is level with the faces in the street –
   Drifting past, drifting past,
   To the beat of weary feet –
While I sorrow for the owners of those faces in the street.

Lawson's sorrow extends both to those who endure the working conditions of business and factory and to those who endure unemployment,

But ah! to dreader things than these our fair young city comes,
For in its heart are growing fast the filthy dens and slums,
Where human forms shall rot away in sites for swine unmeet,
And ghostly faces shall be seen unfit for any street –
   Rotting out, rotting out
   For the lack of air and meat –
In dens of vice and horror that are hidden from the street.

Some of the terms of his final stanza – apathy and heartlessness – are notably held in common with Dransfield's 'Like this for years' but there is one marked difference. Lawson can call on God as final judge: in Dransfield's world 'the system is infallible, does not exist, is/ God, is a computer' (*C.P.*, p. 70).

It is unlikely that Lawson conceived his 'fair young city' in the manner of Peter Porter's 'permanently upright city where/Speech is nature and plants conceive in pots'.[12] His ideal was probably more like the unified society of which Clem Christesen remained an eloquent proponent in 1942:

> The poet, the man who sees the whole while others are fumbling around with the parts, has a vision of Australia as it will be, some day, a land of noble buildings, of craftsmen and creators, of farmers and pastoralists, 'weaving a natural beauty into their lives,' a land leading the world in the tradition of the brotherhood of man.[13]

Porter's ideal city, on the other hand, while including both justice and the aesthetic qualities which Christesen, like Furnley Maurice, locates in architecture, is pre-eminently an Athenian city of conversation and civilization and is defined in opposition to the 'sun-burned truth-teller's world' of Australian culture.[14]

In practice, denial of the tradition of the great *urbs* in Australia is rather more multi-stranded than Porter is obliged to allow for in his witty identification of Australian poetic culture with Les Murray.[15] Some are content to assert the superior reality status of the bush by celebrating just that, leaving the city to be marginalized largely by contemptuous asides or by representations of it as spiritually drought-stricken unable to cope with the revelations that it needs, as in Murray's 'An Absolutely Ordinary Rainbow'. The concession of the superiority of the wisdom of the bush over city smartness can also come from quite surprising sources, as when Max Harris says of the four characters in his 'Incident at the Alice': 'Each revealed his own attitude to life and showed his own kind of wisdom except the city man, who proved to be the foolish one among them.'[16]

Meanwhile, on the pro-city side, there has been a prevailing anxiety that Australia may in fact have no *urbs*, only suburbs, with the true city existing always somewhere else: London, Paris, Rome – or more recently New York. A.D. Hope's 1939 swingeing of 'her five cities, like five teeming sores'[17] has been refined to more domesticated ironies in a poem like John Rowland's 1965 picture of provincial Canberra,[18] but both still pin their hopes for Australian society on nature, with Rowland returning to something of the early romantic vision of the Australian landscape and Hope diverging into the desert, a mythological subset of nature as the oppositional other which has been most powerfully deployed by White in *Voss*.

The picture has been complicated throughout by a factor already mentioned in relation to Lawson's 'Faces in the Street' – the fluidity of boundaries between suburbs and city proper, so that it is not always possible to be sure which is in question when discussion turns to the urban. Joyce Nicholson, writing of the 1964 Adelaide Festival Writers Week, tells us that 'Bruce Dawe opened the discussion with a plea for more poetry about city life and the problems around us rather than the eternal bush or outback.[19] It is for celebrating, or for taking seriously the suburbs, that we remember Dawe, like Alan Wearne.

Dransfield however, is no suburban singer, nor does he seem to have a high regard for those that are, if 'On hearing the first poet in spring' (*C.P.*, p. 284) is any indication. We get a better sense of what is positive (as well as non-suburban) in his own writing if, instead of concentrating on this rather glib satire, we set his 'In the park' beside Gwen Harwood's well-known poem of the same title.[20] While it will no longer shock the bourgeoisie, Harwood's sharply poignant vignette of an encounter which mortifyingly drives home the loss of romance in the realities of motherhood, retains a formal elegance and a sense of closure that is very different from the surrealistic suggestiveness of Dransfield's

> they sit in the park where it is green, where it is quiet
> and green. a few hold their heads, some watch the tiny clouds, how they
> fly. others have brought their sketchbooks; they draw the trees
> singing, they draw each other and the clouds. they are here each day,
> walking from the low buildings, returning with the moon and dream.
> one, who is more adventurous has entered the lake, where it is cool,
> where it is green; she does not see the trees
> or just their pale reflections where her face was.
> her friends tow her to the shore, hair trailing in the water like a mermaid,

they carry her home in state, she will be their queen.
the sketches are left on the grass, to be collected later
by a man with a pointed stick (*C.P.*, p. 222)

In so far as he takes up the *theme* of the city, beyond the kind of incidental use of images drawn from experience of it, Dransfield gravitates towards the rather ominous position that the city is both a major site of modern life and essentially hostile to it. As a major site, it claims attention, is not to be evaded by the polite rituals of colonial poetry. But it is likely to reveal itself to attention, not so much as a moral type of wickedness, or an aesthetic type of artificiality, but in the more contemporary psycho-social terms of alienation, the paradoxes of the lonely crowd, the death wish for anonymity. The poems in which this is most clearly defined, apart from 'Like this for years', are 'The City Theory' and 'Geography I and II'. The former begins with a condition of 'anonymity. perfect black,/ featureless'. Here

... the only gravity
is imperturbable silence, which traffic spoils,
recirculating known roads, probably deserts.
there had been reasons for this shifting
this namelessness, strangeness – some exile state
to which the passport must be common, frail,
worn, and of paper usually a bus ticket
or rent receipt easily lost, but saved.
memorise the writing. all language is the same,
there are only three characters, three words;
some think them colours, or that each
is an expression, which can be shown
by gestures of the hands. you had thought this
a secret, a privilege beyond death, hardwon discovery,
next door, they make your coffee for you,
know its ingredients, the cup you like, and
what to say to you; they know your symbols; to learn this
shatters you. (*C.P.*, p. 118)

'Geography' is less ambivalent, although not a great deal more cheerful, about a loneliness that seems to have at least an immediate cause in the departure of a lover:

the problems of the day. being alone. there
are no people in cities, only strangers, populations,
or the sometimes consolation of familiar
others. it is all other. but people, they do not
live in these lanes and towers. perhaps
back in the distance – you accept the idea and
for a moment the problem is one of geography. (*C.P.*, p. 65)

Although the city itself is 'a windy place to be in Autumn/ and cold', it has not yet shrunk to a single room, and when its inhospitality provokes thoughts that 'the first premise is that we should not have come/this implies that there is somewhere else'. Part III appears to invoke the dualistic formula, answering the question 'where is there to go from that?' with:

in the forest, in unexplored
valleys of the sky, are chapels of pure
vision. there even the desolation of space cannot
sorrow you or imprison (*C.P.*, p. 66)

However, other poems such as 'Outback' represent historical nature as caught up in the horrendous consequences of the economic and political behaviour of our time, so that the very idea of refuge in nature becomes almost as much an illusion as the idea of the sociable city, to which he had conceded a 'perhaps back in the distance' in 'Geography I'. The most explicit treatment of flight from an apocalyptic doom is in 'The Change', a long poem which ends:

total sight now
nothing eaten but earthfood
vegetables fruit
we eat some mushrooms and hallucinate
high on abstractions
& a distance of mountains we start
a colony the air is clean here
the water rainwater
we have music & books & peace
on a radio we listen to the world
death itself & death itself
& the cities be killed & ruined (*C.P.*, p. 98)

Apart from the fact that the ill-fated Paraguayan colony of William Lane's New Australia has made Australians sceptical, the emphasis of the last two lines falls critically on loss and destruction. Indeed it seems an unfortunate point to have reached for someone who wishes to argue for Dransfield's having offered an opportunity for something new in the writing of Australian cities.

Nonetheless, I do want to argue that the Dransfield of *The Inspector of Tides*,[21] with his striking verbal and rhythmic facility and his alertness to both the symbolic values and the social realities of the city, seemed to promise a major city poet for the seventies. I say this with some insistence, being aware that it is not what most of those who praise Dransfield wish to make of him. None of the four poems chosen for discussion by Geoff Page for *Australian Poems in Perspective* is a city poem;[22] Alexander Craig, editor of *Twelve Poets*, insisting that the drug poems are not all, or even the main thing, that there is to Dransfield, praises the very traditional qualities of 'particular sensitivity to Australian light and landscape';[23] while John Tranter writes:

> Michael Dransfield, skilfully evoking a mythical ancestral estate wreathed in an opium twilight – a mood that is almost a type of Transcendental Melancholy – contrasts vividly with Nigel Roberts' colloquial and sometimes cynical rendering of the urban drug scene.[24]

One critic who does, however, consider Dransfield as a city poet – although one whose work is marred by aberrant romanticism – is Andrew Taylor, which is of interest, since Taylor, along with Chris Wallace-Crabbe, has a considerable claim to serious consideration as a city poet.25 Both show that a concern to be a poet of the times, of modern sensibility, was as much to be concerned with finding a style as with finding the city as a subject, and the same is true of Dransfield. Among the poems from *The Inspector of Tides*, 'Colonial Poet' and 'Endsight' politicize poetics as they demonstrate through their construction of A.D Hope as bogeyman, something of the connection (and confusions) that Dransfield was making between literary style, social and personal consciousness, and vision of the world. It is of some import, I think, that the more consistently achieved poem – 'Colonial Poet' – is the one that concentrates explicitly on style:

> today he will write some verses. his schedule
> allows for a poem on his travels, or
> roses, or
> a mythological topic.
> the day is hot so he selects the past/ waterfalls,
> dryads, a god or two. from the filing cabinet
> of his head, in which legends are filed, alphabetically,
> He picks out Hylas and a springside of nymphs. these tiny people
> come to life for him, obediently; the ingredients mix well –
> ....
> ... he sees in the still pool of his verse
> a clear reflection of himself as god.
> he rises, leaving the study, it has served its pannelled purpose; switches off
> his music machine. the record, labelled in flawless french
> L'Apres-midi etc/ returns to yet another file, and his gods and little people
> go home to their woods
> as far now from his mind
> as the toy soldiers of his childhood (*C.P.*, p. 101)

Dransfield works here through parodic description, relying on it to carry implicit criticisms relating to wider issues, just as the key adjective 'colonial' is left to gather pejorative momentum as the poem progresses, until the diminution involved in being *still* a colonial poet (well after Harpur and Kendall, who had no choice) is clinched in the final image of toy soldiers.

In 'Endsight' however, Dransfield takes on a more overtly satiric mode. The unapproved poet is now named, and named moreover as keeping company both odd and bad: Union Carbide, Sir P. Hasluck, Askin, Clutha etc. New questions of ethics, and of the accuracy and cogency of argument are therefore brought into play, especially as one notes that the poetic offence is not one of refusing to oppose what is happening in the world, but of doing so in a style that is declared inappropriate, ineffectual:

> midnights of consciousness. still, and even
> silent, for now the jets are grounded, due to
> lack of visibility, & only random thought & squads of
> landladies' plaster ducks attempt flight. occasionally
> an owl thuds into a building. it is always
> dark now, the air a factory black
> like X-rays of the children's lungs. the coated
> earth is brittle, dead horses rot slowly
> where they fall. using modified
> radar & homing devices, vehicles crowd roads,
> sightless, to carry workers from their
> shelters to factories. a distant, hardly
> safer government issues voluminous
> decrees which litter the town like printed snow.
> also the works of the Official Poets, whose genteel
> iambics chide industrialists
> for making life extinct. (*C.P.*, p. 79)

Dransfield's own style, however, fails to convince us that it is as delinquent to write bad poetry as it is to pollute the atmosphere. A poem which is strongly, even wittily, detailed in its description of the nightmare, becomes hasty and inadequately realized, so that the ending is not tragedy of the absurd, but something remarkably like bathos within the poetry rather than the situation.

The grounds for the kind of literary anger that informs (or deforms) 'Endsight' are positively and powerfully expressed in 'Sub Judice', which also shows a more disturbed and disturbing sense of connections between literature and the world than is suggested in the earlier poem. Here

> ...in the clogged world there is nothing
> but traffic moving/ and drivers/ fleas in their flea society.
> now everything is theirs but love.

The remembered 'other script' of pastoral society tells only of a lost world; 'the maypole becomes/ a dead pine' and in a country become a prison

> the freedom of poets is a choice between images
> we choose the images of what is happening.
> is dynamite enough to change things now? and drugs change

nothing but our health/ the dreams were in our mind from birth/.

a choice of images. and in the world
the someone who arrested you
has choice of victims. (*C.P.*, p. 145)

It is always chancy to call on a poet's extra-poetic words for illumination of our sense of what he was and did as a poet, and Dransfield, although apparently a voracious conversationalist about poetry,[27] left little for the written record: 'My views on poetry are few and private' is the sole 'Statement' afforded in Craig's *12 Poets*. Perhaps he had already learned from his 'Statement' for Shapcott's *Australian Poetry Now*[28] that to say 'I operate on feelings not on thoughts' was to fuel opinions that his poetry stood in need not only of images, but of more consistent and pressing thoughtfulness if it was to develop.[29]

In the event, of course, it is pointless to speculate what Dransfield's development might have been, or whether the drugs that changed his health so finally were formative or destructive for his poetic talent. It might seem that in separating out the 1972 poems for publication in the separate volumes *The Inspector of Tides* and *Drug Poems*,[30] he was making a declaration of his own capacity to keep the drug experience co-terminous rather than dominant, even though one can already see, in 'Start with an image' (*C.P.*, p. 139) an unleashing of simultaneous personal despair and surrealist depersonalization that powerfully over-rides political thinking and/or activism.

It may also seem that I am missing the point that it was exactly being a drug poet that made Dransfield a type of the urban poet of the late 60s and early 70s, moving (and moving, restlessness, is part of the type) between 'shabby city rooms and ramshackle country houses' (*C.P.*, p. xvii). But we have already seen that Tranter, who may be granted some authority for his closeness to the whole scene, associates drugs with Dransfield not as an urban poet, but as the illusionist of Courland Penders, lost world of a putatively ancestral pastoral aristocracy. Rodney Hall sees this, rather, as a central and complex icon:

> There was a 'real' old house belonging, I think, to an uncle which might have triggered his creation. But this, of course, is scarcely the point. Courland Penders was his in imagination as much as the world of the gutter and the chapels of pure vision were his. He relished creating the warmth of an ancestral house crammed with appropriately decaying antiques and vestiges of luxury which carried long histories of meaning and nostalgia. (*C.P.*, p. xix)

That last word could suggest, however, that Dransfield was flirting with an anodyne particularly dangerous for poets. 'Nostalgia' says Vincent

Buckley, 'is the most deceptive of all sentiments for literature. It seems the most poetic and is in fact the least; and if too constantly indulged in, it weakens the poetic vision beyond repair.' [31]

What should be noted is that Courland Penders is present in Dransfield's poetic world from his first volume, *Streets of the Long Voyage* (1970). There, 'Courland Penders: going home' and 'Tapestry at Courland Penders' establish the dominant features of Dransfield's 'icon': its decorativeness and its desolation. In its decorativeness it is 'the romanticism of colours, a mythology of dreamers'; in its desolation it is loss made visible:

> ... No patchwork Herefords
> grazing; no wife or sons; only a crop of brambles; only rabbits to be shot
> from a verandah rail...

But this version of an aristocratic pastoral world has little to do with the mythology of the hardships and simple virtues of bush settlement which I spoke of earlier as the myth of socialized nature in Australian tradition, even though it has had a long, if marginal existence in fiction. It flickers as a tantalizing vision of an inaccessible social reality before Sybylla Melville as she visits her grandmother at Caddagat in *My Brilliant Career*, it briefly occupies the lives of Martin Boyd's Langton family, as they move between it, Brighton and Europe; and it reaches its full flowering as symbol of transience in the works of Patrick White. Glastonbury lies ruined in *The Tree of Man*, Xanadu crumbles around mad Miss Hare in *Riders in the Chariot*, Kudjeri declines into squalor after Elizabeth Hunter deserts it in *The Eye of the Storm*, and although Bogong maintains some hold on the tradition in *The Twyborn Affair*, the Lushington's are childless, and Eddy/Eadie cannot find a place in that world any more than he can take on the protective colour of a working man, or fulfil his truest ambition of 'escaping from himself into a landscape'.[32]

It is 'escaping from too literal company' that we find the poet at the beginning of Dransfield's 'Explorer's Journal' (*C.P.*., p. 35) and this should warn us against making too literal a reading of this poem (or say 'Geography III') as either the record or the promise of experience of the physical world of nature as refuge. When that world appears in an apparently objective reality, it may have been, like the cities, ecologically ravaged and degraded, as in 'Outback' (*C.P.*, p. 23); or, its habitations, like the gold town of 'Desert Fragment' (*C.P.*, p. 245) may have been rendered by history as deserted and desolate as Courland Penders. Moreover, in hinting in 'On the Land' at a reason for the failure of white settlement perhaps more fundamental than heedless industrialization, Dransfield adds another voice to those who, like Judith Wright in 'Niggers' Leap, New England', see no possibility for white Australians to be at one with the land until they face, and in some way pay, the debt of its seizure:

... there is no spring
or autumn here none since the trees
were cut out and the tribes
cut down it brought the land bad luck
we never knew what they told
their young but it must have been
poetry (C.P., p. 178)

Yet here too, as with the city poems, the social conscience runs along with, and often seems to play second fiddle to, a witty nihilism, as in the ironically titled 'Lonely as a Cloud' (*C.P.*, p. 246), which offers the death of 'lost in the bush' as the true solution for those who wish to disappear into the landscape.

One may reasonably ask whether there is any poet who has found a way to sing (let alone celebrate) both the metaphysical and the social city and to see that city and the bush as parts of a continuous being, since that is what I seem to be asking (and not finally receiving) from Dransfield. Perhaps my demand indicates that my mind is indeed set in that synthesizing, moralizing Melbournian cast that so exasperates John Docker, since two of the poets I would suggest as having performed the task are the interesting but erratic Furnley Maurice in his 1934 *Melbourne Odes*[32] and Vincent Buckley in his ambitious long poem 'Golden Builders', first published in *Poetry Australia*.[33] While Furnley Maurice is still usually included in comprehensive anthologies, he has tended not to be noticed in discussions of 'the Australian tradition' except insofar as poems like 'The Agricultural Show, Flemington'(included in *The Collins Book of Australian Poetry*) or 'The Victoria Markets Recollected in Tranquillity' (included in the *New Oxford Book of Australian Verse*) explore intersections of country and city life.[34] But what is distinctive about *Melbourne Odes* is its attempt to represent the city itself as what Bruce Bennett called 'a created world of contending beauty and ugliness' – under which headings one might include both aesthetic idealism and social injustice. 'The Towers at Evening' is one of the very few poems to attempt to do for an Australian city what Wordsworth did for London in 'Upon Westminster Bridge' but it is in the third Ode, 'Upon a Row of Old Boots and Shoes in a Pawnbroker's Window', that Furnley Maurice speaks with a more distinctively Australian idiom, and with a mixture of elements intentionally uneasy, moving in both style and argument towards the jaggedness of experience which is one form of modernism. The Dickensian humour of the sight of the pawnshop window gives way to the bitter ballad of the unemployed, with a bitterness intentionally banal as he wonders 'Could any words mean what their eyes mean'. And this is not in contrast to a distant, more desirable context: Matthew Arnold's Adriatic, breaking in a warm bay 'far, far from here'. It is within a context of lyrical natural beauties, and of the paradoxical occasional civic beauties of architecture:

The towers of Melbourne have been wrought
From rock and trouble and grumbling toil,
Or out of the sliding slush the churning concrete-mixer
Spews into a hideous iron-befangled mould.
But watch those towers from the St. Kilda Road;
Their windows ablaze in the sunset,
The floating towers with their bases muffled in trees
And the trees cooling their feet in the water,
And behind, the long splashes of clouds.

Just, however, as aestheticism seems to triumph, the nagging thought breaks in that 'It's little all that would mean/ To the fellows who pawned their shoes'.

Buckley's 'Golden Builders' is a much more intensely personal vision of contending growth and destruction, love and hatred, although it draws on traditional religion as an informing framework both of ideas and of a rhetoric very different from either Furnley Maurice's romantic aestheticism or his social protest. It is a rhetoric so densely structured that, within the space of this paper, I can only offer assertion rather than analysis. I would comment, however, that the way in which buildings and machines figure in a poem is one mark of an urban consciousness. Early attempts at writing about cities tended to lack a language for these in their own right, and to pass rapidly into describing cities in metaphoric terms drawn from nature – even if nature perverted or monstrous, as it clearly is in Macartney's 'Metropolis'. Judith Wright's 'Typists in the Phoenix Buiding' is a very much more powerful and complex poem than Macartney's, but again it is manipulating a mythological imagery based in nature to portray city sterility, which is antithetical rather than *sui generis*, whereas the machines of Buckley's poem, without being anthropomorphically imagined, function as a force in the ambiguous vitality of his city. It is still however, a force driven by men and the purposes of men: for Dransfield, machines are to be grappled with as elements of experience in their own right – cities, and the rooms of cities, are 'planned for machines/ or for people and machines'. Perhaps the most ominous aspect of machines is the suggestion, wittily made in 'Intelligences, despatches, most secret, from a strange country', that humans are falling silent while machines sing and hum in their 'mechanical language'. They may even come to 'grudge us conversation/ they even let yr voice fade now' ('Geography II).

It is perhaps a sign, although a somewhat annoying one to me personally, of the way in which criticism is now so prolific that it is constantly starting-over that I was unaware when I reached the conclusion that 'Golden Builders' was both a very major city poem[35] and the antithesis of Dransfield's kind of city poem, that others had been in this territory before me. Bruce Bennett, in the article already referred to, places it as the major contemporary poem to match White's novels and Andrew Taylor praises it as 'genuinely mythic', predicting that it will be 'central

– in Australia at least – to the new Romantic poetry'.[35] It is surely an actual compliment to the poem's force that John Tranter, with an editorial eye for the real rivals to his chosen team of players, moves with such vigour to dismiss admirers of this poem by applying to them (and by implication the poem itself) the satirical tag of 'Common-Room Humanism'.[36]

It does not seem to me that Buckley's poem, fine (*pace* Tranter) though it is, has had the influence predicted for it by Taylor, and I doubt if this can be attributed entirely to the continuing hostility of the Sydney 'push'. But one writer who does seem to be in a partial line of descent from Buckley is Conal Fitzpatrick, from whose first volume, *Wollongong Poems*, comes 'Discovering Lasseter',[37] with its striking subversion and conflation of the traditional structural relationships of the symbols of city and desert. For Dransfield, when city and desert come together, it is all too often as common victims of a destructive society, or as re-enforcing symbols of an inhospitable universe. In 'Like this for years' – the poem from his first volume that stands at the beginning of this paper, it is not only the city, but the plains, the desert, the ocean, and language itself that fail to hold. In such circumstances survival can be seen as the ultimate commitment; but there were not too many years for Dransfield to practise it. Let me conclude with a kind of epitaph, written by one of the young poets of that time, that place, who has practised commitment to survival with persistence and élan. This is the end of John Forbes's 'Speed, a pastoral':

> you know Dransfield's line, that once you become a junkie
> you'll never want to be anything else?
> well, I think he died too soon,
> as if he thought drugs were an old-fashioned teacher
> & he was teacher's pet, who just put up his hand
> & said quietly, 'Sir, sir'
> & heroin let him leave the room.[38]

We might extend that to 'And heroin let him leave the city'.

NOTES

1. The text of all Dransfield poems cited is taken from *Michael Dransfield: Collected Poems*, ed. Rodney Hall, St Lucia: University of Queensland Press, 1987. All page references for poems are to that edition, hereafter referred to as *C.P.*
2. Bruce Bennett, *Place, Region and Community* (Townsville: Foundation for Australian Literary Studies, 1985), pp. 56-7. By contrast, the Sydney of *The Tree of Man* is pure type, a 'city of dreadful night,' paradigmatic other to Stan Parker's rural home.
3. What 'Sydney' signifies in Stead's novel is a contentious issue as can be seen in the discussion by Grant McGregor in 'Seven Poor Men of Sydney: The Historical Dimension', *Southerly*, pp. 380-404.
4. A.D. Hope, review of *The Two Fires*, rptd. in Native Companions: *Essays and Comments on Australian Literature 1936-1966* (Sydney: Angus & Robertson, 1974), pp. 79-80.
5. 'Light verse' – that of C.J. Dennis or Kenneth Slessor, for instance, has by no means always been unappreciative of urban life, but it is the 'serious' which has been dominant in characterizing 'the Australian tradition.'
6. Their tone of surprise marks exactly that kind of material which is known but not truly grasped, although the literary neglect of urban life was drawing criticism as early as 1896 in Desmond Byrne's Introduction to *Australian Writers*, rptd. in *The Writer in Australia: A Collection of Literary Documents 1856 to 1964*, ed. John Barnes, (Melbourne: Oxford University Press, 1969), p. 58.
7. Mackellar's poem can indeed be read as an attempt to assert Australia's claim to nature as the romantic sublime as against the more domesticated pastoral nature perceived as characteristic of England.
8. Unlike the folk-ballad squatter mounted on his thoroughbred, literary land-owners from Mary Grant Bruce's David Linton to Patrick White's Harry Courtney tend to be decent fellows (unless unfortunate enough to be involved, like Pritchard's Hugh Watt, with aborigines).
9. From *Where the Dead Men Lie*, 1897; rptd. in numerous anthologies, including *Collins Book of Australian Poetry*, ed. Rodney Hall, (Sydney: Collins, 1981), p. 47.
10. From *Cassandra Paddocks*, 1980; rptd. in *The New Oxford Book of Australian Verse*, ed. Les A. Murray, (Melbourne: Oxford University Press, 1986), p. 297.
11. 'Faces in the Street' 1888, but revised for *Selected Poems*, 1918; frequently rptd. in anthologies, including *The Collins Book of Australian Poetry*, p. 50.
12. Peter Porter, 'On First Looking into Chapman's Hesiod,' from *Living in a Calm Country* (London: Oxford University Press, 1975).
13. C.B. Christesen, 'War on the Intellectual Front,' *Meanjin Papers*, 1942. It is noticeable that Christesen tends, like Furnley Maurice, to use an aesthetic symbol, that of architecture, as a positive sign for the city.
14. Porter's description runs

    ... And the same blunt patriotism,
    A long-winded, emphatic, kelpie yapping
    About our land, our fate, our strange
    And singular way of moon and showers, lakes
    Filling oddly – yes, Australians are Boeotians,
    Hard as headlands, and, to be fair, with days
    As robust as the Scythian wind on stone.
15. Murray's response to Porter's poem in *Australian Poems in Perspective: A Collection of Poems and Critical Commentaries*, ed. P.K. Elkin, (St Lucia: University of

Queensland Press, 1978), drew comment from Porter in 'Country Poetry and Town Poetry: A Debate with Les Murray,' *ALS*, 9, 11 (1979), pp.39-48; Murray's position was then elaborated in 'The Boeotian Strain,' *Kunapipi* 42, 1 (1980), pp. 45-64.

16. Max Harris, Author's Note in *Australian Poets Speak*, ed. Colin Thiele and Ian Mudie, Adelaide: Rigby, 1961, p. 144.
17. A.D. Hope *Collected Poems* (Sydney: Angus & Robertson, 1972), p. 13.
18. John Rowlands, 'Canberra in April' from *The Feast of Ancestors*, 1965; rptd in *The New Oxford Book of Australian Verse*, p. 235.
19. See *Overland* 29 (1964), p. 51.
20. She sits in the park. Her clothes are out of date.
Two children whine and bicker, tug her skirt.
A third draws aimless patterns in the dirt.
Someone she loved once passes by – too late

to feign indifference to that casual nod.
'How nice,' et cetera. 'Time holds great surprises.'
From his neat head unquestionably rises
a small balloon ... 'but for the grace of God...'

They stand a while in flickering light, rehearsing
the children's names and birthdays. 'It's so sweet
to hear their chatter, watch them grow and thrive,'
she says to his departing smile. Then, nursing
the youngest child, sits staring at her feet.
To the wind she says, 'They have eaten me alive.'

21. 'In the Park' was published under the name Walter Lehmann in *The Bulletin*, 1961; rptd. in *Selected Poems* (Sydney: Angus and Robertson), p. 27.
22. *The Inspector of Tides* (St Lucia: University of Queensland Press, 1972).
23. Geoff Page, 'Michael Dransfield,' in *Australian Poems in Perspective* (St Lucia: University of Queensland Press, 1978), pp. 215-31.
24. Alexander Craig, *12 Poets 1950-1970* (Milton, Queensland: Jacaranda Press, 1971), p. 15.
25. John Tranter, ed., *The New Australian Poetry* (St Lucia: Makar Press, 1979), xxvii-xxviii.
26. Andrew Taylor, 'Irrationality Individuality Drug Poetry Romanticism,' *Meanjin* 3 (1972), pp. 373-84.
27. See *C.P.*, p. xviii.
28. *Australian Poetry Now*, ed., Thomas Shapcott, (Melbourne: Sun Books, 1970).
I don't mean simply revision, although if Hall is to be believed, he did little of this; nor do I simply mean ideas – Dransfield had plenty of these, but not everyone might feel as sanguine as Hall in describing a poet thus:
His knowledge of art, music and religion was eclectic to say the least. He took what suited his personal iconography... he showed little sign of wanting to know about orthodox categories, or the details of any narrow specialisation, or even the large-scale intermeshing of movements in art and society. He wanted to remain open to surprise, to an adventure of ideas, to pure movements of insight. (*C.P.*, p. xvii)
29. *Drug Poems* (Melbourne: Sun Books, 1972). Don Anderson's review in *The Bulletin*, March 25, 1972, p. 49, comments on the 'hard, clear, disciplined, fully realised' poems in this volume; but few reviewers have been able to find these qualities in Dransfield's final poems.

poems in this volume; but few reviewers have been able to find these qualities in Dransfield's final poems.

30. Vincent Buckley, 'The Image of Man in Australian Poetry,' rptd. in John Barnes, ed., *The Writer in Australia: A Collection of Literary Documents 1856 to 1964* (Melbourne: Oxford University Press, 1969), p. 281.
31. Patrick White, *The Twyborn Affair* (New York: Penguin Books, 1979), p. 161.
32. Furnley Maurice (Frank Wilmot), *Melbourne Odes* (Melbourne, 1934).
33. First published 1972, this served as the title poem for *Golden Builders and Other Poems* (Sydney: Angus & Robertson, 1976).
34. Les Murray's other selections from his works are a bush-ballad and a short, rather awkwardly abstract personal-philosophy poem
35. It is of course true that it deals, in strict geography, with inner suburbs, and Beate Josephi includes Buckley in her article 'Images of Suburbia in the Poetry of Bruce Dawe, Bruce Beaver, Gwen Harwood, Vincent Buckley.' *Quadrant* 22, 4 (1978), 64-9; but the idea of the city so informs the whole poem that it would seem absurd to treat it as suburban in the sense that, say, Alan Wearne's 'Out There' is suburban by intention.
36. Andrew Taylor, 'Irrationality Individuality Drug Poetry Romanticism,' p. 383.
37. In the Introduction to *The New Australian Poetry*, Tranter constructs a collage of comments approving 'Golden Builders' and comments that the terms are 'appropriate to a work... with specific moral and religious overtones,' but that their language of 'high seriousness' is 'quite inappropriate to most areas of people's lives... a quasi-religious rhetoric... Common-Room Humanism ... apt to sermonize as any other fervid minority belief.' (xxi-xxii)
38. Rptd. in *The New Oxford Book of Australian Verse*, p. 368.
39. John Forbes, 'Speed, a pastoral' from *The Stunned Mullet* (Sydney: Hale & Iremonger, 1988), p. 28.

PETER R: PROUDFOOT

CANBERRA: Landscape and Symbolism in the Parliamentary Triangle

> Mr. Griffin paid particular attention to ... symbolical treatment. His symbolism is of a sociological kind. Everything is placed in relation to everything else in accordance with a curious academic 'system'. The buildings of the future university for example, are planned in concentric circles intended to illustrate the expansion of human knowledge from the fundamental sciences through the theoretical sciences, to the applied sciences, beyond which are 'those spheres where the sciences will be utilised in real life'. Thus, on that part of the rim of the outer circle marked by the two spokes running out from biology, lie surgery, medicine, pharmacy, recreation, athletics ... this is an interesting exposition of the new culture. But it is not architecture. Architects must some day attempt the task of translating the elaborate pattern of lines and figures into three-dimensional form. It is doubtful whether they will succeed.[1]

Canberra has not developed along the lines of other modern capitals such as New Delhi, Chandigarth, Brazilia and Dacca where monumental constructions symbolise the power and authority of centralised government. The quotation above identifies an incipient barrier to the realisation of Walter Burley Griffin's plan and it helps to explain the structured blandness of Canberra's landscape dominated environment.

The early Town Planning movement in Australia was concerned with social welfare, that is to say, with many of the policies related to housing, health and recreation that could contribute to a more egalitarian society. Australia's suburbanisation has been conditioned by this town planning ideology and by many aspects of Ebenezer Howard's Utopian Garden City theory promoted by John Sulman, an English expatriate architect and planner, who became chairman of the Federal Capital Advisory Committee following the departure of Walter Burley Griffin in 1920.[2]

Griffin's competition winning design had provided for Canberra an intricate geometrical pattern of suburban roads which swept around three chief centres unified by three 'axes' derived from the City Beautiful movement and Baroque vista planning: the land axis, the municipal axis, and the water axis which passed through five proposed ornamental basins. Griffin emphasized that, in essence, the plan hinged on axes

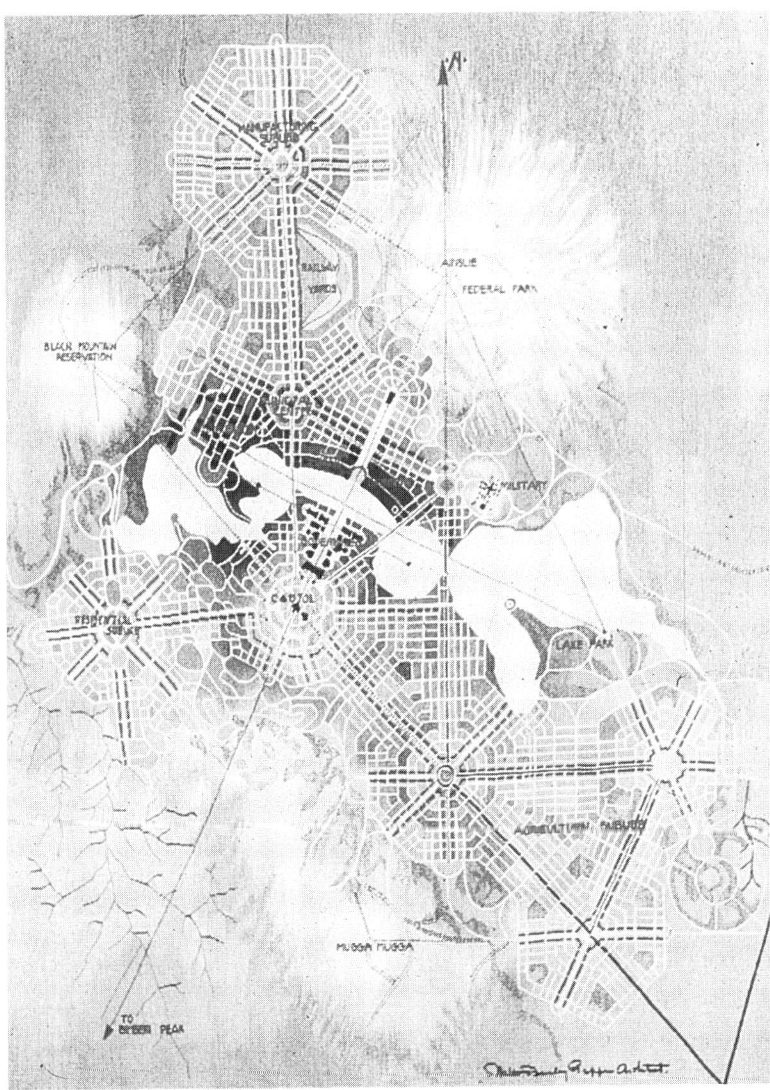

Fig. 1. Walter Burley Griffin's plan: Official Plan for Canberra, 1913.

connecting natural objects: Red Hill, Capital Hill and Camp Hill are on the land axis extending from Mount Ainslie to Bimberi Peak far to the South.[3] In the central area Griffin proposed monumental buildings; a bicameral Parliament House astride Camp Hill and a Capitol on Capital Hill dominating a parliamentary triangle of large public buildings located on terraces. A provisional Parliament House, constructed on the brow of Camp Hill was opened in 1927 but no other monumental construction was envisaged.

In 1930, Keith Hancock writes that

> The plan of Canberra is that of a garden city, in which the garden is more emphasised than the city. It is ten times more spacious than New Delhi. In Australia, more than in any other country, the modern tendency of cities to scatter and spread may operate without check. It is therefore impossible that Australian cities should have 'form' according to the old standards.

and Hancock goes on to say that

> it is true that the paper plan of Canberra is elaborately formal ... But, in Canberra's suburbs, the work of translating the plan into three-dimensional form has already failed. Canberra is springing up in the familiar Australian way as a kind of suburban garden parcelled into plots by a network of paths which have no obvious beginning and lead to no visible end. It is a chaos of prettiness.[4]

Since the 1930s Canberra's suburban landscape imagery has intensified and, in the central area, two generations of idealogues have failed to gain acceptance for Walter Burley Griffin's architectural and civic design proposals. It is clear that both Parliament and the National Capital Development Commission, institutions sensitive to public opinion, are happy with a landscape dominated national capital. Elsewhere, however, monuments of an impressive scale, such as the Jefferson Memorial in Washington, present a symbolic image of a nation.[5]

Tree planting is now the prime space creating function in the Canberra central area. Important recent buildings, such as the High Court and the National Gallery, have been located peripherally in a quasi picturesque setting on the lake shore and their massing is facetted and fragmented so as to exorcise monumental architectural character. The neo-classical National Library (1968) reflects a major point of departure from the Griffin plan where Lord Holford, a British consultant, planned, in 1958, the proposed new Parliament House on the foreshores of the projected lake. In 'a balanced but not symmetrical development' Holford suggested a specific picturesque character for the Parliamentary Triangle. By the early 1970s the picturesque iconography had been reinforced by the removal of the projected Parliament House to Capitol Hill thus proposing an open landscaped national 'Place': the hills north of the lake, Griffin's 'Dress Circle', would then be the enclosure, rather than nearby buildings.[6]

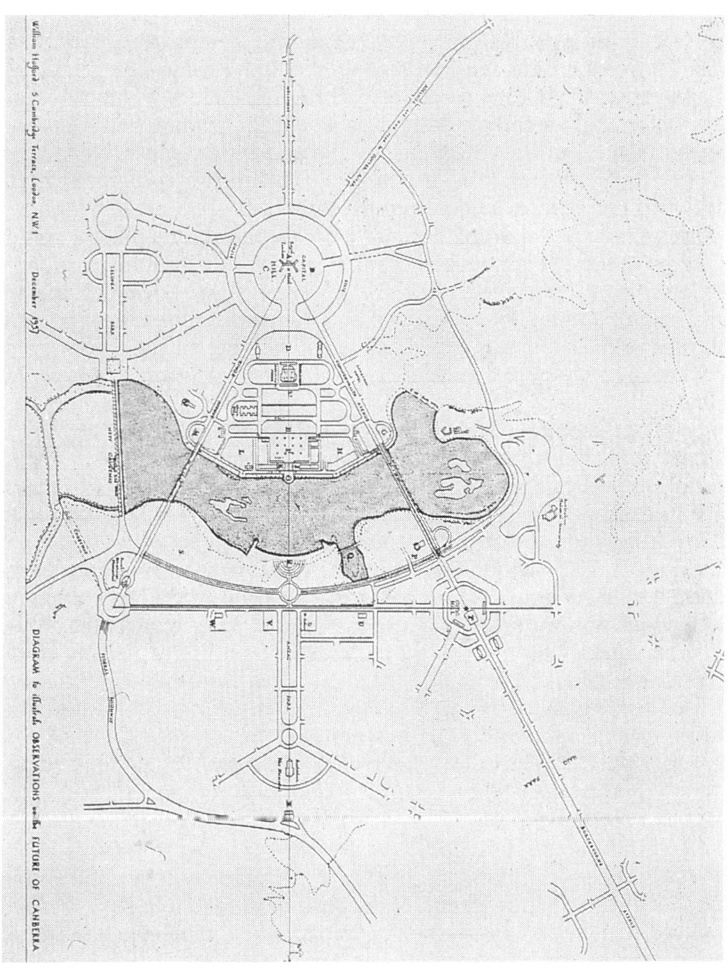

Fig. 2. Plan by William Holford: 1958 – The new Parliament House is located on the lakeshore.

With the proposal to locate the new Parliament House on Capitol Hill there was created 'a real fear of a large and overbearing parliament building towering over the Parliamentary Triangle'. However, the new parliament building by the American architect, Romaldo Giurgola, has not contravened the prevailing landscape imagery. Capital Hill has been removed and then re-stated in the form of two great landscaped hemicycles which conceal the new massing: the landscape character of the central area has been extended into the Hill itself.[7]

Canberra is a special domain under federal control thus it has a certain level of sovereignty over development. It cannot, however, be considered as isolated from Australian city development generally. Underlying the official town planning ideas of social and hygienic improvement was the older idea of the suburban arcadia, already practised in the harbour-side suburbs of Sydney by the middle classes in their villas and ornamental gardens.

Four major cultural themes contributed to the myth of arcady in Australia and the continuing restatement of landscape as a design imperative. Each stems from widely different fields. The first theme emanates from the Romantic Movement with its theory of Natural Rights and the association of Naturalism and the Picturesque with ethical and political ideas. The second stems from the romantic interpretations of the landscape by the painters. The third theme stems from the bush mystique first imposed, not from Australian writers, but by mid-nineteenth century English novelists who transposed the classical concept of Arcady to the antipodes and linked it with an egalitarian ideal impossible in the social structure of England. The fourth theme is implicit in the attempt to translate that egalitarian ideal into practical terms through the Town Planning and City Beautiful movements from the beginning of the twentieth century again emphasising the landscape component, but within a suburban setting.[8]

The cultural themes derived from landscape painting, the evocation of Australia in nineteenth century literature, Utopian concepts, the Picturesque Movement and the legend of the bush-worker as folk-hero, have all influenced and helped unify the Australian ethos, thus engendering an emotional iconography to which our own particular bourgeois might respond. These themes found physical expression in the form and character of the Australian town and suburb. The strengths and weaknesses implicit in these themes have also found expression there. These themes then assumed the imaginative power of national myths. It has been argued that the mythology of a nation does not determine but <u>is</u> its fate from the very beginning. Its history is determined by its mythology and not vice versa. And it is not the material content of mythology that is the problem of importance but rather the intensity with which it is believed. Arcady in Australia was alive as an affirmation of faith in a

Fig. 3. General view of Parliament House.

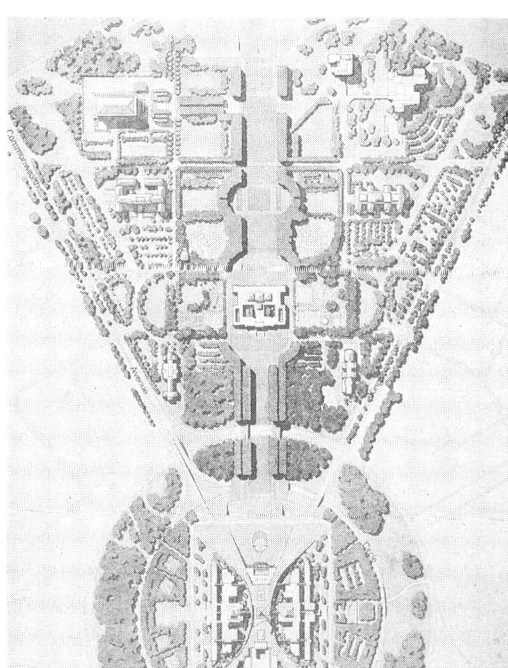

Fig. 4. Plan of Parliamentary Triangle.

myth that was experienced and believed 'as only something endowed with objective reality can be believed'.[9]

In Canberra itself, during the past fifty years, all attempts by planners and architects to realise a positive monumental character in architectural terms have failed. The city is characterised by a picturesque imagery which includes close and distant hills, Lake Burley Griffin, and the continuities arising from strong park systems and homogeneous suburban residential areas. Urban areas are largely obscured by tree growth following a series of Government decisions which eliminated building proposals in the central area, particularly in the Parliamentary triangle. Landscape dominance has been ensured by public protests in opposition to development elsewhere. However, since the competition for the new Parliament House, symbolic issues have been raised by many architects: Romaldo Giurgola himself has attempted to explain the failure of Burley Griffin's 'sociological symbolism'.

> Only buildings with concrete programs produce real places: the attempts often made to work around Griffin's plan of the Parliamentary Triangle area with no program appear inconsequential. Places give form to a site and are suggested by concrete experiences: no design is truly possible without the concrete demands produced by the dynamics of life.[10]

From the 1950s there has been a policy of decentralising firm architectural proposals such as the High Court and the National Gallery within the Parliamentary Triangle. The Gallery site, for example, at first proposed in a prominent location near Camp Hill, was moved to the periphery of the central area, the final building being placed in a picturesque setting on the lake shore near the High Court. No formal structure has been allowed to impinge on the concept of a national 'Place': an open landscaped foreground for the new Parliament House. Architectural monumentality has been exorcised in the new building by the choice of Giurgola's design; the architect has focused with intensity on the theme of landscape design – an unconscious expression of the Arcadian myth in Australia.

Romaldo Giurgola states that

> According to our design 85% of the site is intended to be devoted to landscape, most of which is available to the public. Rather than being an imposition on the site, the Parliament building is generated by the natural state of the land configuration, just as democratic government is not an imposition on the community but rather originates organically from within the populace.[11]

Giurgola's design has assuaged the fears of those who have a real fear of a large and overbearing Parliament building towering over the triangle, and it has placated those who cherish Canberra's 'naturalness'. But there are many Australians who are deeply critical of the picturesque informality and suburban character of the National Capital which has pervaded the central area and been reinforced by the suppression of the Parliament House in a landscaped park. This approach is opposed to the intentions of Burley Griffin who proposed a monumental Capitol. In terms of the site plan, the geometrical construction reads as an extension of Canberra's street patterns. But to critics, the paper pattern of an hexagon or a circle is not an intelligible figure when elevated to a large-scale three dimensional entity. The design becomes invisible. The curves of a street have no formal significance unless there is a just proportion between the width of the street and the height of the buildings which front it. Similarly, street planting is not seen as an effective space dividing medium. All sense of permanence is lost.

The construction of the new Parliament House affirms the dominance of landscape and asserts it as being symbolic of Australianness. There is a further claim by Romaldo Giurgola for heightened significance and symbolism insofar as there is a parallel between Parliament House originating from the 'natural state of the land configuration' and democratic government 'originating organically from within the populace'. In Canberra, the space governs the design whereas in other modern capitals solid, monumental constructions dominate the design. The Parliament House profile reinforces spatial continuity between natural objects in the landscape: a vast gulf lies between it and such modern monuments as the Jefferson Memorial in Washington or Le Corbusier's High Court for the government group at Chandigarth. The Maiden's Parthenon standing up on the Acropolis at Athens was designed to be seen in relation to the Horns of the Hymettos mountains. The space between the natural and man-made forms is essentially a void between opposing solids. These are monuments which enshrine the true spirit of democratic idealism. By placing his building under Capital Hill, lying beneath two landscaped ramped hemicycles, Giurgola has passed over the opportunity for a true parallel with powerful symbols of Western culture.

In his exposition, Romaldo Giurgola seeks to explain the Parliament House design in relation to great buildings and places of the past and in terms of his appreciation of Australian architecture. He argues that '... a building becomes true architecture 'by' ... the making of coherent connections in time, history, and cultural identities, a making which includes all those meanings of the Greek word, 'logos' – 'location', 'place', 'point', 'order', 'reason', 'underlying principle', and 'explanation', among other meanings.' In his article 'Architecture more than a building', Giurgola derives three primary principles and these form the basis for the Parliament House design.

> First, that buildings are not simple material objects, but rather, that buildings should be understood as concepts related to the making of a place.

> Second, that buildings as 'ideas' or 'concepts' contain meanings which are given particular forms of expression by the architects, tradesmen, workers, craftspeople and artists involved in the building's construction. The making of the building therefore produces a field of relationships among these people and their many endeavours involved in the realisation of the place.
>
> Third, that the goal of each building project is to knit together into one concept all of those attendent meanings, thereby making possible for the building's future users and visitors a sense of unity among the building's functional and aesthetic elements, as well as among the physical contributions of all of the designers and workers involved in its making.[12]

There are grave implications concerning Giurgola's 'principles'. A new historical perspective may, at any time, alter the feeling we entertain towards a certain period yet the plastic or concrete arts which these periods produced always remain the same. They remain capable of addressing the same appeal to the physical senses. In contradistinction, Giurgola is claiming an **implied** significance for the Parliament House by overstressing indirect associative elements and discounting the importance of an **apparent** significance. By implication, 'the making of a field of relationships and their many endeavours' together with the incorporation of 'all those attendent meanings' in the building is held to be of greater significance than the immediate apprehension of the building in its visible material, the direct appeal of the qualities of mass, space, line and coherence to the physical senses. It is true to say that, by association, the emotions which a particular building generates can be recalled by everything that can recall that period but Giurgola's 'field of relationships' can be recalled only by events or elements which are generally intangible or evanescent.

In fact, to Giurgola, architecture becomes primarily symbolic and romanticised. It ceases to be an immediate and direct source of enjoyment, and becomes a mediate and indirect one. Romanticism allows the circumstances among which the forms were produced to divert attention from the purely aesthetic character, the sensuous value, of the concrete arts.

In the case of architecture, the architectural design is taken as standing for the period which invented it, and is associated with it, and it is supposed to suggest the general imaginative state, the complex feelings of approval or disapproval, which the idea of the period happens to invoke. It is extremely doubtful how far the abstract characteristics of a society are capable of being embodied in architecture, or, if embodied, how far we can extract them unfalsified, or, if extracted, how far they are relevant to the quality of the work. The whole process is academic and purely literary; its appeal is in the literary value of the idea itself rather than the architecture, or in the act and process of association. Under the romantic influence the interest in architecture becomes symbolic and taste becomes unduly stylistic as is the case with the Parliament House, where the architectural character of the provisional building is repeated in the new work.

In his writing, Giurgola raises important aesthetic and symbolic issues but fails to address their implications.

> As for the second principle, the meanings contained in this building as a concept materialise into the form of the exterior, the sweeping ramps of grass, and the flag mast at the top, as well as into those halls, vestibules and courtyards, where each element is vested with a particular significance which is in turn evocative of a particular function.

This is followed by

> In our building, however, functions, like technology,
> are not overtly celebrated or exploited for aesthetic reasons.[13]

Giurgola's account of his design approach is informative and yet it evades the issue of **apparent** significance. Surely the 'sweeping ramps of grass' veiling the massing of Parliament House and creating a subterranean labyrinth raise significant questions which can affect perceptions of the building as a symbol for cultural values. The 'flag mast at the top' raises many issues about the appropriateness of an identification of parliamentary functions with nationalist ideology and even British imperialism. It can certainly be argued that the geometry of the plan is at variance with Giurgola's perception of Australian architecture as '...an architecture which does not terminate at the periphery of each building...'

Most of Giurgola's writing about the Canberra plan is concerned with the relationship of architecture with nature. Through historical insights into the 'transfer' of geometry into nature, as represented by the Italian and French gardens and 'the alternative view by which naturalness of the organic forms extends within architectural episodes, as in the English landscape', Giurgola is able to view Canberra as a post-industrial artifact: 'a new environment existing as a composite image of social, human, productive and natural factors'. And through an awareness of a new scale and scope of human activities, also influenced by the nineteenth and twentieth century phenomenon of land industrialisation, he convincingly constructs parameters upon which his 'interdependence between built forms and land forms' becomes a 'natural assumption' in the approach to the design of the new Parliament House. With regard to Canberra as a whole, Romaldo Giurgola suggests that we must understand landscape in a different manner from the unproblematic natural order of landform and flora. It seems to me that he considers landscape as a trope or as a figure in a language of civic design. As a trope it has a non-Australian history and it is this history which is employed by architects when they build in remote or rural areas and wish to make a symbolic (not **natural)** gesture towards their site.

Despite Giurgola's rhetoric, there remains the distinct dissatisfaction with the perceivable gap between the aerial plan view and the experience on the ground. In the central area the new Parliament House does not overcome the loss of emotive force and comprehensible order embodied in Walter Burley Griffin's original plan. There also remains a disturbing impression of the erosion of Griffin's Capitol, of an original image diminished; and the Triangle itself, a palimpsest imposed by time on the actions of men who have vacillated between the frantic desire to find something comprehensible to belong to and an equally consuming passion to express their own individuality and act on their own.

Giurgola recognises the power of the 'medieval energy that created Chartres Cathedral', and the 'architecture of the Parthenon ... at a time when Athens had opened its eyes and minds to the view of a new society...'. At a future time, those who wish to avert their eyes from the occluded landscapes of Canberra may find their view winding upwards to the ridges and ravines of the beautifully lifting escarpment of the Monaro Plateau.

> After the City Beautiful and the Pride of Time, it seems rather an anti-climax. There is something very attractive about garden cities but it is difficult to pretend that they are nobler than Pericles' Athens'.[14]

NOTES

1. W.K. Hancock, *Australia* (Brisbane: The Jacaranda Press, 1961), (First published 1930), p.241.
2. J. Sulman, *An Introduction to the Study of Town Planning in Australia*, Government Printer, Sydney, 1921. The City Beautiful ideal, where the dominant images were of monumental buildings, grand plazas and Beaux Arts Vistas, preceded the Garden City movement in Australia. In the 1911-12 Federal Capital International Design Competition most entries proposed a City Beautiful, European style city. As a city planning model,the City Beautiful declined as the Garden City movement gained adherents from 1910 to 1930. See R. Freestone, 'The New Idea; The Garden City as an Urban Environmental Ideal, 1910-1930', *Journal of the Royal Australian Historical Society*, Vol. 73, Part 2, October 1987, pp.94-108. Freestone concludes that the Garden City movement declined after 1930 because '...little was said about improving conditions in areas already built-up.'
3. W.B. Griffin, Report accompanying Design Entry No. 29, 1911; reprinted in Appendix B, *Report from the Select Committee Appointed to Inquire into the Development of Canberra*, September 1955, pp. 93-102.
4. W.K. Hancock, *op.cit*. 'Some aspects of Society in a 'New' Country', pp.240-241.
5. For a comparison of Canberra with other world capitals see *Urban Design International*, Vol. 4, No. 2, 1983; Three world capitals: Canberra, Ottawa and Washington D.C.
6. Sir William Holford's approach is described in 'Observations on the Future Development of Canberra', 1958. See National Capital Planning Commission Report for 1959-64, February 1959. See also N.C.D.C. 'Capital Hill and the Parliamentary Triangle, 1959' and 'The Future Canberra', 1964. Planning policy after 1968 is described in R. Johnson, *Design in Balance*, University of Queensland Press, 1964.
7. The history of planning in Canberra is summarised in R. Pegrum, 'Canberra's Planning', *Architecture Australia*, Vol. 72, No. 5, September 1983, pp.50-59; and landscape history in R. Clough, 'Canberra's Landscape', Idem.
8. See P.R. Proudfoot, 'Arcadia and the Idea of Amenity', *Journal of the Royal Australian Historical Society*, Vol. 72, Part 1, June 1986, pp. 3-18.
9. See Ernst Cassirer, *The Philosophy of Symbolic Fonms*, New Haven, 1965, 3 Vols.
10. R. Giurgola, 'Canberra: a Splendid Place', *Urban Design International*, Vol. 4, No. 2, 1983, p.13.
11. R. Giurgola, 'Architecture, More Than a Building', *Architecture Australia*, Vol. 76, No. 3, May 1987, p.45.
12. Idem.
13. Ibid, p . 46.
14. Hancock, *Australia*, p . 242.

TONY DENHOLM

Paradise Postponed: the Story of the Failure of South Australian Country Towns

By nineteenth-century standards the pinprick communities that appeared on the vast South Australian landscape hardly qualified for urban status. By 1900 no South Australian town outside the Adelaide metropolitan area met the 5000 population criterion usually applied to establish urban status in Britain and there were no sizeable provincial centres like Ballarat and Bendigo in Victoria and Newcastle in New South Wales. Furthermore, the gap between the primary city and the next largest town was considerably greater in South Australia than in other parts of Australia. In 1901 Adelaide had a ratio of 23 persons to every one in the next largest town, Port Pirie, while Melbourne was 11 to one to Ballarat, Perth 10 to one to Freemantle, Sydney 9 to one to Newcastle and Brisbane 7 to one to Rockhampton.[1] The dominance of Adelaide was also more pronounced than that of other capitals: 45 per cent of South Australians lived in Adelaide compared with 41 per centre of Victorians living in Melbourne, 36 per cent of New South Welshmen in Sydney and 24 per cent Queenslanders in Brisbane.[2] More than any other Australian colony South Australia was a one town state The primacy of Adelaide was overwhelming.

Yet this was neither planned nor desired by South Australia's founding fathers. It is ironic that the state which more than any other had 'a tradition of planning in survey and settlement matters and of guiding and controlling expansion'[3] should have ended up with such an urban imbalance. The close settlement envisaged by the Wakefield system, with small scale farming on 80 acre blocks, should have produced clutches of small market towns to service the agricultural exploitation of the other land. Coming from Britain, those who initiated urban development expected to duplicate the tightly knit British urban system with its provincial capitals, its county and market towns and its interlocking network of villages. Except early on and here only in part, this English pattern was never realised. Agriculture in South Australia was different and gave way in large part to pastoralism. As a result the urban settlement of South Australia took off in entirely new directions. Even so in the late nineteenth century South Australia developed 'a comparatively complex regional economy'.[4] To the extent that this economy was based on wheat and copper it should have been conductive to the spread of towns, as both agriculture and mining were labour intensive and required greater servicing than extensive pastoral runs. The extent to which the 80 acre, or at any rate the small farm ideal survived, also aided the foundation and survival of country towns. In the first phase of urbanisation the nucleus of private towns established in the Mount Lofty Ranges and the Lower Mid North came close to the model. However, the proximity of these towns to Adelaide restricted the growth of any one of them into a major regional centre, though Clare came close to it. The chief reasons most frequently advanced for South Australia's lack of large towns are: the relative compactness of the settlement around Adelaide, the accessibility of this hinterland to the capital, and the relative cheapness of transport costs compared with other Australian capitals.[5] In spite of the fact that some 510 towns were founded in South Australia, none came close to challenging the primacy of Adelaide, even after the opening up of the northern wheatlands, the South East, and the Murray Mallee. South Australia was not to have a number of majestic seaports or provincial administrative/social capitals. It did not even acquire modest genteel county towns in spite of the fact that the province was divided into counties like England. How and why did South Australia acquire this different urban pattern – a pattern firmly in place by 1900 and not changed in essentials since? Can we even claim urban status for these tiny communities frequently numbering only a few hundred people? What was life like in these small, and for many of their inhabitants, remote townships? What form did they take and how did they function economically and socially? What kind of lives were lived here? Were they anything more than 'focal points'[6] for the economic exploitation of the land? These are some of the questions worth thinking about. The most obvious but not least important fact is that these towns were set up on a virgin landscape. In medieval Europe many towns were founded on old Roman settlements, which though defunct nevertheless possessed geographical, economic or strategic importance There were no such guidelines in Australia. Aboriginals may have sacred sites and points of concentration but they did not build cities, nor did their tribal life require them. Sites for South Australian towns were not determined by military necessity; there were no hilltop fortifications. Towns did not need walls to defend themselves against hostile native populations; they did not even take the form of outpost forts as in the American West used as military concentration points to coerce Indians. Again, unlike the great period of European town foundation in medieval times, there were no pre-urban nucleii like monasteries, abbeys, and castles sheltering territorial feudal lords, around which so many towns grew to prominence. There were many reasons for the establishment of towns in South Awtralia: some wealthy private individuals subdivided part of their extensive properties and then sold small blocks at great profit to tradesmen whom they induced to settle in order to service their estates or work their mines; governments laid out seaport towns like Robe and Port Augusta, or inland towns like Bordertown in regions and locations vital to the colony's communication with the rest of Australia; German migrants in search of religious freedom built towns for their faith in the hills and in the Barossa Valley. Underlying all these motives however lies the imperative one – the exploitation of the land and its products for profit and progress. South Australia thus shares its urban heritage with large parts of the United States, Canada, South Africa, New Zealand and the rest of Australia in the nineteenth century as capitalists sought out investment and return. Function determines form and South Australia was denied the great variety and complexity of urban forms emanating from the political, religious, military and cultural diversity of Europe. It lacks also the diversity produced by French and Spanish influences in Canada and America, and even the prison features of some towns in N.S.W. and Tasmania.

The ubiquitous grid pattern, it is argued, was a feature of British colonial towns which like those of the Roman empire were laid out as 'geometrical abstractions'.[7] The rectangular geometrical internal subdivision within towns, the regularity of distances between them and the uniform street widths all testify to the bureaucratic dictates of authoritarian rulers. Town creation in Australia, according to Toon, was merely incidental to agricultural production – production that was linked to the demands of the British economy.[8] Given all this it is not surprising that there is a sameness about Australian towns. They were designed to produce cash not culture.

Between 1836 and 1929 some 510 townships had been recognised and of these 370 had been planned by the government. Most remained tiny settlements and some never became anything more than surveyed scratches on the map. Three phases in the urbanisation of South Australia have been identified.[9] The first phase up to 1865 saw the appearance of a number of towns clustered in the Mount Lofty Ranges and the Central Hill district. These were mostly private towns associated with small farming, or, as in the case of Kapunda and Burra, with copper mining. In this first phase private activity was officially encouraged. A Secondary Towns Association was set up in 1838 specifically to sponsor new towns. It was never very successful though Wellington on the River Murray and the now defunct Victoria near Kapunda were the fruits of this enterprise. Much more successful were towns established by leading wealthy settlers on land they acquired by a system known as Special Surveys. Under this scheme individuals requested a government survey of 15000 acres in an area of their choice. They then selected 4000 acres into small town lots and sold them to tradesmen and craftsmen like blacksmiths and carpenters much in demand on their newly developing estates. Angaston, Strathalbyn, Macclesfield and Clare came to life in this way. It is envisaged that these would become like the small market towns of England though in fact only a few, notably Noarlunga and Burra had market places on the English model. Beyond a rudimental layout these towns were not planned as later government towns were. They thus grew outwards from a central core, usually the main street, according to the dictates of time and need. This 'organic' nature accounts for the charm of many hill towns which seem to blend in more naturally with the surrounding countryside, perhaps because they have grown intimately in tandem with human interaction on the landscape.

In this first phase the government was not much interested in established towns except as we have seen certain ports and other vital communication links. Port Lincoln, Port Augusta, Robe, Mannum and Bordertown come into this category. Only a few government towns were associated with agricultural pursuits – Naracoorte 1859, and Gambier Town 1861, were exceptions though both these government towns were attached to existing private foundations and significantly they were located in the pastoral South East of the province. Another exception was with mining. The government town of Burra was grafted onto the mining company towns of Kooringa and Redruth in 1851, and a decade later the government was also involved in the establishment of Moonta, Wallaroo and Kadina.

The second phase from 1870 to 1889 saw the foundation of 161 towns until drought and depression brought a temporary lull to township creation. The government was heavily involved as settlement moved north of Clare and onto both peninsulas in pursuit of wheat crops. After 1864, according to Williams, a radical change occurred in government thinking and towns were surveyed in new areas considered suitable for agriculture.[10] The aim was to have one town in every hundred making it theoretically possible for most farmers to be no more than five miles from the nearest town.[11] The influence of England's close knit network of market centres is still apparent in the thinking behind this policy, which was not altogether unreasonable, for the railway system was not yet extensive enough to make a mockery of the traditional English pre-industrial pattern for the production and exchange of agricultural goods.

At first, however, this new policy was not very successful because rich Adelaide based pastoralists bought up the new town lands at auctions in an attempt to check farming development and what they perceived to be the disruptive influences of shopkeepers and pubs to their own enterprises.[12] However, once the government approved the purchase of town lands on credit, then smaller capitalists – farmers, storesmen, and tradesmen – had a chance to invest, settle and prosper in these new communities set up throughout the State. This was the great period of town foundation when Adelaide's classic grid pattern was stamped all over the countryside, based on Goyder's 1864 adaptation of Light's plan.

As we shall see each new settlement was provided with a core of half-acre lot towns lands, usually square or rectangular in shape. The core was surrounded by a belt of parklands, followed by a further extensive ring of suburban land. One reason for this extraordinary and generous allocation of space stemmed from the enormous optimism of the boom years, especially the late 1870s. As many of these towns were expected to grow into major provincial cities, care was taken to anticipate growth and thus avoid the congestion and squalor which had befallen many English towns. Another less exalted explanation lies in the government's need for money, and town land selling at one time for an average of over £43 per acre was a lucrative source of income.[13] The third phase of town creation from 1900 to 1929 is associated with the revival of the state's economy. In this period 119 new towns were established chiefly on the Eyre Peninsula, on the irrigation lands of the Murray and in the Murray Mallee. Significantly these government towns were not so ambitious in scale. The realities of South Australia's economy had been brought home during the depressed years and the high optimism of the seventies gave way to more sober expectations. This period was strongly influenced too by the thinking of Charles C. Reade, the government's town planner after 1919. He cut down on the extent of parklands and even tackled the sacred cow of the Goyder Grid in his planning. He also initiated the move towards the zoning of town land and the establishment of open space reserves to replace the parkland model of earlier years.

(a) Urban Form

Australian country towns in general have been described as 'dull, repetitive, lacking in personality and image'.[14] This is attributed to military or bureaucratic planners whose desire for uniformity, order and authority triumphed over private endeavours, 'innovators with their desire to maximise every opportunity'.[15] In N.S.W. in 1829, seven years before Light's Adelaide plan, Governor Darling published extensive regulations for the layout of country towns, characterised by grid patterns, uniform street widths and footpaths. Government towns in South Australia conform then to patterns and precedents set, not only in N.S.W. but as the general practice of Imperial town design in the nineteenth century. Only the private towns built in the first phase are exceptions to this rule. South Australia further conforms to general Australian experience in that as in other states the great age for town building occurred between 1850 and 1890. Thus, while Adelaide may boast of its sense of difference as Derek Whitelock sees it, South Australian country towns have much in common with their inter-states counterparts. Like other Australian towns those in South Australia were sited close to water supplies – to rivers or creeks and lakes. Like other Australian towns little attention was paid to the direction of the prevailing wind, the elevation of the sun or other micro-climatic conditions. Given the circumstances under which these towns came to life it is perhaps unreasonable to have expected then the kind of detailed study and consideration now given before urban development takes place. Nevertheless, as South Australia prided itself on having the most ordered settlement and the fact that the role of government was 'remarkably comprehensive'[16] in creating and planning towns, one would expect South Australian towns to be superior in site and form.

Goyder's 1864 plan for township settlements was based on the grid pattern. A core of town land was surrounded, first by a belt of parkland and then a ring of suburban land designed for market gardens. It was a model widely applied with some variations especially in the 1870s and 1880s. Each hundred was provided with 'a bowdlerized Adelaide, shorn of squares, sitting within parklands, astride a river'.[17] Unfortunately, little attention was paid to the environmental variable~ such as the quality of the land, the proximity of the railway or rainfall distribution. All too often the rigid geometrical pattern was imposed on unsuitable flat sites which were frequently surveyed in summer when they appeared suitable. However, when creeks and rivers overflowed in winter the towns became quagmired. The large areas of parkland set aside whilst quite appropriate for major cities, were largely unnecessary in country towns surrounded by hundreds of square miles of open country and fresh air. Though parklands were sometimes used as rubbish dumps or places where stock could be slaughtered, Williams defends them on the grounds that they were used for showgrounds, horse racing and sports fields, as well as providing space for public buildings like hospitals and schools, all of which 'enriched the quality of life and expanded the spirit of community'.[18] No such defence can be made for the surrounding suburban lands. The expectation of course was that these towns would grow into sizeable urban communities which would need to feed themselves, at least in part. The suburban lands were envisaged as market gardens for this purpose, but the amount of land set aside for this purpose was ludicrously excessive. By 1879, 88 of 164 towns had suburban lands of 500 acres or more, but the towns did not grow as expected and even if they had, garden plots within the core, the refrigeration of foodstuffs and improved transport would have made the suburban lands redundant. In fact they did not long survive and most were bought up by local farmers and quickly became inseparable from other farmland. Later planners abandoned the idea.

In the end, in spite of the much vaunted planning by government, South Australian towns were much the same as those in other parts of Australia. According to Jeans, the most common feature of Australian country towns is the principal street, usually part of a through highway around which cluster a core of shops, public buildings and churches. These in turn are surrounded by residencies which fade 'raggedly into outlying paddocks'.[19] This description applies equally to most South Australian towns in spite of the Goyder grid, the parklands and the tuburban belt. The core grid was rarely ever completely built out, and most South Australian towns are centred upon a main through road, which forms a business centre. The uniform size of town blocs would suggest a greater degree of democratization in South Australian towns but as elsewhere some streets and some parts of town became more desirable than others and the social and spatial differentiation came to exist in country towns as in the larger cities.

Toon has identified other features common to the Australian country towns, all of which are shared by those in South Australia. As elsewhere the hotel was the most important building in the town. It was often elaborately decorated and more likely than any other building to keep up with changing fashions, especially in interior decor. Public buildings like court houses, institutes, town halls and post offices were usually built in simple neo-classical styles. Catholic Churches tended to have the most flamboyant followed by Anglicans, Presbyterians and Methodists in descending order of elaboration to the simple meeting halls of other sects. Even Catholic churches were simple in design for the most part and few had lady chapels or pronounced cruciform shapes. In domestic housing too there is considerable uniformity from state to state, with interesting but minor differences. The English cottage with the Indian verandah became the basic model once a town was established enough to have permanent dwellings to replace the temporary wattle and daub, and sacking shanty homes of the first pioneers. There are of course interesting variations even within South Australia itself: the steep sloping roofs and half timbered construction of German cottages in Hahndorf and the Welsh and Cornish cottage styles in the mining towns are good examples. The use of local stone for domestic dwellings as in Mount Gambier also added variety. Nevertheless the basic cottage plan and the ubiquitous verandah are the hallmarks of country town houses. The increased use of iron for roofs and fences increased the uniformity of townscapes by the end of the nineteenth century, however fascinating the subtle but vanishing variations were.

(b) Urban Function

Urbanisation in South Australia is different from that of other states in its failure to produce a crop of medium size provincial towns. Only Mount Gambier really measures up to this status in terms of function and population, though Port Pirie, Port Augusta and perhaps Port Lincoln have some claim. In fact though the largest towns outside Adelaide before 1900 were neither provincial pastoral centres nor outports, but mining communities. Even so copper could not match gold and the whole Moonta-Wallaroo-Kadina area with a population peak of 15672 in 1876 could not rival the Victorian gold town of Ballarat whose population in 1861 was over 22000. Ballarat's growing and larger population led to the creation of a social and economic infrastructure which enabled it to retain its status as a provincial centre long after gold had ceased to provide its main livelihood. The ports were perhaps South Australia's best hope for provincial greatness. Port Augusta hoped to become the Liverpool of the south but failed. Port Pirie made a run with a population of around 9000 in 1911 but, as Hirst gloomily remarks, Pirie like Moonta and Kadina was 'a working class town in desolate surroundings with little to recommend it'.[20]

We have come to accept the failure of South Australian towns to become provincial centres as inevitable. They are seen as the victims of Adelaide's successful commercial dominance; its stranglehold on transport, and its virtual monopoly of high level services like banking, insurance and legal advice prevented the substantial development of these vital functions elsewhere. Changing technology, especially the telegraph and the railway, reinforced Adelaide's position. Period droughts, economic slumps and reluctant migrants added to the problems of the country towns. Their failure may have been inevitable but for a brief period this was not thought to be the case. We have noted the optimism which led governments to engage upon a spate of town building in the 1870s. This optimism was not without foundation. For a short time from the 1850s to the 1870s the population in the country grew more rapidly than that of Adelaide; in the 1871 census Adelaide and its suburbs had less than one third of the state's population but by 1900 it was nearly one half. The rapid growth of Australian capital cities especially after 1871 at the expense of the countryside was noted at the time as a distinctive feature of Australian urbanisation in general.[21] But for a while the country kept its natural increase in population and acquired more as tradesmen and storekeepers moved into old and new country towns, to service expanding agriculture and industry. It looked as if the dreams of the founding fathers might be realised.

It appears that a number of towns were on the point of take off into sustained growth as measured by the variety and range of their functions. This is where functional analyses of towns like those made by M. Collins[22] in a recent doctoral dissertation are so valuable as they allow the historian to chart the economic and social well-being of a community. It is possible to discover when a town 'peaked' in terms of its range of occupations and functions. Greater precision in tracking the fortunes of country towns is thus now possible, and many more towns need to be studied in this way before any conclusion can be drawn. What we can say is that in the late nineteenth century many small towns boasted a great variety of occupations and functions, many of which have been long since lost: doctors, teachers, solicitors, auctioneers, stock and station agents, insurance brokers, bankers, blacksmiths, undertakers, builders, butchers, bakers, coach and buggy makers, tanners, shoemakers, confectioners and sometimes booksellers, newspaper editors and printers. In many towns there were factories making agricultural implements and cordials, breweries, flour mills, silos and in the ports, jetties, warehouses and customs and excise facilities. After the coming of the railway many towns accommodated linesmen, porters, signalmen and station masters.

What can one say about the nature of these tiny urban communities with population ranging from a hundred or so to a few thousand? What were their strengths to set against their many weaknesses? The essential function of a town is the production and exchange of goods and services. Where this is apparent there is urban life, where it is absent there is decline and depopulation. At first a number of towns in South Australia like Clare achieved some temporary success in the production of goods. Initially, distance from Adelaide ensured a measure of independence. However, some industries previously situated in the country confined themselves more and more to Adelaide. There were for example 43 breweries in South Australia in 1868, 33 of which were located in country towns. By 1919 however there were 9 left and 5 of these were in Adelaide. Of course the early ones were smaller but they provided work not only for the skilled men who made the beer but for labourers and transport workers as well. The story is similar with milling. In 1879 there were 109 flour mills in the state, 103 of which were in the country. During the depression of the eighties the number dropped to 80 and subsequently the Adelaide Milling and Mercantile Company began to dominate the industry until by 1917 there were only 40 mills left in the country. Agricultural implement manufacturers survived best. There were 57 of these in country towns in 1870 but their number declined to 18 in 1896 on account of the agricultural depression, though with the revival on the land early in this century their number bounded back to 51 in 1917.[23] Here we can clearly see the precarious nature of industrial activity in country towns dependent so completely on agricultural fortunes. Of course all these enterprises – brewing, milling and implement manufacture – were small scale businesses generally. Nevertheless, the employment of even six to ten men made a significant contribution to the economic life of these fragile towns. While they were processing the products of their hinterland, or else comprehensively servicing those who produced agricultural goods, they remained viable even vibrant communities. However, they were essentially parasitic and their fortunes fluctuated to the same rhythms as their hinterlands.

This is not to say that attempts weren't made to generate varied economic activity, and some towns showed remarkable capacities for survival even after the first cause for their settlement had been lost. Mintaro's slate kept the town going long after it had ceased to be an important bullocky stop. Goolwa survived the decline of its river trade which followed the building of the railway to Morgan, at first by building barges, and later as a resort and retirement centre. Clare developed viticulture and fruit growing on a large scale after it lost its unique position as capital of the north when the wheat frontier moved on. Kapunda, Mannum and Mount Barker owe much to their substantial agricultural machinery works which survived the vicissitudes of boom and slump years. Others like Port Augusta, Peterborough and Gladstone wrapped themselves around the railways. Nevertheless for the most part towns remained service areas for surrounding pastoral or agricultural regions. Generally those that failed to process agricultural products or otherwise significantly involve themselves in the exchange or transshipment of these goods faced inevitable decline.

Reasons most frequently advanced for the failure of South Australia to generate a network of viable provincial centers and country towns are both economic and social. At first one is tempted to look at the co-relationship between the slowdown in the number of new towns and the population growths of the old ones in the 1890s, with two late nineteenth century phenomena – the depression from the mid 1880s and the completion of the railway network. Does the answer lie here? Maybe, but one must remember that country people overcame the depression and diversified. Wheat still remained the chief crop but dairying, horticulture and viticulture flourished.

Furthermore, irrigation schemes spawned a crop of citrus and fruit growing towns in the riverland early in this century.[24] However, the fact remains that even when prosperity returned to the countryside the towns did not grow substantially. Were the railways responsible? The arrival of a railway in a town was a mixed blessing. Most town people anticipating greater business were happy to have a railway. However, in breaking down the tyranny of distance which had brought these communities to life the railway which at first breathed life into the towns ultimately sucked life out of many of them and their market and exchange functions declined as Adelaide-based merchants telegraphed the movement of goods. The trains now trundled through the town replacing the bullock wagons which previously rested or stayed overnight en route from mine, woolshed, or silo, to the coast.

Migrants from Europe were reluctant to move out into the inhospitable countryside so unlike the gentle, welcoming landscapes of home. They were used to city life, found employment and housing available in Adelaide and were thus content to stay there. Only second generation Australian born it is suggested were game enough to pioneer the country towns.

Other arguments centre on the dominant economic and social role of Adelaide. All communications were based on Adelaide; at first the road network and then the telegraph by which Adelaide businessmen were able to 'control the movement of money and goods hour by hour throughout the colony'.[25] It was unnecessary to have merchants on the spot as transactions could be directed from Adelaide. The railway network reinforced this pattern. By 1870 the line to Kapunda and Burra was actually carrying more wheat than copper to Port Adelaide thus replacing the old bullocky copper trail from Kapunda to Port Wakefield. However, the reorientation of the rail network to link the northern wheatlands with the gulf ports was a promising move in the direction of decentralisation. Hirst shows that by 1880 only 46 per cent of exported wheat passed through Port Adelaide. Unfortunately however, there were no merchants of sufficient standing in the gulf ports to take advantage of this and large Adelaide firms still controlled the export trade. Hirst claims that the outports might have done better if the export of wheat had been in the small quantities required by the eastern states. As it were, most wheat exported from the late 1860s was bound for the large British market which required commensurate amounts of capital as well as large scale exporting experience and expertise none of which was available in these port towns. Even luck was against Port Augusta. It exported 15 per cent of South Australia's wool in the 1870s and 1880s but a decline in wool prices in the nineties destroyed this potential.[26] Similarly the Murray River ports were choked off by Adelaide's direct rail links to Milang and Murray Bridge. Only Mount Gambier and the ports of the South East resisted Adelaide, exporting 15 per cent of South Australian wool as late at 1917. Mount Gambier gained by the railway and became a major supplier of potatoes to Adelaide from 1880. It had been forced to look to Adelaide rather than to Victoria by protectionist legislation in 1866. Its distance from Adelaide at the hub of a distinctive pastoral district allowed it to grow and function as a provincial centre bringing other towns – ports like Robe and farming communities like Penola within its orbit. Outports also suffered as coastal trade dried up. With the exception of the two peninsulas the railways replaced coastal vessels and road haulage as carriers of goods to country towns. Undoubtedly then Adelaide's communication stranglehold, along with its near monopoly of commercial and financial power, explain in part the failure of other centres to rival it.

Hirst's analysis of the social relationships between Adelaide and the country has some bearing on our discussion. He argues that influential local leadership was weak due to the fact that most of the country wealth makers chose to live in Adelaide, or were otherwise absentees.[27] Neither the rich miners nor the pastoralists for the most part lived in or close to country towns, some of which they had actually founded. This is especially true once the pastoralists had established themselves and could safely leave the running of their estates to agents. They were often overseas or busy attending to their other preoccupations in Adelaide, and this was truer of the second generation than the first.[28] Most pastoralists were city born gentlemen, lawyers like the Downers and Elders or merchants like the Barr Smiths. They took up leases to run sheep but they did not for the most part take up lives of country gentlemen. Rather they ran their many and varied business interests from the comfort of Adelaide. Some exceptions were the Bowmans and Mortlocks of Martindale Hall who in all respects sought to replicate the life of the country gentry of England with hunting, cricket and house parties. Others like the Stirlings of Strathalbyn and Angas in Angaston were patrons of their towns, but these towns were close to Adelaide. In the South East, however, more of the wealthy landowners lived on their properties and involved themselves in the social life of the community, running hunts, balls and patronising the churches in local towns. Generally though, the gentry were absentees. They were not sufficiently interested or long enough resident in local towns to nurture and succour them. They were not identified with provincial life and thus less inclined to use their influence to foster them. This is in marked contrast to the situation in England where the local gentry were deeply involved socially and politically with provincial towns. In England the gentry aided the economies of countless market towns by their patronage of local tradesmen and their social activities brought towns a measure of culture and sophistication. Generally in South Australia the rich pastoralists neglected the country towns. This was no less true of mining communities. Mining towns were dominated by companies which left the day to day running of the mines to managers, foremen and other salaried officials. The men who grew fat on their labours lived in Adelaide mansions and showed little interest in the urban communities growing up around their mines. All this confirms the view that small towns were simply seen as instruments for processing the agricultural and mineral wealth of the countryside. Profit and progress were paramount. Those who made the profits cared little about the kind of societies emerging in the towns. Social amenities were left chiefly to the government, the churches or the local townsfolk themselves.

The elites who ran South Australian towns in the late nineteenth century were then not the great landowners but local tradesmen, shopkeepers, professionals and relatively small farmers. It was left to them to make what they could of their towns with the limited resources at their disposal. They faced enormous difficulties because Adelaide exercised a social and cultural dominance as well as an economic one. All the 'best' people lived in Adelaide. Society was centred in the capital, and country people as much as city folk looked to Adelaide to provide the major diversion, entertainments and many facilities. The Royal Agricultural Show was held in Adelaide twice a year in February and September attracting hordes of country pople who came to display their stock and produce and assess those of others. The railway made it relatively easy to travel to Adelaide. Adelaide dominated many important services needed occasionally by countrymen and women. The best doctors were there. In the 1870s the only hospitals outside Adelaide were in Mont Gambier, Port Augusta, Port Lincoln and Wallaroo. All medical specialists, however, were in the capital. There were no government secondary schools in country towns until 1907, though many had private grammar schools. Nevertheless, the tradition of well-to-do country people sending their children to one of the major colleges in town began early, and still continues. Hirst stresses the importance of Adelaide's social dominance. Even with the onset of democracy when their political position was no longer taken for granted, the South Australian elite did not retire to their country properties to sulk, but rather stayed on in town and became even more active in newly developing roles as patrons of the Zoo, the Botanical Gardens, the University and the learned societies. All these ties kept good society firmly in Adelaide.[29]

Another problem for the country town was keeping its people once it had got them. Farmers were constantly on the move in search of new land, at first to the northern wheatlands, then to the peninsulas, even beyond Goyder's line, and after the turn of the century to the irrigation towns and the Murray Mallee. This mobility did not help the stability of towns – storekeepers, blacksmiths and other service tradesmen could lose their livelihoods if even a few farmers moved on. It needed only a handful of people to leave these tiny towns to make it impossible for service traders to make a living. Thus the lineal development of town – the gradual build-up of services and functions which was a common feature in the history of small market centres in England is frequently missing in South Australia. There was nothing to fall back on if the mine closed or the farmers left. No great ruined abbey existed to attract the tourist, no elegant spa or prestigious school attracted custom. These towns had little beyond the mineral and agricultural wealth of their hinterland to sustain them, and the many ruins of these settlements are eloquent testimony to the precarious nature of their existence. The farmers, even if they stayed, were never too far from Adelaide where they could go for legal consultations, medical treatment or commercial advice. Hirst has shown that in 1910 the average distance of farmers from the nearest port was 242 miles in N.S.W., 149 in Victoria, but only 60 miles in South Australia.[30] No great mountain range hampered the easy access of farmers to Adelaide for markets, higher goods and services. Even when they retired, farmers often chose to settle in Adelaide rather than in the community among whom they had spent their working live. They were not so attached to their land, had not the same connections as their English counterparts who rarely left the district or even the farm when they became too old to work. Thus towns were deprived of the constant succour that a committed permanent resident farming community could provide.

One further problem that faced many small towns was competition from near neighbours, especially when transport improvements reduced the viability of a number of tiny communities grouped close together. This is even true of towns in rich agricultural districts like the Barossa Valley where Nuriootpa, Tanunda and Angaston were in very close proximity. Fortune smiled however on these towns and, as a recent study has shown, they overcame their difficulties by exercising a measure of functional specialisation ensuring each one some important sustaining role.[31]

Small towns laboured then under many difficulties and hazards. This should not, however, blind us to the successes many enjoyed, if only for a brief period in their histories. Historians have largely ignored the rich social lives people in these communities made for themselves in the last decades of the nineteenth century and the first two of this one. Much of the character and quality of small town life is lost if we restrict our investigations to their economic functions. Thrown back on their own resources those townsfolk who could not afford the time or the money to go to Adelaide developed many and varied cultural, sporting and sociable activities to enrich their lives. Churches were all important both for townsfolk and neighbouring farmers and their families, as were hotels, sporting clubs and the ubiquitous institutes with their libraries and reading rooms. Schoolteachers from the 1870s, doctors and clergymen of all denominations brought a measure of learning and culture. Sunday schools, church picnics and brass bands brought pleasure to many along with football, cricket and gun clubs. Most towns boasted a racing or hunt club and women's organisations mostly associated with the church or temperance movements flourished. The men (for it was the men) who ran these towns were chiefly storekeepers, tradesmen, professionals like solicitors, journalists and hotel proprietors along with the well-established farmers in the hinterland. They ran their towns as mayors, councillors and J.P.s. They met frequently as Freemasons, Oddfellows and Foresters. They were lay preachers or office holders in their churches. They presided over the fortunes of agricultural societies, jockey clubs and local sports teams. They gave leadership to the labourers, the farm workers and the railwaymen for whom the town was the chief focus of their lives. Before the motor car their lives were bounded by the town in a way unimaginable since. Nascent civic pride fostered by sporting rivalries with nearby towns created a community spirit still much in evidence in country towns today. The elite who organised and presided over these activities enjoyed their status as a result of their wealth or social standing. They can be identified with some accuracy in the *Encyclopedia of South Australia* (1909), compiled by H.T. Burgess.

In this work Burgess provided a brief description of most towns in South Australia followed by a list of their prominent citizens with details of their backgrounds, occupations and local interests. It is an invaluable source for discovering the nature of the elites who controlled the government and economy of country towns. It has not been possible to determine how Burgess came by the names or the details of those he chose to include. He may have consulted directories or approached well known local people for their advice. Certainly the extent of personal details included suggests that he obtained the co-operation of his subjects, and to this extent his entries may be something of a self-proclaimed elite. Schoolteachers and clergymen are notably absent, perhaps because they moved around from place to place frequently, but chiefly because Burgess was perhaps more interested in providing a profile of the business life of the towns. However, in spite of these drawbacks, Burgess's entries give us vital dues about the kinds of men who dominated the political, economic and social life of our country communities early in the twentieth century.

An analysis of some 450 individuals from 23 towns provides a fairly accurate sample of the whole as they include a wide variety of towns and were chosen for their geographical spread. They are: Angaston, Burra, Clare, Cawler, Jamestown, Kadina, Kapunda, Maitland, Millicent, Mount Barker, Moonta, Morgan, Mount Gambier, Naracoorte, Peterborough, Port Augusta, Port Lincoln, Port Pirie, Renmark, Strathalbyn, Tanunda, Victor Harbor and Wallaroo. The study shows that 62 per cent of these leading citizens were born in Australia and 72.5 per cent were involved in non-agricultural occupations. The latter figure is particularly interesting because it suggests that the prevailing voice in the towns was that of the business community rather than the farmers. Some 35.5 per cent were, or had been, members of local councils and 17.7 per cent were, or had been, J.P.s. Some, of course, were both. Of the 450 only one was a member of the South Australian parliament, and a further 5 had been. This underlines the fact that these men were not drawn from the highest ranks of South Australian society and perhaps reflects on the political weakness of country towns in the higher deliberations of the state. It also reinforces Hirst's view that the countryside was deprived of powerful leadership.

The profile of religious adherence is also interesting though only a quarter of those surveyed indicated their denominational affiliation. Of these however, 53 per cent were Methodists, 25 per cent Anglicans, and 24 per cent other non-Catholics, chiefly Presbyterians and Baptists. Not one of the 450 acknowledged himself to be a Roman Catholic. As for their social activities, over half belonged to a fraternal organisation of some kind and frequently they belonged to more than one. Freemasons were the largest group claiming 24 per cent membership of the total; 12 per cent were Oddfellows, 7 per cent Foresters and 4 per cent Rechabites. A further 3 per cent belonged to other groups, chiefly the Druids. These figures clearly indicate a protestant, indeed mainly Methodist ascendancy, and suggest that through the agency of fraternal societies the town elites were a closely knit group whose business interests were reinforced by social ties. Figures for other kinds of social activity are not so impressive. Some 28.6 per cent had past or present involvement with sporting pursuits, 19.7 per cent had past or present membership of local Agricultural and/or Horticultural societies, and 19.5 per cent were official past or present office holders of the Institute. Over a quarter then had been or were involved in sporting activities and a fifth had at some time concerned themselves with the broader cultural life of the community.

There is plenty of evidence then to suggest that vital purposeful lives were lived in South Australian country towns, many of which survived the depression years and had adjusted to new or diminished roles. Their elites may have been dull, lacking wealth and perhaps also the vision to create vibrant communities, but they pursued their tasks and fulfilled their duties as they saw fit. They provided leadership and supervised a wide range of social activities to sustain themselves and others.

Though geography, economics and transport innovation conspired to destroy the high hopes once entertained for country towns, they had survived and some had flourished in a harsh environment. Townsfolk had nurtured civic pride in their communities and saw themselves as part of, but distinct from, the surrounding countryside. The intense localism which had been the great strength of English country towns was never as much in evidence in South Australia whose markets were from the beginning geared to international trade. Nevertheless, in the space of eighty years several hundred towns had been created and loyalties fostered. While these towns were places of production and exchange, however limited, they survived. When they became simply places of consumption they lost their life force. The railway was the first to take them along this road, but the internal combustion engine and the metalled highway completed their journey. Some now exist only to serve the motor vehicles passing through. The petrol station is no substitute for the mill, the mine or the manufacturer.

NOTES

1. J.W. McCarthy & C.B. Schedvin, *Australian Capital Cities* (Sydney, 1978), p. 113.
2. S. Glynn, *Urbanisation in Australian History* (Melbourne, 1970), p. 29.
3. M. Williams, *The Making of the South Australian Landscape* (London, 1974), p. 334.
4. McCarthy and Schedvin, *op.cit.*, p.25.
5. *Ibid.*, p. 25.
6. Williams, *op.cit.*, p.334.
7. J. Toon in the Introduction to P.Cox & W. Stacey, *Historic Towns of Australia* (Sydney, 1973).
8. *Ibid.*, p. 14.
9. Williams, *op.cit.*, pp. 335-349.
10. *Ibid.*, p. 344.
11. *Ibid.*, p. 348
12. *Ibid.*, p.344.
13. *Ibid.*, p. 374.
14. Cox and Stacey, *op.cit.*, p. 11.
16. Williams, *op.cit.*, p. 335.
17. A. Hutchings & R. Bunker (eds), *With Conscious Purpose: A History of Town Planning in South Australia* (Adelaide, 1986), p. 25.
18. Williams, *op.cit.*, p. 365.
19. D.N. Jeans, *An Historical Geography of New South Wales to 1901* (Sydney, 1972), p. 308.
20. J.B. Hirst, *Adelaide and the Country 1870-1917* (Melbourne, 1973), p. 22.
21. A. Weber, *The Growth of Cities in the Nineteenth Century* (New York, 1903), pp. 138-139.
22. M. Collins, 'Pre-Industrial Towns: A Spatial and Functional Analysis' (Ph.D. thesis, University of Adelaide, 1985).
23. Hirst, *op.cit.*, p. 30.
24. *Ibid.*, p. 56.
25. *Ibid.*, p.31.
26. *Ibid.*, p. 25.
27. *Ibid.*, pp. 10-19.
28. E. Williams, *A Way of Life: The Pastoral Families of the Central Hill Country of South Australia* (Adelaide, 1980), pp. 75-102.
29. Hirst, *op.cit*, pp. 45-47.
30. *Ibid.*, p. 64.
31. L. Weiland, 'A Functional and Occupational Analysis of Nuriootpa and its Relationship to Greenock, Tanunda and Angaston' (B.A. Hons thesis, University of Adelaide, 1987).

RODERICK J. LAWRENCE

Colonial Houses And Domestic Life in South Australia, 1836 - 1900

INTRODUCTION

There are diverse interpretations of vernacular domestic architecture; for example, scholars have undertaken an aesthetic/formalist interpretation; a typological analysis; a study according to evolutionary theory; explanations using social and geographical diffusionism; physical explanations (such as building techniques, materials, site and climate); social explanations (including household demography, economy and defence); and/or socio-cultural factors (such as religious practices and collective spatial images).[1] With respect to the subject of this paper, it may appear that social and geographical diffusionism is the most relevant perspective. However, each of the seven listed interpretations can be instructive for the analysis of vernacular buildings in general, and particularly with respect to the development of domestic architecture in Australia.

There are few buildings which remain from the early period of colonial settlement in Australia. Furthermore, the historical documents concerned with town planning and house design in the colonies have generally been limited to the presentation of building facades and street-scapes in accord with the picturesque tradition. Nonetheless, apart from these isolated colonial buildings which still exist, and apart from maps, paintings and engravings, there are the official and private manuscripts which have recorded the designs of houses in Australia from the earliest years of settlement.[2]

It is invaluable to consult all of these sources no matter how few they may be because, in tandem with fieldwork studies of surviving vernacular buildings, such documents provide a complementary analysis of how domestic architecture evolved. This is equally applicable in each of the Australian states, although the vernacular architecture is not the same. In this paper the method will be briefly illustrated with respect to South Australia.

METHODOLOGY

The first settlement of Australia at Sydney Cove in January 1788 was the genesis for the future development of the English penal colony. The development of that colony into a nation need not be described here. However, the model of culture change used to understand the derivation of Australian domestic architecture will acknowledge that the history of house forms has been an undetachable component of a specific socio-cultural, political and geographical context. This model can be illustrated by the study of the interaction between the images and ideas of the primary parent culture – British society – and the specific requirements of the settlers who were transplanted to this completely different place. In the Australian context, the nomadic aboriginals, unlike the Boers, for example, had a social and cultural heritage without a substantial material culture: furthermore, the interaction between the settlers and the aborigines was, and still is, minimal. This study is therefore different from the explanation of 'how two different cultures have interacted at the Cape'.[3]

In the Australian context, the important concept to grasp is the adaptation and transformation of specific European cultural predispositions, according to economic, social and political circumstances in the colony. In this respect the content of the colonial culture, and notably its architecture has unique attributes. It is a culture which is founded upon its own institutions, which have regulated the structure, actions and social relations in Australian society. This interpretation contrasts with the widely accepted viewpoint that Australia became a provincial British society following the importation of immigrants, institutions, and material culture from Britain. Such an interpretation fails to account for many other influences: for example the integration of ethnic groups from Germany during the earliest years of settlement in South Australia; the granting of political rights to most men prior to 1850 and to women after 1894, and the specific economic growth of Australia in which the majority of the population have participated. These and other influences have produced a society and culture different from that in Great Britain. These differences have been expressed in Australian speech, dress, and social customs. A distinct culture has developed during the last two centuries and the dissimilarities between it and the British prototype have become more evident as each decade has unfolded.

Moreover, this interpretation is quite different from that which is primarily concerned with *symbolism,* as illustrated by the thesis of Rapport.[4] Rapport upholds that the houses of the early English settlers in Australia were reproductions of what had been common in Britain, because they had a high symbolic value. Such an interpretation ignores two fundamental themes: firstly, the kind of 'technological transfer' that existed between Britain, other European countries and Australia within the global context of colonialism; and secondly, how the Australian experience is related to economic, technological and social developments concerning domestic architecture at an international level.

There is a growing interest concerning the exchange of construction technologies and design principles between the motherland and the English colonies. In one study, Herbert has examined the development of prefabricated building techniques and the evolution of indigenous colonial architecture in Australia and South Africa during the nineteenth century.[5] Here, however, the focus will be upon the exchange of ideas rather than equipment or techniques. To establish that focus, the subject ought to be discussed within the wider framework of colonialism, as Gubler noted:

'Colonialism...involves a complex set of interactions between the "mother country" and the overseas territories. In matters of architecture, this relationship cannot be reduced to a simple shuttle movement: the importation of picturesque exotic styles would correspond to the exportation of the 'mother country's' schemes of composition.'[6]

The principle is ably illustrated by the provision of reticulated water supply in the majority of residential suburbs in the main Australian cities many years prior to the same provision in the main towns in England.

Finally, the importance of a temporal dimension ought to be stressed, because the culture of both the parent and the colonial societies changed during the nineteenth and twentieth centuries. A study of the evolving relationship between domestic architecture and economic, social and political factors is crucial, because the parent and colonial culture served as normative models until the influence from North America became significant during the last half of the nineteenth century, and again after the Second world war.

The method of study adopted in this paper addresses each of these themes. It is founded upon a dual approach that includes both spatial and ethnographic analyses which employ an historical or temporal perspective. Such a method acknowledges that the study of the development of Australian domestic architecture poses two methodological problems; firstly, the endurance of buildings enables people to experience their physical and symbolic characteristics during a relatively long period of time; secondly, during the course of time buildings not only undergo physical transformations but also their meanings and uses change.[7] In other terms, in architecture the relationship between Space and time is a transactional process between building form and social factors, between continuity and change, between permanence and flexibility.

Having established this important principle the spatial and ethnographic analyses are founded upon:

i) fieldwork studies of the design, the construction and furnishing of dwellings built at various dates since the settlement of South Australia; and
ii) analysis of diverse documentary sources, which not only consider the design and construction of houses but also record how they were used by their residents in bygone years.

This method will now be briefly illustrated with respect to the development of domestic architecture in South Australia.

THE MORPHOGENESIS OF HOUSE FORMS IN SOUTH AUSTRALIA

The evolution of domestic architecture in Australia must acknowledge the foundation of separate and distinct colonies each of which became a political State and then a member of the Australian Federation.

The foundation of South Australia in 1836 was exceptional in several respects. For example, unlike New South Wales, or Tasmania, it was a free-planned settlement; there were no convicts and relatively few Irishmen emigrated to South Australia, but there was an influx of Scottish and German settlers. Furthermore, the City of Adelaide was consciously planned by Colonel William Light and George Gibbon Wakefield's principles of land tenure here employed.

Such demographic, economic and political characteristics generated differences between the colonization of this and the other States. These differences were obvious late in the nineteenth century, as some monographs written at that time have recorded.[8] Moreover, there were important topographical differences and the availability of building materials varied, as these monographs have noted. Given this diversity it is instructive to examine how the development of domestic architecture occurred with respect to building construction and techniques, the layout or organization of rooms, and the use of domestic appliances and furniture.

BUILDING CONSTRUCTION AND TECHNIQUES

The development of domestic architecture in South Australia is particularly interesting owing to the cultural diversity of the pioneers and the conscious emphasis given to town planning. The contribution of these two factors is still evident today from the scant numbers of vernacular buildings constructed about 1850 in diverse regions of South Australia.[9] These buildings illustrate a variety of construction techniques including simple masonry walling (employing random rubble, limestone and sun-dried bricks) timber construction (using post and beam construction, half-timber framed walling and split-gum framing), and diverse roofing materials, including bark, thatch, slate and corrugated iron sheeting.

At first sight, it becomes clear that these materials were used according to their availability, yet the fact that a range of materials and construction methods were employed concurrently suggests that such a simple explanation, tied to physical factors alone, is not as pregnant or pertinent as interpretations of diffusionism and socio-cultural factors. As fieldwork alone can reveal, in the same settlement either English, Scottish or German lores were practised (or modified) according to the availability of building material, and local topographical and climatic conditions. Thus in the German settlements in the Mount Lofty Ranges both the construction techniques and the house plans were transported by the settlers from their native country: even the layout of the rural town was reused.[10] To these Lutherans it was vernacular architecture reemployed in South Australia, whereas to a Scottish or English settler it was foreign.

During the last half of the 19th century 'hybrid' architectural forms were built to adapt to local conditions; the addition of verandahs ably illustrates an attempt to respond to a local climate quite different from that in Europe.[11] Moreover, fieldwork has revealed that, irrespective of the kinds of building materials used, by the end of the 19th century construction techniques that had been transposed from Europe were modified.[12] In sum, people with diverse cultural origins borrowed (or exchanged) 'rules of thumb' about house building. This was an internal indigenous development which occurred according to social interaction between the pioneers, and the merits and pitfalls of their building lores when transposed to a different context.

On the other hand, by the beginning of this century, the influx of external influences had also been well established. On the one hand, there was a continual stream of immigrants who commonly transplanted their own habits and material culture;[13] on the other hand, beginning in 1837, there was a proliferation of publications about domestic architecture in the colony.[14] These publications have been given the general title of 'Pattern Books' and some authors, including the Scot J.C. London, explicitly wrote about house building in the colonies from 1833.[15]

Apart from the transfer of architectural ideas by word and the image of model plans, Herbert has studied how prefabricated building systems were transported to Australia during the nineteenth century.[16] During the first decade of settlement in South Australia portable cottages were erected, including those by two London manufacturers; advertisements including model plans (with prices and options) were published in the *South Australian Record* from 1837. Furthermore, in 1837 Trinity Church was erected, and in 1840 a meeting house for the Society of Friends was constructed employing a portable prefabricated building kit.[17] According to Herbert's research, by 1850 the advertisements and the demand for this kind of dwelling were almost insignificant compared with the 1840s. In this respect the influence of external factors was counteracted by internal ones, notably the increased affluence of the settlers and the availability of construction materials, domestic appliances and furnishing.

THE ORGANIZATION OF DOMESTIC SPACE

Although the dwellings constructed soon after the settlement of South Australia were tents or one-roomed huts, within a decade many more substantial structures with at least two rooms existed. In general, fieldwork has indicated that it was most likely that the earliest houses grew from one- or two-roomed timber or stone structures, then verandahs were added and, sometimes, enclosed to create additional rooms.[18]

From these meagre beginnings the standard of domestic construction and facilities improved rapidly. By 1880 houses had four or six main rooms, and it was common for the kitchen, bathroom and toilet to be detached at the rear:

> ...the favourite type of Australian house is laid out in an oblong block bisected by a three to eight foot passage. The first door on one side as you go in is the drawing room, on the other (side) the dining room. Then follow the bedrooms, etc., with the kitchen and scullery at the end of the passage, or sometimes in a lean-to at right angles to the hinder part of the house proper. This kind of cottage is almost universal in Adelaide amongst the middle and upper middle classes and invariable in the working-class throughout Australia.[19]

The descriptions of houses which authors have recorded throughout the 19th century indicate that the development of domestic architecture did not follow preestablished house types in Europe, especially Britain, from whence the majority of settlers emigrated. Furthermore, it is important to underline that indigenous house forms developed despite the explicit models evoked by building regulations that were introduced in London from 1667 and then transposed to English provincial towns and the colonial states of Australia. These building regulations prescribed building plans, construction methods and materials, and the standard plan layout was copied with or without modifications when built in South Australia; it is commonly known as the single-fronted cottage or row house. Hence, it is possible to represent two predominant house types which are shown in Figure 1. Nonetheless, such broad classifications of buildings need many qualifications because alone, they cannot account for the development of houses and household life in South Australia in a comprehensive way. The complexity of this subject is illustrated by the evolving design and use of kitchens during the nineteenth and twentieth centuries.[20]

Initially, as Twopenny noted, it was not uncommon for houses occupied by English settlers to have a kitchen, washroom and toilet detached from the main living rooms of the house. These service rooms then became

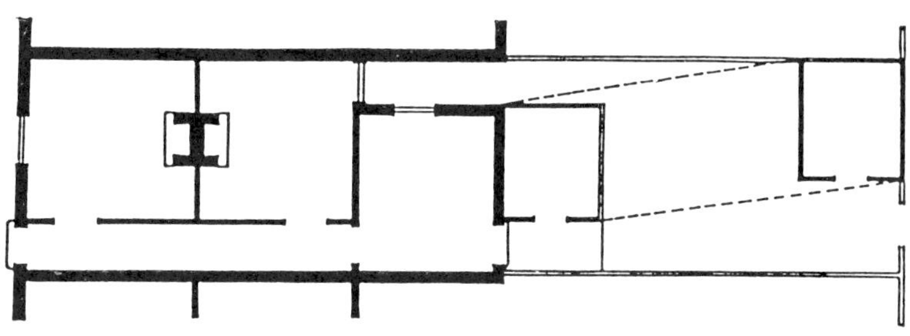

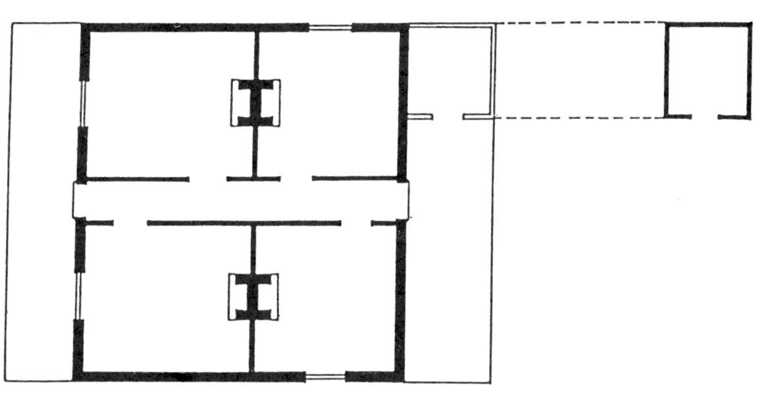

Figure 1

attached to the back of the house (sometimes only being accessible from the back verandah). Later they became integrated under the main roof of the house. In contrast, the houses occupied by Cornish miners did not have detached kitchens, but rooms for cooking and eating under the main roof, as shown in one group of dwellings built in the township of Burra during the mid-1840s reproduced in Figure 2 and 3. In stark contrast to the Cornish, German settlers in Bethany (and other settlements in the Adelaide Hills) constructed houses with a *schwarzekuche* (a black kitchen) in the centre of the dwelling. Despite the hot climate by European standards, the construction and use of a *schwarzekuche* for smoking meats illustrates the direct transposition of architectural elements and domestic cooking practices by the German settlers. One example of this transposition is shown in Figure 3 .

It is instructive to compare the cooking facilities of Cornish, German and English settlers in order to highlight the important symbolic value attributed to the domestic hearth. The archetypal value and connotation of the hearth cannot be divorced from the symbolism of the home. In this respect, despite the hot climate, these German settlers chose to keep traditional cooking practices in the Province of South Australia, rather than suppressing these remnants of life back in the Motherland.

This example of the kitchen and domestic cooking practices could be supplemented by comparisons of the layout and construction of houses built by other ethnic groups, the layout of their townships, and the relationship between public and private buildings to the street alignment. Unfortunately, space does not permit the inclusion of these comparisons here. Consequently, the next section will examine the meanings and uses of domestic appliances and furniture.

DOMESTIC APPLIANCES AND FURNITURE

In Australia, as in many other countries during the first half of the 19th century, most buildings including those for domestic purposes had very little service equipment. A typical house in Australia at that time was heated by open fires and lit by lamps or candles. Furthermore, the cooking equipment was minimal, as authors including Twopenny have tabled. Initially the pioneers only had open fires for cooking; then from 1840 the influence of domestic technology upon the development of domestic architecture was substantial.

The first significant innovation was cast-iron so that 'by the forties cast iron stoves and fireplace grates found their way into the kitchens and drawing rooms.'[21] Moreover, research has indicated that the influence of overseas countries apart from Britain was significant after 1850: apparently neither English nor European cooking stoves were as popular as those imported from North America.[22] While imported appliances were

Figure 2

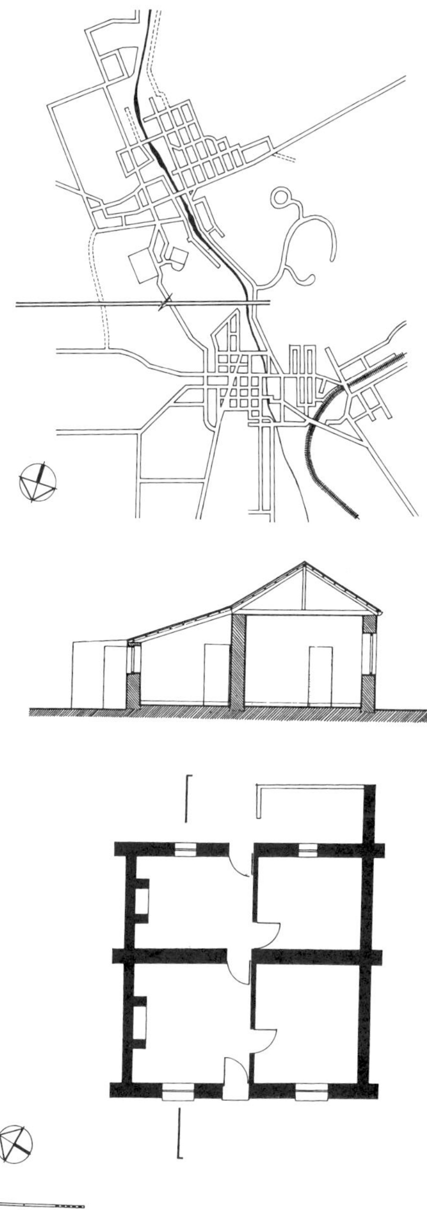

Figure 3

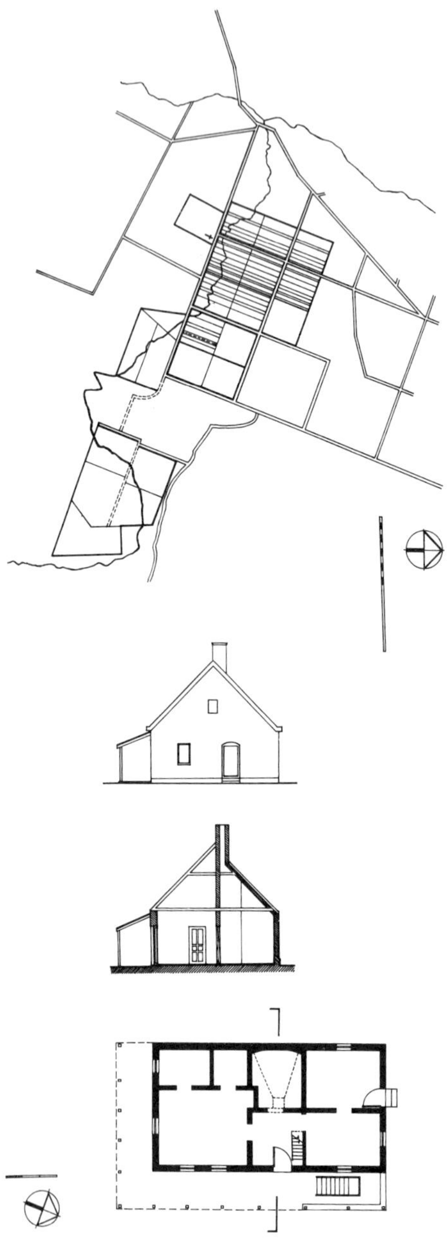

Figure 4

Figure 5

dominant it has also been concluded that when these products were manufactured in Australia they followed the designs of these foreign models.[23] This early trend has been evident from the mid-nineteenth century until today. Nonetheless, what is of particular interest is that in spite of this custom, domestic architecture did not initiate the spatial ordering of rooms which contained similar appliances in Britain or North America.

There are numerous public and private documents that describe the furnishing and use of rooms in houses that were occupied as early as 1850. Indeed, there are archives of private correspondence concerning this subject. For example, when Mr. Joseph Elliott of Jeffcott street, North Adelaide wrote to his mother in Britain in August 1860, he not only sketched the design of his house and all the furniture therein, but also described each item of furniture and the use of rooms.[24] There are several manuscripts of this kind written by the pioneers, which are available for consultation and warrant analysis.

The Elliott family lived in a double-fronted cottage of the type illustrated in Figure 1. On either side of the passage, after entering the front door, was the parlour (on the left) and the main bedroom (on the right): behind the parlour was the kitchen; behind the main bedroom was the sitting room.

Joseph Elliott drew all the furniture in these rooms. Although this is informative, his description is more so, given that it accounts for past and present uses of specific items, for example, the baby's cradle or out in the main bedroom:

> Now the next thing we jump into is the Cradle or as we call it the cot, but I beg your pardon it is too small to jump into – so we'll look at it only – & while looking at it may please remember that our poor (Jamey) was ill & died in that same cot! And we know he has got a richer cot in Heaven – would to Heaven we were all as sure! All the babies have slept & *cried* in it & (Mister) Joseph has lately slept very well in it. And Miss Beppy contrives some mornings to cram herself into it when she is tired of her own. It is covered with a patchwork quilt – octagon – commenced by Elizabeth and finished by Becky. And by the side of the cradle is a chair with rockers of my own manufacture ...[25]

This description reveals that for Elliott the cradle or cot evokes both previous and contemporary experiences of childbearing. He associates a matrix of events with it, including the birth of several children and the death of one. In this sense this item of furniture has unique associations and meaning for him. However, it is inadequate not to extend this text analysis further to include the social or cultural characteristics of this furniture. In general, beds are archetypal domestic objects with social values related to family unity and continuity, and stages of the life-cycle including birth, procreation and death. Thus, in the context of the Australian pioneers, beds including the baby's cot evoke positive associations with one's heritage. Therefore, the meaning of the cradle described in this context can be fully grasped only by the superposition of the social values and conventions and the unique personal values accumulated through an individual's experience. In sum, analysis of written narratives can lead to an understanding of the interaction between cultural and personal values and meanings invested in the home, household objects and household life in a bygone era.

INTO THE TWENTIETH CENTURY

The development of domestic architecture in South Australia has been briefly outlined according to findings from fieldwork studies and the analysis of documentary sources.. The same dual approach is equally valid for the development of domestic architecture during this century although the factors involved and the rates of change have been different. Thus it would be possible to interpret the import of model plans of the Californian bungalow (which became a dominant style for houses constructed between 1900 and 1918); in like manner it would be possible to trace the development of appliances, the influence of international and local architectural and planning ideals, and whether the emancipation of women impinged upon their role in the home including the way they used kitchen facilities. Moreover, it would be instructive to analyze how the influx of immigrants from various European countries included the transposition or adaption of socio-cultural customs related to the design and use of domestic space, and what modifications occurred when they were confronted with foreign house forms in Australia. This analysis would necessitate ethnographic research, or fieldwork different from that used to study houses built many years ago.

SYNTHESIS

This ongoing study of colonial houses and domestic life in South Australia indicates that there were numerous factors associated with the development of vernacular houses and daily life during the late nineteenth century. Owing to the complexity of the subject, it is instructive to consider the pertinence of the seven recurrent interpretations of vernacular buildings mentioned in the introduction.

(i) The aesthetic/formalist interpretation has been used to examine the origins and development of house planning in Australia especially those components of Georgian architecture in Britain that were transposed to Australia. The main object of study is the aesthetic composition facades of many large mansions, whereas there is rarely any account of the majority of colonial houses that did not rely on these aesthetic conventions.

The study reported in this article suggests that the houses of diverse ethnic groups in South Australia reflected the customs of vernacular buildings in the regions from which the pioneers emigrated, but not in the simplistic manner of copied designs found in architectural pattern books. Furthermore, additions and modifications to houses apparently overlook stylistic conventions, because other factors were deemed to be of greater importance.

(ii) The typological approach has been applied to analyze houses, as briefly illustrated in this article and elsewhere, but many qualifications are required. Nonetheless, this approach indicates that the housing stock was more heterogeneous in the mid-nineteenth century than in 1900, and an important aim of this study is to understand why this occurred.

(iii) Evolutionary theory may not seem pertinent for the study of colonial houses in South Australia owing to the relatively short time since the foundation of the British Province. This point-of-view should not underrate the range and volume of developments that have occurred, especially with respect to construction techniques, availability of materials and services, and the supply of equipment and services.

(iv) Social and geographical diffusionism appear to be useful analytical concepts for the interpretation of colonial houses in South Australia. This study shows that English, Cornish and German lores, amongst others, were practised simultaneously according to the availability of building materials, local topographical and climatic conditions, as well as a limited number of statutory regulations. Thus in Bethany, the layout of the township, house plans and construction techniques were transposed by the pioneers from their native country. However, in subsequent years hybrid architectural forms were constructed. This process shows that people with different cultural backgrounds borrowed or exchanged 'rules of thumb' about house constructions. This was an indigenous development that occurred according to the social interaction between pioneers.

(v) Physical explanations have been widely used to explain developments in house planning and construction. The inclusion of cellars, and the addition of verandahs have been attributed to climatic factors. Yet, careful site analysis reveals that verandahs were not only added to protect northern walls of houses from harsh summer sun, but also to eastern, western and even southern facades. This suggests that factors other than climate were involved. Given that verandahs are commonly built on facades that overlook streets, they can be interpreted as transition spaces between inside and outside, and public and private domains. In this way, the verandah can regulate access between the inside and outside of houses.

(vi) Social and economic factors are implicated in the development of colonial houses and domestic life from several points-of-view. This study illustrates that the size, construction and furnishing of houses developed and became more elaborate as economic circumstances in the colony improved. These developments occurred in tandem with the provision of public services, and a growing choice of building materials and tradesmen.

(vii) Cultural factors have also been associated with the design and use of colonial houses. A comparison of dwellings inhabited by English, Cornish and German settlers not only illustrates the pertinence of examining how and why cultural variables are implicated in house planning but also in what ways these factors may be modified by socio-economic and political factors, such as restrictions on the use of timber as a building material in Bethany. During the last half of the nineteenth century, the influence of transposed cultural customs became less pertinent, owing to a natural decline in the numbers of first generation immigrants, and a subsequent increase in younger generations who often had no personal experience of houses and domestic life in 'the Motherlands'.

CONCLUSION

This study illustrates that a wide range of factors, but cultural ones in particular, can account for the development of colonial domestic architecture and household life in South Australia from 1836. The approach briefly presented here contradicts some recurrent interpretations of the history of housing in Australia, in general, and within South Australia in particular, especially those that only consider the population and built environment in terms of a dominant and uniform British culture. This study indicates that the colonization of South Australia (and indeed Australia generally), and the development of houses and household life in each of the colonies, can no longer be justifiably interpreted *solely* in terms of an homogeneous residential environment that reflects English taste and preferences typified by Georgian design. Today there is ample evidence to show how public edifices differed in their formal composition from the houses built by pioneers, and that to a large extent, this divergence stemmed from the ways in which migrants from diverse ethnic groups reused, modified and eventually exchanged house designs, construction techniques and domestic practices in the colony.

NOTES

1. Lawrence, R., 'The Interpretation of vernacular architecture', *Vernacular Architecture* (14) 1983, pp. 19-28.
2. Angus, G., *Savage Life and Scenes in Australia and New Zealand* (London: Smith and Elder, 1847) (Facsimile Edition, 1968).
3. Lewcock, R., *Early nineteenth century architecture in South Africa: a study of the interaction of two cultures, 1795-1837*. (Capetown: Blakema, 1963).
4. Rapoport, A., *House form and culture* (Englewood Cliffs, N.J.: Prentice Hall, 1969).
5. Herbert, G., *Pioneers of Prefabrication: the British contribution to the nineteenth century* (Baltimore: John Hopkins University Press, 1970).
6. Gubler, J., 'Architecture and colonialism', *Lotus* 26, 1980; pp 5-19.
7. Bonta, J., *Architecture and its Interpretation* (London: Lund Humphries, 1979).
8. Twopenny, R., *Town Life in Australia* (London: Elliot Stock, 1883).
9. Berry, D. and Gilbert, S., *Pioneer Building Techniques in South Australia* (Adelaide: Gilbert Partners, 1981).
10. Young, G. et al, *Early German Settlements in the Barossa Valley, South Australia* (Adelaide, 1978).
    Young, G. et al, *Hahndorf* (Adelaide, 1981, 2 volumes)
11. Sumner, R., 'The tropical bungalow – the search for an indigenous Australian architecture', *Australian Journal of Art* 1, 1978; pp 27-30.
12. Berry, D. and Gilbert, S., *Pioneer Building Techniques in South Australia* (Adelaide: Gilbert Partners, 1981).
13. Hodder, E., *The History of South Australia* (London: Sampson, Low and Marston, 1893).
14. Summerson, J., *Heavenly mansions* (London: Norton, 1948).
15. Loudon, J.C., *An encyclopedia of cottage, farm and villa architecture* (London: Longman and Longman, 1833).
16. Herbert, G., *Pioneers of prefabrication: the British contribution to the nineteenth century* (Baltimore: John Hopkins University Press, 1978).
17. Laikve, G. 'A survey report on the Meeting House of the Society of Friends, Pennington Terrace, North Adelaide' (University of Adelaide: School of Architecture, 1963).
18. Berry, D. and Gilbert, S., *Pioneer Building Techniques in South Australia* (Adelaide: Gilbert Partners, 1981).
19. Twopenny, R., *Town Life in Australia* (London: Elliot Stock, 1883).
20. Lawrence, R., 'Domestic space and society: a cross-cultural study', *Comparative Studies in Society and History* 24 (1) 1982; pp 104-130.
21. Freeland, J., *Architecture in Australia: a history* (Ringwood, Victoria: Penguin Press, 1972), p. 108.
22. Lewis, M., Tradition and Innovation in Victorian Building, 1801-1865. A thesis submitted for the degree of Doctor of Philosophy. (Melbourne, University of Melbourne: Melbourne, Faculty of Architecture, 1972).
23. Boyd, R., *Australia's home: its origins, builders and occupiers* (Ringwood, Victoria: Penguin Press, 1968).
24. Manuscript held in the State Archives of South Australia, North Terrace, Adelaide.
25. Boyd, R., *Australia's Rome: its origins, builders and occupiers* (Ringwood, Victoria: Penguin Press, 1968).

ARNIS SIKSNA

Australian Urban Space Heritage : the Distinctive Townscape of Settlers in a New Land

(a) INTRODUCTION

Celebration of the Australian Bicentennial was an opportune time to consider questions of national identity. It might be appropriate to examine whether we have succeeded in creating urban spaces and townscapes that have distinctly Australian traits. Two broad determinants – one physical and the other cultural – have shaped the way Australians built their towns and cities.

The major physical determinant has been the fact that most Australian towns were initially planned by government, and were laid out in regular, grid patterns orientated to the cardinal directions. Furthermore the streets, blocks and the individual lots were very generous in size. (See Appendix). Although the dimensions vary, there is also a great deal of consistency in lot widths of 20 metres, block lengths of 200 metres, and street widths of 20 metres and 30 metres which recur in many Australian towns in different states.

The detailed development of buildings and spaces was strongly influenced by the widespread adoption of the verandah as a means of adapting to the climate and the common use of materials easily transportable from England, such as corrugated iron, and cast-iron lacework decoration.

Consequently numerous Australian towns share the same orientation, the same basic dimensions, and often the same materials. Equally, the people who built them shared similar attitudes to the new land, its landscape, its vegetation and held common memories of the countries they had left behind.

The perceptions and responses of the early settlers have been examined by several authors (Rapoport 1972; Seddon & Davis 1976; Jeans & Spearritt 1980; Bolton 1981). These cultural determinants can be summarised as:

(a) the need to adjust to the new land and yet at the same time to civilise it

(b) the need to retain an affinity with their previous culture and land. The tension between previous cultural factors on the one hand, and local environmental factors on the other, pervaded most of the town building efforts throughout the 19th century (Siksna 1981, pp. 121-123). The tendency was to adhere to European building forms, and to modify them only as much as climate, or other circumstances, demanded. For comfort in the harsh climate towns needed greenery and shade, but the streets, parks and gardens were planted mostly with non-Australian species. These were arranged in formal, ornamental patterns so as to conform to European perceptions, and to create the illusion that the landscape and townscape had been civilised (Richards 1982).

Against this common background several typical urban spaces emerged in Australian cities and towns:

- main streets
- terraced streets
- avenue streets/boulevards
- lanes and little streets
- arcades
- green squares

Their distinctive traits will be identified in the following discussion, which relates primarily to the urban spaces as they evolved, and reached full development, in the 19th century. Some, such as main streets, have lost much of their historical form in the last fifty years and others, such as lanes, have not been used in recent urban planning practice. Nevertheless, all these typical spaces can still be found in many present day urban environments.

Australian country towns often display these spaces more fully and vividly than the larger cities (Hall 1980; Siksna 1981). They are important reminders of Australian urban space heritage and for this reason are frequently used as examples in the following discussion.

(b) THE MAIN STREET

The main streets of country towns constitute the most widespread and distinctive urban space type in Australia. Its physical characteristics are very simple and easily recognisable. It is a space of generous width – usually about 30 metres, rarely less than 20 metres. The several lanes for vehicular traffic are bordered by a strip devoted to parking on both sides of the street. The wide footpaths are covered almost continuously by verandahs or awnings to provide shade in hot summers and protection from rain. The street space is enclosed by one and two storey buildings, and is often planted with rows of trees and shrubs – either adjoining the footpath, or in the central part of the street (Armstrong & Burton 1986, pp. 18-19; Walker 1981, pp. 1-45 to 1-46). Main street is thus composed of a set of distinctive and interlinked spaces, which break down the considerable width into smaller functional units and human scaled spaces. Despite the overall simplicity, main street is a complex urban space type that evolved in a coherent and durable form, yet expressed regional differences and diversity of detailed character.

Main street occurs in three basic variations, deriving from the different means of handling the large central section of the space.

(i) Single central space – The space between the two footpaths forms an unbroken expanse devoted to moving and parked vehicles. The parked cars, and the row of trees which is often planted adjacent to the footpath, structure the large space at its edges. [Examples -Hay, Moree, Glen Innes, Tamworth in N.S.W.; Hamilton, Beechworth in Vic.; Maryborough, Laidley in Queensland].

(ii) Central space divided by trees or planted median strip – A central row of trees or a narrow, planted median separates the carriageways. [Examples – Coonabarabran, Camden in N.S.W.; Warwick, Goondiwindi in Queensland]. In other cases the median strip is wider and contains plantings of trees, shrubs and grass and/or provides for a central row of car parking [Examples – Gatton, Toowoomba in Queensland].

(iii) Linear central park – In some cases, particularly where the street width exceeds 30 metres, the middle part is developed as a linear park strip. It is planted with two or more rows of trees, ornamental shrubs and flowers, and often also contains bandstands, gazebos, fountains, statues, monuments and seating. [Examples largely in Victorian towns – Mildura, Camperdown, Terang, Ballarat].

Historically, the basic elements of main street also recur in the main shopping streets of the older suburbs and even of the centres of capital cities – only the height of buildings enclosing the streets varies.

The distinctive qualities of country town main streets were gradually refined during the 19th century, and reached their fullest expression in the early part of the 20th century. A photo of Peel Street, the main street of Tamworth, N.S.W., taken in 1906 shows an elegant and delightful urban space where lace-like cast-iron verandahs cover the footpaths and are complemented by a line of mature trees providing shade for the horse-drawn carriages on the roadway. Many such streets existed throughout Australia and were admirably related to the way the people of the countryside used them. A study of country towns in Victoria (McIntyre and McIntyre 1944) demonstrates the vital community function of main street as a business forum and social meeting place, and the particular role that its detailed spatial treatment – its pavement, street trees, fountains etc. – plays in its efficiency as a social centre.

Main streets still perform much the same social functions today but, sadly, have lost some distinctive physical features – verandah posts, cast-iron decorations, and street trees have disappeared to make way for less effective cantilevered awnings, and parking meter stumps. Nevertheless the main streets of Australian country towns have shown a remarkable robustness in adapting their essential form to changing conditions.

(c) THE TERRACED STREET

As a building and urban space type the terraced street has similarities with British prototypes, but has developed original Australian characteristics. These streets resulted from the first wave of urban intensification in areas adjoining the central parts of the capital cities. In successive building booms of the 19th century, the large blocks and lots established by the original government town layouts were subdivided by speculative private developers into a finer mesh of street networks, and smaller lots suited for row houses (Kelly 1978).

The terraced streets in Sydney are sometimes as narrow as 9 metres and rarely wider than 20 metres. This led to the creation of intimate, residential scaled street spaces which were further reinforced by the size and detailed treatment of the terrace houses lining the street. Unlike the large upper and middle class terrace houses of Britain, Australian terrace houses were built to cater for the growing working class population. They were much more modest in size and single or two storeys in height.

The terrace houses generally have a small front yard, or at least a front verandah, which forms an interface between the private space of the house and the public space of the street, and serves the socialising and territorial needs of their residents. (Gehl 1980). This simple spatial form is elaborated by the rich detailing of the cast-iron verandahs and balconies that are such a characteristic feature of the Australian terrace house.

(d) THE AVENUE STREET/BOULEVARD

In contrast to the intimate nature of the terraced street, many residential streets in the more affluent areas of Australian cities and country towns in the 19th century were developed in the form of spacious, graceful tree lined avenues as a setting for the suburban detached house.

The streets were generally far wider than needed for residential purposes. All secondary streets of towns laid out in N.S.W. and Queensland under Governor Darling's regulations are about 25 metres wide. In Adelaide and Melbourne most residential streets exceed 20 metres, and some are as wide as 30 metres. This excessive width provided enormous scope for landscape treatment on the grand scale. Many of the inner and middle ring suburbs of Melbourne, Adelaide and Sydney, and also the larger and more prosperous country towns in several states, have used this opportunity to create distinctive tree and shrub lined residential streets. (Armstrong & Burton 1986, pp. 17-18; Walker 1981, pp. 1-44 to 1-45).

The treatment usually adopted is one of simple avenue type planting of trees in a row alongside both footpaths. In the narrower streets this provides a sheltered canopy for pedestrians and a green tunnel-like corridor for vehicular movement. [Examples – Logan Street, Tenterfield, N.S.W.; George Street, East Melbourne; Abbott Street, New Farm and Laurel Avenue, Chelmer in Brisbane; most of the streets in North Adelaide]. In the wider streets the footpath canopy is achieved, but the wide carriageway separates the tree rows to create green walls to the space, but also allowing views of the sky and the distant landscape. [Examples – Ballarat, Mildura in Victoria; Warwick, Toowoomba in Queensland]. In some towns, such as Tamworth, N.S.W. the planting treatment varies – in one street rows of trees are placed on both sides; in another, they are placed on one side only; while in streets on steeper ground the two carriageways are separated by a row of trees planted in the central median.

In some inner suburbs even grander avenue effects were achieved. The most notable examples exist in the Adelaide suburbs of Norwood and Rose Park. (Williams 1974, pp. 445-446). Their major streets, 30 to 40 metres wide, are developed in the form of a central linear park strip having two or more rows of trees, ornamental flower beds and monuments. [Examples – Osmond Terrace, Norwood; Alexandra Avenue and Prescott Terrace, Rose Park].

Avenue planting was also used to create distinctive approach routes to the city centre. Melbourne has the most notable boulevard type main road system. The roads are about 60 metres wide and are treated as a set of interlinked spaces – a central through traffic route, often with a central median separating the carriageways, and two service roads giving local access on either side, and separated by a median strip from the through route. The through route sometimes also carries tram lines. The median strips are planted with one or two rows of trees, usually elms, planes, and ash. [Examples – St.Kilda Road, Victoria Parade, Royal Parade]. Other cities have not developed such comprehensive systems but similar boulevards were developed in Adelaide [North Terrace, Anzac Parade, Frome Road, King William Road] and Sydney [Anzac Parade].

The boulevard also appears in a more rural version as an avenue type approach route to a country town. (Armstrong and Burton 1986, pp.9-12, 23; Spencer 1986). Many examples exist throughout Australia, the most notable being the 14km long memorial avenue which leads into Ballarat. [Other examples – Tenterfield, Coonabarabran, Jugiong in N.S.W.].

Though obviously influenced by European models these avenue streets and boulevards are nevertheless uniquely Australian. Their European ancestry is reflected in the exotic nature of the deciduous trees that were almost inevitably used during the 19th century (Spencer 1986). What makes them Australian is the generous width of the street; the widely spaced detached buildings and the relatively minor role these play in defining spatial form; the contribution made by private gardens; and the fact that in most cases the verges and medians are planted with grass, rather than being paved or gravelled as they usually are in Europe. These residential environments and boulevards represent an elegant response to the suburban lifestyle of Australians, to the climatically dictated need for shade and greenery in the hot summers, and the psychological need to create a civilised and European image in a harsh new land.

(e) THE LANES AND LITTLE STREETS

The enormous size of the blocks and lots created by the initial government town layouts, inevitably called for the introduction of additional, smaller streets as urban development intensified. Sometimes a system of service lanes was already included in the initial layout. These smaller streets fall into two general categories:

(a) Planned, regular street systems – Generally parallel to the main and secondary streets, and provided throughout the town plan. They are relatively narrow – 10 metres in Melbourne; 6 metres in Warwick, Queensland.

(b) Unplanned, irregular laneways – Introduced haphazardly in response to land sub-division and development intensification, mostly by private developers within the limitations of the original land ownership patterns. They vary in width (3 metres to 10 metres) and configuration – some are straight connections of two major streets; others are awkward, dog-leg or dead end laneways giving only service access. (Examples – Most of the subsequent laneway pattern within the original blocks of Adelaide, Brisbane, Melbourne, Sydney).

Each of these categories is associated with both residential development and commercial development, giving rise to further spatial sub-types. In all cases they express 'the front and back' distinction of the activities they serve. They are also a vital reflection of the spontaneous, informal growth processes of the city and thus of particular importance in introducing organic and humanising traits into the otherwise regular, ordered layouts of Australian towns and cities. The irregular laneways and alleys succeed in imparting the intimacy and human scale qualities of European urban areas, which cannot be achieved in the regular, broad urban spaces of Australian cities and towns.

The residential lanes of country towns often extend for several blocks in a continuous line. The lots and houses are often smaller, and sometimes the lanes provide only rear access to lots fronting the larger street. The lanes are sometimes unpaved or are unevenly paved; different types of fences are employed; there is a general air of seclusion and informality which contributes to a distinct rural flavour. [Examples – Warwick, Qld. and Tamworth N.S.W. where they are called 'avenues'; Glen Innes and Tenterfield, N.S.W. where they are called 'lanes'].

The laneways in inner suburban areas of Sydney and Melbourne are similar to the country lanes in width and pattern, but are mostly used as rear access lanes to terraced houses. They are generally lined by back fences, sheds and garage doors. [Examples – Laneways in Paddington and Glebe in Sydney, Carlton in Melbourne]. Before the introduction of sewerage systems, the back lanes were functionally necessary both in cities and in country towns for the collection of sanitary pans from backyard 'dunnies'. [Examples -Mitchell Lane, Glebe in Sydney].

The 'little streets' of Melbourne, 10 metres wide and alternating with the parallel major streets, were included in the original town layout to give rear access. They have acquired an interesting spatial form – a canyon like, but intimate space with bustling activity at street level, which at the same time has a grand scale because of the undulating topography which allows extensive views along the streets. David Martin (1969, pp. 4,5) has described them as follows: 'It was one of those narrow one-way streets wafered between the main thoroughfare which give the city area of Melbourne its character. Always crowded, it reminded me of a bazaar robbed of its Eastern trappings. Beautiful it was not .... but it had a certain relaxed, neutral pleasantness ....'

(f) THE ARCADE

Just as the terraced street is a smaller scaled version of its British counterpart, so the Australian shopping arcade can be distinguished from the grander European models in a similar way. Arcades made their appearance in Australian cities soon after their introduction in Europe (Heath and Moore 1963; Garside and White 1963). Their development was both facilitated and confined by the original land subdivision pattern in different cities.

The arcades of the 19th century are generally narrow, and run straight between two major streets. [Examples – Strand Arcade, Sydney; Royal Arcade, Melbourne; Adelaide Arcade, Adelaide], but sometimes they are L-shaped [Block Arcade, Melbourne]. Very rarely do they form a more extensive system, such as occupying a whole city block or giving access to several surrounding streets [Example – Queen Victoria Building, Sydney]. The heights of the arcades rarely exceed two storeys. Even where they do, they maintain an intimate scale, contributed partly by their narrowness, but even more so by the elaborate cast iron detailing of the balconies and roof-skylights, and the richly patterned and coloured flooring tiles.

(g) THE GARDEN SQUARES

Squares were rarely provided in the initial layout of Australian towns. Few have survived to the present day, and examples of urban squares in the European manner are very rare.

The 19th century town or city is characterised by a regular city block sized piece of ground being developed as a garden (Armstrong & Burton 1986, pp. 22-23; Walker 1981, pp. 1-46 to 1-48; Richards 1982). They are generally treated as a mini botanical garden in which a variety of non-native trees and floral displays is arranged in a simple, compact, regular arrangement. Often they contain a fountain, a bandstand, a war memorial or statues. [Examples – Leslie Park, Warwick, Qld.; Princes Square, Launceston, Tasmania; Victoria Park, Forbes, N.S.W.; Belmore Square, Goulburn, N.S.W.; Johnstone Park, Geelong, Vic.] An interesting exception is the formal planting of eucalypts in the riverside park at Coonabarabran, N.S.W.

These spaces are essentially 'garden squares'. Their shape is very often square or rectangular and is taken arbitrarily out of the grid layout of streets. The term therefore reflects the geometrical shape, its arbitrary selection and its landscaped treatment as opposed to the consciously defined, enclosed and hard paved 'urban square' of Europe. Leftover spaces at the awkward junctions of two differently oriented grids are often treated as 'garden triangles'. [Examples – Brisbane, Sydney]. The squares of Adelaide, although more consciously planned as part of the city layout, still conform to the type in the sense that they are vast spaces, treated as ornamental gardens in the urban grid pattern.

(h) THE DISTINCTIVE TOWNSCAPE OF SETTLERS IN A NEW LAND

It took less than a hundred years for the typical urban space types to emerge and to be refined into workable and often elegant forms. The forms may not stand comparison with the sophisticated urban spaces of Europe, but they effectively express Australian lifestyles and spatial perceptions. What are the general qualities of these spatial types and their overall townscape effect?

Firstly, they carry a general feeling of spaciousness – the spaces feel generous, at times they may even be considered too vast for the purpose they serve, and seem to reflect an Australian preference for unconfined, loosely defined spaces.

Secondly, the space does not contain, but neither does it connect properly to the surrounding landscape. Almost every urban space in Australia reveals the vast empty space beyond it – an expanse of sky; a distant landscape or seascape. Yet the views are not exploited for aesthetic effect – they just present themselves in a haphazard way. Unlike the contrived European vistas in towns and gardens, the view from Australian urban spaces seems unconnected to the urban scene within the settlement.

Thirdly, the spatial pattern and overall townscape has a somewhat vague and neutral nature lacking firm organisation or a clear focus (Hall 1980, p. 44). This is mainly contributed by the grid layout of streets, which is organised by the cardinal directions rather than by the topography or surrounding natural features. The absence of urban squares, and the haphazard placing of garden squares, compounds the egalitarian nature of the layout. The town may be full of nicely developed individual urban spaces, but it will rarely have a special place – of intensive use; of deep meaning; of outstanding character that stands as a focus for the whole town.

Although the Australian town lacks the European town square, it does have an effective community social place in the form of the extended, broad main street. The extended place, rather than the square, seems to be the preferred urban focus in Australia – the traditional form of main street is now being reflected in the new pedestrian malls of city centres.

(i) CONCLUSION

The 19th century heritage of Australian urban space has produced a rich stock of prototypes that provide a sound foundation for developing contemporary urban forms. Almost all these typical spaces have been used by urban designers in the recent few years to create urban environments which link our past and present in a meaningful way. The two hundred years of urban settlement in Australia show how quickly our urban identity was established in the first century, and also how this identity has been partly destroyed by neglect and by the importation of overseas models of urban forms during the latter part of the second century. The bicentennial commemoration serves as a timely reminder that historical continuity is a vital ingredient of national identity in all its forms, including that of our urban environment.

APPENDIX STREET, BLOCK AND LOT DIMENSIONS OF SOME AUSTRALIAN CITIES AND TOWNS

	Lot Size (metres)	Block Size (metres)	Street Widths (metres)		
			Main Street	Secondary Streets	Other Streets
* Adelaide, SA	65 x 65	523 x 131	40	30	20
* Brisbane, Qld	20 x 45	200 x 90	20	20	20
* Melbourne, Vic	20 x 95	200 x 95	30	30	10
(1) NSW Towns	20 x 100	200 x 200	30	26	26
(2) Qld Towns	20 x 50	200 x 100	40	30	30
(3) SA Towns	40 x 50	160 x 100	30	30	30

NOTES

* Dimensions of the layout of the initial parts, now the Central Business Districts, of these cities.

(1) Applies to most N.S.W. towns laid out after Governor Darling's Regulations were published in 1829, and also to some Queensland towns laid out prior to 1860 under these regulations.

(2) Applies to most Queensland towns particularly those laid out in accordance with successive 'General Directions for the Guidance of Surveyors' which were first published in 1878.

(3) Applies to those South Australian and Northern Territory towns laid out in accordance with Surveyor General Goyder's instructions published in 1864.

REFERENCES

H. Armstrong & D. Burton, *Street Tree Survey N.S.W. Country Towns* (Sydney: School of Landscape Architecture, University of New South Wales, 1986).

G. Bolton, *Spoils and Spoilers : Australians Make Their Environment 1788-1980* (Sydney: George Allen & Unwin, 1981).

J. Garside & D. White, 'Arcades of Melbourne', *Architecture in Australia*, Vol.52 (1963), No.2, 80-84.

J. Gehl, 'The Residential Street Environment', *Built Environment*, Vol.6 (1980), No.1, 51-61.

R. Hall, 'An Australian Country Townscape', *Landscape*, Vol.24 (1980), No.2, 41-48.

T. Heath, & T. Moore, 'Sydney's Arcades : An Historical Note', *Architecture in Australia*, Vol.52 (1963), No.2, 85-90.

D.N. Jeans & P. Spearritt, *The Open Air Museum : The Cultural Landscape of N.S.W.* (Sydney: George Allen & Unwin, 1980). pp. 1-7.

M. Kelly, *Paddock Full of Houses* (Sydney: Doak Press, 1978).

D. Martin, *Where a Man Belongs* (North Melbourne: Cassell Australia, 1969).

A.J. & J.J. McIntyre, *Country Towns of Victoria : A Social Survey*. Melbourne: Melbourne University Press, 1944). pp. 18-48.

Australia as Human Setting, edited by A. Rapoport (Sydney: Angus & Robertson, 1972).

O. Richards, 'A Fairer Athens and a Freer Rome – Historic Public Gardens in Perth W.A.', *Heritage Australia*. Winter 1982 (1982). pp. 66-69.

Man and Landscape in Australia : Towards an Ecological Vision, edited by G. Seddon & M. Davis (Canberra: A.G.P.S., 1976)

A. Siksna, 'Understanding Australian Urban Space : The Lesson of Country Towns'. *Proceedings of the 1981 Conference of the Australian & New Zealand Architectural Science Association, Canberra, October 1981* (Canberra: ANZAScA., 1981), pp. 121-127.

R. Spencer, 'Fashions in Street Tree Planting in Victoria', *Landscape Australia*, Vol.8 (1986), No.4, pp. 304-309.

M. Walker, *Historic Towns in Queensland : An Introductory Study* (Brisbane: The National Trust of Queensland, 1981).

M. Williams, *The Making of the South Australian Landscape* (London: Academic Press, 1974).

HELEN THOMSON

Catherine Helen Spence: City Woman

Catherine Spence became a city woman in a relatively unique way: born in rural Scotland, she arrived in Adelaide in 1839 on her 14th birthday, when the colony was only three years old. As Spence matured, Adelaide grew, and its pioneers were uniquely privileged in the intimacy of their involvement with social and political institutions as they were gradually established. The special implications of this for a woman of ability were at first not understood by Spence. She records the Spence family's arrival in 1839: 'When we sat down on a log in Light Square, waiting till my father brought the key of the wooden house in Gilles Street, in spite of the dignity of my 14 years just attained, I had a good cry.'[1]

By the time she wrote her Autobiography in 1910, the year of her death, Spence was aware that her own and Adelaide's simultaneous growth had liberated her out of the constricting private sphere of nineteenth century womanhood into a richly rewarding public life undreamt of her in her girlhood. Spence became a novelist, journalist, preacher, public speaker, political candidate, essayist and social reformer, in many cases being the first Australian woman to adopt these roles. In every case, the city was an essential enabling factor, not just any city, although Spence understood very well that gender and class-related constraints were weaker in colonial cities than elsewhere, but specifically Adelaide.

This Australian city had two essential differences to the other colonial cities: it never accepted convicts, and it was carefully planned on Wakefield's principles of selling land in small parcels and encouraging family emigration. To its early settlers Adelaide must have seemed to have utopian potential, and although, as I shall show, Spence was to shift some of her utopian hopes into a fictional context later in her life, in part a reaction of disappointment with the reality, even in 1910 she could write enthusiastically of Adelaide's founding:

> It is sometimes counted as a reproach that South Australia was founded by doctrinaires and that we retain traces of our origin; to me it is our glory. In the land laws and the immigration laws it struck out a new path, and sought to

> found a new community where the sexes should be equal, and where land, labour, and capital should work harmoniously together.[2]

The interesting result of this conviction is that we cannot separate Spence's idea of the city from the utopian. The idea is inseparable from the ideal, and when we look at Spence's fiction in particular, for that is where many of her ideas are worked out in most detail, this becomes clear.

She wrote in two fictional modes (excepting one work of religious speculation, a kind of Bunyanesque Free-thinking work called *An Agnostic's Progress from the Known to the Unknown*). The first mode was conventional realism, the second, utopian fiction. There may well have been a degree of disillusionment with the 19th century city in the shift from one to another, as I shall argue. But in the realistic novels, all of them set in both the old and new worlds, partly in order to cater for more than the small colonial market for fiction, it is specifically the city of Adelaide which plays a starring role. Even in her first novel, *Clara Morison; a tale of South Australia during the gold fever*, published in 1854, when the town still consisted of straggling, muddy streets and small outlying farms, when it had already weathered a depression in the 1840's and was facing another serious set-back as nearly all its able-bodied men left for the Victorian goldfields, Spence voices her characteristic optimism in its closing pages:

> I think that the discovery of these goldfields will throw us at once into a more advanced state; I do not mean of morals, but it will bring us improvements in arts and sciences: we shall have steam and railways; towns will grow suddenly into cities; population will increase at an unexampled rate; and not only diggers and speculators will come to our shores, but men of intellect and enterprise.[3]

These words are not spoken by the heroine, Clara Morison, but by a character called Margaret Elliott, who Spence confessed was a portrait of herself. In this first novel Spence evolved a strategy which she was to employ in her later fiction as well. This was to give her novel a conventional courtship and marriage romance plot, but in a realistic setting which contained a sub-plot with characters drawn from real life and owing nothing to the conventions of fiction. Clara Morison, an explicit Cinderella figure with sources as remote as Samuel Richardson's *Pamela* and as recent as Charlotte Bronte's *Jane Eyre*, marries her Australian prince, who is a grazier. Sent out to Adelaide on the death of her father by a heartless but respectable middle-class uncle, Clara must become a domestic servant to survive, and regains her middle-class position only upon the discovery of cousins in the Elliott family, and ultimately, respectable marriage.

The Elliotts demonstate the uniquely colonial and for women ironically liberating fact that in a servant-starved colony, middle-class women could perform domestic work, and even earn their own living if necessary, without forfeiting their social respectability, as would be the case with their English counterparts. Margaret Elliott, like Spence herself, chooses not to marry and instead to study law with her brother with a view to assisting and shaping political reform in the city of Adelaide. Nowhere else, even in Australia, did such opportunities exist. The letters written by the male Elliots from the Victorian goldfields, give a picture of Melbourne in chaos as people flood in from all over the world. The city is an overcrowded, near-lawless mess; the land is locked up by squatting interests. Adelaide seems a haven of civilization, its city may be small, but it has been meticulously planned by Colonel Light, and its small farms promise to become the country's bread-basket. Thus the utopian strain is carried through in notions of orderly civic growth as well as personal liberation of female lives.

Catherine Spence was unique in sharing her personal growth as a public woman with that of a colonial city, but in understanding that female liberation was dependent upon an urban setting, she was the precursor of a later generation of Australian women writers. Barbara Baynton exorcised the horrors of bush life, for women, in her *Bush Studies*, and beat a strategic retreat to Sydney and then London. Rosa Praed survived a pioneering Queensland childhood, then permanently left it behind for Brisbane and London. Louisa Lawson and Mary Gilmore were two more brilliant women who also understood urban life was a necessary pre-requisite for liberation.

The bottom line of all this was of course economic. Financial independence was the Holy Grail of 19th century womanhood. Sometimes, as in the case of Barbara Baynton, a succession of wealthy husbands and an astute instinct for investment did the trick. But Catherine Spence, who chose to remain single, understood only too well that her society had, with the exception of working-class women, made paid employment and respectability mutually exclusive. She had a very good understanding of economics, as her newspaper writings revealed. But what Adelaide deprived her of was a first-hand knowledge of industrial capitalism. This gap in her knowledge was in fact an enabling factor in her utopianism. An almost universal characteristic of 19th century utopian fiction is its essentially Arcadian nature: a setting which returns to notions of a fruitful and benevolent natural world in which man lives in harmony and health, both mental and physical. Pre-industrial Adelaide had the potential for an ideal city, and Spence did not see the consequent limitations on the growth of wealth and capital as a disadvantage.

Yet when we look again at *Clara Morison*, certain contradictions emerge. One is the sheer fragility of Adelaide when its men leave during the gold-rushes. The local economy is devastated, although on the other hand it provided the opportunity for women to step into men's roles. Yet Spence also suggested that the thriving small-farm economy which produced food crops rather than wool, could make fortunes for farmers who understood the implications of Victoria's population explosion. However she's not really interested in farming. Instead she sees opportunities for her own family as much as her fictional characters, in the steady growth of civil administration, banking and commerce, traditional occupations for the urban middle-class. Furthermore, even at this early stage in her writing career she assumes a distinctly partisan Australian position on the question of rural capital investment in Australia.

No character is more despised in *Clara Morison* than Mr. Dent, who from an *English* point of view makes ideal use of colonial opportunities. He makes money out of a sheep farm in South Australia, then sells out and with his capital conveniently increased by an inheritance, purchases himself an estate and a place back in England's aristocratic and leisured class. Spence held his social climbing in contempt, since she understood Australia's main advantage to be its less rigid and stultifying class divisions, but she also saw the removal of his capital, sorely needed in South Australia, as virtual robbery.

The only capital possessed by single women like Catherine Spence was their education, and society did not value that very highly. In her youth, Spence adopted the familiar role of governess, going out at 17 to teach for 6 pence an hour, but she abandoned that thankless task as soon as she could. She was 53 before she had a regular job, as outside contributor to the *Adelaide Register*. Her journalism provided her not only with an income, but an opportunity to comment on and analyse a wide range of subjects. Here is a list of just some of them: compulsory education, taxation, marriage laws, literary criticism, electoral reform, social class, organised charity, dress reform, co-operative stores, criminal law, female wages, girls' reformatories, civil service reform, national insurance, building societies, socialism and communism, Henry George's Land Tax, capitalism and banking, democracy, the Selection Acts, liberalism: the list could go on and on, but its breadth indicates Spence's active participation in all the intellectual concerns of her day.

There is nothing gendered about her interests here, but running through almost everything she wrote was a constant concern for social justice, an encouragement of reform not conservatism, and a particular awareness of the legally disadvantaged position of women and children in her society. Her irrepressible optimism was rewarded by her witnessing, over a long life, many of her cherished reforms come to pass. But her idealism was always one leap ahead of reality: utopia always lies ahead, although Spence was aware she occupied a mid-point in a century of unprecedented change.

In 1878 she published in the South Australian Register a series of articles entitled 'Some Social Aspects of South Australian Life'. Looking back to Adelaide's early days she sees its reversion to a relatively primitive economic model as vital to shaping egalitarian values:

> The Wakefield system of colonization had been extolled as sure to avert the crisis which all colonies had previously gone through, for the simultaneous arrival in due proportions of capital and labour was expected to secure steady and industrial progress. But neither labour nor capital was employed to produce anything. Instead of the two male and two female immigrants being employed on the eighty-acre section they were ostensibly sent to cultivate for the purchaser, they were employed in building houses for themselves and others in Adelaide, and when that failed – when capital was drained for food supplies – on costly Government works paid for in bills on England, afterwards protested. It was well for South Australia that the crisis did come, that Government works were stopped, and people driven to the country. Everybody took simultaneously to farming and gardening, flocks and herds increased in number – faster than the consumers of beef and mutton – and the result was a time of almost fabulous cheapness and an extraordinary scarcity of money. The necessaries of life were produced in super abundance, the comforts were slowly reached, and the luxuries had to be done without. There was very little difference in the actual circumstances of different classes – some had property and some had none; but property was unsaleable for money, and barter only exchanged one unsaleable article for another. Nobody employed hired labour who could possibly do the work himself, and everyone had to turn his or her hand to a great deal of miscellaneous work, most of which would be called menial and degrading in an older community, where large classes have been from time immemorial set apart for drudgery, and where other classes would rather sacrifice anything than take a part of it ...
>
> In the early days of a free colony we see something of the Utopia, where man learns the usefulness, the dignity and the blessedness of labour, where work is paid for according to its hardness and its disagreeableness, and not after the standard of overcrowded countries where bread is dear and human life and strength cheap.[4]

This was a temporary stage of Adelaide's development (it in fact describes the 1840's crisis and depression), but Spence understood it to be crucial in the development of an ideal national character. She re-iterated this in the fictional form of her 1865 novel *Mr. Hogarth's Will,* which has the problem of women's employment as its central concern. The fictional structure is almost the same as *Clara Morison's,* but the first half of the novel is set in England, and a contrast in employment opportunities for women, between the old and new societies, is made. The disinherited heroines Jane and Elsie Melville, provided with 'masculine' educations which prove quite useless in the market-place, must go into service (though of a superior kind to Clara's) to survive, before immigration to Adelaide is followed by marriage. Again it is the sub-plot and alternative heroines who reflect other realities. The unmarried Miss Thomson (based on a real-life aunt of Spence's) runs the most successful farm in her part of Scotland. Also unmarried is Peggy Walker, a washerwoman who supports five orphaned nieces and nephews and their aged grandparent. Hard work in service and the purchase of a small shop for her by a grateful employer in Adelaide, have made Peggy's life comfortable, but she returns to Scotland on the death of her sister, and manages to survive financially by selling her labour as a washerwoman. She also returns to Adelaide and relative prosperity before the novel ends.

Jane and Elsie's painful and unsuccessful search for work – Jane is told when applying for a book-keeping job for which she is thoroughly trained, ... 'what would be the consequence if all the clever women like yourself were to thrust themselves into masculine avocations? Do you not see that the competition would reduce the earnings of men, and then there would be fewer who could afford to marry?'[5]– and Peggy Walker's success in finding working-class employment, spell out the class\gender trap for women. Peggy also explodes the comfortable male presumption that only men had financial dependents. The happy ending for them all is provided, uniquely, by Adelaide, the colonial city where class distinctions are weakened, where women are valued as citizens, and where labour has an appropriate value given to it.

1865, the year in which Spence published *Mr. Hogarth's Will,* was also the year in which the generosity of two of her friends, who had made money from investing in South Australia's copper mines, paid for a return visit to England and Scotland for her. The trip only confirmed her opinion of the superiority of her colonial society. On going back to Melrose, the village of her birth, she was amused to find herself pitied: 'They grieved that I had been banished from the romantic associations and the high civilization of Melrose to rough it in the wilds, while my heart was full of thankfulness that I had moved to the wider spaces and the more varied activities of a new and progressive colony.'[6] When she visited Edinburgh and then London, once again her comparisons with Adelaide and South Australia were always to the advantage of the colony. Her booklet on the Hare system of proportional representation, *A Plea for Pure Democracy,* written in 1859, opened many doors for her in London, including that of John Stuart Mill.

In reference to electoral reform she said in her *Autobiography*: 'I had a feeling that in our new colonies the reform would meet with less obstruction than in old countries bound by precedent and prejudiced by vested interests. Parliament was the preserve of the wealthy in the United Kingdom. There was no property qualification for the candidate in South Australia, and we had manhood suffrage.'[7]

Three decades later South Australia was the first state to introduce female suffrage, and by that time Spence had thrown her considerable influence behind the suffragette movement. When she first met John Stuart Mill in 1865 she found him, at that time, more enthusiastic about women's rights than she was herself: 'For myself, I considered electoral reform on the Hare system of more value than the enfranchisement of women, and was not eager for the doubling of the electors in number, especially as the new voters would probably be more ignorant and more apathetic than the old.'[8]

She shared this opinion with George Eliot, whom she also met in 1865, but she was to change her mind, and eventually received, in 1895, just before South Australia's historic first universal suffrage election, a letter from the National Council of Women of the United States, congratulating her on the success of her work in the cause of women's suffrage.

In the intervening years Spence threw herself into a variety of reformist activities, philanthropic, economic, political and literary. She developed her skills as a public speaker, preaching more than 100 sermons in the Unitarian Church she had joined after thankfully abandoning the Calvinism of her youth and its dogma of predestination: 'The doctrine of innate human depravity is one of the most paralysing dogmas that human fear invented or priestcraft encouraged' she commented in her *Autobiography*.[9] Her consequent conviction that environment was the crucial aspect of moral development was part of her lifelong utopianism. She was also prepared to travel anywhere to speak on her major pre-occupation, proportional representation or 'effective voting' as she was to call it. In 1893, at the age of 68, she left for America as a Government Commissioner and delegate to the Great World's Fair Congresses in Chicago.

Her travels through America and its cities broadened and deepened her ideas and introduced her to many prominent Americans of the time. Her reflections on America, her liking for this new society, reveal again not only her bias, her preference for the new over the old, but her essentially urban pre-occupations:

> Intelligence and not wealth I found to be the passport to social life among the Americans I met ... The homeliness and unostentatiousness of the middleclass American were captivating. My interests have always been in people and in the things that make for human happiness or misery rather than in the beauties of Nature, art, or architecture. I want to know how the people live, what wages are, what the amount of comfort they can buy; how the people are fed, taught, amused; how the burden of taxation falls; how justice is executed; how much or how little liberty the people enjoy.[10]

The failure of Spence's efforts to introduce proportional representation was ironical because of the very reform it was intended to bring about. Its introduction would have weakened party politics, but Spence was to witness, with great disappointment, the replication of old world political parties in South Australia. She records her original high hopes for the new Labour Party:

> Before I left for America I saw the growing power and strength of the Labour Party. I rejoiced that a new star had arisen in the political firmament. I looked to it as a party that would support every cause that tended towards righteousness. I expected it, as a reform party, to take up effective voting, because effective voting was reform. I hoped that a party whose motto was 'Trust the People' would have adopted a reform by means of which alone it would be possible for the people to gain control over its Legislature and its Government. Alas! for human hopes that depend on parties for their realization![11]

As an electoral reformer Spence needed the city for two reasons. It was where the governing body was itself to be found, and it was where most of the voters were to be found. Her American tour only intensified her zeal for effective voting, as she found there already well entrenched, a tyrannous and corrupt party system. However there, as in Australia, existing Party interests ultimately doomed her reform.

When she spoke of her interest in the mechanisms of society, what we would today called sociology, she was again not only defining an urban pre-occupation, but disclaiming a taste for the aesthetic aspects of life. This was a weakness she was well aware of: she actively disliked music, for example, in an era which defined itself culturally very much in terms of music, both domestic and public. Some critics of her fiction have decried the lack of artistic sophistication in her writing, sensing perhaps that the novel in Spence's hands was a means to an end rather than an end in itself.

For these and other reasons, her switch to the utopian mode from the conventions of realism in her fiction, is a very interesting one. Some initial points need to be made about this. First of all, despite the gradual realisation of many of the reforms she worked for, a fictional utopia represented both an acceleration of the sometimes painfully slow rate of real reform, and a blueprint for the ideal society itself. Secondly, both her utopias reflected cultural loss as part of the necessary price for social reform. Her society in *Handfasted,* in its utilitarian evolution, had lost its ability to produce music, decorative arts or literature. Spence was well aware that the feeling and impulse behind great art was very often precisely the result of the suffering endured in a flawed, as opposed to perfect, society. Thirdly, Spence as a utopian moved, as did all her fellow-utopians of the same period, from the Arcadian ideal of societies remote in time and\or space from the realities of 19th century life, towards the more complex problems of urban, industrialised life. Thus *Handfasted* is set in a remote valley in Central America, peopled by Scots immigrants cut off from the world for generations, isolated both geographically and historically. But *A Week in the Future,* written in 1888, surveys London in 1988, chosen precisely because that city represents the maximum degree of difficulty for reform.

A 1971 article written by a Monash geographer, Joe Powell, on utopias in the 19th century, describes the necessary transference of utopia from rural to urban settings:

> ... the simple ideas expounded by the utopists could never be widely realized in the increasing pace of industrialization and urbanization of that startling century. Strange, remote and 'unknown' societies, perhaps on uncharted islands, were frequent motifs; but the elementary geographical isolation which was necessary for the preservation of fictional communities had become far too unreal by the mid-point of such a progressive era. Thereafter this could only be conceived as a fantastic literary device, and as a form of utopian expression it declined considerably in power.
>
> Towards the end of the 19th century, the utopists made a fresh assault. The new breed returned to the emphasis upon institutional structures in a highly centralized complex. Whereas the earliest writers had expected that either religion or science would provide the force and binding thread of centralized organization, the utopias of the late nineteenth-early twentieth centuries described the centralization of economic activity within society – in a period of unrestrained individualism and free enterprise, they were anticipating nationalization and the Welfare State.[12]

Two things distinguish the earlier *Handfasted* from the later *A Week in the Future*. One is industrialization; the mythical country of Columba in *Handfasted* has a rural economy and some mining, an image in fact of early South Australia's economy. The other is a more radical feminism in the former novel. Handfasting, the practice of trial marriage of a year and a day, allows Spence to sweep away all vestiges of her own society's double sexual standard. There is no illegitimacy in Columba, in fact the children of handfasted unions which are not followed by marriage are privileged by superior education and become the country's administrative elite. There is also no prostitution, nor any of the social ostracism which the 19th century inflicted on sexually active but unmarried women. Essential to the workings of this liberated sexuality is economic independence for women, and this is assured by the practice of alloting land to every adult citizen regardless of sex.

Furthermore, this society has had a matriarchal founder, a Frenchwoman of the 18th century whose ideal society takes shape in direct reaction to her own youthful suffering from the constraints of an unhappy marriage, Calvinism and sexism. Needless to say, all this was too radical for 1879, and the judges of the novel competition to which Spence submitted the manuscript of *Handfasted* rejected it as 'calculated to loosen the marriage tie – it was too socialistic, and consequently dangerous'[13] It was 1984 before it was published.

Nearly a decade later, Spence wrote the much less original and radical *A Week in the Future*, and tackled the problems of the 19th century city. Her ideas came primarily from Jane Hume Clapperton's book *Scientific Meliorism and the Evolution of Happiness* which Spence had reviewed for the South Australian *Register* in 1887. These ideas in turn had their source in the evolutionary ideas of Charles Darwin and Herbert Spencer, the Social Darwinists and neo-Malthusians. Lesley Ljungdahl, who has produced a bi-centennial edition of *A Week in the Future*, describes its theoretical background in these terms:

> Scientific meliorism stressed that gradual evolution and adaptation of a superior race could be achieved by changing the moral nature of society through a scientific knowledge of heredity, education and environment. It is an essentially optimistic faith in society's potential capacity for improvement which now may seem rather naive in its simplicity ... Spence stresses an ethical evolutionary process ... which would ultimately create superior social conditions.[14]

Abandoning altogether in this work the conventions of romantic fiction, Spence describes a clean, uncrowded London, rationally organized into co-operative homes, with a strictly controlled population and equality between the sexes. Like most utopian writers Spence is little interested in the actual struggle and process by which the transition from individualism to collectivism, from capitalism to socialism, is brought about. There are some aspects of her future society to which subsequent history has given sinister significance, such as its ruthless euthenasia, the elimination of both the mentally deficient and the criminally insane. But of more interest is its reversionary character, for Spence's vision of the year in which we are now living has much in common with her picture of early Adelaide society. What this ultimately indicates is the empirical limitations of the colonial city, I think. Despite her wide theoretical reading and intelligent analyses and discussions of political and economic theories, 19th century Adelaide provided a relatively primitive, or simple, model of the city for Spence .

In her lifetime, at least, Adelaide did not develop the sophisticated complexities of many other post-industrial urban structures. Its essentially rural economy sustained the Arcadian possibilities dear to utopians. Adelaide in 1839 had certainly represented a fresh start, and the intelligent, optimistic and energetic young girl who grew up with the city itself, was herself an emblem for its best possibilities. She achieved a great deal in her lifetime, and South Australia can rightfully boast of its many progressive social and political initiatives. But the reform dearest to Spence's heart, proportional representation was never achieved in that State. It would however be quite false to describe her life in any other terms than that of success, she was a truly remarkable woman. Yet in the end I am reminded of the failure of a fellow-socialist and utopian, William Lane, who abandoned another Australian city to attempt the creation of a real-life utopia in Paraguay. It failed, but Sydney has flourished. What would these idealists make of their post-colonial cities at the 200 year mark, I wonder.

NOTES

1. *Catherine Helen Spence: An Autobiography* (Adelaide: Libraries Board of South Australia, 1967), p. 17.
2. *Autobiography*, p. 14.
3. Clara Morison: *a Tale of South Australia during the gold fever*, in *Catherine Helen Spence* (Portable Australian Authors series), edited by Helen Thomson. St. Lucia: University of Queensland Press, 1987, p. 395.
4. *Catherine Helen Spence* (Portable Australian Authors), p. 527-8.
5. *Mr. Hogarth's Will*, edited by Helen Thomson. Ringwood: Penguin, 1988, p. 38-9.
6. *Autobiography*, p. 34.
7. *Ibid.*, p. 37
8. *Ibid.*, p. 41.
9. *Ibid.*, p. 63.
10. *Ibid.*, p. 70.
11. *Ibid.*, p. 95.
12. 'Utopia, Millennium and the Co-Operative Ideal: A Behavioural Matrix in the Settlement Process', *The Australian Geographer*, XI, 6 (1971), p. 608.
13. *Op. Cit.*, p. 63
14. *A Week in the Future*, Catherine Helen Spence's 1888 Forecast of Life in 1988, with Introduction and Notes by Lesley Durrell Ljungdahl. Sydney: Hale and Iremonger, 1987, p. 12.

CARL BRIDGE

Gentlemen and Mechanics: Public Libraries and Reading in Colonial Adelaide, 1836-1884

South Australia was unique among the Australian colonies in its provision of a library for public use right from the colony's foundation. Just as the colony's founders carefully planned their system of land sales, their city and much else, so also did they provide a library to help educate the citizens of their new so-called 'enlightened' and 'progressive' society; a means both to gentle the masses and to improve and sustain the 'mental culture' of their masters. However, social and economic realities cut across the founders' utilitarian dream. Gentlemen colonists wanted an exclusive and expensive reading club; the artisans, clerks and mechanics wished for reading classes, entertainments and the cheapest possible reading matter. Rival institutions were founded and both failed. Finally there was a marriage of convenience between the two which was cemented by a government subsidy. But who was to dictate purchasing policy and strike balances between classes and books and between books for entertainment and those for instruction? Should borrowing be permitted? And how would the gentlemen bear rubbing shoulders with the general public? The marriage lasted thirty years, during which time these questions were never resolved to the satisfaction of all parties, and in 1884 the government stepped in to arrange the divorce. The story enables us to probe the purposes and practices of public library provision in colonial Adelaide and in so doing illuminate some of the social and political sensibilities of mid-nineteenth century Adelaideans.

(a) The Utilitarian Dream

A library was part of the earliest plans for the colony framed in 1831 and, though one was not specifically mentioned in the South Australia Act of 1834, one of the first moves of the gentlemen colonists was to meet in London in Adelphi Terrace, the Strand, on 29 August 1834, to form the South Australian Literary and Scientific Association.[1] The ten gentlemen who formed the association included: Osmond Gilles, a 46 year old London wool-trader of Huguenot descent and with republican tendencies who later became the colony's first treasurer; Edward Wright, also 46, a surgeon recently dismissed from London's Bethlehem Hospital for drunkenness; John Brown (33), a non-conformist London wine merchant recently bankrupt; Robert Gouger (31) a radical journalist interested in colonisation questions and in the colonial secretaryship; Richard Davies Hanson (29), a lawyer whose radical politics and non-conformity had led to his dismissal from his law firm – he aspired to the judgeship; and G.S. Kingston (27), an Irish republican engineer and surveyor.[2]

Hanson was chosen to deliver at the next meeting an inaugural address setting out the association's ideals. In a considered philosophical discourse he argued that while the Wakefield system of co-ordinated land sales and systematic migration of capital and labour would meet their 'physical wants', the library would fill their 'intellectual wants', and so help prevent a 'retrograde' step in civilisation. In their 'improved circumstances' in the new colony, gentlemen members would have time to cultivate their minds. The colonist would have 'far more leisure than he could command in his native country' where 'increasing difficulties' had forced his emigration by 'paralyzing' his 'decaying fortunes'. In South Australia concentrated settlement on the Wakefield model, plus 'the personal character of many who will be among its founders', would make a literary society more appropriate than in sparsely-settled, convict New South Wales. Knowledge, moreover, had a specific role to play in the colony:

> It may, I believe, be fearlessly stated that the many never go wrong unless from ignorance ... There is diffused among the labouring classes an idea that their interests are opposed to the interest of the capitalist, that the profit of the capitalist is a fraud upon the labourer, and that the productive class, as they claim exclusively to be considered, is injured in exact proportion to the gains of the other classes ... I think that it might easily be shown that the real interests of all classes are identical ... But it is obvious, that among those who go out as labourers we must expect to have many who are deeply imbued with the doctrines now prevalent among the class to which they belong ... [I]t will therefore behove us to take care that an antidote is provided.[3]

Hanson believed that once the propertyless were taught the cast-iron laws of political economy they would get down to work, save, and slowly promote themselves into the propertied class by the sweat of their now-educated brows. Education would give 'the power of indefinitely [*sic*] extending the fields of production' so that all would be free of 'physical want' and be aware of 'the whole circle of their social duties'. 'With an instructed people we may hope to found a reasonable community.'[4]

This was a wondrous vision of an ideal capitalist society, replete with a library to teach recalcitrant labourers the error of their ways by imbuing them with the scientific laws of Smithian economics. But there was a fatal flaw. When the gentlemen came to make the rules for their association they made them those of an exclusive club: a high admission fee of 10s.

6d.; two guineas a year subscription in advance; nomination by two members, and election by vote, including exclusion by one black ball in ten. Ladies were to be invited to the monthly conversaziones but were not to be permitted membership in their own right. There is no record of how Hanson proposed to teach his humble mechanics the right economic gospel when the library membership was to be restricted in such ways – the fees alone amounted to a week's wages for many labourers! Even the worthies in Hanson's audience proved very reluctant to renew their subscriptions at the end of the first year.[5] User-pays principles and gentlemanly exclusiveness cut right across the utilitarian dream of a library fully accessible to the public.

And what of the bookstock? Gouger began the collection by donating 82 volumes. Virtually all were contemporary works of a practical nature, useful for intending emigrants. The books included Bischoff's *Van Diemen's Land,* Pickering's *Inquiries of an Emigrant,* Bliss on *The Statistics of Canada,* and *Remarks on Trial by Jury in New South Wales.* Gouger's books were later supplemented by a series of 20 religious tracts donated by J.H. Angas. Certainly the bookstock did not display the range of books one would expect to find in a nineteenth century club library – classics, poetry, history, popular science. Most of the income went on hiring the rooms for meetings, the rest on incidentals.[6] No new books were purchased before the 'library' was packed into an iron chest and shipped off to South Australia in May 1836. Only 40 of the 546 initial colonists had bothered to join the Literary Association.[7]

(b) Rival Organisations

It was to be two years before the chest was opened. In June 1838, the Literary Association never having met on South Australian soil, it was decided to form a mechanics' institute, and make use of the books. While five of the former gentlemen subscribers remained on the new committee, the other sixteen members of it were men of a different class, including a builder, a house painter, a grocer and a publican. The new subscription was set at 24s. a year, payable at 6s. a quarter; that is it was within the grasp of the aristocracy of labour, those who could afford respectability. There was no joining fee and anybody who could pay could join. Classes in the 'three Rs' were envisaged, the books were placed in the schoolroom and a part-time librarian appointed. But still the formula was not right. Barely a hundred joined and the money raised was not enough to pay the librarian, hire the rooms for the library, classes and monthly lectures and entertainments, and then buy sufficient books – a bound book often cost a guinea in the 1840s – to keep interest up. The classes soon failed, since those people who could afford the shilling or two a week usually could already read, write and do sums and not enough of the 20 per cent of the adult population who were illiterate and innumerate could afford to pay.

The first Mechanics' Institute collapsed in 1840, was revived, and collapsed again in 1842 during the colony's depression.[8]

In October 1844, when the economy began to recover, the wealthy members of the old Literary Association met to form a new gentlemen's library, the South Australian Subscription Library. Like similar institutions in England it was essentially a reading club for the well-to-do. Two guineas in advance, blackballing, and admission by ballot all returned. The first rooms were in the Club House (later the Adelaide Club) and the librarian was a law clerk on the handsome part-time remuneration of £52 a year. They secured the old Mechanics' Institute bookstock from the pawnbroker Da Costa for £20. All meetings were held during daylight hours, a further sign that mechanics and tradesmen were to be excluded. The new gentlemen's Subscription Library never had more than 120 members.[9]

'Quintus Curtius Horatius' was soon complaining in the *South Australian*:

> Does it not occur to the gentlemen who have the management of the institution ... that there may be many to whom it would be most desirable to throw open the doors of the Subscription Library – who may not have, or who cannot afford the means? Is it not notorious that the class who would derive most benefit from access to the Library ... are ordinarily not much burdened with superfluous cash? To make no provision ... is ... very illiberal and exhibits the Muses in a very unsocial light.[10]

There was no reply.

Doran's Eagle Tavern in Hindley Street was not a likely spot for the members of the Club to gather, but it was there in August 1847 at 7.30 in the evening that 'a most spirited group of mechanics' and 'several gentlemen' met to discuss the resuscitation of the Mechanics' Institute. They included clerks, shopkeepers, journalists, a chemist, an auctioneer and an ironmonger. They agreed on £1 a year fee, payable at 5s. a quarter, and an open-door membership policy. The librarian would receive £25 a year, half the salary the Subscription Library paid. Classes now were to be in art, music, French, German and chemistry. As the English social historian J.F.C. Harrison has observed, such an appeal was 'to the new clientele of clerks and shopkeepers who wanted not science and the disciplines of study, but the opportunity of a little of the cultural elegance which they noted in their superiors'. Of course, they asked the gentlemen for the books back and failed to secure them. Nevertheless, within a year, by which time the new Mechanics' Institute had 300 members, the faltering gentlemen's Subscription Library had asked for an amalgamation. The proposal was accepted.[11]

(c) A Marriage of Convenience

In its early years the marriage of the two institutions was not harmonious. Lectures were interrupted, one newspaper complained, by 'ill-bred' persons 'stamping' and 'hissing' as in 'pot-houses', counting out the speakers at the monthly conversaziones in order to hurry on the musical entertainment that was always included in the programme to assure the serious lecturer of a good audience and to give the subscribers their money's worth. A reply drew attention to the 'clergy, landlords and employers' who had swamped the library, introducing a new 'aristocratic tone' which discouraged 'the people'. 'Jack Plane' railed against the 'miserable exclusiveness of a few "library gentlemen" and their pitiful parasites who would fain lock up science and lay an embargo on literature'. Another upbraided the librarian for 'his over-refined and supercilious' manner. Yet another was upset that 'sufficient care is not taken as to the admission of members... Persons not having a passport to respectable society should not be suffered to be on the Committee'. But they needed each others' money, and the income from the concerts after lectures, to pay the rent on the rooms and to purchase enough books to keep the library viable.[12]

Soon after the merger the first printed catalogue and regulations were published. They are an insight into the sort of library it was. There were 2,000 volumes, 300 of them novels, 140 travel books, 200 history, 100 sciences. It was, on the whole, heavy fare. The novels included all of Scott and Dickens, Bulwer Lytton, G.P.R. James and Hannah More; the histories, Burke, Grote, Machiavelli and J.D. Lang. Other sections included Paley's *Natural Theology* and Southey's *Sheep and Wool*. The essays of Carlyle, Bacon, Lamb and Hazlitt were there, as were the works of Milton and Shakespeare. There were none of the cheap popular romances that dominated the borrowing of English commercial circulating libraries at the time. The committee obviously took themselves very seriously and bought to educate rather than to entertain.[13]

Only the librarian was permitted to take the books from the shelves. Lengths of loans were determined by distance lived from the library and the size of the book: borrowers who lived ten miles out could borrow folios for a month, duodecimos for a fortnight; city dwellers could borrow them for three weeks and one week respectively. Just one book could be borrowed at a time. Overdue fines were 4d. a day for big books, 2d. for small ones. Lending books to friends carried a 5s. fine. Hats and coats were not to be worn in the reading room, whips and sticks were not to be placed under chairs and tables. Smoking was forbidden. Interestingly, dogs were allowed into the library with their owners until one was locked in overnight in 1864; children under 13 years old were banned in 1859. The children were readmitted in 1915; the dogs are still waiting. Overseas newspapers, the most sought-after commodity in this pre-telegraph period, had a half-hour limit per reader; local papers which were shorter, fifteen minutes. Apart from personal letters, the library was the disseminator of news from the Mother Country and a social centre where news on any person, matter or thing could be obtained.[14]

Money continued to be in short supply and membership fluctuated with the economy. In 1854 another generation of Committee members – J.H. Clark, company secretary of *The Register*, Benjamin Babbage, vigneron and engineer, and Robert Mann, Advocate-General of the colony, devised a new scheme to finance the library. In New South Wales, Victoria and Tasmania the government had subsidised the mechanics' institutes for some years. Clark, Babbage and Mann decided to put the Library at the 'public's' disposal in return both for a subsidy of £1,000 per annum – to pay salaries and buy books – and for a new institute building to house them. Their scheme was accepted by the Government in 1856 and remained in force until 1884. The new, rent-free building was opened in 1861.[15]

The most remarkable characteristics of the new arrangement were its system of management and its treatment of subscribers as against public readers. The institute was to be managed by a committee part-nominated by Government and part-elected by £1 subscribers. In Clark's words, these subscribers would provide 'the advantages of a private institution over a mere public concern', in that they would make certain that their money was well-spent. Subscribers would have their own private reading room and be able to borrow books and have a say in purchasing policy and staffing. The general public would have access to books only on the premises. Opening a public reading room to all would be an 'inducement to withdraw from the public house', and it was hoped that once the public picked up the habit of reading they might consider becoming subscribers.[16]

(d) The Readers and their Reading Habits

Fortunately the borrowing and attendance registers for 1861 and half of 1862 survive and from them the names and addresses of borrowers (subscribers) and registered readers (the public) can be obtained and the types and frequencies of books borrowed can be determined.

TABLE

MALE SUBSCRIBERS AND READERS BY OCCUPATION, 1860s[17]

Class	1866 Census%	Subscribers%	Readers%
Professionals	4.5	15	14
Artisans	24.0	17	26
Shopkeepers	7.0	12	10
Merchants/Agents	0.5	5	3
Gentlemen	0.5	5	7
Clerks/Shop Assistants	4.0	35	26
Labourers	38.0	--	10
Farmers/Pastoralists	17.0	5	2
Others	4.5	6	2

Among the subscribers, gentlemen and merchants were ten times more prevalent than they were in the population at large, clerks and shop assistants nine times, shopkeepers twice. Artisans were slightly under-represented, farmers more so and labourers not at all. It was very much a lower middle-class institution – clerks, artisans and shopkeepers account for two-thirds of the subscribers. Nearly all of them had city addresses – their workplaces – which helps to explain the farmers' under-representation. The non-paying readers' profile echoes the subscribers' profile other than for artisans and labourers who obviously would have made up a higher proportion of the subscribers had they been able to afford the £1 fee. The virtual absence of women is explained by the fact that subscriptions were regarded as family subscriptions. Hence a female relative would use the ticket of the male head of the household. The handful of women subscribers in their own right were those without a male subscriber's ticket to use. Further, in the period under discussion, public library reading rooms were regarded as unseemly places for respectable women to frequent. For instance, when the South Australian Institute secretary visited the Melbourne Public Library in 1873, he noted only four women among the 200 readers present. In Adelaide gentlewomen were often ushered into a small annex to read in privacy. And it was a common pattern in Adelaide for a male member of the family to borrow books for the women. Even Catherine Helen Spence, the famous novelist and feminist, recalls her brother doing this for her in the 1840s.[18]

The most prolific borrower in the 1860s was a Mr Bastard, who borrowed two or three novels each day. He obviously did a great deal of reading on the job, which is not surprising when you discover that he was Superintendent of the Adelaide Swimming Baths, just a short walk along North Terrace near Parliament House.[19]

The 1861 printed catalogue shows that roughly a third of the 9,824 books were novels – the other most numerous classes being General Literature (essays, letters, etc.) a seventh; Geography and Travels, a further seventh; scientific works, an eighth. And in addition 54 periodicals and newspapers were subscribed to. All sections showed an increase in variety. Among the novels, the two Brontes, Dumas and Austen now appear. G.P.R. James and Miss Gore were the best represented, each with 38 titles, followed by Trollope with 33, Fenimore Cooper with 29 and Captain Marryat with 22. The subscribers' clamorous demand for light entertaining fiction was being recognised with a spate of titles such as *Scalp Hunters, Devoted, Manfrone the One-Handed Monk, Married not Mated, The Ensnared, Memoirs of a Femme de Chambre, The Devil's Elixir, Quicksands,* and *Matrimonial Shipwrecks.* At the other end of the spectrum the library spent several hundred pounds on the eight sumptuous volumes of Gould's *Birds of Australia,* not for loan.[20]

Subscribers' borrowing habits confirm that, despite many loud disclaimers to the contrary, it was primarily a library for light and entertaining reading. The pattern for each month is regular. Two-thirds of the borrowings were novels, with the next most popular classes the related ones of travels, essays, memoirs, history, biography and periodicals (which were really serialised forms of the earlier categories). Together novels and general literature made up a mammoth 97 per cent of the borrowings; serious and scientific literature a meagre 3 per cent. Book circulation was high at 57,564 in 1865: on average each book was borrowed five times and each subscriber borrowed 57 books a year.[21]

If we disregard the unbalanced reading diet, the Adelaide library experience was, for its time, a success story for the reading public that was repeated right across the colony. By 1884 there were 113 country and suburban institutes with 6,185 subscribers. The Adelaide Institute had 37,000 volumes, the other 96,000, and 157 boxes of books, each with 50 books in it, were in circulation between the central institute and the others, 23 of them containing books in the German language. There was still room for improvement with one library book for every three South Australians and, if we allow for subscriptions being family ones, only a tenth of the population could borrow books, but this was twice the rate of 1856 and there were now three times the books per head of population. As each of the institutes attracted Government subsidies the bookstocks were available for the use on the premises by all citizens.[22]

(e) Divorce

However, were these readers fulfilling Hanson's prophecy and learning to be useful citizens, or were they merely entertaining themselves with the nineteenth century equivalents to our *Rambo* or to the television soap operas? As with the debate today about the effects of video violence, many opposed the reading of the yellow-backed romantic novels, and voices were raised in protest in the 1860s and 1870s that the Government was subsidising private entertainment at the expense of public education. They echoed Sheridan: 'Madam, a circulating library ... is an evergreen tree of diabolical knowledge! ... And depend upon it, ... they who are so fond of handling the leaves will long for the fruit at last'. A plan to force borrowers to borrow another work along with each novel was rejected as too offensive, but the doubts remained.[23]

In 1874 Parliament finally decided that all Government money would be spent solely on reference books and in 1884 these were placed in a new Adelaide Public Library building and the circulating library split off, once more becoming essentially a private institution.[24] Unfortunately the romantic novels became the standard fare of the new circulating library, while the new Public Library, though it had many splendid books, insisted that they be used only on the premises. (At least the Adelaide Public Library kept the classical novelists on its shelves; when the Sydney Library decided to throw away its fiction in 1869 they dispensed with all without fear or favour, Dickens and Lytton included.)[25] Such was the Government's new determination not to subsidise pleasure that this arrangement lasted over half a century: Adelaide's citizens lost the opportunity of borrowing other than novels until 1946, by which time all the other Australian capital cities had had their own truly public circulating libraries for some time. The nineteenth century lead was frittered away.[26]

(f) Consequences

The gentlemen colonists' utopian plan to create a library that would be an engine of culture, social progress and social control was put into practice in ways they had not envisaged. Certainly it was a remarkable success in that Adelaideans were better supplied with library books of all sorts than residents of any other Australian capital city in the nineteenth century.[27] But the model colony was no egalitarian literary paradise. The gentlemen colonists' desire to assert their social superiority over the common herd led them to form an exclusive reading club. The respectable artisans, shopkeepers and clerks then founded their own institution which, by charging fees, in its turn excluded others even further down the social scale. Social sensibilities, too, meant that respectable women had only limited access to the books. Non-members were only begrudgingly allowed to use books on the premises as a sort of charity in return for government subsidy. The library's rules, not the contents of its books, became an instrument of social control. Contrary to Hanson's predictions, the need to attract fee-paying members meant that the lowest common denominator in reading taste came to apply, and light, amusing literature predominated over worthy educational books. In the end the circulating library was judged to be a private institution, for entertainment, Government support for it virtually ceased and the educational books were locked up in a new citadel of knowledge on North Terrace, further restricting the public's access.

Social distinctions, utilitarian user-pays notions, the subscribers' addiction to romantic novels, and finally the Government's determination to be seen to provide only serious educational books, made the establishment in Adelaide of a proper public lending library, in the modern sense, impossible. Adelaide has always prided itself in its sobriety, respectability and individual enterprise; but we can now see that these values produced losers as well as winners, and had costs as well as benefits. Today it is accepted that public money spent on books for the entertainment and leisure of all in the community is not wasted. Extraordinary as it seems, nobody in that nineteenth-century library debate appears to have realised that to amuse is often the best way to instruct. But then, philosophical radicals have never been noted for their sense of humour.

NOTES

1. Minute Book of the South Australian Literary and Scientific Association, South Australian Archives, [hereafter SAA], 31, 379a.
2. See their entries in D. Pike (ed.), *Australian Dictionary of Biography*, vols. 1-4, (Melbourne: Melbourne University Press, 1966-72).
3. Minute Book, *op. cit.*
4. *Ibid.*
5. *Ibid.*
6. See W. H. Langham, *In the Beginning* (Adelaide: Hassell Press, 1936), pp. 13-15, and T. Horton James, *Six Months in South Australia*, Public Libraries Board of South Australia, facsimile no. 18, 1962 (1st. pub., London, 1838), p. 172.
7. Minute Book, *op. cit.*, and D. Pike, *Paradise of Dissent* (Melbourne: Melbourne University Press, 1957).
8. *Southern Australian*, 30 June 1838; C. Bridge, *A Trunk Full of Books. A History of the State Library of South Australia and its Forerunners* (Adelaide: Wakefield Press, 1986), pp 10-11.
9. *Southern Australia*, 11 and 18 October 1844; *South Australian*, 26 November 1844, 25 April 1845; *Register*, 7 January 1845.
10. *South Australian*, 2 May 1845.
11. *Ibid.*, 10 August 1847. Minute Book of the Adelaide Mechanics' Insitute, 1847-9, SAA, 1423. J. F. C. Harrison, *Early Victorian Britain* (London: Sphere, 1979), p. 178.
12. *Register*, 8 July, 16 September 1848, 9 July 1850; *Adelaide Times*, 22 January 1849.
13. *Catalogue of Books Belonging to the South Australian Literary and Mechanics' Institute* (Adelaide: South Australian Literary and Mechanics' Insitute, 1848). For a discussion of British circulating libraries, and libraries generally, see G. L. Griest, *Mudie's Library and the Victorian Novel* (London: David and Charles, 1970), and Thomas Kelly's two books: *Early Public Libraries* (London: Library Association, 1966), and *A History of the Public Library in Britain* (London: Library Association, 1973).
14. *Catalogue*, *op. cit.*
15. See South Australian Parliament Papers, 1854, no. 80.
16. *Ibid.*
17. The census information is from J. Ramsay, 'Culture and Society in South Australia, 1857-66' (B.A. Hons thesis, University of Adelaide, 1963); the occupations and descriptions of subscribers and readers are based on the Subscribers Book and the Day Book, SAA, GRG 19/97, 1 and 2.
18. Secretary's Report of a Visit to Melbourne, 1873, SAA, GRG 19/164. C. H. Spence, *Autobiography* (Adelaide: Register, 1910), p. 20.
19. See the Borrowing Registers for 1861 and half of 1862, SAA, GRG 19/115/1-3.
20. South Australian Institute Catalogue, 1861, SAA, GRG 19/255.
21. From my analysis of the Borrowing Registers, *op. cit.*
22. South Australian Institute Annual Reports, 1856-84, SAA, GRG 19/369.
23. T. Sheridan, *The Rivals*, 1775, act 1, scene ii; R. S. Benham to Institute Board, 7 January 1869, SAA, GRG 19/185; Bridge, *op. cit.*, ch. 5.
24. South Australian Parliamentary Papers, 1874, no. 150.
25. Deborah Campbell, 'Culture and the Colonial City: A Study in Ideas, Attitudes and Institutions in Sydney, 1870-90' (Ph. D. thesis, University of New South Wales, 1982), p. 152.
26. See Bridge, *op. cit.*, chs. 11-14.
27. *Ibid.*, chs. 4-6, argue this case.

JOHN BARNES

The Artist and the Mechanic: Joseph Furphy and John Longstaff as Fellow-Townsmen

'Shepparton, *a la* Byron, woke up to find itself famous on a recent morning when the Sydney *Bulletin* office finished the printing of 297 pages of the deep, gritty philosophy contained in the volume, *Such is Life*, from the pen of "Tom Collins".' So begins a review of Joseph Furphy's novel in the *Shepparton News* of 21 August 1903. One does not look for sophisticated literary criticism in country newspapers, but this review has a particular interest because it offers a local perspective on the writer and his work. By the time *Such is Life* was published Furphy had lived in the town almost exactly twenty years, long enough one would have thought to be a familiar figure to the 2000 or so inhabitants. However, as the reviewer (probably the editor of the paper) goes on to point out, Furphy was far from being well known to his neighbours and was certainly not a literary identity:

> The quiet, self-effacing, short-spoken man is but very little known in his own town, beyond his own immediate circle, but even a hasty glance through the closely printed volume, and a perusal of a passage here and there shows that we have in our midst a distinctly Australian philosopher, who, while he has been fashioning the implements for our fields has also been carefully moulding in his own brain gems of thought for committal to the diary which now sees the light of day in the volume, *Such is Life*.

The family name of 'Furphy' was very well known in Shepparton and beyond, but it was associated with agricultural machinery rather than literature. When at the age of 40 Joseph came to Shepparton it was to work in his brother's foundry, and he continued to work there, even when his own sons had set up a rival establishment in the town. The residents of Shepparton knew the author of *Such is Life* – if they knew him at all – as a mechanic in Furphy's Foundry, the brother of the genial, upright, practical but literary John Furphy, the proprietor of the Foundry, a leading townsman whose business success and Christian piety were publicly acknowledged on all sides. In the eyes of most Shepparton residents, then, *Such is Life* was remarkable for having been produced by a mechanic, a bookish man it is true, but a man who had failed – or appeared to have failed – in the struggle to make a career of his own, a man who earned his living by working as a hand in his brother's foundry.

Although the reviewer in the *Shepparton News* was friendly and found things to praise – 'the musings of an Australian Socrates'; 'written in a distinctly new Australian graceful style'; 'Tom Collins has struck a new path in Australian literature' – he obviously found the book hard-going, and was joking in saying that it had made Shepparton famous. The same newspaper was not joking, however, when the previous year it headed an item about John Longstaff, formerly of Shepparton, 'The Pinnacle of Fame'. The occasion was the commissioning (by Earl Beauchamp, Governor of New South Wales from 1899 to 1901 and Henry Lawson's benefactor) of a portrait of King Edward VII in his coronation robes. The announcement of this commission brought another – a public subscription for a companion portrait of the Queen in her coronation robes. Longstaff's acceptance by the official establishment and by fashionable society in London as well as in Australia dazzled his former associates. 'An Old Schoolmate' wrote to the *Shepparton News* on 10 June 1902:

> Our old Shepparton friend, Artist John Longstaff, has reached the pinnacle of fame. Invited to Court, and commissioned to paint pictures of both King Edward and Queen Alexandra. The old wooden schoolhouse in Fryers Street never dreamt that it sheltered such a future genius, who spent a big part of his lesson hours in caricaturing in humorous fashion prominent people and passing events, to be posted on his favourite hoarding – the old tree near the river.

Longstaff's success was visible and easily understood, and the citizens of Shepparton identified with his success and congratulated themselves on having nurtured a genius.

Furphy and Longstaff were of different generations, but they came to prominence in the period of surging nationalism at the end of the nineteenth century. Both Australian-born, they have been seen as significant in the forming of an Australian cultural identity. Their names have not been linked directly, although they were associated with the same country town over the same period; it is more than likely that young John Longstaff never spoke with the older man, and registered him only as the ineffectual brother of his father's great friend, Mr. John Furphy. John Longstaff's name is, however, forever linked with that of Henry Lawson, and for two reasons. Lawson's favourite painting was Longstaff's 'Breaking the News', which hung in the *Bulletin* office for many years. In an essay, 'If I could Paint' (1899), Lawson declared 'I'd be prouder of a picture like "Breaking the News" than of a hundred exquisite alleged studies in the nude...', and his enthusiastic references to details show how well he knew the painting. He was 'already a worshipper of John Longstaff because of his picture "Breaking the News"'[1] when the editor of the *Bulletin*, J.F. Archibald, commissioned Longstaff to paint Lawson's portrait. The resulting portrait, certainly one of Longstaff's best works, added to his reputation, and Lawson was later to write a poem about the Longstaff portraits in the Sydney Art Gallery entitled 'The King and Queen and I.' Longstaff had a wide range of acquaintances, and he and Lawson had a number of mutual friends in the *Bulletin* circle. It is characteristic of him that he could obey the summons of the Queen to be present at Court ('Black velvet-knee breeches etc. etc. and a sword!'[2]) and include a casual mention of the occasion in a letter to his friend Randolph Bedford, an avowed republican. He mixed easily in the best society, enjoying the privileges accorded the artist by those wishing to have their portraits painted; and although he was not wealthy he lived a comfortable life such as writers like Lawson and Furphy never knew. A writer in *The Lone Hand*[3] described him as an Australian who had 'made good', and that perhaps gets closest to what it was about him that his contemporaries so admired. In being accepted by the Old World, in becoming part of the art establishment in London, Longstaff could be seen as helping Australians to throw off their feelings of colonial inferiority. As the writer in *The Lone Hand* put it, 'In the difficult art world of Paris and London he challenged comparison with those who had been reared in the atmosphere of art, who had breathed its rarefied air all their lives'. This is an attitude which does not conform to the programmatic radical nationalism of *Bulletin* writers, of which Furphy was an exponent, and seems at odds with the political values of the *Bulletin*. Yet the *Bulletin* itself in the same year that it published *Such is Life* singled out Longstaff as 'standing far above other Australian born painters', and pronounced his painting, 'The Bush Fire', to be 'the most memorable picture of Australia yet painted' (3 January 1903). This may reflect Archibald's taste, which raises the interesting question of how far there is a coherent *Bulletin* view of Australian culture in the nineties. Equally relevant to this general issue, perhaps, is the fact that Archibald had no liking for *Such is Life*, and but for the pressure of the editor of the Red Page, A.G. Stephens, would probably not have published it.

Leaving aside such speculations which cannot be pursued here, there is no doubt that Longstaff was a popular painter, and that in their enthusiasm for 'Breaking the News' Lawson and Archibald were with the majority. That student painting, which was widely reproduced, won Longstaff the first Travelling Scholarship of the Art School of the National Gallery in 1887, enabling him to go abroad to study painting. That he was the *first* recipient is very relevant: in the eyes of his contemporaries it gave him a particular importance as a pioneer. In 1899 a writer in the Socialist *Tocsin*, calling Longstaff 'the most masterful artist that Australia has so far produced', pointed to the kind of responsibility that the Scholarship carried:

> In returning to his native land, Longstaff completely fulfilled the chief object of the Scholarship, which was to educate the best Australian artists at the world's leading schools in order that they might come back to Australia and influence Art and artists by their spirit and prestige. That he has done this is proved by the position he occupies today.4

From this point of view the patronage of the wealthy and the famous, the royal portraits, the hanging of Longstaff's paintings in Royal Academy exhibitions and other marks of his prestige in the Old World, were causes for rejoicing by those who regarded themselves as Australian nationalists. Here was concrete proof that Australians were capable of meeting the standards of the civilized world. This kind of nationalism (with which most of us would be very familiar) most often finds its focus in the performing arts and in sport, the essential criterion of success being performance or craftsmanship rather than individuality of vision and attitude. It was said of Longstaff that he would be 'Australia's first Old Master', and the remark epitomizes the fundamentally conservative attitude that underlay the admiration of him as well as the fundamentally conservative attitude that he himself had towards art.

It isn't part of my purpose to trace Longstaff's career in any detail, but it is relevant to note the kind of success that he had. At the age of 25 he had won the Travelling Scholarship, and although he experienced hard times – largely as a result of marrying before he had the means to support a wife and family – by the age of 40 (when he received the commissions for the royal portraits) he had made his name as a portrait painter. In 1901 he had received the valuable Gilbee Bequest to paint in England a picture commemorating Burke and Wills; from 1902 onward he was exhibiting at the Royal Academy; in 1918 he became an Official War Artist with the A.I.F. in France; between 1925 and 1935 he won the Archibald Prize five times; in 1928 he became the first Australian artist to be knighted; from 1937 till his death in 1941 he was the first President of the Australian Academy of Art. There were other honours and positions, all testifying to his prestige in the public eye, and to his own popularity as a man. He was 'bluff, breezy Jack, popular wherever he goes'[5], and he was one of the elect - an Australian artist, prepared to speak for Australian art. Of his later life Bernard Smith has written: 'For twenty years he became the hearty and complaisant embodiment of art officialdom in Australia'[6]. The short-lived Australian Academy that he headed was modelled on the Royal Academy, with the aim of bringing all Australian artists together in the one organization, which would have official recognition and set standards - which, in practice, meant opposing modernism in painting. The prime mover was Longstaff's friend, R.G. Menzies, then Attorney General and later Prime Minister, whose view was: 'Great art speaks a language which every intelligent person can understand. The people who call themselves modernists speak a different language'[7]. Like Longstaff,

Menzies had grown up in a Victorian country town, a fact which may have a bearing on their similarity of views of art and the politics of art.

To become an artist Longstaff had had to flout his father's authority and to resist his father's attempts to make a business man of him. According to John Longstaff's biographer, Nina Murdoch, Ralph Longstaff was exasperated by his adolescent son's failure to settle down to work at any of the jobs procured for him, and actively opposed his painting. She adds an anecdote which is all too believable:

> Local feeling ran generally in sympathy with Mr. Longstaff, the point of view being best expressed when one good wife, eyeing John's vigorous physique, admonished him with: 'Fancy a great lump like you wanting to be an artist! I'm surprised at you, Jack!'[8]

He eventually got his chance to study painting when the head of the Melbourne importing business, in which his father had placed him, was persuaded that he had talent. Ralph Longstaff in his turn was persuaded. His son's later career was all that he could have hoped for.

On the face of it, the story of John Longstaff's becoming an artist is the story of the talented youth defying the materialism and philistinism of his home environment and succeeding in the metropolis. The values of the country town, which his father epitomized, were an obstacle to be overcome. It is a familiar enough pattern in Australian cultural history, where the only hope of being an artist has until recent times so often depended upon being able to go to the city, with the trip abroad to complete the process of emancipation and development. To pursue his vocation Longstaff had to leave his home and eventually his country, and, as again is so often the case, in doing so he became a hero to those whom he left behind.

From the perspective of the country town, Longstaff's success was seen as reflecting glory upon the town itself, and his upward progress was chronicled very fully in the local newspapers. At the end of 1883, for instance, the *Shepparton News* noted the first distribution of prizes for students at the National Gallery and recorded with pride that 'the second prize, value £20, was awarded to the son of our respected resident, Mr. Longstaff'. By 1885 the newspaper was calling him 'our rising young artist', a phrase that was repeated in later years. When in 1887 he was awarded the Travelling Scholarship, a group of townspeople arranged a banquet at which they presented him with a diamond ring (which they presumably thought an appropriate gift for an artist). The Mechanics' Institute asked for the prize-winning painting, 'Breaking the News', to be exhibited in Shepparton. He was now acclaimed by Shepparton as a worthy son. At the banquet he had responded to the presentation with exactly the sort of thing that his hosts wanted to hear:

> It has been said that a prophet hath no honour in his own country. This cannot be the case with regards to Shepparton. I am only afraid that you do me too much honour ...[9]

He had identified himself with the town, and the town eagerly accepted the honour and identified with him. He was now 'Our Shepparton Artist', and reports of his work abroad appeared in the local newspapers from time to time. Articles about him in other journals were reproduced in the local newspapers so that local people might know 'how the painter is regarded by men capable of judging their fellow men'[10]. Fame abroad made Longstaff all the dearer to Shepparton. When in 1911 he made a trip from London on his own to visit his aged parents he was given a civic welcome, at which the local orators vied with each other in the art of the cliche', his health was drunk, 'For he's a Jolly Good Fellow' was sung, and he was given a large laurel wreath. Appropriately enough, the local brass band escorted him from the railway station playing 'See the Conquering Hero Comes'.

Longstaff said all the appropriate things on such occasions and played to perfection the role of the Artist as the public expected it to be played. As an artist he was set apart, and as an Australian Artist who had gained fame abroad, he was in a special category. 'There is no mistaking the genius in him', confided the reporter on the *Shepparton Advertiser* who interviewed Longstaff and looked into his 'rapturous, dancing, scintillating eyes' during the brief 1911 visit[11]. The lavish praise, the deference, the almost reverential treatment of Longstaff on this occasion by the local dignitaries were manifestations of pride rather than any interest in art and culture, and there is a teasing irony in the fact that the town intended Longstaff's portrait of his father to be the nucleus of the future art gallery.

Against the success story of John Longstaff I want to set the contrasting story of Joseph Furphy. The linking of the two names is less arbitrary than it may seem, because the two families had so much in common and were so representative of local attitudes. When in 1908 a new Methodist church was being built, the congregation decided to have not one but two foundation stones, asking Ralph Longstaff to lay one (with the inscription 'God is Light') and John Furphy the other (his inscription being 'God is Love'). They were accorded this honour because they had been pioneers of Methodism – Longstaff with the Wesleyan Methodists and Furphy with the United Free Methodists – from the very beginnings of the town.

The Furphys were of Northern Irish origin, John's parents having emigrated to Victoria straight after their marriage. They were farming people, John being the only member of the family who did not settle on the land. Having served an apprenticeship to a blacksmith in Kyneton, he set up on his own account, moving from there to Shepparton in 1873. As closer settlement proceeded in the fertile Goulburn valley, Shepparton on the site of the main crossing of the Goulburn river, became the centre of the farming and fruit growing district; and so began the process of expansion that has continued to the present. The description of the town given by 'The Vagabond' as part of a series in the Melbourne *Arqus* (20 September 1884) emphasizes the prosperity that resulted from the development of wheat growing in the Goulburn Valley:

> A genuine air of prosperity surrounds Shepparton. The buildings do not appear to have been built for a day. Their solidity impresses us after the flimsy pack-of-card dwellings we have lately seen in many places. The streets are broad and the citizens hasten along them as if time were money[12].

Making allowance for the superficiality of the quick impression, this is a fair enough characterization of the place, in which small traders and manufacturers like Ralph Longstaff and John Furphy were civic and religious leaders. The latter was admired for his enterprise in setting up a foundry, which had become one of the largest industries in the town by the time Joseph joined his brother in 1883. John was inventive and saw the need to adapt farming machinery to local conditions, having considerable success with his patented grain stripper. His most significant invention was the water-cart, for which he received orders from all over the colony and the Riverina region of New South Wales. These carts, with his name painted on the tank in large letters, made his name a household word in many farming areas. Although he was a successful business man, a self-made man deeply imbued with the Protestant work ethic, he believed in cultivating the spirit, and one gets the impression that he was happiest in the various public activities he took on – talks and recitations to literary and self-improvement societies, committee work for the Mechanics' Institute, being a Commissioner on the local Urban Water Trust, a leader of Local Option and, most important of all, preaching to Methodist congregations and writing for the Salvation Army paper, *The War Cry*. To Shepparton he was a public figure, 'that ever genial and always popular gentleman', known for his 'ready wit and quaint humour' as well as his good works and his business drive[13]. Politically he was conservative, but unlike Ralph Longstaff he tended to steer clear of local politicking and the Honorary Bench.

Ralph Longstaff, whose 'Emporium of Fashion' was advertised in the same papers that carried articles on his artist-son, was a less sympathetic figure than John Furphy. Born in Durham in 1826, he had come to Australia in 1852 attracted by the gold discoveries, and after a few years of mining tried farming, then set up as a builder and contractor at Clunes, before he moved in 1873 to Shepparton where he was at first farmer and builder and undertaker as well as storekeeper. According to one reminiscence, as he reached the level ground where stood the few buildings that then comprised the township, he heard the ringing of Furphy's anvil. At Shepparton he prospered, having the satisfaction of taking one of his sons into the business, while another became the local pharmacist. He appears to have been a man of rigid outlook, emotionally repressed, and without the charm that his famous son possessed. Mrs. Longstaff, who was Highland-born, was a freer, more emotional and more creative personality, with a sense of humour that survived a strict Presbyterian upbringing. Something of what she endured is indicated by John Longstaff's biographer:

> Once on being asked in the arch manner of the period: 'And what is your husband's pet name for you?' she replied: 'He never calls me by name.'
> 'But supposing you were out of sight?'
> 'He'd simply say: "are you there?"'[14]

Patriarchal Ralph Longstaff JP, Licensing Magistrate, trustee of the Mechanics' Institute, trustee of Wesley Hall, chairman of this and member of that committee, was a pillar of the community. On the jubilee of the Eureka Stockade, he described how he and his companions who were working a claim on the Ballarat field avoided any involvement with the protesting diggers:

> Mr. Longstaff and his party took no active part in the movement, but steadily worked their claim, and watched the progress of events. There was always the fear that, if the diggers got the upper hand for the time, their claims would be taken from them, so it was decided to hold aloof from the rioters as much as possible. Mr. Longstaff did not take part in the meetings on Bakery Hill and Eureka, but he was present at the burning down of Bentley's hotel, and was sufficiently close to get his digger's blue shirt on fire ... The Durham party was working a rich claim at the time, and they will scarcely be blamed for giving it more thought than the insurrection, with which they had no sympathy[15].

In his attitudes towards Eureka and towards social issues generally, Longstaff was a conservative. He and Furphy could both be called 'wowsers', but their outlook on religious and social questions was probably shared by the great majority of the citizens of Shepparton over the period that Joseph Furphy lived there.

When Joseph arrived in 1883 the population of the town was over 1000, and by the time he left in 1904 it was over 2000. Furphy's Foundry was one of the growing businesses in the early 1880s (by 1889 it had 37 employees), which made it easier for John – a man with a strong sense of family responsibilities and a disposition to be charitable – to help his brother who was destitute, with a wife and three children to support. Joseph had settled on the land in the same district of Central Victoria as his parents and the others of the family in 1869, but by 1877 he had lost his property and was working as a carrier. About 1880 he moved his wife and children to Hay in the Riverina, and over the next few years was comparatively prosperous, at one stage having two bullock teams. By late

1883, however, he had lost his means of livelihood, his bullocks having perished in the severe drought. This latest in the series of failures that made up his life marked the end of Furphy's attempt to achieve the family ideal of being an independent property owner. As a mechanic in his brother's foundry he had, as he once observed, '16 hours off out of the 24'[16]: with regular hours he was able to set about his own education – and eventually to realize his ambition to be a writer, a spare-time writer.

Such is Life is a work of fiction drawing upon Furphy's experiences before he came to Shepparton. Set in Riverina and Northern Victoria, it is written from the perspective of a traveller – Tom Collins is supposedly a N.S.W. civil servant with a job that involves his riding to various Riverina stations – who is nevertheless part of a community. Tom Collins has no wife or dependents, and no fixed place of abode, or none that the reader hears of. Most of the action takes place out of doors, the most sociable occasions being campfire gatherings of bullockies (such as Furphy himself had once been). Tom Collins lives a life very different from that Furphy was leading in Shepparton, and one might well be tempted to conclude that his experience of Shepparton was irrelevant to the novel.

In Shepparton his closest friends were two fellow-workers in the foundry; they lacked his literary capacity and were his inferiors intellectually, but they shared his enthusiasm for the Sydney *Bulletin* and his Socialism. He was for a time in the mutual improvement association of the Church of Christ, and he was a constant member of the Mechanics' Institute, being on the committee most of the time. In the mid-nineties, about the time he was starting to write the final copy of his novel, he had a few contributions in the local newspapers under the pseudonym of 'Tom Collins', which he used for contributions to the *Bulletin* from 1893 onward. He was, in a small way, a *Bulletin* identity under his pen-name, contributing prose paragraphs and short articles as well as verse, but in Shepparton he was in the shadow of his 'Right Rev. elder brother'. In *Such is Life* his political and religious attitudes were of an unorthodox kind which his brother would not have approved of, and the whole book implicitly rejects what John Furphy and Ralph Longstaff stood for. Only occasionally is there an overt reference, as in the burlesque Introduction (which the *Shepparton News* thought 'cynical') when he writes: 'It has been pointed out to me that the prizes of civilization – Municipal dignity, Churchwardenship, the Honorary Bench, and so forth – do not wait upon avowed comradeship with people who can by no management of hyperbole be called respectable'. Furphy's attitude to country towns was summed up in a remark to a fellow contributor to the Bulletin with whom he corresponded: 'Bushmen – and especially plainsmen – cannot realise, without experience, the superficiality of townsmen's thoughts and conversation.'[16a] To John Furphy and Ralph Longstaff Shepparton was a congenial place in which to live. To Joseph Furphy, despite the advantage of a library and the existence of various literary and debating societies, the town held no real attraction. He was a comparatively lonely and isolated figure, but in *Such is Life* he created images of sociability in his accounts of the gatherings of bushmen who live on the track away from towns and cities.

The pictures of the Riverina in *Such is Life* are highly selective – which is hardly surprising but perhaps seldom given due weight by readers. The perspective is that of the landless rather than the landowners; life on the station is seen from the outside and mostly at a considerable distance; the experiences of women are on the margin of the picture; there is little of the domestic and family life of the characters; and the life of the towns – Hay, after all, was a thriving centre of both rail and river traffic in the region – is out of view. The actual portrayal of the bullockies and their everyday working lives gives little hint of the economic and political struggles of the period. In 1880, for instance, there was a Carriers' Union at Hay which called a strike over the terms proposed by the agents for land carriage; but it is hard to imagine Furphy's bullockies involved in such activities. Furphy's Riverina is an almost timeless world, remote from the concerns of Shepparton and such go-ahead places; and for all the hardship experienced by the bullockies it is an attractive world of independent-minded individuals who, however blindly, choose their own fates.

A piece of advice which Furphy gave to Cecil Winter ('Riverina') who was then working on a Riverina station is relevant to Furphy's own treatment of his experience:

> You won't always be on the voiceless plain; but when the actuality becomes a memory, you will see Riverina with clearer artistic vision, purified from all sordidness, and transfigured to poetic use...as an illustration, you remember 'Gilrooney's' Riverina, as seen through the golden haze of Memory, from some narrow lodging in Sydney.[17]

In *Such is Life* Furphy was drawing on a chapter of his life that was closed. (The date at which the events of the novel are supposed to begin is, I suspect, the exact date on which Furphy himself became 'unemployed'.) I have argued elsewhere that a concern with 'the Coming Australian' runs through the novel, and bears on his portrayal of Tom Collins as a man of learning and philosophic depth[18]. In Chapter II there is an expression of his nationalism ('It is not in our cities or townships, it is not in our agricultural or mining areas, that the Australian attains full consciousness of his own nationality; it is in places like this...') which he feels most strongly out on the Riverina plains. Speaking through Tom Collins, Furphy voices his idealism: 'Then think how immeasurably higher are the possibilities of a Future than the memories of any Past since history began.' And of course Rigby expounds the Christian Socialist vision by which Furphy believed that the future should be shaped. But it was not a vision that could be expressed except in talk and in essays. *Such is Life* does not register the changing historical reality of Australian life, but a version of the past. It was one thing to speculate on the future, and to believe, as Furphy said,

> that the first public duty of every born or adoptive Australian is to bear a hand in building up an independent and common sense civilization; while his first private duty is to pursue Australian virtues and vices, in contradistinction to those of the Northern Hemisphere[19].

but it was another to give substance to such fine sentiments. The world of *Such is Life* was not readily accessible to readers, the style and structure made demands for which they were unprepared. The reviewer in the *Shepparton News* rightly warned that the reader 'who grabs this volume to pass away a dull evening, as he would with the airy sketches of Steele Rudd, will be disappointed'. Although Furphy was creating a version of 'the bush', which was emerging as the most persuasive myth of Australia, it was not a version that won the kind of self-recognition that Lawson or Paterson won.

Furphy's description of *Such is Life* (in his letter to Archibald asking for advice on how to get it published) – 'temper, democratic; bias, offensively Australian' – associated the work with the literary nationalism of the *Bulletin*. And the eventual publication of the novel by the *Bulletin* was an appropriate acknowledgement of relationship between the Sydney journal and Furphy's vision of a future Australia. Equally, the lack of enthusiasm shown by his fellow-townsmen revealed Furphy's isolation from the very people who were, in so many ways, shaping that future at the turn of the century.

In places like Shepparton, all over the continent, there was a very real concern with what was 'Australian' and with the sort of society that was being created. The arts were not neglected: there were literary and debating societies which had readings and discussions of Australian writers; the Mechanics' Institute libraries contained volumes by such new writers as Lawson, Paterson, Rudd, and Dyson as well as older colonial writers; there were philharmonic societies and dramatic groups, and so on. Essays read to local societies were sometimes reproduced in full by newspapers, as when a schoolmaster spoke on 'Australian Characteristics' to the Shepparton branch of the Australian Natives Association in 1904. The speaker was of the opinion that 'we have no literature worthy of the name', and that 'there is little by which we can judge of the difference between a Native and an Englishman'. He knew of *Such is Life* but he mentioned the book - without naming it – to make a point about Australian speech habits:

> A Shepparton gentleman has written a book. A friend of mine calls it 'intensely Australian'. What does he mean? Simply that the characters in the book use beastly

> language. And we must confess that this penchant for slang and for 'swear words' is on the increase, and should be sternly put down.[20]

The schoolmaster's incomprehension of Furphy's work was no greater than that of the general public.

Such is Life had few readers until the 1940s, when universities discovered the richness of its craftsmanship, but it was a key work in the thinking of such nationalists as Vance Palmer in the 1920s and 1930s, and was later an important source for Russell Ward in constructing 'The Australian Legend'. The sort of nationalism of which the book is the major document was, I suggest, less a reflection of what Furphy's neighbours and fellow mechanics felt than a reflection of what he hoped that they would feel. His fellow workers (apart from his two close friends) were not eager for his views: fifty-five years after *Such is Life* appeared, Claud Gent, who had been 'just a fellow worker and saw Joe every day for 12 months in the year' recalled that 'I didn't know or perhaps care that he was an author' and wrote that what he remembered was 'Joe as a very quiet old chap just done his work and never interfered with any one ...[21] The overt social and political attitudes of *Such is Life* are a conscious and deeply meditated rejection of those which prevailed in the society to which Furphy belonged, but Shepparton hardly registered either the man or his views.

The writing of *Such is Life* was in itself a kind of triumph for the Shepparton mechanic but to the people among whom he lived it remained virtually an unread curiosity. The respectable citizens of Shepparton were no less committed to an ideal of Australia than was Furphy, but it was a different ideal. They unconsciously expressed their kind of Australianness in their readiness to identify with a fashionable portrait painter in far-off London and their neglect of the radical, literary mechanic in their midst. Longstaff remained 'Our Shepparton Artist' wherever he was and whatever he painted, but Furphy was never 'Our Shepparton Writer'.

NOTES

1. Henry Lawson, 'The Longstaff Portrait', *Autobiographical and Other Writings 1887-1922*, ed. Colin Roderick (Sydney: Angus and Robertson, 1972), p. 218.
2. John Longstaff letter to Randolph Bedford, 19 June 1903. Edward Dyson Papers, State Library of Victoria.
3. 'Good Australians: John Longstaff', *The Lone Hand*, 1 September 1911, pp. 411-3. The article was in an unsigned 'series of Character Studies of Australians – born or made – whose public services have, in larger or smaller degree, benefited the Commonwealth'.
4. The *Tocsin* article was reprinted in the *Shepparton News*, 29 September 1899.
5. 'Adele' (pseud.), 'Artist John Longstaff', *Shepparton Advertiser*, 21 February 1904.
6. Bernard Smith, *Australian Painting 1788-1960*, Melbourne, O.U.P., 1962, p. 189.
7. *Argus*, 23 April 1937. Quoted in R. Haese, *Rebels and Precursors: The Revolutionary Years of Australian Art* (Ringwood: Allen Lane, 1981), p. 41.
8. Nina Murdoch, *Portrait in Youth of Sir John Longstaff 1861-1941* (Sydney: Angus and Robertson, 1948, p. 42.
9. *Shepparton News*, 9 August 1887.
10. *Shepparton News*, 29 September 1899.
11. *Shepparton Advertiser*, 10 March 1911.
12. 'One town ruined by private enterprise and another saved', *Argus*, 20 September 1884, *Vagabond Country: Australian Bush & Town Life in the Victorian Age*, ed. Michael Cannon (Melbourne: Hyland House, 1981), p. 32.
13. These phrases from the *Shepparton News* are representative of the way in which John Furphy was perceived in the nineties.
14. Nina Murdoch, *op. cit.*, p. 4.
15. 'Reminiscences of a Pioneer', *Shepparton Advertiser*, 13 December 1904.
16. Letter to Cecil Winter, 23 September 1903, State Library of Victoria.

16a. Letter to Cecil Winter, 28 July 1904, State Library of Virgaina

17. Letter to Cecil Winter, undated [October 1904], State Library of Victoria.
18. '"Every man can write at least one book": Joseph Furphy', paper delivered to Cultural History Seminar, Australian National University, 26 June 1988; published in *Australian Cultural History*, No. 8, 1989, pp. 7-23.
19. Quoted in a *Bulletin* article, reprinted in the *Shepparton News*, 8 March 1904.
20. *Shepparton News*, 22 July 1904. The speaker, W.C. Anderson, was head teacher at the Central Shepparton State School and an active member of the ANA.
21. Letter to John K. Ewers, 29 July 1958. (Copy supplied by Ewers family.)

FRANK DAVIDSON

The Search for a Colonial Metropolis: Martin Boyd and the Myth of The Noble Settler.

The concept of the metropolis is intimately bound up with the concept of the region; in its turn, the concept of the region presupposes a focus of consciousness. Unless we are to speak of imposed political boundaries, the identification of a region suggests some inherent social unification, which we know to exist but which it is hard to define exactly. In geographical terms, a region implies the existence of an economic metropolis; in social terms, regionalism implies the existence of a cultural metropolis, which may or may not equate exactly with an economic one. Moreover, a metropolis may imply subordinate regional centres or foci.

It has become a truism, in the consideration of writing produced in the colonial condition, that the colonised region plays counterpart to its dominant metropolis. Alienation from the metropolis, through either exile or estrangement, produces cultural dislocation, an identity crisis in the colonised region, followed by the acknowledgement there of biculturalism or cultural hybridization, and the eventual discarding of those metropolitan codes that the colonial region finds that it can function without. In theory, a new independent culture finally emerges. What can be overlooked, as one observes this process, is the extent to which adaptation can modify metropolitan or imperial models, to a degree that will find them acceptable as new endemic culture. In considering the developing sense of an Australian culture, it would be arguable that Australia's cities, where aspirations towards culture in the metropolitan sense were often remarked, might exhibit more deference to a metropolitan model than would the Australian outback or the bush. But, as Bruce Bennett has observed of the present situation in Australia: 'The common expectation of metropolitan elites that other centres will conform to their values or style can exist only if the other centres are prepared for this to happen.'[1] Bennett was commenting in part on the dispute for cultural pre-eminence in Australia of its two largest cities, Sydney and Melbourne; a tussle that has gone on since the time, over 100 years ago, when Melbourne briefly overtook Sydney in size and centripetal economic influence. A major piece of Melbourne's armoury in this persistent half-frivolous, half-serious quasi-metropolitan posturing, is the output of the novelist Martin Boyd.

There is less evidence of an intra-Australian regionalism in Melbourne today, than there was in the years after the colony at Port Phillip Bay was founded. Unlike Sydney and Van Diemen's Land the settlement had a significant concentration of free settlers. It was also cut off from those earlier centres by distance. The small 19th century elite in Melbourne was chronicled in retrospect by Martin Boyd, the process of which he began in *The Montforts* (1928). His fiction in a general sense can be found to show some evidence of conflict between the cultural projections of England and the cultural impulses of Australia.

In *The Montforts* in particular the indication is that even amongst English gentry transplanted to Australia, the Australianness that they acquire might eventually prevail over their Englishness. Precisely the same phenomenon had been occurring to gentlefolk in real life for some time before Boyd wrote, as the life of the 19th century novelist Ada Cambridge testifies. After thirty years in Australia (ten of them living in Melbourne), when she and her husband went to England for a holiday in 1903, Cambridge found that she had 'become an Australian' and eventually she returned to live permanently in Melbourne.

In the pattern of Martin Boyd's infant and childhood experiences can be found the source of the erroneous idea that he deprecated Australia and embraced Britain and British culture at Australia's expense. It is true he was born at Lucerne in Switzerland, in 1893, but his family returned to Australia while he was still a young child and between the ages of 8 and 13 he lived at Sandringham, on Port Phillip Bay, which was then no more than a tiny hamlet of about half a dozen houses. Boyd recalled: 'We had the undisturbed use of a mile of golden beach, and tea-tree covered cliffs. An arcadian horse-tram trundled twice a day along the road to Black Rock and Beaumaris, and twice a day it went off the rails.'[2] His use of the word 'arcadian' in this context relates not only to his recollection of a golden childhood, but also to his perception of Australia as a land in which a new civilization could be cradled.

In both his autobiography and his fiction Boyd looks towards Europe as the generating source of civilization, but it is a Europe seen through the screen of his family's identity as expatriate English gentry, with a consequent unreality in his perception of the European model. He refers to the discovery in his family's country house, near Melbourne, of the trigger which had set off his production of *The Cardboard Crown* (1952) and the three novels following it: 'I found there my grandmother's diaries of most of her married life, especially of the years in Europe preceding my birth, so glamorous in my childhood imagination.'[3]

One might ask, what was the glamorous Europe that Boyd's imagination led him to see? In common with other Australians of his generation, he had an idealised perception, in particular of England, which reflected his family's colonial experience and their place in British metropolitan society. He records the significance he attached to the substantial houses of his grandparents in Melbourne, and the 'frontier' they defined for him: 'The greener lawns, fatter buds, the damper, darker soil of the gardens in St Kilda and Brighton satisfied in me some nostalgia for a fertile terrain. There was a field dotted with gum-trees which we passed on the way to Brighton and which I regarded as the frontier of civilisation.'[4]

He refers to the sense, shared by others of his generation, that Australia had no identity of its own; it is significant that upon being brought into contact with an aspect of French history, he is 'dumb with shame', having thought up till that moment that all history was English. Any evidence of man's occupation of Australia is seen purely in terms of the history of its European settlement; and for this reason, Tasmania (previously Van Diemen's Land) is looked upon favourably, not only because the family went there for summer holidays each year but because: 'it had more feeling of history than Victoria. Many of the houses were Georgian and the villages, woods and orchards along the River Derwent were very picturesque. The ruined church of the convict settlement at Port Arthur was the Australian equivalent of Glastonbury.'[5]

The idea of a culture growing up in Australia which is at once both derivative of British culture and decidedly different from it is strongly presented in *The Montforts* as I have argued elsewhere to the conclusion that Boyd acknowledges the difference and foresees that an Australian culture must eventually prevail in Australia. In this respect, Boyd advances the position of Henry Kingsley, whose Sam Buckley, created about 70 years earlier, had uttered his pronouncement rejecting the colonial in favour of the metropolitan:

> I want to buy back the acres of my forefathers...my father could do it, but will not. He and my mother have severed every tie with the old country, ... but with me it is different ... I want to throw in my lot heart and hand with the greatest nation in the world. I don't want to be young Sam Buckley of Baroona. I want to be the Buckley of Clere. Is it not a noble ambition?[6]

Sam Buckley's use in this context of the word 'noble' refers us directly to components of the British metropolitan culture which are important to the later novelist Martin Boyd. These components are the English ancestral estate with its great house, and the social hierarchy of which the historically landed gentry were the crowning layer. Both Kingsley and Boyd in terms of these components are rendering into Australian literature what could be called the myth of the noble settler.

As far as I am aware, this myth was first identified by G A Wilkes in *The Stockyard and The Croquet Lawn* (1982), where Wilkes described its features in terms of the system of values espoused by Kingsley in *Geoffrey Hamlyn*: the testing in the wilderness of the noble and the innocent, resulting in the strengthening of their characters and the assurance of their prosperity. In *The Montforts*, Boyd draws from his own family history a narrative which echoes this myth, but moderates it towards a more realistic expression. Although Kingsley's Buckley family and Boyd's Montfort family are roughly contemporaneous settlers in Australia, the separation by 70 or so years of the two authors produces different aspects of the myth.

In the case of the Buckleys, Australia is still a desperate resort. Success there is a means of recovery of the place that had been lost or obscured in England. Boyd also makes use of this aspect of the myth in *Lucinda Brayford* (1946) in which Australia is judged to be a suitable destination for William Vane, caught cheating at cards at Cambridge. For this transgression of the code of the 'gentleman', he is exiled to Australia quite as irrecoverably as any member of the convict class might have been. In ironic counterpoint much later in that story, William's prosperous Australian grazier son Fred, visiting England, goes home to Australia in disgust when the only public notice he is accorded in London is a brief report in 'The Times' of his motor accident in Regent Street. However, the social fabric supporting the myth is still strong enough in Edwardian Australia for Fred to glory in the marriage of his daughter Lucinda with the British aristocrat Hugo Brayford. Lucinda, in going to England as Hugo's wife, enacts the same role in the myth as Kingsley's Sam Buckley had done in the 1850s. In the return to it of these natural aristocrats Sam and Lucinda, the cultural metropolis has claimed the fairest blooms of its colonial region. In the case of Boyd's Montfort family, the realistic destiny of the settler is not his triumphant return to England from exile, as it was for Sam Buckley, but his satisfactory progression towards reconstitution as an Australian. This illustrates a different aspect of the noble settler myth: his contribution towards the evolution of an endemic Australian culture.

This is an aspect of the 'gentleman settler' that the social historian Paul de Serville claims has been unfairly overlooked in Australian cultural studies. De Serville states:

> So much has been made of the egalitarian tradition in Australian society that it has overshadowed the existence of an older code, that of the gentleman. Transplanted from the British Isles by earlier settlers, the code of the gentleman was upheld in each of the colonies and flourished despite many vicissitudes. It has contributed much to the diversity of Australian life. In a country nominally dedicated to the

> proposition of equality, the beliefs of the gentleman have been dismissed by some as effete, undemocratic and un-Australian. That they have survived at all in such an unsympathetic climate indicates an intrinsic strength. The power exercised by the code of honour was every bit as strong as that wielded later by the cult of mateship.[7]

The Montforts offers a view of one such settler as he tosses and turns in his bunk on the journey out to Port Phillip. Henry Montfort is prepared to leave the ancestral home and to face the rigours of colonial experience, but there is always the metropolitan backstop to safeguard this experience. In his musings he refers to icons of British metropolitan culture; the institution of the English country house, the Public School, the University:

> Henry regretted most, perhaps, Farleigh-Scudamore, and the fact that his children could not grow up in the English countryside, would never again play in the paternal woods and barns. They would grow up as Australians. The two boys would have to go to an Australian school. It was hard to imagine what kind of school there could be in Australia. Simon had written to say that there was talk of a grammar school being founded in Melbourne for the sons of gentlemen. An Australian grammar school for the sons of a Westminster family! The prospect was not attractive, but if he were to be an earnest colonist he must accept without complaint the colonist's limitations. Later if he were successful, the boys might come home to Oxford.[8]

While Oxford clearly represents in Henry's perceptions an important metropolitan component, to which access can be kept open for those of the gentleman class, his wife Letitia's reaction to her first contact with Melbourne raises another consideration, one that is more immediate to the colonial life of gentlefolk, and to women in particular. It is the consideration of whether or not adequate forms are available in the colony for the constitution of 'civilization' and therefore whether or not the society of gentlefolk may be maintained under the colonial conditions. Letitia's bonnet and crinoline preface this question as Boyd describes her preparations to step ashore representing the imperial thrust:

> Letitia donned her smartest bonnet and her widest crinoline and came on deck before breakfast and eagerly scanned the shore, which here was nothing but low sand-flats, covered with stunted trees. There were a few stone-built houses at Williamstown, belonging to the harbour authorities. Across the bay on the Melbourne side were some small tenements and wooden jetties for landing. Henry came up and told her that Melbourne lay two miles inland from those jetties. Her heart sank. It was worse, far worse than she had expected. She felt as if she had been dealt a blow from which it would be impossible to recover. Hope had left her. It was true, then, that she had to renounce all those things which made life pleasant, gentle society and elegant homes. What civilization could lie beyond those tenements and barren sands?[9]

The answer to Letitia's question comes when the Montforts traverse the new settlement: 'mean streets surrounded by piggeries and cow-pens', and a Collins Street 'ill-made and not yet free of the stumps of trees'. In short, there is no sign of 'civilization' in Melbourne; or so it seems at first contact. Not until the party arrives at the new house of Simon Montfort, who has preceded his brother Henry to the Port Phillip settlement, where Letitia finds the accommodation 'elegant and far more fashionable than she had expected', is there some sign of a revision of Letitia's initial impressions. Her apprehension of exile from civilization reflects the need of colonial society to seek out and to reaffirm those qualities that marked people off as 'ladies and gentlemen'; qualities without which in their view 'society' could not function adequately.

De Serville's classification of Port Phillip society confirms three general groupings of 'gentlemen', the first consisting of gentlemen of good family, the second of gentlemen by profession or commission, the third of gentlemen by upbringing. The novelist Ada Cambridge indicates in *The Three Miss Kings* the female counterpart of de Serville's 'gentleman', in her introductory sketch of Elizabeth King: 'A noble figure she was tall, strong, perfect in proportion, fine in texture, full of natural dignity and grace...the product of several generations of healthy and cultured people, and therefore a truly well-bred woman.'[10]

Similarly, in the world of Martin Boyd's fiction the placing of people in society is a duty undertaken in the interests of good society; in *The Montforts* Boyd illustrates the effect of the Victorian gold-rush on people of the sort represented in de Serville's first category, gentleman of good family:

> Up to 1851 new arrivals had nearly all been men of good family who had come to try their fortunes on the land. They were adventurous, of fine physique, moderate erudition, and good manners. They were mostly related to, or had letters of introduction to, the families which were already settled, and were received with open arms as welcome additions to the society of Port Phillip. But now the ladies of Melbourne were wont to look askance at any new arrival and inquire into his antecedents.[11]

The merging of the grades of gentility is observed in *The Montforts* when Amy Montfort, daughter of Henry and Letitia, marries Thomas Allman. Thomas is described as 'heavy in face and in manner', and his departure from the ideal gentleman of good family is carefully catalogued. He is adventurous to the extent of going to the goldfields, where he has success, but his poverty of spirit brings him back to Melbourne to start life in an office. He lacks natural physical grace, his conversation is limited to political subjects, and his manners are unwittingly boorish. Nevertheless, he represents the second category of gentlemen, accorded the rank by his profession of the law.

The conversation between Amy's parents, discussing Thomas' proposal, places the Montforts' colonial circle in relation to the metropolis they have left behind:

> 'But is he a gentleman?' Letitia had cried.
> 'Well, in Australia, yes', said Henry.
> 'But she could never take him home. He would be like old Skinner, who was given a baronetcy on the condition that he never settled in England.'[12]

In reverse form and set at a later time, we see in turn the placing of Lucinda Vane's Australian family by the English aristocrat Hugo Brayford:

> '...Are the parents vulgar or anything? Mama seemed a bit breezy at the dance last night.'
> 'No. They're not exactly vulgar. I believe Mrs Vane has quite good English connections...I should say the Vanes are rather like rich manufacturing people at home, but with worse voices and better horses, which amply makes up for it.'[13]

In the Boyd canon there is ample evidence of cultural dislocations between Australian and English society, but there is also a consistent projection of the natural growth of cultural differences in Australia itself. Essentially, regionalism shows in the way that those with an unimpeded access to metropolitan culture, eye the differences spawned in colonial society.

One of these differences, in the displacement of the gentry from their habitual setting and their transplantation to the Australian colony, is brought about by the liberating effect of this transplantation. In the case of Hugo and Lucinda, this is represented by an incident during their honeymoon when they drive out into the countryside and climb to the top of a hill where they make love:

> They sat down to rest after the climb. Lucinda lay back and closed her eyes against the sun, white and blinding in the mid-heaven. Hugo began to make love to her. At first she tried to restrain him, because of the time and place. But then the time and place, the high and piercing sun, the stark earth, seemed to fuse in her body a wild desire. A kind of ferocity seized them, a joy that passed beyond endurance to pain. She felt that she was consumed by the sun itself, by some principle of life that immolated her body in an act of new creation.[14]

In the narrative pattern of *Lucinda Brayford* it is ironic that the illumination of this incident is a transitory one; it is the last event in the story before Lucinda must leave Australia, and neither Hugo nor Lucinda ever refers to it again. Hugo, only an exploitative British visitor to Australia, is untouched by the creative moment; Lucinda, henceforth swallowed up in English life, is cut off from her native surroundings, and denied further responses to them as she slowly takes on the cultural identity of an English gentlewoman, required of her by life in British aristocratic society.

However Letitia Montfort, travelling in the opposite direction, from the English cultural context to the Australian, illustrates the effects of a reverse transplantation. On the Montforts' arrival in Melbourne, a party is given to which are invited the friends and neighbours who constitute 'society'. Amongst them is an exiled Spanish nobleman Don Gomez. When he sings at the party Letitia is charmed. A mild flirtation ensues:

> Letitia herself would not have approved of it in Bedford Square. But this slight social gaiety and the admiration she evoked, and the discovery of persons of distinction and refinement, coming after months of privation and disappointment, gave her a new and, perhaps, rather alarming sense of exhilaration. As people are apt to do in a foreign country, feeling that there are present no competent critics of their behaviour, she discarded some of the reserve which in Bloomsbury she would have thought decorous.[15]

For all her characteristics as a conventional English 'lady', Letitia is already on the way to cultural hybridization, in that some years later, now Lady Montfort and the wife of the Chief Justice, we see her abandoning Victorian propriety to the extent of taking the leading hand in the elopement of Don Gomez' daughter - with a 'gentleman' of course, but, all the same, she has engaged in a form of behaviour that would have been unthinkable in her previous English context.

Within the condition of colonial exile, as we may say it is represented in *The Montforts* and elsewhere in Boyd's writings, the social unification of the gentry class marks out an enclave or 'region' within the colonial culture. But the gentry class is susceptible to cultural modification in the colonial situation, just as are other social classes. British metropolitan culture had provided in Australian society the idea of an upper class; to which, as G C Bolton has pointed out, the gradually prospering colonials of lesser origins aspired. Bolton claims: '...only the superficial trimmings of British upper-class manners were welcomed by the colonial elite. Knighthoods and Government House levees soothed their social aspirations, but when it came to a question of political or economic action the naked prejudices of an Australian interest group were expected to prevail.'[16]

It was against precisely just such concerns with the trimmings rather than with the core of gentle conduct that Martin Boyd reacted strongly in his writing, in autobiography and also in fiction. In *The Montforts* can be seen not only the extent to which the metropolis casts its influence into the colony, but a serious consideration by Boyd of how a particular colonial condition produced modifying effects on the patterns of attitude and behaviour brought from the metropolitan culture. These changes are attributable to the liberating influence of contact with a new land and different cultures, as in the effect on Letitia of her friendship with Don Gomez; on the opportunities for personal advancement open to the sufficiently adventurous settler and, not least, the retreating realities of the metropolitan culture into the idealised perceptions of it which, as Boyd admitted in his autobiography, he himself held until his own experiences in Europe proved to him otherwise in his 'life-long search for the non-existent abiding city'.

NOTES

1. Bruce Bennett, *Place, Region and Community* (James Cook University of North-Queensland: Foundation for Australian Studies, 1984), p. 5.
2. Martin Boyd, *Day of My Delight: An Anglo-Australian Memoir* (Melbourne: Landsdowne, 1965), p. 3. This, the second autobiography, reissues and continues Boyd's account of his own life published in *A Single Flame*, (1939).
3. Martin Boyd, 'Preoccupations and Intentions', *Southerly*, No. 2 of 1968. The article was canvassed by the editor, G A Wilkes, in reply to attacks made on Boyd's writing in *Southerly* No.4 of 1966.
4. *Day of My Delight*, p. 5.
5. *Ibid.*, p. 18.
6. Henry Kingsley, *The Recollections of Geoffrey Hamlyn* (London: J M Dent & Sons, 1924), pp. 438-439. First published 1859.
7. Paul de Serville, *Port Phillip Gentlemen* (Melbourne: Oxford University Press, 1980), p. 14.
8. Martin Boyd, *The Montforts* (Melbourne: Penguin Australia, 1986), p. 12. All further references are to this edition.
9. *Ibid.*, p. 21.
10. Ada Cambridge, *The Three Miss Kings* (London: Virago Press, 1987), p. 3. First published by Wm Heinemann, London, 1891 and Melville, Mullon and Slade, Melbourne 1891.
11. *The Montforts*, p. 37.
12. *Ibid.*, p. 59.
13. *Lucinda Brayford* (Melbourne: Penguin Australia, 1985), p. 120.
14. *Ibid.*, p. 141.
15. *The Montforts*, p. 27.
16. G. C. Bolton, 'The Idea of a Colonial Aristocracy', *Historical Studies* No. 13 (1968) p. 325. Bolton takes what he calls 'the crudest of yardsticks' to determine the composition of an Australian upper social group: inclusion in books of social reference such as Burke's *Landed Gentry*.

STEPHEN ALOMES

Class, Cities and Colonies: The Dominance of Local Elites in Australian Society 1880-1960

In the old world of Europe it is easy to have a vision of Australia as a land of nature and openness, a sun-drenched land in which freedom and opportunity, and careers open to talent, are available to all except Aboriginal Australians and kangaroos. Old images of mateship and bush egalitarianism and new images of hedonistic happiness have been implicit in the Bicentennial trumpet fanfares, if not in the origins myth replayed endlessly in the celebration of First Fleets and/or Tall Ships. Cliches appeal to a troubled northern hemisphere while simultaneously providing an excuse for self-congratulation in an unsettled and changing Australia.

The reality is different in the Australia of the new rich and of growing poverty – the Australia with a more unequal distribution of wealth than in most O.E.C.D. countries. It also was different. My thesis is that from the 1880s until at least the 1960s Australian society was a class society; economically, socially and culturally (and most of the time politically), it was dominated by the six capital city elites with the support of the middle classes. Despite the brevity of post-invasion Australian history, city elites and rural graziers, who were linked in the colonial establishments, dominated Australian society. The occasional tendency towards a social democracy of manners, the conflict between upper and lower houses in State and colonial parliaments, the strength of the labour movement, Federal politics itself and the regional variations only slightly qualified this pattern of colonial city state dominance.

In the small space available to me I will delineate the outlines of this argument, the broad brush strokes and contrasts of Albert Tucker being more appropriate than the fine detail of those who paint on a smaller canvas.

The economic centrality of wool and minerals exports and the integration of pastoral, financial and commercial capital was culturally reinforced by a society and culture which was linked to Home Counties Britain (as well as the City of London) by British forms and titles and centered locally at Government House.[1] Since the division by social rank between officers and settlers and convicts, between exclusives and emancipists in the convict colony of N.S.W., the social divide had been present as had the integration of pastoral, financial and commercial capital. Although the emancipist son W.C. Wentworth's dream of a 'bunyip aristocracy' in a titled Upper House was not realised the Legislative Councils continued to hold a degree of social and political power on a limited franchise for up to a century after responsible government in most colonies and states. In Max Neutze's summary 'the six state/colonial capitals' were 'the centre of government and the commercial life of their colonies'; in turn they 'looked directly to London rather than to a leading city in Australia.'[2]

The integration of rural and urban elites through wool had its social expression in the gentleman's club (first formed to provide city lodgings for squatters) and had its leisured expressions including horse racing, the hunt and polo and garden parties and balls. Town and Country balls also proved useful for ensuring suitable matches between the well-heeled, and ideally respectable, offspring of polite society.

The formation of elite society continued, even with the challenges to established wealth and the recurring appearances of new money. The integration of new generations of nouveau riches into the Establishment is a process that denies neither the existence of an Establishment nor the exclusion of the bulk of society from it. The challenges of the sons of the emancipists to the 'Exclusives', of the new rich of the gold generation to the 'Port Phillip Gentlemen' in the 1850s, the appearance of the new rich in mining, land speculation, retailing and manufacturing of the late nineteenth century, (including the Baillieus and Myer) were all reflections of that process. Some were not to be accepted as in the case of the Myers who were blackballed by the Melbourne Club or the member of the Holden manufacturing family in Adelaide who was also similarly excluded by the Adelaide Club.[3] Nor would all be landowners or capitalists: a society with strong commercial economic activities offered a place for managers and the strength of the government bureaucracy offered a role for senior public servants who also received knighthoods; to this must be added the status of the professions, particularly medicine and law. Australian society may have had fewer barriers of accent and social mores to upward mobility than some others (and the right habits could be learned) but nonetheless from the 1880s to 1960 a learned southern English accent with an Australian inflection was a decided social asset.

The formation of elite society occurred not only through the social and cultural rituals of polite society but through the elaboration of necessary institutions for its reproduction. The consolidation of the private schools (or 'public schools' as they were known in Victoria), the professionalisation of medicine and the expansion and consolidation of the legal profession and of professional and commercial white collar work all provided solid foundations for middle class and upper middle class decency. Although the labour shortages encouraged Jack and Jill to think that they were as good as their master, and electoral and social reform was achieved by lower houses, social democratic tendencies were unwelcome to many, and even many middle class liberals sought the values of respectability and the 'gentleman' as well as, or over, those of reform. In the more turbulent and conservative years of the new century such tendencies would become increasingly apparent.

The evolution of separate elite societies in the six colonies left a legacy of land, wealth and names which are with us still, even though the grand houses and country estates have sometimes passed into the respectable hands of the National Trust and some of the urban estates have passed through the hands of the real estate agents and developers. In Western Australia, the successful squatting family the Duracks, the mercantile-commercial Hacketts and other well-known names such as the Drake-Brockmans and Lee-Steeres were paralleled on a smaller scale in Tasmania by the pastoral Burburys and the Camerons and the urban Dobson and Allport families; and in South Australia by the Barr-Smiths, Downers, Bonythons, Duttons, Angases, Hawkers, and Simpsons; and in Victoria by the Clarkes, Armytages, Chirnsides, Manifolds and Fairbairns and in N.S.W. by the Macarthur-Onslows and Whites and the urban Windeyers and Streets; and in Queensland by the Halls, Persses and McConnels. To the traditional pastoral, legal and commercial elites would be added such new money from the 1880s as the Baillieus and that of newer manufacturers including Holden in Adelaide and the Nicholas 'Aspro' family in Victoria; yet they too knew the social importance of land, a Nicholas son acquiring the de rigeur Western District property. Mining, manufacturing and self-made men were all part of the story of the evolution of the colonial Establishments.[4]

In an illuminating study of that Australian upper class at its Edwardian peak, and before its relative decline, Michael Cannon has delineated its social dominance and its authority over the institutions and rituals of respectable middle-class society. Its role was central in the universities and the private schools, in the golf and tennis clubs (Prime Minister S.M. Bruce's father was the founder of the Royal Melbourne Golf Club in 1891)[5] in the links to Oxbridge, the British Medical Association and to the Inns of Court as well as in presentation to or investiture at the Royal Court itself, in gentlemanly equestrian sport and in the new automobile clubs which often won the title 'royal' and in the gatherings of 'society'. This class set a standard for the aspiring middle classes. 'Leadership', to use a term of which not only Dr. J.R. Darling of Geelong Grammar would have approved, extended through the universities and university colleges, the professions, business of course, the armed services, politics (although only sometimes the upper houses) to the political nether world of Right secret armies. The upper class notion of 'noblesse oblige' or 'service' (to use a traditional word which would eventually be popularised and later Rotarianised) also issued in service of King and Country and Empire in war. Many of those from upper class society, such as S.M. Bruce, Charles Hawker and the later General Sir John Hackett, would serve, especially in the first world war, in the British forces, for they had been working or pursuing a military career in Britain.[6] From the upper class or upper middle class world (the question of nomenclature is important but difficult to resolve) would also come the laureates of their society such as Mary Durack and its dissidents including the poet, communist and folklorist J.F. Manifold, the republican and literary critic Geoffrey Dutton and the novelist Patrick White.

The Edwardian autumn of which Cannon writes was a prelude to relative decline; Baron Clarke's Rupertswood and the Chirnsides' Werribee Park would decline socially and architecturally between the wars as they were sold to the Catholic Church which sought a different kind of rigidity. Servants had become more expensive and as always bad seasons or poor prices for commodities could make life a little harder for new 'old' wealth. Yet in the era which I have termed the 'Dominion Culture', the years from 1900 to 1940 or perhaps even to 1960, the upper class elite, through its social and cultural forms and its economic and political values would influence the wider middle class society.[7] Values, forms and networks which persisted in the colonial capitals, and their wider worlds for most of the twentieth century, were evolving in the late nineteenth century.

Economic and demographic realities provided the basis for this society and culture. A smaller primary industry workforce (26%) than in other settler societies (e.g. Canada 48%), the greater dominance of the cities (Melbourne had 41% of the colony of Victoria's population in 1891; in the other colonies Sydney had 35%, Adelaide had 31% and Perth 33%)[8], the growing tertiary workforce (in finance, commerce, the public service, transport and the professions) and declining social and geographical mobility in the era of Dominion Culture bolstered localism and middle class hegemony. Although many clerks longed to be with Clancy of the Overflow increasingly the Australian reality was one of the 'dingy little office' rather than droving somewhere on the Lachlan.

Not until it slowly began to change in the early 1960s was the character of the enlarged elite discerned in critiques by four intellectual 'new boys', the immigrant social scientists, Hugo Wolfsohn and Sol Encel and the Sydney journalists, Donald Horne and Craig McGregor, in their diagnoses of the Australian condition. Hugo Wolfsohn wrote of the 'ideology--makers', the 'judges, leading clergymen, some business leaders and military men, a small band of university professors and college heads'. He believed that their 'conservative values, largely a third-rate imitation of the paternalistic postures of the 19th century British upper class, must have an inhibiting influence on the scope of social and cultural policy'. But this was only the ideological expression of a larger social world, provincial in its localism as well as in its cultural derivativeness; a world characterised by 'the institutionalization of mediocrity'.[9]

Although, in the symbolic triangle of empire and provincialism, that of land, colonial capital city and Britain, this world was distinctively Australian, it can also be placed in a larger context. E.J. Hobsbawm has argued that 1870-1914 was a crucial period in the invention of middle class, working class and national traditions in Western society; it was the period of the establishment of national middle class elites through processes of class definition and differentiation, of organisation and social consolidation. Drawing on aristocratic forms and pretensions, new measures were introduced in middle class life – secondary schooling, which fused association with potential fluidity, supplemented by amateur sport and through the Headmasters' Conference, public school sport; university colleges in Britain, student 'Korps' in Germany and fraternities in the US were all important.[10] In Australia too similar processes reflected the expansion and ritualisation of a larger middle class society. 'Middle class and upper middle class] domination over professional life[11] was strengthened, not only by the expansion of the professions but also by one of the few large private school systems oriented towards social status in the settler societies of the new world. Amateur sport (especially Old Boys football, the Rugby Union - Rugby League class division in NSW) and the gentlemanly and later lady-like sports of lawn tennis and golf reinforced these processes. In the southern states the authority of Establishment society over even 'professional' football paralleled its authority over cricket, rowing and athletics more generally.[12]

In the different Australian capitals it was through racing clubs, gentlemen's clubs, the BMA and the legal worlds in buildings named 'Temple Court' or 'Selborne Chambers' that such society worked. The links between Town and Country and between Town and Gown and the P & O liners which took better-off citizens to London for the Season, for Ascot and Lords, if not presentation at Court, reflected a provincial and colonial elite society.[13] While in the smaller cities, lawyers and surgeons had a status more elevated than in the two great centres of capital, Melbourne and Sydney, the knighthood, or even the Order of the British Empire, was a shared aspiration for many good citizens.

What were the social values of this enlarged elite? Its values fused the social pretention of the colonial upper class of the world's greatest Empire with the suburban respectability which they also derived from Britain. Although liberal sides could be found, generally they looked down on the working classes and on the merely and roughly 'Australian'. Only when treated as a 'colonial' in Britain or over important matters like cricket did the Australian component of their British-Australianness become sometimes predominant. This was a mono-cultural elite characterised by male dominance but with an important social role for the 'lady'.[14] It was through the family, through the rituals and occasions of society and through dress (both were the province of the lady) that its values would be negotiated and maintained and it would reproduce itself. Had the events of World War I, the Easter Uprising in Ireland and the Conscription referenda not occurred it might perhaps have been more open to the upper middle class Catholics as it would eventually become in the 1960s and after. It had little time for foreigners (as reflected in the B.M.A's attitude to foreign doctors in the 1930s and 1940s) and it was ready, through the GPS schools and the universities, to fight them in 1914-18.[15] Similarly it provided strike-breakers and paramilitary secret army troops in the class conflicts of 1919-22 and 1929-32. City and country were linked in the squattocratic splendour of Streeton pastorals and in the pioneer (rather than egalitarian) bush myth manifested in so many memorials and also in the rural hill-stations to which the upper middle class retreated in summer – to Mt. Macedon from Melbourne, to the Adelaide Hills from Adelaide and to Bowral from Sydney. The middle classes, too, wisely made for cooler climes during the oppressive summer, striking out for the nearer Blue Mountains in Sydney and the Dandenongs in Melbourne. Culturally, the orientation of the enlarged elite was to Britain from which most books came, and to which most Australian writers felt either compelled to go or desirous of going.

Intellectually, the enlarged elite was derivative, English empiricism being exacerbated by dutiful provincialism. It was a society which preferred the expert to the intellectual, the practical man to the thinker and it was unduly dependent on British precedent and visiting British expertise. This was in part because so few resources had keen put into the universities which between the wars took even more of the merely local product rather than the imported proconsuls from Britain. Not surprisingly, Australian foreign policy between the wars came mainly from London while critical thinking about Australia developed only slightly through such new forums as the Australian Institute of Political Science and the Australian Institute of International Affairs which fused a desire for critical thought with the respectability, if not the complacency, of middle and upper middle class Australia. It is possible to see these patterns of derivativeness as part of a larger problem of intellectual provincialism in Australia. In a society in which 'who you know' becomes more important than 'what you know', whether the 'who' is a local authority or a visiting expert from Britain, then ideas have lost much of their own intellectual warrant. What authority the ideas have and where they come from becomes more important than how you know or think or understand. In a provincial society, in which the 1930s economists, for example, applied British ideas and administrative reformers did the same, information is more valued than ideas, empiricism is more important than theory and analysis and the expert is so much more practical, inevitably, than the intellectual.[16]

What, it may be asked, were the political implications of the situation? How can it be related to the rise of the Labour parties (for they differed in the several states), to reforming liberalism, to ruling ideologies of

Progress and regionalism, to the fractions of capital, to Federal politics which transcended the states in its Labor-non-Labor divides and to political decisions in general? While political scientists and political historians can happily leave out society when they write those who suggest a social-cultural hegemony cannot rest easily on suggestions of political rule by osmosis. Perhaps, if in another Danish town, one could reply that 'there is more in Heaven and earth than is heard of in your philosophy, Horatio'.

However, legitimate, but not fundamental, qualifications must be recognised – the Queensland differences – regionalism, religion and Queensland's branch-plant economy and raw material processing mentalité; the Tasmanian and South Australian variations - the role of government and its support of industrialisation, greater and lesser non-metropolitan influence; and the NSW emphases – Labour, industrialisation and a state of corruption. The use by conservative society of political professionals from Menzies to Peacock and the low-key role of many establishment men (Bruce and Hawker and later Fraser were exceptions) offers a further clarification. So too does the slow incorporation into parts of society of the retailers and the manufacturers in the new century such as the Myers, the descendants of Simcha Baevski, or Sidney Myer. Yet the argument stands that the terms of debate were set by this Establishment society in an initially imperial and colonial context. To use a traditional Australian argument the team which dictates terms usually wins the game. Given the dominance of conservative governments in Australia federally, and in most States for most of the century, and the tame cat nature of even most state Labor governments which were committed only to solid administration and progress, the Establishment and the old middle class with which it was related held great power in the era of Dominion Culture.

The workings of the Establishment in South Australia have been analysed in several fascinating chapters in *The Flinders History of South Australia*, a three volume work perhaps only a little more known in most Australian states than it is in Denmark. Dirk van Dissel has painted a masterly collective portrait of 'The Adelaide Gentry, between 1850-1920'. Urban as well as rural, as befitted the city-state, the Adelaide gentry had 'many of the trappings of its English counterpart' with which it 'prized its historic and social connections'. In his words

> Most of the gentry and such patrician politicians as Charles Hawker and Sir Alexander Downer were very conscious of their membership of a wider society centred on England. These links were reinforced by frequent visits, intermarriage, and presentation at Court which persisted until the 1950s.
>
> Government House played an important role in maintaining the social connections with England. Members of the gentry felt at ease there; they were frequently invited there for luncheons, dinners, garden parties and children's parties and there many

> of their daughters made their debut. The gentry, in turn, entertained vice-regal parties ... on the sea front at Glenelg... or at country properties such as Wellington Lodge near Meningie
> ... This remained so till about 1965...
> Overseas observers noted that the Adelaide Club, founded in 1863, provided another link with Great Britain. 'Where is the core of the British Empire?... In the Adelaide Club you will find the answer.' At a time when many Australians referred to England as 'home', it was probably the gentry who retained closest emotional ties with the mother country.[17]

And it might be added, in a melancholy footnote, that the Adelaide Club did not serve Australian wines until 1947.

This respectable society combined solidarity and exclusiveness with an openness necessary in an immigrant society which also relied on economic and technological change for its development. It also had its moments of liberalism in the late nineteenth century (in the reforms initiated by Downer and Kingston in South Australia and by Sir John Hackett in Western Australia) and its cultural pretensions as Adelaide sought to be the Athens of the south, before it discovered in the 1980s that more lucre could be won through becoming the Estoril of the south, with Grand Prix and casino. In fact in a changing South Australia unions between old pastoral wealth and new commercial and industrial wealth and also vice-regal connections reflected the interaction between society and economics.[18]

The role of such institutions as the major clubs, the leading City Council and The University (and in all Australian cities there are still people who put that definite article in block capitals) was central to social and political processes. When the geographer at Adelaide University, Archibald Grenfell Price was invited by two pillars of the Establishment, C.A.S Hawker and W.G. Duncan, to organise the Emergency Committee to defend South Australian government against the perils of Langism during the political conflicts of the 1930s Great Depression, the matter was raised over lunch in the Adelaide Club, while the university granted him leave for this important work[19]

Nor was the commercial and business world in which the elite were involved narrowly South Australian. Van Dissel shows a high proportion of the gentry held directorships in key foreign and local companies in insurance, banking, shipping, pastoral finance, brewing and mining.[20] In asking why the Australian elites were comparatively poor when put against the British, American, Canadian and South African elites W.D. Rubinstein has noted that their lack of ownership of major banks, insurance companies and other financial institutions is part of the story. In a colonial structure these were often British institutions with some Australian directors and even large mineral/industrial companies such as BHP would have a strong British connection despite their Australian base. Rubinstein is interested in the paradox of how this 'drongo midget elite' (a sobriquet he gives them for their limited skill in amassing wealth) would so dominate Australian society for so long.[21] The once radical social scientist and now neo-conservative, John Playford, has suggested that the powerful 'informal decision making' of the Adelaide Club has been overstated. His argument is that since only nine out of eighteen members of the Legislative Council were members in 1880 and 5-18 in 1910, 18-46 members of the House of Assembly in 1880 and 2-54 in 1910 and 5-20 MLCs in 1968-70 the Club's influence was insignificant. Only five out of the seventeen cabinet ministers in the administrations of his uncle, Sir Thomas Playford between 1938 and 1965, were members, and so on... The Adelaide Club, he argues, sought only to pursue the 'gracious living' of the late nineteenth century. Perhaps those with a less subjective viewpoint might draw different conclusions.[22]

Yet there is something in a footnote to Playford's argument. He points out that many of the industrialists and the prominent public servants so central to the industrialisation of South Australia were not members. Although one can list industrialists and public servants in other states who have become members of the appropriate club there is an argument that they stood at times outside of the club, because of Australia taking on the British distaste for manufacturing and the reservations of capitalists and professionals about merely salaried employees. But that is too large a question to go into here. So too are the difficult questions of the relationship between local elites and the elaboration of national mining, manufacturing and commercial firms and that other related complex question of the divisions between the different fractions of capital as reflected in the fights over government support for primary industry and secondary industry between the wars. The dominance, as T.H. Irving suggests, of pastoral capital amongst Australian millionaires does however indicate that the predominant values of Australian society between the wars, in economics as well as ideology, were associated with the Empire and the land, even more than with the idea of imperial manufacturing in Australia.[23]

Having surveyed the origins of the enlarged upper middle class establishment, the relationships between the elite and middle class professionals and its values, it must now be asked as to how it has worked and what is its legacy in the late twentieth century? In city societies it worked mainly through social networks established through school, suburb and family, which were arguably stronger in Melbourne, Adelaide and Perth than in Sydney or Brisbane. In an evolving, expanding immigrant society (in which the only bluebloods with long lineages are aboriginal) wealth could buy acceptance for the next generation through private schooling at least, although anti-semitism qualified such openness. In the years after World War II the expansion of the tertiary sector of the economy, and the expansion of the secondary schools and later the universities offered new opportunities for upward mobility; scholarships allowed lower middle class Catholics and the children of the skilled and semi-skilled working classes to enter the universities and to obtain jobs as teachers. The later expansion of the universities would provide positions for not only the products of private schools, but also for some from the selective high schools (which imitated the GPS schools) and for others from the suburbs. There was now a place for upper middle class and middle class women, especially those with the right contacts and connections; marriage and an avocation was not the only way of ensuring a standard to which one was accustomed or of moving up the social scale for women. One cannot underestimate here the importance of education in offering a new route to social mobility for the lower middle classes and for women after 1945. Perhaps it was in the opportunities for social mobility and the barriers to it that the enlarged elite had its greatest power.

Localism cannot be underestimated in this process although there have been important exceptions. Even with the rise of national and international institutions since the 1960s, localism has left its legacy. Despite such innovations as jet travel, standard gauge rail between the capitals, television and radio networking, direct-dial telephones and improved roads, despite the 1960s role of the then progressive *Australian* newspaper, despite the political dominance of the Federal parliament and the role of the international money market in determining Australian economic and social policy, localism or state/colonial parochialism and its enclosed social worlds is still important.

In the universities in the 1960s the scenario of the prodigal son (and later daughter) returned from Oxbridge was particularly strong. 'First class minds' and 'high flyers' were sent abroad for finishing like the sons and daughters of the gentry and then returned to their rightful positions along with imperial pro-consuls, themselves sometimes talented but sometimes sent out with 'good enough for the colonies' references. One, perhaps typical, Arts Faculty department in a larger, older capital city university had, in 1987, among its twenty-six staff, thirteen from overseas, eight local boys and girls and only five from the other Australian states.

In the law, where separate bars and large legal firms operated until recently, a similar localism prevailed. Arguably, in law, as in other fields, given the periods necessary for career development its generational legacy is still with us. The students of the 1940s and 1950s are now at the peak of their career paths. The Victorian Supreme Court in early 1988 had only one state school boy out of its twentyfour judges, only one from interstate, only one postwar migrant and no women. Some of those changes had been rung in recent years by the Cain Labor Government. Even in the larger arena of the High Court this century, according to Eddy Neumann's 1973 study,

> the typical High Court Justice is a male white Protestant raised in Sydney or Melbourne ... and of British ethnic origins. He is also from upper middle rather than

> upper class background ... He usually goes to a high status high school (usually private) and then to Sydney or Melbourne university where he has a brilliant academic record.[24]

In business, in companies of national and international capital, the pattern has continued until recently. In March 1988 it was remarked that 'the board of BHP, [Melbourne's] leading business house, is peopled by men versed in war cries on the banks of the Barwon River every April' (the private schools Head of the River rowing). Here too, however, is change. 'The Big Australian', BHP, had always represented the connections between the land, Melbourne, mining and the City of London (perhaps up to a quarter of its shares had been held on the London Stock Exchange at times) while its Board has traditionally had a great number of pastoralists and graziers amongst its members. But today, in the spirit of managerialism, it has added several executives to the board.[25]

In politics, the Victorian Labor government has six out of sixteen cabinet ministers from private schools compared to the Opposition front bench's 11-20 while in Federal politics the Labor ministry of the 1980s has had more Oxford graduates than the Gorton and the Fraser governments. Victorian Governors as well as Melbourne University Vice-Chancellors are still usually Melbourne Club members. In an *Age* supplement entitled 'Who Shapes Melbourne?' a picture was given of change and continuity. One account which expressed the older values of Melbourne declared: 'Knot the Old School Tie around a childhood neck and in Melbourne it stays there forever. A typical lineage runs: Melbourne Grammar, Melbourne University, Melbourne Club, Melbourne Cemetery'.[26] Perhaps this view is confirmed by the fact that in 1988 the new, and American titled, Alumni Association of Melbourne University was running tours of the adjoining land across the road, in part to look at those graduates who have at last crossed the River Styx.

The world is moving, however, although slowly. If similar things can be said of Adelaide and of Perth and of Upper North Shore Sydney, change is in the air. Ruth Ostrow has written of the mostly European 'new boys' in business who have transformed transport, packaging, the rag trade and other industries and now own many of the mansions of Toorak and Bellevue Hill.[27] The new money of Perth and Sydney and the now wealth of sons of society such as Rupert Murdoch and the less well-born John Elliott has brought change. So too have the international companies with which they also deal, increasingly American and Japanese as well as British. The change is symbolised in Melbourne by the company advertising and private boxes which dominate the Carlton football ground, a place which hosts the Carlton Football Club which has been seen by many observers as challenging the dominance of the Melbourne Club. It is, in the *Age*'s summary,

> a reflection of the great broadening of our business elite, the increasing wealth and influence of our ethnic communities, and the influx of overseas business people, especially into the financial services area, since the deregulation introduced by the Federal Government.

'It's like another Melbourne Club without the restrictions and old world conservatism' remarks one executive, while the Jewish millionaire businessman Dick Pratt is pleased that 'there are no barriers at Carlton except of course you have to be pretty wealthy to pay $1000 each week for the privilege of watching a game of football'.[28]

We now live in a changing international world. In 1988 this was a world in which the Hyde Park Barracks Social History museum was hosting, on Australia Day, a history of Coke exhibition (which left out Pepsi and every other soft drink company),[29] a world in which many retail signs in European cities are in trendy English and Adelaide is considering putting its street signs in the new tourist language, Japanese. It is a world characterised by McDonaldisation, the one hundred restaurants in London and those of Paris, and of the cities of Denmark and Australia. It is a world of the print and satellite media empires of Rupert Murdoch which cover not only the newspapers of the Australian capitals and of New York and London, but, through his Sky Channel, much of Europe; it is a world which John Elliott seeks to Fosterise, using a company which is based on the old Tasmanian, South Australian and Victorian companies of the food processors, IXL, the stock and station agents and wool dealers, Elders, and Carlton and United Breweries. It is a world of international and multi-national companies including the transport empires of Sir Peter Abeles' TNT and of managerial opportunities for middle class women as well as men. In the rapidly expanding area of finance neither class nor education are always essential for those who know how to make bucks in the money market. In this changing world the 1990s might see Paul Keating as Australia's first Yuppie Prime Minister, his Sydney working class origins as much disguised as his French pronunciation.

We live today in the world of the internationalisation of capital, of media and of consumer culture. Yet that old Australian world, not that of egalitarianism and mateship but of the patronage networks and the suburban conventionality of the old middle class and upper middle class, has not entirely departed. In its local environment, the world of class, cities and colonies, has influence yet.

NOTES

1. See Stephen Alomes, *A Nation at Last? The Changing Character of Australian Nationalism 1880-1988*, (Sydney: Angus & Robertson, 1988) chapters 3,7.
2. Max Neutze, 'City, Country, Town: Australian Peculiarities', *Australian Cultural History*, 4 (1985), p. 10
3. John Playford, 'The Adelaide Club and Politics' in Dean Jaensch, ed. *The Flinders History of South Australia: Political History* (Adelaide: Wakefield Press, 1986), p. 289.
4. Michael Cannon, *The Long Last Summer: Australia's Upper Class Before the Great War* (Melbourne: Nelson, 1985), Introduction.
5. *Age*, 8.12.87 (article on Garry Mansfield, *A History of Golf in Victoria*, Melbourne, 1987).
6. Cecil Edwards, *Bruce of Melbourne: Man of Two Worlds* (London: Heinemann,1965)
7. *A Nation at Last?*, chapters 3,7.
8. John McCarty, 'The Seven Colonies of Australasia in 1891', *Tasmanian Historical Research Association P & P*, 29,4 (December 1982), pp. 14-15, 9-10.
9. Hugo Wolfsohn, 'The Ideology Makers' in Henry Mayer (ed), *Australian Politics* (Melbourne: Cheshire, 1966), pp. 76,79-80. Sol Encel, *Equality and Authority: A Study of Class, Status and Power in Australia*, (Melbourne: Cheshire, 1970); Donald Horne, *The Lucky Country* (Melbourne: Penguin, 1964); Craig McGregor, *Profile of Australia* (Melbourne: Penguin, 1968), ch.4.
10. Eric Hobsbawm, 'Mass-Producing Traditions: Europe, 1870-1914' in E.J. Hobsbawm and T.O. Ranger, eds., *The Invention of Tradition* (Cambridge: Cambridge University Press, 1983) especially pp. 291-303; The economic historians P.J. Cain and A.G. Hopkins have also discerned from 1850 to 1945 in Britain the dominance of a Home Counties elite based on 'gentlemanly capitalism', comprising landed money, the City of London and the middle classes. Their description of its social forms and institutions is instantly recognisable to a student of 'Dominion Culture' elites in Australia:

    The values of the elite were shaped by the shared experience of a revitalised public school education, were reinforced by intermarriage and were put on display in 'society' circles in London where a patriotic association with the monarchy could also be proclaimed (P.J. Cain and A.G. Hopkins, 'Gentlemanly Capitalism and British Expansion Overseas II: new imperialism, 1850-1945', *Economic History Review*, XL,I, Feb. 1987, pp. 2-3).

11. Graeme Davison, *The Rise and Fall of Marvellous Melbourne*, (Melbourne: Melbourne University Press, 1979), p. 96; Paul J. Boreham, Alec Pemberton and Paul Wilson, eds., *The Professions in Australia: A Critical Appraisal* (St Lucia, University of Queensland Press, 1976), pp. 44,47.
12. Brian Stoddart, 'Sport' in Jim Davidson (ed.), *The Sydney-Melbourne Book* (Sydney: George Allen & Unwin, 1986) especially pp. 250-254. Elite theory in several of its forms discerns a connection between the elite and the larger middle class which supports it (eg. Mosca, see T.B. Bottomore, *Elites and Society*, (Harmondsworth: Penguin, 1964), p. 13. It also discerns social and political elites which may be distinct or interconnected (Pareto and Mosca, see Bottomore, p. 17). The Gramscian influenced concept of elite social and ideological, and therefore political, hegemony implicit in my analysis differs from the pluralist concept of elites which informs the

data collected in John Higley, Desley Deacon and Don Smart, *Elites in Australia* (London: Routledge and Kegan Paul, 1979).

13. Stephen Alomes, *op. cit.*, pp. 73-81.
14. See Michael Cannon, *op. cit.*, pp. 50-51, 159-162.
15. Stephen Alomes, *op. cit.*, pp. 54-56, 62-66, 89-93.
16. Stephen Alomes, 'Intellectuals as Publicists: 1920s to 1940s' in Brian Head and James Walter, eds., *Intellectual Movements and Australian Society*, (Melbourne: Oxford University Press, 1988). A.F. Davies, 'Intellectuals in Politics', in his *Essays in Political Sociology*, (Melbourne: Cheshire, 1972), p. 29.
17. Dirk van Dissel, 'The Adelaide Gentry, 1850-1920' in Eric Richards, ed., *The Flinders History of South Australia: Social History* (Adelaide: Wakefield Press, 1986), p. 335.
18. van Dissel, *op. cit.*, p. 335. He also notes the move towards establishment religions as Congregationalists became Anglicans as they moved up the social scale.
19. Alomes, *A Nation at Last?*, p. 91.
20. van Dissel, *op. cit.*
21. W.D. Rubinstein, 'Elites in Australian History', 1980 paper. When published in Robert Manne, ed., *The New Conservatism in Australia* (Melbourne: Oxford U.P., 1982), p. 80 the colourful first adjective was omitted.
22. John Playford, *op. cit.*, pp. 289-291.
23. T.H. Irving, 'Class', *Australians: A Historical Dictionary* (Sydney: Fairfax, Syme and Weldon, 1987), p. 78.
24. *Age*, 2.3.1988; Melbourne *Herald*, 'The Who's Who of the Supreme Court' 18.11.1987; Eddy Neumann, *The High Court of Australia: A Collective Portrait 1903-1972* (second edition) (Sydney: Sydney University Department of Government and Public Administration, 1973). pp. 105, 81.
25. *Age*, 2.3.1988, 20.9.1988.
26. 'Who Shapes Melbourne', *Age*, 2 .3.1988.
27. Ruth Ostrow, *The New Boy Network: Taking Over Corporate Australia* (Richmond: Heinemann, 1987).
28. *Age*, 2.3.1988.
29. The Social History museum is part of the entrepreneurial sponsor orientated and postmodernist-loving (but NSW Government) Powerhouse Museum.

LIONEL FROST

Suburbia and Inner Cities

The suburbanization and resulting physical and spatial form of Australian cities is best understood in a broad comparative context. Studies of individual cases, as is the preference of urban history specialists, tend to beg most of the interesting historical questions. In what sense is a city's physical form unique or typical? And what factors contribute to the differences? Such issues are beyond the scope of local studies 'wrapped in a cocoon of uniqueness'.[1] The historian engaged in 'deep' research into a particular place, like the person who lives all his/her life in the one town, often tends to regard local conditions as 'normal', and therefore not requiring explanation. Furthermore, such historians may be unable to detect the absence of events which were common in other places. Comparative work, whereby a number of cities are examined with the intention of identifying more general trends and sorting the causal factors which account for the divergence from or conformity to those trends, remains relatively rare.

In all of Australia's large cities there were powerful forces making for suburbanization. Australia's immigrants, almost solely of British origin, brought with them an overwhelming preference for living in a suburban setting. This Anglo-Saxon desire for privacy, attainable only by living away from the commotion and smells of crowded, rapidly growing urban areas, gained great popularity in the century preceding the First World War. The suburbanite could shield his wife and family from urban disease, crime, and immorality. The ideal suburb was 'a marriage of town and country': tranquil and private, located in districts with pleasant views and fresh air, yet still within a convenient ride or even walk of central city workplaces.[2]

The inhabitants of Australian cities, by and large employed in providing various commercial services for a prosperous export sector, or in supplying the services needed by other urban inhabitants (the 'taking in of each other's washing'), enjoyed for the most part the high average incomes which the cost of suburban living required.[3] N.G. Butlin's index of Australian per capita real consumption from the 1860s shows a sustained increase until the late 1880s. Moreover, the figures in the 1860s are between 50 and 100 per cent higher than those of Britain and the United States.[4] Unlike European and most American cities, there was no large industrial proletariat, and no pool of illiterate former peasants, unable to demand anything but substandard shelter. Furthermore, much of the infrastructure required for suburban development, such as railways and water supply systems, was provided by colonial governments and financed by overseas borrowings.

In terms of culture, economic function, and politics, the major Australian cities were like peas in a pod, but physically there was in the nineteenth century no such thing as 'An Australian City'. Today our major cities are broadly similar, dominated by a vast sprawl of suburbs round a downtown core, but in the nineteenth century they were physically and spatially of two contrasting types. Sydney, Brisbane, and Hobart were compact, land-intensive cities which more closely resembled those of Britain, Europe, and eastern North America, than they did the other Australian cities. Melbourne, Adelaide, and Perth were of far lower density, with sprawling suburbs like those of the American West.[5] This paper briefly sketches the characteristics of the two sets of cities, and offers an explanation for the bifurcation.

Despite the very marked nineteenth-century expansion of the suburban edge of English and North American cities, the majority of the urban population lived within walking distance or a short tram ride of the central business district and other places of employment. Roughly equivalent to what is known in Australia as the 'inner city', these districts offered shelter which was at best compact, and at worst, abominably overcrowded and dirty. In American cities, 'streetcar suburbs' typically consisted of around 10 houses per acre, either two- or three-storey terraces or detached cottages, each perhaps housing two or three families. Terrace houses, as many as 60 or more per acre, were the norm in English cities. They were usually smaller than their American counterparts, but more likely to be occupied by a single family. Some of these housing districts had been built specifically for working-class occupation, others were former low-density suburbs which the middle classes had built and since abandoned. These slabs of closely-packed housing, with their invariably inadequate water supply and sewerage systems, offered little, if any respite from the sounds and smells of urban life. High rates of population growth could easily turn them into slums, by making it profitable for owners and tenants to subdivide or sublet property.

The true suburbs, usually at the very edge of the metropolis, were invariably accessible only to upper-income groups. Middle-class suburbia, after all, was what Fishman calls a 'bourgeois utopia', deliberately excluding worker housing (except that required by local service sector workers), as well as factories and other sources of lower-class employment.[6]

Sydney was the Australian city in which English visitors felt most at home. It reminded H.M. Franklyn of Bristol, Exeter, Southampton, and 'here and there' of Genoa.[7] 'Everything in Sydney', observed the journalist John Stanley James ('The Vagabond'), was 'built after the English fashion'.[8] The city and surrounding districts were dominated by terrace houses, while clusters of poor quality, overcrowded dwellings were tucked away in courts and alleys in or near the city core.

Sydney was a microcosm of the physical pattern of growth exhibited in high-density nineteenth-century cities. As the metropolitan population climbed from 138,000 to 400,000 between 1871 and 1891, the physical fabric of the districts immediately beyond the core degenerated as a growing number of workers crowded into the existing housing stock. The shortfall of new housing behind population growth in Sydney during the last two decades of the century was of similar magnitude to that of high-density North American cities such as Chicago, Boston, Cleveland, and Toronto. In a study of Sydney aptly titled *Rising Damp*, Shirley Fitzgerald writes that the 1870s and 1880s 'witnessed the steady deterioration of the physical environment as rapid urban growth proceeded without adequate provision of the amenities likely to preserve the quality of living and the basic health of the citizens'.[9] This was not, of course, a unique phenomenon. Fitzgerald's conclusion might easily be applied to, say, Liverpool, Glasgow, Berlin, Cincinnati, or in fact any number of British, European, and American cities which had faced the stress of surging population growth.

Part of the problem lay with the city's location on one of the numerous small, hilly peninsulas which jutted into the magnificent harbour at Port Jackson. Aesthetically, this was one of the world's great city sites, but one which gave little elbow room for the dockside, commercial, manufacturing, and residential areas of what was to become a major metropolis. Brisbane was similarly hemmed in by a tight bend in the wide Brisbane River, while Hobart was so close to its port 'that ships seem to be anchored in the streets'.[10]

As Sydney's public transport system developed, a number of problems made access to the suburban edge costly and difficult, thereby retarding the provision of new and spacious housing. The expense and inconvenience of omnibuses and ferries confined their usage to the upper middle classes. The New South Wales Parliament, dominated by rural interests, under-invested in Sydney's infrastructure. There was until 1906 no railway terminus convenient to the central business district. A network of tramways was built but did not reach the narrow, crooked, and traffic-choked central city.

The majority of the population – including many well-paid workers – were as a result forced to live within walking distance of their place of employment. The competition for shelter in these inner city areas naturally forced rents up: in the district above Sydney Cove known as The Rocks, rents were often twice as high as for comparable suburban housing.[11] High rents forced those of limited or precarious means to sublet their dwellings or take in lodgers, or accept defective shelter, lacking adequate space or drainage. The physical fabric of districts which had initially housed a mixture of middle- and working-class inhabitants, such as Woolloomooloo, Darlinghurst, and The Rocks, had by 1890 clearly declined. Here, in the low-lying areas near sewer and drainage outlets, were some of the developed world's most dreadful slums.[12]

In the new middle-class suburbs within a reasonable omnibus ride of the city, such as Paddington, landowners could offer narrow lots suitable for only terrace houses, and still find buyers.[13] By 1881 some 83 per cent of the population lived in the central slums and adjoining terrace house suburbs that included Balmain, Leichardt, Annandale, Glebe, Newtown, Redfern, Erskineville, and Paddington, most of them within a two mile radius. For almost all of nineteenth-century Sydney's inhabitants, 'home' was a terrace house not too far from Sydney Cove.

By contrast, Melbourne, Adelaide, and Perth exemplified a new configuration of city growth, which resulted as settlement was pushed westward across the plains and prairies of North America, and spread over the arable portions of Australia and New Zealand, mainly in the second half of the nineteenth century. The new cities, instead of developing physically as virtually transplanted European cities, took on a distinct and novel urban form. They were of arrestingly low density, and coped with very rapid rates of population growth by spreading outwards through the replication of suburbs of detached, single-family houses. In so doing they largely avoided urban congestion and its problems. The present writer has elsewhere dubbed this major region of cities the 'New Urban Frontier'.[14]

The cities of the New Urban Frontier accommodated bursts of substantial population growth while developing only minor slum districts. What cities such as Los Angeles, Denver, Vancouver, Auckland, and Adelaide had in common was that the opportunities they offered for suburbanization spread from the elite to the lower ranks at an extraordinarily rapid rate, with the central business district being surrounded by low-density suburbs for both the working and middle classes. Even poorly-drained, innately undesirable inner city areas, such as Collingwood in Melbourne, maintained their low-density character, as the section of the population unable to take up better quality dwellings elsewhere was intrinsically small. Furthermore, the accessibility of distant suburban subdivisions meant that middle-class suburbs close to the city centre, such as North Adelaide and Norwood, did not crumble into slums under the pressure of population growth.

In 1890 Melbourne and Sydney were of roughly similar population, but the metropolitan area of Sydney, as defined by the New South Wales Government Statistician, covered barely half that of Melbourne. In this respect, Sydney was more closely analogous to compact English

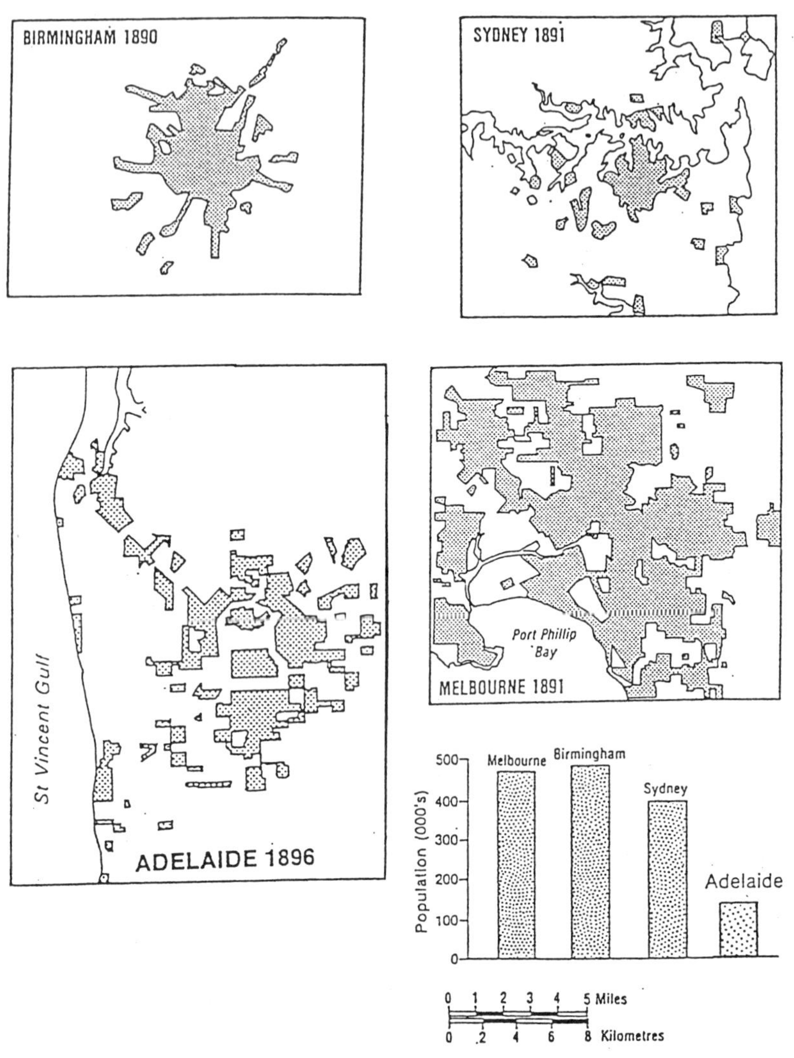

Fig. 1. Built-up area of Melbourne, Sydney, Adelaide, and Birmingham. (Sources: Graeme Davison, *The Rise and Fall of Marvellous Melbourne* (Melbourne, 1978), 1 E.C. Fry, 'The Growth of Sydney', in J.W. McCarty and C.B. Schedvin (eds.), *Australian Capi Cities: Historical Essays* (sydney, 1978), 34; Michael Williams, The *Making of the South Australi Landscape* (London, 1974), 418; Peter Hall *et al.*, The *Containment of Urban England* (Londo 1973), 81.)

cities such as Birmingham. Adelaide sprawled almost as far as Melbourne, despite being far less populous. The South Australian capital was a remarkably out-sized city, which in terms of geographical setting and physical form resembled nothing so much as pre-automobile Los Angeles.[15]

Sydney's most densely populated municipality in 1890 had an average population density of 79 persons per acre; Melbourne's averaged only 37. Half of the population of metropolitan Sydney lived in municipalities where densities averaged over 30 per acre, compared to only 14 per cent in Melbourne, and none in Adelaide and Perth, where the peak density was a mere 10 per acre.[16] One visitor to Sydney observed that while it 'curls in upon itself; Melbourne grows outward'.[17] 'Sydney, with all its natural beauty, is huddled up and dirty', Melbourne's *Daily Telegraph* told its readers in 1888. 'Its people are satisfied to live in crowded streets, ... [whereas] Melbourne reaches out like an octopus.'[18]

In Melbourne, Adelaide, and Perth the basic residential unit was the detached, single-storey dwelling, occupied by a single family and set on a fairly large lot. The suburbs where the bulk of the population lived usually developed gradually. Open spaces and unsold house lots were abundant. Worker housing, despite its sheer drabness, was relatively spacious and private. With such a predominance of large lots, the housing stock was spared the shock of major fire damage which was a common feature of premodern and some industrial cities.[19] This fire safety permitted the construction of simple wooden dwellings, being made progressively cheaper by new building methods and lower-cost materials. Single-storey houses generally do not require extra space and building materials for stairs, and can be more easily built with less substantial foundations that multi-storey dwellings. The cost advantage of building single-storey cottages in wood was substantial, provided land was sufficiently cheap to encourage the purchase of sites large enough for such housing. By the 1890s a four-roomed house was around 50 per cent dearer in brick terrace Sydney than in weatherboard cottage Melbourne.[20] Large lots with cesspits at the rear could also provide a cheap and fairly adequate solution to the public health problems of city growth, provided adequate supplies of piped water were available. The inhabitants of the New Frontier cities in general eschewed the convenience and social liveliness of more compact cities for the privacy and conformity of suburban life.

What permitted the building of these unusually sprawling cities? Such suburbanization *en masse* required two conditions to be met: first, high average incomes were needed to meet the heavy capital requirements of suburbia; and second, easy access to distant suburban subdivisions depended on the efficiency of the public transport system. Unless *both* these requirements were met, suburbanization would be greatly retarded. Thus in high-income cities such as Sydney, unsatisfactory public transport arrangements forced even well-paid workers to reside in or near the city core. Although many North American cities built superb mass transit systems, low incomes condemned the bulk of the population to ramshackle inner city housing.

A common feature of Australia's New Frontier cities is that their founders sited them some distance – up to 10 miles – from their deep-water harbour. This made early rail links between port and city a virtual necessity. City layouts provided ample space for rail termini close to the central business district, while the generally wide streets facilitated the introduction and operation of tramways. Melbourne, Adelaide, and Perth possessed a solid foundation for a comprehensive public transport network well before entering their boom period of population growth. The three cities were therefore 'born decentralized'.

As Melbourne's population boomed in the 1880s and homesites close to the city centre became more scarce, the public transport system was easily and effectively extended to provide access to cheap peripheral land. The Victorian Parliament extended rail lines to distant suburban tracts, well in advance of population.[21] A similar situation prevailed in Adelaide in the 1870s, and Perth in the 1890s. Horse-drawn trams to Adelaide's south and east, together with the railway to Port Adelaide, increased building activity in older districts and turned villages into thriving suburbs. The railway to Fremantle provided the key corridor of Perth's suburban expansion.

The physical and environmental contrast between the private, suburban cities of Melbourne, Adelaide, and Perth, and the more compact cities of Sydney, Brisbane, and Hobart has been generally overlooked by historians because of their typical focus on a particular case. Such broad patterns of city growth cannot be detected by the *ad infinitum* replication of close-up studies. Comparative analysis casts new light on the burgeoning literature dealing with Australia's major cities. Much of the revisionist literature which seeks to replace the conventional optimistic picture of nineteenth-century Australian affluence with a more pessimistic view of the quality of urban life comes from Sydney.[22] The scholarly histories of Melbourne are in general more optimistic.[23] These differing interpretations may perhaps be attributed to the historians' respective ideological biases, but here this seems an unconvincing explanation. Rather, it seems the specialist urban historians of Sydney and Melbourne have come to different conclusions because the physical environment of the two cities was so dissimilar.

NOTES

1. Oliver Knight, 'Towards an Understanding of the Western Town', *Western Historical Quarterly*, 4 (1973), p. 27.

2. See Robert Fishman, *Bourgeois Utopias: The Rise and Fall of Suburbia* (New York: Basic Books, 1987), passim. For a survey of the American experience, see Kenneth T. Jackson, *Crabgrass Frontier: The Suburbanization of the United States* (New York: Oxford U.P., 1985).
3. These costs are heavy both for the individual in terms of the extra land, building materials, and commuting costs required, and for society in terms of the heavy infrastructural requirement of providing roads, pipes, wires, and other services to far-flung homesites.
4. N.G. Butlin, 'Long-run Trends in Australian Per Capita Consumption', in K.J. Hancock (ed), *The National Income and Social Welfare* (Melbourne; Cheshire, 1965), 8.
5. This distinction is made in Lionel Frost, *The New Urban Frontier: Urbanisation and City-Building in Australasia and the American West* (Sydney: New South Wales U.P., 1991).
6. Fishman, *Bourgeois Utopias*, passim.
7. H.M. Franklyn, *A Glance at Australia* in 1880 (Melbourne: Victorian Review Publishing Co., 1881), p. 30.
8. John Stanley James, *The Vagabond Papers*, Abridged edn., ed. M. Cannon. (Melbourne: Melbourne U.P., 1877-8), p. 56.
9. Shirley Fitzgerald, *Rising Damp: Sydney 1870-90* (Melbourne: Oxford U.P., 1987), p. 226.
10. Donald Horne, *The Lucky Country* (Ringwood, Vic.: Penguin, 1964), p. 54.
11. Graeme Davison, 'The Capital Cities', in G. Davison, J.W. McCarty, and A. McLeary (eds.), *Australians 1888* (Broadway, N.S.W.: Fairfax, Syme, and Weldon Associates, 1987), p. 203.
12. See for example Max Kelly, 'Picturesque and Pestilential: The Sydney Slum Observed 1860-1900', in M. Kelly (ed.), *Nineteenth Century Sydney: Essays in Urban History* (Sydney: Sydney U.P., 1978).
13. See Max Kelly, *Paddock Full of Houses: Paddington 1840-1890* (Sydney: Doak Press, 1978), passim.
14. Frost, *The New Urban Frontier.*
15. See the maps in Frost, *The New Urban Frontier*, p. 25, p. 27.
16. Data calculated from Statistical Registers.
17. Quoted by Davison, 'The Capital Cities', p. 220
18. *Daily Telegraph* (Melbourne), 26 November 1888.
19. L.E. Frost and E.L. Jones, 'The Fire Gap and the Greater Durability of Nineteenth-Century Cities', *Planning Perspectives*, 4 (1989), pp. 333-47.
20. R.V. Jackson, 'Owner-Occupation of Houses in Sydney, 1871 to 1891', *Australian Economic History Review*, 14 (1974), pp. 145-6.
21. See Graeme Davison, *The Rise and Fall of Marvellous Melbourne* (Melbourne: Melbourne U.P., 1978), Ch. 7.
22. See for example Fitzgerald, *Rising Damp*; Kelly, 'Picturesque and Pestilential'. See also the review of literature in Max Kelly, 'Nineteenth Century Sydney: "Beautiful Certainly; Not Bountiful"', in J. Davidson, (ed.), *The Sydney-Melbourne Book* (Sydney: Allen & Unain, 1986).
23. See for example Davison, *Marvellous Melbourne*; Tony Dingle, *The Victorians: Settling* (McMahons Point: Fairfax, Syme, and Weldon Associates, 1984), Ch. 8; John Lack, 'Footscray: An Industrial Suburban Community' (Ph.D. Thesis, Monash University, 1976).

RENATE HOWE

Far from a Worker's Paradise; Social and Economic Change in Melbourne's Inner Suburbs 1890s - 1940s

Melbourne's reputation is that of the suburban city par excellence. That reputation was reinforced in the 1970s in widely read books by historians Graeme Davison, *The Rise and Fall of 'Marvellous Melbourne'*, and Hugh Stretton, *Ideas for Australian Cities*, which emphasised the popularity and attraction of Melbourne's suburbs. Responding to the criticisms of writers such as Robin Boyd that Melbourne's suburbs were sterile, soulless environments, Davison and Stretton emphasised the creativity of the suburban environment, reminding readers that Melbournians had always voted with their feet in showing an overwhelming preference for suburban living. However, Davison acknowledged that while the suburban ethos was widely shared attainment of the suburban ideal depended on the fulfillment of a number of material conditions 'notably a reasonably spacious dwelling, access to the natural refreshment of a secluded garden setting, the security of home ownership and an income sufficient to support a family with some degree of comfort and leisure'.[1] This paper will argue that for a significant proportion of Melbourne's residents, the suburban ideal was impossible to attain no matter how much they might desire it. The reality of their life and labour raises questions about claims of the high standard of living of the working classes and the egalitarianism of Australian society on which the advantages of the new world cities over those of the old fundamentally rested.

From 1890 to 1940 Melbourne can be divided into three sectors – the villa suburbs to the south and east, the working family suburbs to the north and west and the inner suburbs circling the central city area. Of these three sectors the residents of the villa suburbs came closest to attaining the material pre-conditions for the suburban ideal as spelt out by Davison. Although the villa and the working family suburbs had the largest increases in population in the period of the 1880s and 90s more people lived in the inner suburbs, than in either of the other sectors. Assigning local government areas to the three sectors of the city from

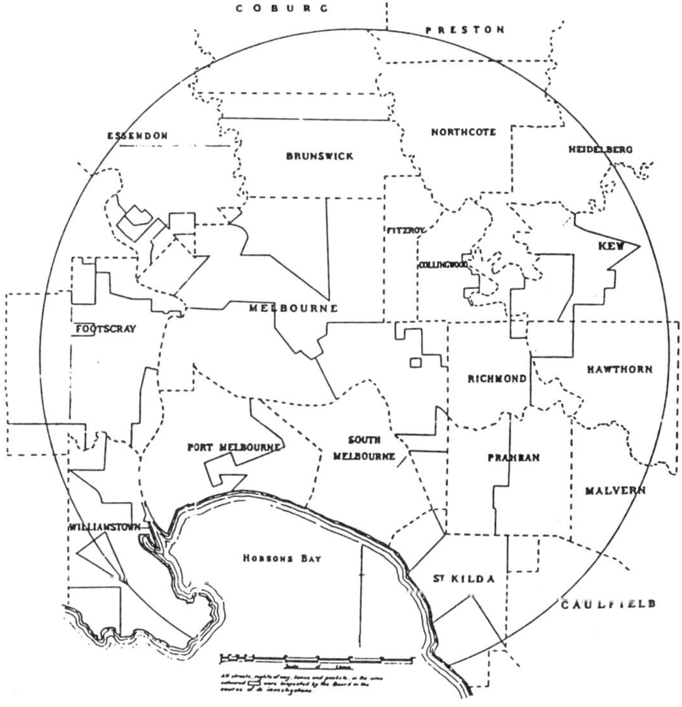

Fig. 1. Map of Melbourne within 5-mile radius of city centre. Each street, right-of-way, lane and pocket in the shaded areas was inspected by HISAB in the course of its investigations. (*First Report HISAB* 1937).

population numbers provided for 1911 in the *Commonwealth Year Book,* approximately 307,561 residents of Melbourne lived in the inner city, 126,955 in the working family suburbs and 155,951 in the villa-suburbs.[2] Over half of Melbourne's population lived in the inner suburbs and many more travelled to the inner suburbs to work. In terms of the number of residents, in terms of their economic importance to the metropolis and in terms of their political significance, the inner suburbs have been central to Melbourne's history. Of the three sectors of the city, the inner suburban sector has the most complex history, undergoing significant social and economic changes in the fifty year period. The extent of the differences between inner suburbs was often overlooked after the expansion of industry in the 1880s filled in the areas of open space that had separated the early towns. The inner suburban sector of the city came to be viewed as an undifferentiated industrial zone rather than as a circle of distinctive, inter-related communities. Yet an understanding of the distinctiveness of inner suburbs is central to an understanding of class relations in Melbourne; a distinctiveness that resulted from differing social and economic origins reinforced by each suburb's status as a separate local government area. Although North Melbourne, Flemington and Kensington were amalgamated with the Melbourne City Council in 1904, all other suburbs successfully resisted attempts to amalgamate municipalities including the latest initiatives of the Victorian government in 1986.

As the period of early development has been so significant it is instructive to examine some of these social and economic differences from census material for 1857 and 1861 for the suburbs included in this study – Fitzroy, Collingwood, Flemington and Kensington, North Melbourne, Port Melbourne, South Melbourne and Richmond.

Table 1 - Percentage of workforce in selected occupational categories, 1857.[3]

	Professions/ Merchants	Clerk/Shop Assistants	Labourers
Fitzroy	0.3	8.3	4.8
Collingwood	2.9	5.0	8.9
North Melbourne	3.3	6.9	9.6
Port Melbourne	2.3	3.2	13.3
Richmond	4.6	7.2	8.4
South Melbourne	3.3	7.9	12.0

Source: Census of Victoria 1857.

Table 1 indicates that there was a range of occupations in each suburb but within this range significant differences have emerged as early as the first reliable Victorian Census of 1857. The close proximity of Fitzroy to the central area of Melbourne and the suburb's own vigorous commercial life is indicated in the higher proportion of its workforce in the professions/merchants and clerks/shop assistants categories compared with other inner suburbs. Fitzroy also has the smallest proportion of labourers, (4.8%) reflecting the low demand for unskilled labour in the suburb. The highest percentages of labourers (13.3% and 12%) live in South and Port Melbourne because of their proximity to the wharves. In Collingwood, labourers employed in the noxious industries along the river outnumber those in the other two occupational categories. Richmond has the most evenly balanced population profile, sharing characteristics with Collingwood in the number of unskilled workers employed in noxious industries and of Fitzroy in attracting merchants, professionals and clerks because of proximity to the city.

Related to this occupational difference between suburbs was the differences in ethnic background evident in Table 2.

Table 2 - Percentage of population by birthplace, 1861.

	England	Ireland	Scotland	Wales	Native Born	Other
Fitzroy	41	14	11	1	30	3
Collingwood	42	12	10	1	31	5
Flem./Kens.	32	19	12	1	35	
North Melb.	29	22	15	1	31	2
Melbourne	32	23	11	1	26	7
Port Melb.	42	14	9	1	27	7
South Melb.	38	16	10	1	30	5
Richmond	42	15	7	1	32	3

Source: Census of Victoria 1861.

The Irish-born are most evident in the northern inner suburbs of North Melbourne and Flemington/Kensington. North Melbourne and South Melbourne were popular suburbs for the ubiquitous Scottish-born engineers, working in the maritime industries of South Melbourne and the engineering workshops of North Melbourne. Fitzroy, Collingwood and especially Port Melbourne had a population of predominantly English--born background, although as Table 3 suggests there were differences in the social background of the English-born between these suburbs. Fitzroy and Collingwood have more Wesleyan Methodists than Port Melbourne while Fitzroy's 10 per cent of 'Other Protestants' were adherents of minor

Methodist and Baptist churches, reinforcing the evidence in Table 1 of the predominance in Fitzroy of skilled workers, small businessman, clerks and shopkeepers.

Table 3 - Percentages of Denominations, 1861.

	C of E	Presby.	Wes. Meth.	Other Prot.	R.C.	Jews	Other
Fitzroy	43	15	12	10	14	2	4
Collingwood	47	14	10	5	18	0	6
Flem./Kens.	49	20	6	3	20	0	2
North Melb.	37	20	8	5	28	0	2
Melbourne	38	14	5	7	29	3	4
Port Melb.	57	12	7	5	18	0	1
South Melb.	42	21	6	6	19	0	6
Richmond	51	10	6	10	19	0	4

Source: Census of Victoria 1861.

The Irish were the most visible ethnic group in inner suburban Melbourne. Compared with American cities of this period there was no significant migration from Scandinavia and Germany to Melbourne. By the turn of the century the Irish and the children of Irish born parents were 34 percent in North Melbourne and 25.8 per cent in Richmond, comparable proportions to the influential Irish enclaves of some American cities.[4]

The ethnic background of early residents influenced the later development of the suburbs. In Fitzroy the existence of a Wesleyan congregation, chapel and school attracted returning gold diggers with a Wesleyan background to that suburb, while the Irish migrants of the 1860s settled in areas where not only unskilled work but also Catholic churches and schools were located. Bernard Barrett, in a study of the early development of Collingwood, argues that the poorest gold rush immigrants were attracted because the area was outside the Melbourne City Council building code enabling the construction of makeshift dwellings. He suggests that it was availability of an unskilled residential labour force that first attracted industry to Collingwood and questions historical interpretations of Melbourne's inner suburbs as a ring of once affluent areas which declined when their socially mobile residents moved to the villa and working family suburbs after the 1890s. Collingwood was born poor and remained poor.[5]

The different economic and social structure of inner suburbs meant differences in living and working conditions, class relations and the ability to achieve the suburban ideal. This is evident in a brief case study of

Fitzroy focussing on the years after the depressions of the 1890s and 1930s, which devastated the inner suburban sector.

In the 1880s, the period of 'Marvellous Melbourne' Fitzroy along with other inner suburbs, experienced considerable residential, commercial and industrial development. Initially, it seemed that these changes would not effect the social and political consensus, the co-operative social relations, that had been characteristic of Fitzroy's early development under the paternalistic leadership of the suburb's Wesleyan elite. Although industries and commercial establishments expanded introducing new work practices and machinery, capital and management was still largely drawn from within the suburb and the scale of the re-developed industries was not large. For instance, J.G. Porta established a small factory making bellows in the 1860s.[6]

In the 1880s his son took over the management and re-built 'especially designed' premises measuring 33′ by 120′ on the George Street site. The latest machinery and appliances were installed, the firm employing nine to ten workers. When Mr. T. Randell, who in 1867 had established the Victorian Steam Washboard works in Rose Street, died, two employees, William and Harry Western, took over as partners. Enterprisingly they added the manufacture of 'American thermometers' to that of knife boards and washboards in the 66′ by 130′ factory employing five in 1886.

The central area of Fitzroy became the focus for carriage-building and medium-sized machine works. William Dalrymple's carriage works at the corner of Fitzroy and Westgarth Streets employed 18-25 workers, in a building 66′ by 100′. W. and A. Powell began their carriage works with four workers in 1884. By 1902 they employed 40 and had built new works covering one and a half acres. Grayson and Sons at the corner of Johnston and Young Streets had commenced in 1868 and moved to its new premises (65′ by 100′) in 1887. The firm employed nine workers and manufactured a steam engine of its own invention.

The boot and shoe factories were larger, and employed more unskilled workers including large numbers of young women. Johannes Yager who had established a factory in 1872 had by the 1880s installed gas power and the latest machinery. Yager employed 150 workers in his two storey Kerr Street factory. His former partner, Robert Hurst built a new two storey factory on the Heidelberg Road, North Fitzroy, in 1884 employing 100. The Acme Shirt Company in Victoria Street, prided itself on having put the sweater out of work by establishing a factory 'upon the best possible lines, with every facility for the comfort and convenience of the worker'. Located in a three-storey building, the factory employed around 220 workers in the 1890s, a high proportion of them women.

Brunswick street, Fitzroy's 'High Street', also changed in the 1880s as the small shop-keeper gave way to larger commercial firms. By 1890 Moran and Cato's grocery business had 34 suburban branches and had moved into importing and manufacturing. At the new headquarters on the corner of Victoria and Brunswick Street, a large staff, many of them women, were employed to manufacture, pack, bottle and label products for the suburban grocery stores. The firm continued to be owned and managed by the families who had started the first grocery shop.

The increased demand for unskilled labour in Fitzroy as a result of such changes was largely met by a young female labour force. There was a loss of skilled and semi-skilled workers moving to the working family suburbs to the north and west in the last two decades of the nineteenth century.[7] However, the expansion of industry in Fitzroy did not result in the class tensions of some other inner suburbs. There was not the insecurity of large-scale casual employment as in South, West, North and Port Melbourne around waterfront and railyards. The largest Fitzroy factories had far fewer workers than the 500 plus employed in many South and North Melbourne engineering factories. Fitzroy had neither the extensive sweating associated with the clothing industry in Melbourne nor the identification with one industry as had the boot and shoe industry with Collingwood.

The extent of interaction between social classes is evident in a comparison of Fitzroy with Richmond. Janet McCalman's history of Richmond underlines the tension between the Protestant and Roman Catholic community which dominated that suburb's history.[8] McCalman has also identified the division between those casually employed and those in regular employment – the regular and respectable versus the casual and rough – as one of the most distinguishing features of Richmond's social life. Fitzroy, which had neither a large Roman Catholic community nor a large casual labour force largely avoided sharp divisions in the late nineteenth century.

It was a measure of Fitzroy's consensus that the suburb returned Liberal protectionist candidates to the Victorian Parliament, a platform in tune with the social ethos and economic advantage of Fitzroy's manufacturers and workforce. In 1892 a Fitzroy branch of the new Progressive Political League [PPL] was formed, the forerunner of the Australian Labour Party. As in other inner suburbs, the League endorsed two candidates to oppose Fitzroy's long standing Parliamentary members – Albert Tucker and Robert Best in the election of that year. After an acrimonious election, Best and Tucker were returned; as the local Fitzroy paper noted 'the great bulk of the citizens of Fitzroy ... do not want to set up class distinctions here.'[9] It was another ten years before the first PPL candidate, J.W. Billson, was successful with the Fitzroy electorate.

The different nature of class relations in Fitzroy compared with other inner suburbs is reflected in this delay in electing a labour member to the Victorian Parliament. Richmond and Collingwood had elected workingmen as members before the 1892 election and members of the North Melbourne PPL branch had contested the 1886 election. After the election of 1892, Fitzroy and Port Melbourne were the only inner suburbs not to be represented by a PPL member and Port Melbourne elected a PPL member at the next election in 1894. Fitzroy's record in local government is even more distinctive. In neighbouring, Richmond and Collingwood the 'Wren machine' largely based on those suburbs with substantial Irish populations, was well entrenched by the turn of the century, while Richmond elected a Labour Mayor in 1913. The base of the Wren machine was in the suburbs of Collingwood, Richmond and Carlton, leap frogging Fitzroy where it had only a marginal influence.[10]

Part of the explanation for this political distinctiveness is the increasingly depressed and demoralised nature of Fitzroy's social development after the First World War. In this period it was fragmentation rather than consensus which came to distinguish social and economic relations in the suburb. The suburb emerged from the depression of the thirties with bitter memories of poverty and evictions, a run-down housing stock and an expanded industrial base. While many factories remained small others had expanded into large manufacturing establishments employing an unskilled workforce. In Central Ward, MacRobertson's confectionery factory had spread over an acre of former residential development and was known as the Great White City.

In 1939 Fitzroy was the smallest and most densely populated suburb in Victoria housing a population of 30,650 on 923 acres, an average of 33.2 persons to the acre; the density for Melbourne as a whole was 5 persons to the acre.

The Census statistic underestimates the extent of overcrowding as most of Fitzroy's population was resident in the East and West Wards. This overcrowding was made worse in the initial stages of the war as the Exhibition Building was used for housing American soldiers and airforcemen while every available room in Fitzroy was taken over by servicemen.

Where Fitzroy had been among the elite among the inner suburbs of the nineteenth century, because of the number of houses with more than six rooms (17% in 1881 compared with 6% in Collingwood), in the 1930s and 40s these larger houses located in the older part of the suburb were subdivided into makeshift flats or became boarding houses contributing to Fitzroy's attraction for the poorest social groups.

Families who had depended on sustenance (the Victorian version of the dole) since the depression crowded into the houses. There was a large proportion of single parent families as men left to fight in the war. Rural aboriginals who moved to Melbourne to work in defence industries during the war were also attracted by the rooming-house accommodation. By 1949 approximately 300 aboriginals were living in Fitzroy terraces in George, little George, Gertrude and Gore Street. The availability of large cheap houses in Fitzroy also attracted young single males mainly from Italy and Greece, the forerunners of Melbourne's large post-war migration. The men were shift workers, sharing a bed with a companion who worked an earlier or later shift. Largely unskilled workers they worked in manufacturing industry, transport, or as outdoor labourers.[11]

These disparate networks contributed to the lack of political clout of the labour movement in Fitzroy. Their presence was reflected in the predominance of tenants, unskilled workers, high rents, overcrowding, dilapidated dwellings and poor services, especially in East and Central Wards revealed in the Fitzroy interviews in a Metropolitan Survey conducted between September 1941 and January 1943 by Professor W. Prest of the Commerce Faculty at Melbourne University. Comments marked on records of Fitzroy interviews include 'renovation badly needed'. 'rain-through ceiling, w.c. not functioning', 'house is deplorable'. One house in Gore Street sub-let to an aboriginal family is described as in a 'bad state ... damp and bug-infested ... in last rain, water came over ground through passage into bedroom. Water near door was electrically charged.' At 72 Kerr Street the interviewer drew a diagram to show how five adults and their children lived in four small rooms.[12]

The social and economic changes of the inter-war period in Fitzroy demonstrate that the increasingly unskilled and causal labour force could not attain the material requirements for the suburban lifestyle as spelt out by Davison; the reasonably spacious dwelling, access to garden space, home ownership and a sufficient income to support a family with some degree of comfort and leisure. Other pockets of Melbourne's inner suburbs were similarly disadvantaged. A survey conducted by the Housing Investigation and Slum Abolition Board in 1937 showed that all inner suburbs had substantial pockets of appalling poverty and living conditions similar to those outlined in the case study of Fitzroy.[13] The HISAB commissioned an external survey of 85,779 dwellings in a five mile radius of the GPO (see Map) and on the basis of this external assessment 7,330 houses were identified as being in a sufficiently dilapidated condition to warrant a special internal survey and social census. Most of these houses were located in the inner suburban sector of the city and the working people's suburbs, suggesting that not all of those who had moved to this sector from the inner suburbs had necessarily moved significantly closer to the suburban ideal. Nearly all the houses surveyed had leaking roots, 32 percent had been built on the ground and lacked ventilation, 27 per cent of houses had no electricity or gas, 87 per cent of the houses were without kitchen sinks, 32 per cent without bathrooms and 51 per cent without washhouses. The social census of residents revealed that compared with residents in the villa suburbs there were considerably higher rates of juvenile delinquency infectious diseases and infant mortality. The Board's Report concluded that "the slum problem is largely a problem of poverty". Few houses (8.5 per cent) were owner occupied and 64.7 per cent of the male residents were casual and unskilled workers while the average family income was well below the basic wage. The Report concluded that this group could only achieve the suburban

Fig. 2. Photograph from Housing Investigation and Slum Abolition Board Report, 1936-37 showing industrial and residential development in inner suburbian Melbourne.

life-style through rental subsidies and housing provided by the state and recommended the establishment of a state housing authority.

The conditions outlined by the HISAB Report were the culmination of a long period of social and economic change in Melbourne's inner suburbs and effected a substantial proportion of the city's population over fifty years. Nor were such conditions confined to Melbourne. In her study of Sydney from 1870-90, Shirley Fitzgerald reaches similar conclusions for this earlier period in relation to the extent of low incomes, low home ownership rates, poor health, a polluted environment and restricted opportunities for mobility in jobs or housing.

> ... it cannot be denied that the idea of the detached house, with garden, in the suburbs, was the goal of many people, and important in the imagery of what constituted the good life in Sydney... The ubiquitous terrace house, was both symbolic of the rift between dream and reality, and in real terms generated health problems associated with close living.[14]

The conclusion of her book, *Rising Damp* questions the 'conventional wisdom' that labour was in demand and wages high in Australian colonial cities.

Sydney had a larger casual labour force than Melbourne and a larger proportion of its population living in inner city areas. In both cities the residents of these areas, especially the unskilled, casually employed and women workers, lived and worked in conditions remarkably similar to their counterparts in the old world. It would seem that a substantial proportion of the population of Australia's two largest cities could not attain the material conditions necessary for the suburban life style. If Melbournians voted with their feet for life in the suburbs, their steps were directed by social class while a sizeable proportion were left marching on the spot.

Fig. 3. Fitzroy from the Town Hall, c. 1910.

NOTES

1. Graeme Davison, *The Rise and Fall of 'Marvellous Melbourne'* (Melbourne: Melbourne University Press, 1978); Hugh Stretton, *Ideas for Australian Cities* (Melbourne: Georgian House, 1970).
2. *Official Year Book of the Commonwealth of Australia, 1901-1919*, 'Population of Principal Local Government Areas in the Commonwealth 3rd April 1911', pp. 114-15.
3. Tables 1, 2 and 3 draw on information in Lesley Fricker, 'Aspects of Melbourne's Nineteenth Century Urbanisation process', Ph.D, Melbourne University, 1978, pp. 395, 428. In Table 1, statistics on Flemington/Kensington could not be distinguished in the census data.
4. Sue Coffey, 'Hotham Ethnic group and class structure, 1855-1890, Honours thesis, Department of History, University of Melbourne, 1973.
5. Bernard Barrett, *The Inner Suburbs* (Melbourne: Melbourne University Press, 1971).
6. Information on factories from Alexander Sutherland, *Victoria and its Metropolis* (Melbourne, 1888) and *Cyclopaedia of Victoria* (Melbourne, 1902).
7. Lesley Fricker, 'Aspects of Melbourne's Nineteenth Century Urbanisation Process'.
8. Janet McCalman, *Struggletown; Public. and Private Life in Richmond, 1900-1965* (Melbourne, 1984).
9. Alan Jordan, 'Fitzroy in the Grim Nineties', November, 1971. Typescript, Fitzroy Public Library, pp. 43-46.
10. The most comprehensive account of the Wren machine and its operations in inner city Melbourne can be found in Frank Hardy's novel, *Power Without Glory*.
11. A fuller account of these groups can be found in my chapter 'Together but Different; A Study of Communities', in *Fitzroy: Melbourne's First Suburb* (Melbourne: Hyland House, 1989).
12. Metropolitan Social Survey, September 1941 - January 1943, University of Melbourne Archives.
13. Victoria, *First Report. Housing Investigation and Slum Abolition Board*, 1937.
14. Shirley Fitzgerald, *Rising Damp, Sydney 1870-90*, (Melbourne: Oxford University Press, 1986), p. 227.

SHURLEE L. SWAIN

Besmirching Our Reputation

– a study of the interaction between sectarianism and charity in the provincial city of Geelong, Victoria

As Michael Hogan notes in *The Sectarian Strand*, ethnic, class and sectarian identifications were so intertwined in the early history of white settlement in Australia that their influences are difficult to unravel.[1] In Geelong, the second major point of settlement in Victoria, sectarianism gained the upper hand, dividing the town into two separate worlds, the barriers between which were not to be broken down for over one hundred years.

Charity has long been recognised as an exercise in power as well as benevolence. The notion of the rich using their wealth to control the behaviour of the poor is not new but in nineteenth century Geelong charity also became a means by which the Protestant establishment was able to exercise control over the predominantly Catholic poor. By continuing to exclude influential Catholics from the committees which controlled the major charities in the town Protestants were able to keep sectarianism alive until the late 1950s.

Geelong was not unique in excluding Catholics from participation in its so-called non-sectarian Christian charities. In Melbourne the Catholic press was always on the alert for any instances of this 'offensive system of proselytism under the guise of a charitable institution' and had cause to condemn such organisations as the Servants' Home and the growing network of ragged schools in this regard.[2] Catholics did not dispute the right of the Protestant churches to establish charities for their own followers but fiercely resisted all attempts 'to entice from us the poor, and, comparatively speaking, unprotected portion of the Catholic flock'.[3] The strength of this reaction made it necessary for at least token upper class Catholics to be included on the committees of the mainstream charities. Dependent on a continuing Government grant and substantial contributions from the community, few charities could afford to alienate such a large body of potential supporters. Though children's charities remained divided by religion, hospitals, institutions for the elderly and most of the local ladies' benevolent societies, which provided the bulk of the outdoor relief in Melbourne, included prominent Catholics on their governing committees.

Geelong was, from its earliest days, a deeply divided community in which Catholics had little influence and no local mouthpiece. Settled initially as an offshoot of Tasmania, it was a popular haven for ex-convicts, many of whom were of Irish Catholic origin. They were concentrated in the developing working class areas of the town, down near the waterfront in the lanes and alleys off Corio street and in the emerging industrial area along the Barwon river. By contrast the Wesleyans, many of whom had been leaders in the first settlement, had had far greater financial success. They had established large homes on the hills overlooking Corio Bay, particularly in the emerging suburb of Newtown, where they could be well away from the bustle but still within walking distance of their places of business. While St Mary's Church was to dominate the hill in the centre of the town it was its neighbour, the much smaller Yarra street Wesleyan church, which had the more influential congregation.

Geelong was a major point of entry and a service town for the goldfields and during the decade 1851-61 it trebled its population. This influx of population did little to break down divisions in the town. Statistics as to place of birth show little variation between the different sections of the town but this was not the case with religious affiliation. In Barwon Ward, the south side of the town, there were 1102 Catholics, 30% population and only 526 of Wesleyan or other Methodist persuasion (14%). In Bellarine, around the port, there were 760 Catholics (26%) and only 200 Wesleyans (7%). By contrast the borough of Newtown and Chilwell had 942 Wesleyans (19%) to only 788 Catholics (16%).[4] Of the total Catholic population of the town 57% were concentrated in the Barwon and Bellarine wards with only 23% having made the move to the borough of Newtown and Chilwell. Forty-seven per cent of the Wesleyans were in the borough and only 36% were in the two down-town wards.[5]

Over the next ten years, though the population remained stagnant, the town became more spread out. Many working class families set up house in the new suburb of Ashby or Geelong West. However, relatively few Catholics participated in this move. In 1871 42% of the Catholics were still concentrated in Bellarine and Barwon wards with only 23% living in the new suburb and a further 22% in the borough of Newtown and Chilwell. Only 20% Wesleyans and other Methodists were now in the two town wards, with 27% in Newtown and Chilwell and 32% in Geelong West, which was home to a significant number of Primitive Methodists.[6] Ten years later the differences, though narrowing, were still quite apparent.[7]

Though a small group of Wesleyans dominated business in the town they were not the largest Protestant group. This honour went to the Anglicans who by 1861 had three well established congregations in the elite areas of the town plus mission churches in the working class districts. There was also a significant settlement of Scottish Presbyterians, many with Western District connections, and a much smaller number of Baptists and Congregationalists. Whatever their doctrinal differences, all of these groups shared a commitment to Evangelical Christianity and were able to cooperate on the various charities which developed in the post-gold years. Catholics however were almost universally excluded.

The sectarian division was apparent from the start though it is difficult to disentangle from class and ethnic differences. Dr Alexander Thomson, who had come over as surgeon to the Port Phillip Association, claimed that the Irish were 'utterly useless ... intellectually inferior even to the aborigines'.[8] However in the early years there is no suggestion of proselysation; the two communities seemed content to live separate lives. During the 1840s both the Anglicans and the Catholics established local societies for the relief of destitution amongst their own congregations however attempts, prior to the gold rush, to bring the community together to found a local hospital had been unsuccessful. A second attempt, in 1850, led to the establishment, two years later, of a Hospital and Benevolent Asylum on a hill to the east of the town. The original committee included the two Catholic priests in the town, but no Catholic laymen, a tradition which was to continue for the rest of the century. Though the inclusion of the clergy ensured community wide financial support for the institution, the Protestant establishment dominated decision making. Sectarian fighting reached a peak during the first world war when Protestant committee members used their numbers to ban any form of gambling at Hospital fundraising functions, leaving the Catholics clearly labelled as defenders of vice and sin.[9]

It was a similar dispute which had led to the demise of the only other non-denominational charity in the town. The Geelong and Western District Ladies' Benevolent Association, which had its origin in the Anglican Christ Church Ladies' Visiting Society, did come to include a small number of Catholics on its committee, though 'suitable' candidates were difficult to find. Always a rather tense arrangement this finally broke down in 1871 after a dispute as to whether raffles should be allowed at the annual fete. The Committee called a meeting of clergy, all Protestant, at which it was agreed that in future the Association would rely on concerts sponsored by the main Protestant churches in the town as a substitute for the money previously raised by gambling.[10] As a result the Catholic members, who had organised the raffles, left the committee and went on to establish a local branch of the St Vincent de Paul Society to care for the Catholic poor.[11]

As in Melbourne, children's charities were always administered along denominational lines. The Geelong and Western District Protestant Orphanage was erected on a hill overlooking the Moorabool River in 1855. Two years later Dean Hayes sponsored the first Catholic Orphanage. Initially a mixed institution under lay management it was taken over by the Sisters of Mercy in 1859. Three years later the sisters moved to their own property in the heart of Newtown where they ran a convent school for girls which catered for the female orphans and later industrial school girls as well. The boys returned to lay management but also moved to a

Fig. 1. Remains of mixed working class district. Corio St., Geelong.

Fig. 2. Working class housing – lane off Corio St., Geelong.

Fig. 3. Newtown home, Geelong

hill-top site in Newtown where in 1878 the Christian Brothers arrived to take charge.[12]

By 1870 these three institutions accommodated almost 300 children between them but there were a further 400-500 children under Government control in the two industrial schools, one in the old Immigrants' Depot, the other in an unused portion of the Geelong Gaol. The early attempts of the local Traders' and Citizens' Association to have the schools established in Geelong had nearly come to grief because of disputes as to which clergy would have access to the children. These difficulties were only overcome when the main combatants were reassured that in all such institutions Protestants and Catholics were kept apart with separate staff and separate chaplains to avoid any accusations of proselytism.

The decision of the Government to dismantle the industrial schools and board-out all the wards with private families provided an excuse for another outbreak of sectarianism in the Geelong charity scene. In order to establish local ladies' committees to recruit potential foster parents and supervise boarding out placements the Neglected Children's Department worked through the established Ladies' Benevolent Societies which in most regions included Catholics and Protestants. However, by this stage, the Geelong Association had no Catholic members and the ladies saw no necessity to move outside their own social circle to form the new boarding-out committee. Not surprisingly the Catholic priests were suspicious of the new scheme and refused to co-operate with the local committee. As potential foster parents required a reference from their clergyman this non-cooperation effectively prevented the local committee finding appropriate homes for the Catholic children in the Geelong Industrial Schools. The difficulty was unique to Geelong and diminished the contribution which the town was able to make to the boarding-out scheme.[13]

The small number of Catholics who had found financial success in Geelong were clearly unwelcome amongst the predominantly Protestant upper and middle classes. The large number of Catholics who remained working class and poor were at best objects of pity, at worst a threat to public morality. On both counts they came to be seen as legitimate targets for evangelisation, for only by embracing Protestantism could they be released from their lives of poverty and vice. 'There is in the Town of Geelong a large and increasing number of poor and neglected children, whose physical and moral cultivation claims the attention and sympathy of the whole Christian community', declared a group of ladies and clergymen who, towards the end of 1863, founded the first ragged school in the town.[14] They were of course all Protestants and the movement they were setting out to establish owed much to the Evangelical missions which were in the vanguard of the Protestant response to the growing cities of England. The Ragged School Association adopted a similar pattern employing Biblewomen to visit the parents of the pupils and was later sponsoring a Female Refuge to rescue their older sisters who had gone astray.

Speaking at the 1870 Annual Meeting of the Association the Rev T. McK. Fraser declared that he 'believed in the Agency because it was thoroughly unsectarian; the work was supported and carried on in a catholic spirit, and that was why it was supported by all the clergymen in the town, no matter of what denomination'. He was followed by Rev A.J. Campbell who regaled his audience with an anecdote about a Catholic priest who had tried to prevent a woman from reading her Bible.[15] Two years later this pattern was repeated when the Rev McKenzie, speaking in praise of the Biblewomen, reminded his audience that 'the Church of Rome had made use of the services of women, and it was by the skilful use of women's agency they kept up the importance of the church; but by shutting women up in nunneries he maintained they perverted their use'. Rev Bunning, a Baptist minister just off the boat from England, praised the organisation as one in which 'Christians of every denomination could unite together' and the Rev Mr Watkins in concluding the gathering 'thanked God that bigotry was diminished' in the town.

In the opinion of the supporters of the Ragged Schools' Association and Biblewomen's Mission, Catholics were clearly not included amongst the ranks of true Christians. They were the local equivalent of the ignorant heathen, in need of conversion as much as they needed charitable relief. Indeed the Biblewomen dispensed no charitable relief but rather hefty lashings of prayer and Bible reading, lessons in thrift and right living and assistance in caring for the sick and the elderly. 'The Biblewomens' Agency', said Rev James Bickford, 'went ... to the root of evil. They endeavoured to make the next generation better than that which it succeeded.'[16] By better one presumes he meant Protestant, sober, thrifty and hard-working, all the virtues which these middle class Evangelicals wanted the poor to espouse.

The Ragged Schools aimed to inculcate habits of order, cleanliness and industry in the children by teaching reading, writing and arithmetic, with a heavy emphasis on biblical instruction. In later years boys were taught a trade while girls were instructed in knitting, sewing, mending and darning to prepare them for their role as mothers of the next generation. Children of the Roman Catholic religion formed a large element, reported the Treasurer of the Association at the 1867 Annual Meeting. They were educated, fed, clothed and kept away from the temptations of the street all for the 'fabulous low rate of 30 shillings per annum'.[18]

It was the desire to rescue an older age group from the temptations of the street that led the association into its next venture; the foundation of a female refuge. There is little evidence to suggest that Geelong was in dire need of such an institution but many evangelical missions in England had set up rescue homes and Geelong was not to be left behind. The reports that the Biblewomen brought back of life in and around Corio street convinced the Committee members that it was an environment in which no young girl could remain pure. Adjacent to the port, the street was home to several brothels established during the gold rush years. These establishments and the ever present streetwalkers posed a continuing affront to middle class morality. In such an environment there was no room for the innocent.

The Refuge, established, in 1868, some five miles to the north of the town, was, however, never rushed with customers. 'There was not an unfortunate girl or woman in Geelong that need stay out on these cold miserable nights; the door of the Refuge was always open to them, and they could all receive a hearty welcome and a seat at a warm fireside', said the Rev A.J. Campbell at the 1870 Annual Meeting.[19] He neglected to mention that they would also be expected to promise to stay until the Matron was convinced that they had seen the error of their ways, working in the laundry to wash away their sinfulness. The institution made no impact on prostitution in the town. Indeed the Biblewomen were reluctant to accept such women into the home for fear they would corrupt their ideal clientele, young girls who had only just begun on the downward path.

Many of the young girls who did come found the regime far too strict. 'I won't be a nun' shouted Mary Flanagan when she was reprimanded for trying to add flounces to a dress she was making.[20] Nineteen year old Sarah, after twenty months inside, made her escape by 'leaping over the enclosure in the presence of the matron'. She returned immediately to life on the streets where two of her friends celebrated her return by taking her to the nearest public house and treating her to a pint of beer.[21] Fifteen year old Mary Ann O'Neil ran away after one day when she was sent to the Refuge on the order of the court. She had run away from home frequently over the previous three years and found the prospect of an indefinite period within the walls beyond contemplation.

Mary Ann was a particular prize to the ladies of the committee, doubly at risk because of her Catholicism. Although the Catholic church had no equivalent institution in the town arrangements had been made to have her sent to a convent school. However the expense was more than her parents could afford and the Protestant institution was free.[22] While the Refuge accepted girls without regard to creed it was conducted along Protestant Evangelical principles. Until the Salvation Army opened a Rescue Home in the town in 1884 the ladies had the female rescue field to themselves and were keen to use this advantage to bring more young women to the true religion. 'Although the Refuge had no great successes of which to boast', they proclaimed at their annual meeting in 1870, 'it had made the deliverance of those who had wasted their all in notorious living, and who, in the depth of their wretchedness, 'had come to themselves', a possibility, and would compare favourably with any similar institution in the colony'.[23]

Fig. 4. Geelong Female Refuge (previously part of the industrial school buildings).

Increased competition combined with a continuing lack of success was to lead to a change of function for the Refuge before the century came to an end. Rev Walter Eddy, a Baptist minister new to the town in 1889, brought new spirit to the Refuge Committee. As the Geelong Hospital had no maternity ward it had been the custom to send any of the inmates who were pregnant to Melbourne for their confinements. In return the Refuge accepted mothers and babies from the Carlton Refuge whenever it was overcrowded. Eddy suggested that if the Refuge were to construct its own maternity ward all this travelling would be eliminated and the institution might find a new usefulness. The small maternity ward which opened in 1891 was to give the ailing institution a new lease of life.

Along with providing maternity facilities Eddy vowed to rigorously pursue the men who had caused the young girls to fall. His first opportunity to put his philosophy into practice came when a young woman by the name of Louise was ready to leave the refuge and return to work. Unable to pay to have her child boarded out she sought to have him admitted to the care of the Neglected Children's Department. Speaking on her behalf before the court Rev Eddy claimed that she had been a respectable girl prior to the birth of her child. Now her life was in ruins while her seducer walked free, leaving their son to become a charge upon the state. When questioned by the magistrate Louise named as her seducer a prominent manufacturer, a justice of the peace and one of the few Catholics who had donated to the Refuge in the past. He chose to defend the case but, failing to convince a majority of the seven magistrates on the bench, he was ordered to pay 7/6 per week to the Neglected Children's Department. Flushed with success, Walter Eddy was delighted to announce that the Refuge's honorary solicitors would

> take legal action on behalf of any inmates of the Refuge against any individual to whom can be clearly traced the paternity of any child brought to or born in the Refuge, and compel him to assist in the maintenance of his offspring. The committee hoped that this procedure may assist in stopping girls on the threshold of a downward course; and will also save others from seduction by those who will hesitate to run the risk of subsequent expense.[24]

However none of the young mothers could equal Louise's stunning coup and few seducers were ever pursued.

The period between the wars saw a lessening of sectarian conflict in Geelong. However the gulf between the two communities was, if anything, wider than it had been in the early years. Across Australia Catholics and Protestants lived in different worlds, a social and religious segregation which, Patrick O'Farrell suggests, 'was an arrangement satisfactory to both parties'.[25] Campion argues that the apparent peace

Fig. 5. Geelong and Western District Protestant Orphanage: Herne Hill.

Fig. 6. "Glastonbury" Geelong and Western District Orphanage, Belmont (1930, 17).

disguised a continuing Anti-Catholicism, 'a muted underground phenomenon that spoke most eloquently in its silences'.[26] Within Geelong there appeared to be a new amity abroad. The three orphanages were rebuilt between 1926 and 1939, close to each other but well to the west of the town, and the Female Refuge was replaced on its old site by a thoroughly modern babies' home.[27] In each case the fundraising committee had representatives of all the major denominations. When, in the face of the depression, steps were taken to coordinate local charities, representatives of the Catholic organisations were always included.[28] When the Protestant Council of Churches again raised a protest against the reliance on gambling at the annual hospital Gala Day its calls fell on deaf ears.[29] The depression highlighted class divisions in the town and sectarian differences were temporarily put aside but the barriers between the two communities were not broken down.

With the return to prosperity in the early war years some of the old sectarian divisions were revived. An offer by a Mr P.C. Monaghan to sponsor an appeal to provide Christmas treats for all the institutions in the town brought a hasty rebuke from a representative of the Protestant organisations. The Freemasons, he said, provided a well-loaded Christmas tree for both institutions and no further help was needed.[30] In 1944 the Babies' Home Committee chose to take the high moral ground over gambling, refusing to accept the proceeds of the Eastern Beach Easter Carnival.

> We feel that the financial success of an effort of this nature is largely dependent upon raising money by dubious means not condoned by many supporters of our Home, and that, further, the welfare of the forty babies in our care is too sacred for us to discharge our obligation to them by erecting a number of spinning wheels. In other words, we feel that the public of Geelong will support our efforts to finance our Home without resort to gambling.[31]

The subsequent appeal was a resounding success as leading Protestants, anxious to display their solidarity with the Committee's stand, flocked to the support of the Home.

Despite a superficial appearance of amity Bethany Babies' Home remained an aggressively Protestant organisation. Committee membership was not open to Catholics, though prominent Jewish women were acceptable. Catholics were also ineligible for entry into the Mothercraft Training school though they were frequently employed on the domestic staff, usually for low wages in return for board, lodging and child care. Even in the early 1950s it was considered unthinkable that a Catholic could make a suitable teacher for the new kindergarten. However, unlike the Protestant Orphanage, Bethany continued to take in women and children of all creeds. It was now the only institution of its kind in the area and one of only two or three such homes outside the metropolitan area. Throughout the Babies' Home years just under 30% children in the Home were listed as Catholic. Yet as an approved adoption agency Bethany would only accept applications from Protestant couples. Unless they had made arrangements through a Melbourne agency, Catholic mothers whose babies were delivered at the Geelong Hospital were usually sent to Bethany, where arrangements were made to place their children in impeccable Protestant homes. Many children who were not originally intended for adoption were also placed in this way. Committee members were very reluctant to see a Bethany baby move on to another institution so mothers were strongly urged to consent to adoption if they had no way of supporting their child.

Sectarianism is no longer a force in Geelong society and when committee members from the 1950s are asked why it was so persistent in the early post-war years they seem rather shamefaced. 'We simply didn't know any Catholics', they reply but there is also a hidden suggestion that should one Catholic have been invited into the charmed circle they would have brought in their friends and taken over. The sectarianism of the 1950s was but one symptom of the decline of the old elite in Geelong society. 'Once we were very well known', said Bethany treasurer R.G.Farrow when the agency faced closure in 1976, 'but Geelong grew so quickly'.[32] What he meant was that in the post war world when religion was no longer a vital force in the lives of most of the people, the old elite based around the leading Protestant churches in the town was no longer relevant. New alliances needed to be formed and they were to be alliances based far more on wealth than on sectarian preferences.

NOTES

1. M. Hogan, *The Sectarian Strand*, (Ringwood: Penguin, 1987), p.29.
2. M. Pawsey, *The Popish Plot* (Manly, 1983), p.11-12.
3. *Ibid*, p.12.
4. These figures almost certainly overstate the Catholic presence in the upper class areas as the borough included the working class area of Chilwell as well as the prestigious Newtown.
5. Census of Victoria, 1861, *Votes and Proceedings of the Victorian Legislative Assembly 1864*, vol.2, p.149.
6. Census of Victoria, 1871, *VPP*, 1872, vol 2, p.888ff.
7. For 1881 and following the census provides statistics for municipalities rather than wards hence disguising differences within the town of Geelong. By this stage Geelong was home to 55% of the Catholic population of the three municipalities but only 45% of the Wesleyans and other Methodists. 28% Wesleyans and 22% Catholics lived in Newtown and Chilwell and the remaining 26% Wesleyans and 23% Catholics resided in Geelong West. *VPP* 1882-3, Vol.3, p.456ff.
8. Quoted in P. O'Farrell, *The Irish in Australia* (Kensington, 1987), p.72.
9. *Geelong Advertiser*, 14 January 1915, 7 November 1917.
10. *Ibid*, 14 September 1871, 5 October 1871.
11. *Ibid.*, 22 June 1874.
12. *Ibid.*, 19 September 1914.
13. *Ibid.*, 4 February 1873, 27 May 1873.
14. *Ibid.*, 14 November 1863.
15. *Ibid.*, 5 August 1870.
16. *Ibid.*, 21 August 1872.
17. *Ibid.*, 12 September 1867.
18. *Ibid.*
19. *Ibid.*, 5 August 1870.
20. *Ibid.*, 6 October 1870.
21. *Ibid.*, 16 March 1871.
22. *Ibid.*, 15 May 1888.
23. *Ibid.*, 5 August 1870.
24. *Ibid.*, 8 August 1891.
25. P. O'Farrell, *The Catholic Church and Community: An Australian History* (N.S.W.: Kensington, 1985), p. 352.
26. E. Campion, *Rockchoppers: Growing Up Catholic in Australia* (Ringwood, 1982), p.94.
27. This move is particularly significant in the case of the Catholic institutions for it marks the final separation of the orphanage children from the middle class Catholic boys and girls who attended the prestigious schools which took over their previous Newtown locations
28. *Geelong Advertiser*, 31 July 1930.
29. *Ibid.*, 28. June 1933.
30. *Ibid.*, 18 December 1939.
31. *Ibid.*, 26 February 1944.
32. Bethany Babies' Home Minute Book, 7 May 1976.

JOHN RICKARD

The Importance of Being Victorian

I must confess that this paper had its origins in another bicentennial conference sponsored by two Victorian institutions, the Royal Historical Society of Victoria and the History Institute, Victoria. The title of that conference, 'The Victorian Contribution to Nationhood', struck me as curious: why should it be pertinent to isolate and identify the *Victorian* contribution to nationhood? Indeed, was it not mildly subversive of the Bicentenary as an allegedly national occasion to be trumpeting the particular contribution of Victoria? This led me to ponder the nature of Victorian self-awareness and Victorian patriotism and their relationship to Australian identity and nationalism. My justification for presenting this paper to a conference on 'Populous Places' is that in opposition to the tradition of bush nationalism, which has so often claimed the attention of historians and myth makers, Victorian patriotism had a strong urban dimension.

Although, in recent years, there has been an increasing interest in the specificity of region and place, and although the pre-bicentennial parade of state sesquicentenaries has born its historical fruit, the colony or state as a focus for loyalty and sentiment has seemed to be something of an embarrassment to the narrative of nationalism, and is usually treated dismissively. Two recent books on nationalism illustrate this in different ways. Stephen Alomes in *A Nation At Last?* talks fleetingly about 'regional rivalries' and 'parochialism', and notes that 'the primary affiliations of many Australians to state over nation were expressed in sport and advertising'.[1] On the other hand in *The Rise of Colonial Nationalism* John Eddy and Deryck Schreuder, reflecting the concerns of Richard Jebb which provide the focus for the contributing essays, are really discussing not *colonial* but *dominion* nationalism. In his essay on 'Australia' Eddy does argue that 'the small colonial nations' which had grown out of the original 'penal farm' were, by the late 1890s, 'sufficiently confident of their own identities, as well as of the things they had in common, to be engaged in the forging of a federal pact which would lay the foundations of a modern nation-state'. Yet he goes on to quote John Foster Fraser, writing in 1910, that 'you drop from imperialism to something like parochialism in Australia with little of the real national spirit intervening'. (This observation of the English journalist must be something of a favourite: Alomes also uses it, while I, too, must own to having exploited it.)[2]

'Parochialism', like 'provincialism', can be used to cover a multitude of sins. Those resisting federation were often characterised as negatively parochial: on the other hand H.B. Higgins, arguing against the adoption of the Constitution in 1897, saw the equal representation of the States in the Senate as a symptom of provincialism.[3] Even the advocates of States' Rights have argued their case more in terms of 'checks and balances' than the virtues of State loyalty. The Bicentenary has, of necessity, given rise to much soul searching about national identity and Australians' self perception of themselves and their society. Even that old skeleton in the cupboard, the cultural cringe, was dusted down and brought out as a warning to us all in the wake of the failure of the bicentennial musical 'Manning Clark's History of Australia'. But the nexus between state and federal, between colonial and dominion, and between regional and national sentiment, has been little explored. The assumption has tended to remain that the two are in competition.

I shall argue that the relationship between the two foci for loyalty and sentiment is much more complex than this. Each colony had a separate history, and therefore a distinctive perspective on submerging itself in the Australian project. Their sense of their own identity also varied. Nowhere is this better demonstrated than in the comparison between New South Wales and Victoria. As the original European colony New South Wales, however small in numbers and area of settlement, was, to all intents and purposes Australia , as Matthew Flinders in 1814 proposed the continent should be called. The establishment of the Swan River Colony and South Australia first modified such an identification: both these colonies were separate and distinct from New South Wales from their inception. Van Diemen's Land, although originally governed as part of New South Wales, was from 1825 effectively independent of the parent settlement. Victoria and Queensland, however, had to win their separation from New South Wales, the mother colony being dismembered to create them. In terms, then, of their sense of their own origins, the colonies could be said to fall into three categories: New South Wales, the mother colony, which sees its boundaries ever shrinking till it constitutes a rump; Western Australia and South Australia and (to a lesser extent) Tasmania, which can trace a continuous identity; and Victoria and Queensland, which are born of separation (and which, interestingly, both take their name from Queen Victoria).

Peter Spearritt has argued that the end result of the process of separation has left New South Wales with little sense of its own identity as a State. Nor did the formal creation of Victoria and Queensland put an end to the psychological disintegration. The fringes of the State look outwards rather than inwards: northern New South Wales to Brisbane, the Riverina to Melbourne, and Broken Hill to Adelaide. Even the growth of Canberra, creating a powerful regional centre which is not part of New South Wales, can be seen as weakening the State's sense of identity. Spearritt nominates

New South Wales as the 'on-existent state'.[4] The other side to this coin, however, is that New South Wales tended to retain a sense of its being the mother colony, and to that extent still somehow identified with the totality of Australia. Thus in 1888 Sir Henry Parkes made his own centennial gesture by introducing legislation to rename New South Wales Australia. When the other colonies angrily denounced this attempt to appropriate the name 'Australia', Parkes loftily explained that ever since Flinders had first suggested the application of 'Australia' to the continent 'the name has been used interchangeably with the name of New South Wales'. In the event Parkes gave up the bill in exchange for the G.C.M.G. bestowed upon him by the New South Wales governor.[5] In similar fashion Sydney's historical society has always styled itself the Royal Australian Historical Society. That the present bicentenary is also New South Wales' bicentenary further sustains the identification of the State with Australia. And Sydney's ability to project its landmarks as symbols of Australia – the Harbour Bridge, the Opera House – has the incidental effect of making the State seem an unnecessary intermediary.

Victoria, on the other hand, born of separation from the mother colony, has always experienced a greater need to define and assert its own identity. Much of the character of Victorian self-awareness was determined by the boom growth of the period from 1851 to 1890. The institution of a policy of tariff protection, explicitly designed to retain and build upon the sudden prosperity of the gold rushes, was vital. This involved a rejection of the free trade, laissez-faire orthodoxy of Great Britain, to which New South Wales adhered; protection also naturally lent itself to, indeed, even required the rhetoric of nationalism. 'Marvellous Melbourne' bore testimony to Victorians' sense of their own achievement. When in 1888 Victoria chose to mark New South Wales' centenary with the Exhibition which the mother colony could not itself afford to put on, it was a typical piece of Victorian oneupmanship. The depression of the 1890s was, of course, to have a profound effect on Victorian self perceptions, and also, as we shall see, on Victorian attitudes to federation, but it did not obliterate Victoria's sense of its own historical identity.

It is worth noting, for example, that the art gallery in Melbourne is the *National* Gallery of Victoria. And while Sydney historians proclaimed an *Australian* Historical Society, I suspect that their Melbourne brothers and sisters actually preferred the idea of a *Victorian* Historical Society. When in 1913, twelve years after the birth of the Commonwealth, Henry Gyles Turner published his account of Eureka, and called it *Our Own Little Rebellion* the title suggested a measure of pride flavoured with a hint of apology for nominating this episode for the national pantheon. But while Turner expressed regret that the rising generation in Australia showed little interest in history, we should not assume that by 'Our Own' Turner meant 'Australia's Own'. Noting the impact of the colonies' support for Britain in the Boer War, Turner observed:

> In this spirit it is worth while to place on record a definite and impartial account of our own little Victorian Rebellion, when the enthusiasm for the military was of a very different kind to that which was in evidence during the South African War.[6]

Even after the formal achievement of nationhood, Eureka remained 'our own little Victorian Rebellion'. I often wonder, too, what one is to make of that remarkable inscription on the Shrine of Remembrance:

> THIS MONUMENT WAS ERECTED BY A GRATEFUL PEOPLE TO THE HONOURED MEMORY OF THE MEN AND WOMEN OF VICTORIA WHO SERVED THE EMPIRE IN THE GREAT WAR OF 1914-1918.[7]

Wasn't Australia supposed to have been there somewhere too? Here the nexus is a direct one between 'the men and women of Victoria' and 'the Empire', and any sense that they may also have served Australia is curiously but deliberately excluded.

The conclusion to be drawn from these stray bits of evidence is not, however, that Victorians were weak in Australian nationalism, or that they necessarily elevated a sense of Victorian above Australian identity. In the federal referenda of 1898-9 Victoria led the way in federalist enthusiasm. In 1898 Victoria recorded the highest 'Yes' vote, 89.25%, of all the colonies, and although in 1899 little Tasmania marginally eclipsed Victoria, Victoria was the only colony where a majority of those qualified to vote (53.13%) actually voted 'Yes', there being, of course, no compulsory voting. What I want to argue here is that there was a particular relationship between Victorians' attitude to their colony or state and their attitude to their nation which was unique. I intend to look briefly at the organisation chiefly associated with the cause of federation in Victoria, the Australian Natives' Association, and then at Victoria's leading apostle of that cause, Alfred Deakin.

The Australian Natives' Association was founded in 1871 at a meeting held at Grimwade's Hotel in Elizabeth Street as a friendly society for the native born. It's ideological commitment to nativism was, as Marian Aveling has shown, minimal in these early years: rather, its emergence reflected a view that just as immigrants had their 'national' societies (such as the Order of St Andrew and the Hibernian Catholic Benefit Society) there was no reason why the native born should not form a friendly society on a similar basis. But in the 1870s only the Ballarat branch showed any interest in native rights and characteristics.[8] Substantial expansion did not begin until the mid-eighties: by 1890 there were over 8,000 members; by the turn of the century close to 19,000. By the 1890s the aims of the Association were seen as threefold: according to a blurb in 1898 'its first object is to instil into its members the principle of Thrift', which related to its role as a benefits society. The Association was also dedicated to 'the mental improvement of its members', and much time was given to determining what was called the 'syllabus'. And by this time it had undertaken the role of federal missionary. As *Advance Australia* put it, 'the patriotic feelings of a people must have a directing force if they are to accomplish any good, and it is precisely this force that the A.N.A. supplies'.[9] It was a cardinal rule of the A.N.A. (Rule 49 in fact) that religion was not a subject for discussion. 'We inquire into no man's religion. We allow no religious discussion. We have no secret signs. All our meetings are open to the public. Religion and the morality it dictated could not help but intrude at times, however, as in the controversy about the Association's Art Union.[10]

There was in all this much that reflected Victoria's colonial inheritance. The whole concept of an organisation for the native born made more dramatic sense in generational terms in Victoria, where there had been such a large and sudden immigration in the 1850s. The emphasis on thrift and mental improvement accorded well with the values of the gold rush generation, whose children most of the native born were. The A.N.A. was particularly strong in the goldfields communities. The barring of religion only makes sense in the light of the community's denominational balance and the legacy of sectarianism from the educational settlement of 1872. An organisation which defined itself in terms of the native-born could not risk further limiting its appeal, particularly if it claimed to be 'national'. The federal cause, however, provided the A.N.A., if only briefly, with something akin to religious fervour. Marian Aveling calls her section on the Association's contribution to the 1898 campaign, 'The Faith Militant'.[11] Although the A.N.A. carefully eschewed party politics, its ideology was in accord with the liberal protectionist tradition which had dominated Victorian politics, and which had done much to articulate the Victorian identity.

While the A.N.A. was the Australian Natives Association, 'Australian' was not so much a territorial claim as an elucidation of the *raison d'etre*. To a large extent it was really the Victorian Association for Australian Natives. True, the Association tended to make national claims. The journal *The Advance Australia*, launching its first issue on 26 January 1897, purported to be 'a national newspaper': 'We belong to no province in particular ... We are not Victorian or South Australian in our proclivities; neither do we incline to New South Wales.' Curious, then, that all it's advertising should be derived from Melbourne businesses (who sometime just gave their address as 'City'), and that virtually all the branch news it published should be Victorian. There had of course been serious attempts to export the A.N.A. to other colonies which had a limited meassure of success. New South Wales, however, defied the Association's colonisation. Partly this was because New South Wales law did not encourage the A.N.A. kind of friendly society; but partly it was because, as J.L. Purves admitted, in the mother colony 'an institution ... [being] of Victorian origin is reason enough for its being left severely alone'. So *Advance Australia* could quote as an accolade Barton's declaration in 1898 that 'if I had a body of men such as the A.N.A. to aid me, I would have no fears for the result of the approaching poll.'[12] And where the A.N.A. did succeed in exporting itself, it seemed often, as in the case of Western Australia, to be the work of emigrating Victorians.

What I am suggesting, then, is that the A.N.A. was in a very basic cultural sense a Victorian rather than an Australian institution. It's rationale as a society for the native born was conditioned by the Victorian experience; and even its campaigning for federation, sincere and dedicated though it might have been, represented a Victorian perspective on both the practicalities of constitution making and the construction of a national ideology. It was not appropriate for an organisation like the A.N.A. to dwell on the selfish, economic benefits of federation – the expectation, for example, that Victorian manufacturers would benefit from an Australia--wide market – but the economic malaise of the 1890s provided the context for the Victorian campaign. In the wake of industrial strife and collapsing building societies and banks, the achieving of federation promised economic encouragement and reassurance. And after a decade which had seen a net loss of 110,000, mostly, as H.G. Turner put it, able-bodied adults',[13] federation in an emotional sense offered Victoria the prospect of reclaiming its own. One should not be surprised by the contrast between Victoria, where, after the brief flurry of behind the scenes alarm in 1898 which brought the Victorian government and the *Age* into line, support for federation was overwhelming, and New South Wales where the issue was immensely divisive. Federation fitted much more comfortably into the Victorian political – and economic – agenda than it did for New South Wales.

Even in a cultural sense, the federal cause was temperamentally suited to the Victorian outlook. The defining of the Victorian experience and the pride in the colony's achievements could easily be transferred to the new arena, with little sense of conflict or tension. So Bernard O'Dowd could point to the potential national significance of Victoria's own little rebellion:

> What the plain of Runnymede is to England, what the Sacred Mount was to the Roman plebeians, what Bannockburn used to mean to Scotland, and what Bunker's Hill is to the United States, so is the Eureka Stockade to Victoria, nay, to Australia. .. that it hasn't yet been properly sung, is no credit to the fibre or the patriotism of our Victorian poets.

Here O'Dowd is still defining Eureka as a Victorian event, a cause for Victorian patriotism; but he is also nominating it for an Australian recognition as well. But he does so, not because what is Victorian today (this was 1897) will be Australian tomorrow, but because Eureka, he argues, directly affected other colonies too. 'It is to the Eureka Stockade we owe our Victorian freedom', O'Dowd asserts, and 'it has had its indirect effect in causing the English Government to accord similar rights to the other colonies'.[14] Eureka was thus Victoria's gift to the other colonies, and, hence, to the future nation, but it remained Victoria's. It might also be observed that Eureka could be characterised as an urban event even if its Ballarat setting was a primitive one.

Alfred Deakin was Victoria's foremost federalist. At a time when he was very much the colony's coming man, he withdrew from the mainstream of politics in the 1890s and devoted himself to the federal cause. Federation had, for him, a personal as well as political significance. Deakin was a native-born Victorian and effectively a patron of the A.N.A. When he made his first trip to Europe for the Jubilee in 1887 he seemed determined not to be dazzled, and in telling his sister Catherine of the sights, made, for a Victorian, the obvious local comparison:

> As for Paris and London you have their miniature in Melbourne. Raise the houses three or four stories and increase the size of public buildings in proportion – clean the streets and quadruple the traffic and you have Paris. Put only one storey on the houses, have the streets not quite so clean, and a good deal older and twist and tangle all the straight ways and you have London. It is enormous in its extent more than anything else.[15]

By the time of the 1897-8 Convention Deakin had had almost twenty years experience of Victorian politics. Originally a free-trader, Deakin was converted to protection by David Syme, who had taken an interest in him when he had tried his hand with some casual journalism for the *Age*. This conversion was significant enough for Deakin to recall the place if not the time – it was as we crossed the old Prince's Bridge one evening , in the course of which he had, he acknowledged, 'crossed the fiscal Rubicon'.[16] Deakin made a dramatic entry (if, in a sense, a false start) into the Victorian Legislative Assembly at the tender age of twenty-two; he was still not twenty-seven when he became a cabinet minister. David Syme remained an important patron, as, indeed, he tended to be for any liberal protectionist of note in Victoria; but in Deakin's case the relationship had something of a personal basis. So Deakin can be seen as being in a symbolic relationship with two important Victorian institutions – the A.N.A. and the *Age*.

Of course Deakin was also to some extent unusual in that he was an intellectual and a cosmopolitan – a man of wide interests who would have preferred success as a writer rather than as a politician. There were those who thought his real calling was as a religious leader. (As late as 1905 Herbert Brookes could tell the man he addressed in correspondence as 'Dear Master', 'Politics is not *your* element great as has been your success – Religion is.)[17] Deakin's private religious life provides a fascinating counterpoint to his public life, but it is unusual more in the nature of its documentation rather than in the mere fact of its existence. And it needs also to be seen in the context of Deakin as a modern – for the range of his intellectual concerns was strikingly modern: education, the rights of women, comparative religion, health, hygeine; even his youthful interest in spiritualism had a modern impulse. It is no surprise that he should have been a loyal supporter of Charles Strong's Australian Church. In 1890 Deakin penned a remarkable testament for the guidance of his daughters in the event of his death, setting out the principles for their upbringing. It began with religion – he wanted his children 'brought up religiously, but as far as possible apart from sectarianism' – but embraced education, pastimes, exercise, diet, marriage. He desired, for example, that 'they be qualified for some professional work by which they may be enabled to earn a livelihood', and expressly approved medicine as a possible occupation. On the other hand he desired 'the home to be the centre of their thoughts, enjoyments, and ambitions', for 'within yourselves and your home you can make a city of refuge, a Garden of Eden, from which you can pluck flowers to scatter in the world'.[18] Deakin's own family experience was, in one sense, decidedly modern, for he was one of only two children, and he and Pattie Browne, whom he married at the age of twenty-five (she was nineteen), brought up three daughters. On more than one occasion in later years Deakin attributed tensions within the tightly knit family circle to the greater intensity of relationships within such a nuclear family.

It is true of course that Deakin's perspective on these concerns and issues was necessarily provincial, in the sense that he had, for the most part, to interpret them in the setting of the infant colony of Victoria, but it seems to me a little unfair to label him, as Manning Clark has, as 'at heart ... a provincial without an inkling of the wider loyalties made possible by the rapid developments in production, transport and communication'.[19] Deakin had a world view; in his omniverous reading he read also in French; and he was, for an Australian of his generation, well travelled. Apart from the several imperial journeys to the heart of the empire, he had been to Fiji, India and the United States. His daughters were encouraged to travel. Both Stella and Vera pursued their studies in London and Berlin; Vera in Budapest as well. If anyone was to transcend the petty – well, perhaps not so petty – provincial economic rivaries which the federal debate exposed – it would be Deakin, the intellectual and man of conscience. In Victoria he was looked to as the moral and ideological voice of federalism, and of the nationalism underpinning it.

Deakin's separation from the political mainstream in the 1890s, his sense of apartness, no doubt helped him adopt this role. But one should not underestimate his skills as an orator, which were appropriate to anyone charged with the responsibility of articulating national sentiment. Deakin was not a demagogue. As a speaker he was not a thunderer who overwhelmed an audience with dramatic rhetoric: if a phrase might suggest the apparent quality of his oratory it is perhaps 'seductive eloquence'. The Queensland conservative, St Ledger recalled hearing Deakin for the first time at a federalist meeting in southern Queensland:

> ... it was in the fiery glow, the irresistible rush of his occasional perorations (so to speak) that one recognised the power and magnetism of his hold on the imagination of his audience... There is this remarkable feature in his speeches; there is never a halt in the rush of his ideas, the flow and torrent of his words. Each word comes instantaneously, in its proper time, to its proper place. There has been the instantaneous rejection of the wrong or less suitable word and the selection of the right and more suitable word, and so the stream gathers in strength and broadens out in beauty and harmony with the whole landscape he has painted before your very eyes ... [20]

In a very real sense Deakin, particularly when preaching to the converted, was able to elevate those less articulate than himself to a level of discourse which gave the cause a dignity and purpose it would otherwise have lacked. Deakin's famous late night address to the Bendigo banquet of the A.N.A. in March 1898 was a case in point. The argument concerning the significance of this speech in influencing the course of the federal campaign in Victoria is not relevant here: the point is that the speech was remembered by those who heard it as a decisive and climactic moment, an experience which succeeded in articulating their commitment. It was brief, simple and eloquent. 'I recognise that the united Australia yet to be can only come to be with the consent of and by the efforts of the Australian-born,' he began. 'I propose to speak to Australians simply as an Australian.' Deakin's message essentially was that in the international as well as national context, 'it's time': 'Let us recognise that we live in an unstable era, and that, if we fail in the hour of crisis, we may never be able to recall our lost national opportunities'. He concluded with an appeal to campaign 'without any attempt at intimidation, without taking advantage of sectionalism, but in the purest and broadest spirit of Australian unity':

This cause dignifies every one of its servants and all efforts that are made in its behalf. The contest in which you are about to engage is one in which it is a privilege to be enrolled. It lifts your labours to the loftiest political levels, where they may be inspired with the purest patriotic passion for national life and being. Remember the stirring appeal of the young poet of genius, so recently lost to us in Bendigo, and whose grave is not yet green in your midst. His dying lips warned us of our present need and future duty, and pointed to the true Australian goal –

> Our country's garment
> With hands unfilial we have basely rent
> With petty variance our souls are spent,
> And ancient kinship under foot is trod:

> O let us rise, – united, – penitent, –
> And be one people, – mighty, serving God![21]

These lines were much quoted in 1897-8, but the poet William Gay having died at the age of thirty-two in Bendigo a mere three months earlier made them peculiarly apt for the occasion. Deakin had the ability of infusing the often pedestrian campaign for federation with a sense of nobility.

However Deakin was also a politician and a Victorian. It was arresting and dramatic to tell his audience that he spoke to them simply as an Australian , but he was also a Victorian speaking to the Victorian members of a fundamentally Victorian organisation. Deakin prayed for federation, but he also prayed for his country, by which he seems to have meant Victoria. After the success of the 1898 referendum in Victoria he gave thanks to the 'Father of Nations' – 'Enable us to pursue the cause of unity in spite of the obstacles which at present appear to beset our path' – then he added 'elsewhere' to make clear that he meant New South Wales where the minimum required 'Yes' vote had not been achieved. At the end of 1900, and on the very eve of the Commonwealth he craved for 'Thy blessings for my wife & children family country nation race & universe'.[22] All encompassing, rather in the manner of a child putting the address on the top of a letter, but the distinction between 'my country' and 'my nation' appears to be the distinction between Victoria and Australia. Federation did not mean that he ceased to be a Victorian. To Brookes in 1899 he confessed that

> What I am most concerned about at present is to preserve our local industries or at least to let them slide down a gentle declivity into lower duties if we cannot maintain them as I hope we will. That is the first aim of a Victorian as I understand his obligations.[23]

Becoming an Australian did not mean that you ceased to be a Victorian: indeed we need to be reminded that that was the whole point of a federation. As Deakin, in the guise of the journalist for the London *Morning Post* put it, writing, interestingly enough, the day after he had prayed for his country, nation, race and universe:

> Not even an Act of the Imperial Parliament can remove by its fiat the antagonisms of thought, aim and situation existing among the scattered four millions of independent Australian Britons who are taking their destinies into their own hands on a far greater scale than they have been hitherto accustomed to essay. Because they are enriched by the acquisition of a Federal in addition to a State citizenship they will not be at once inspired with Federal feelings. There will be no complete break with their past.[24]

But Deakin seemed to be saying that there *should* be no complete break with their past. They were not losing their State citizenship: they were being 'enriched' by gaining another.

Deakin's noble rhetoric disguised the extent to which the great success of the federal referenda in Victoria was the product of efficient stage management. It is not profitable to speculate what the situation might have been if the Turner Government and the *Age* had come out against the Bill: the significant thing is that behind the scenes pressure, in which Deakin played an important role, helped mobilise both behind the Bill, so that Higgins, McLean and the Trades Hall were left to fight a lonely and hopeless campaign against the adoption of the Constitution. The case of the *Age* is of interest. Richard Jebb, who arrived in Australia in 1899, saw the *Age* as having more 'continental influence' than the *Sydney Morning Herald* 'just because its protectionist standpoint was Australian rather than English'. He assumed (wrongly) that the *Age* was 'naturally' federalist; but he saw it as being 'nationalist also, in the sense of encouraging the sentiment of pan-Australian patriotism, as an antidote to the idea, industriously circulated from the Sydney press offices, that federation was nothing else than a manufacturers' conspiracy engineered in Melbourne'. Jebb seemed to appreciate that such an *Age* brand of 'pan-Australian patriotism' might confirm the worst Sydney fears, for he conceded that 'the nationalism of the *Age*, having been developed not *a priori* but in support of a particular fiscal policy, has not always been of a pronounced character in regard to other than commercial questions.'[25] Deakin himself in later years was to see the *Age* as provincial in its outlook, a captive of the Victorian nationalism of its past.

Nevertheless the fact that the *Age*, for all its lack of enthusiasm for federation, felt bound in the end to support it, points to the forces which linked Victoria's future to the Australian project. Victoria was neatly positioned to take up the federal cause. It was large enough to be a vital component of any federation, and its liberal political tradition meant that it would have an important role to play in arguing and shaping the Constitution. But as an offspring of New South Wales it could claim some affinity with the experience of the smaller colonies. Federation could be seen as celebrating Victoria's Oedipus complex: for if it was technically not feasible to murder its father, John Bull, it could at least marry the Mother Colony.

At an economic level Protection symbolised the nexus between Victoria's well being and that of the new Commonwealth. Protection also helped generate the colonial nationalism which meant that the Victorian advocates of federation approached the issue with a relatively united sense of their colony's interests. But at an ideological level Victorian pride in the colony's achievement, which was no doubt aided by its spatial compactness compared with most other colonies, rehearsed many of the items which would take their place on the Australian agenda. It is no accident, surely, that the pervading spirit of the Commonwealth's first decade was not Edmund Barton or George Reid, but Alfred Deakin - not simply because of his talents as a leader and skills as a politician, but because he was strategically placed to define the national priorities of the new Australia. Victorian patriotism helped articulate and sustain Australian patriotism. Eureka, like Protection, would be part of the package. Yet the sense of local community, and of its old colonial ties with 'Home', could still sometimes render the Australian perspective irrelevant – hence the inscription on the Shrine of Remembrance.

The collapse of the 1890s meant that it made good economic sense for Victorians to invest in the Australian project. The colony's ethos, so well encapsulated in the A.N.A. – bourgeois, liberal, urban, self-improving and self conscious – was therefore exploited in the interest of the larger cause. Federation in this sense became the Victorian project. Perhaps New South Wales was right to be suspicious of this 'hidden agenda'. Yet once the deed was done, once the union was accomplished, the colonies, now States, could still maintain their old roles: federation simply provided a new forum within which they could be played out. So New South Wales could still strike attitudes and psychologically project itself – if chiefly to itself – as Australia; while Victoria could continue to work assiduously to make the Commonwealth serve its purpose. Nowhere is this better demonstrated than in the Victorian monopoly of Anti-Labor leadership.

In its concern with economic recovery and local industries, the Victorian investment in Australian nationalism could be seen as mere political pragmatism, but in the hands of a Deakin, or even an A.N.A., it was capable of taking flight as ideology. Such a nationalism was not bound to the Bush, even if it could afford to look with a benign eye on *Bulletin* journalism (the *Bulletin* was, after all, protectionist!) and Heidelberg pastoral images. Its essential urbanism, which had its source as much in in the goldfields inheritance of Ballarat and Bendigo as in the showpiece of 'Marvellous Melbourne', keyed in easily with nineteenth century ideas of improvement and progress. If the urban dream turned sour in the 1890s its impulse could be productively redirected into the federal movement, which was, ironically perhaps, ultimately to be responsible for the idea of Canberra.

As the Bicentenary, not before time, draws to a close, it is salutory to remind ourselves that nationalism, whether Victorian or Australian, is a mixed blessing, if a blessing at all. Nationalism always seeks to simplify, to compel. Nationalism can also be very perverse. It has the habit of not doing what you might want it to do – like helping sustain a 'Yes' vote in constitutional referendums – while on the other hand it easily lends itself to slogans like 'All For Australia', 'Australia First' and 'One Australia'. If parochialism is too readily characterised as a vice, nationalism is too easily assumed to be a virtue.

And with the rhetoric of 1988 still ringing in our ears it should be noted that Victoria has not allowed itself to be unduly carried away by the Bicentenary; indeed, Victorian interest in the event has been modest, if not minimal. Is it significant that in 1988, unlike 1888, it is Brisbane, not Melbourne, which has staged Expo?

NOTES

1. Stephen Alomes, *A Nation at Last? The Changing Character of Australian Nationalism 1880-1988* (North Ryde, 1988), pp. 47-8.
2. Eddy and Schreuder, *The Rise of Colonial Nationalism: Australia, New Zealand, Canada and South Africa first assert their nationalities, 1880-1914* (Sydney, 1988), pp. 133, 135; Alomes, *op. cit.*, p. 48; Rickard, *Australia: A Cultural History* (London, 1988), p. 116.
3. Rickard, *H.B. Higgins: The Rebel as Judge* (Sydney, 1984), p. 102.
4. 'New South Wales: The Non-Existent State?', *Meanjin*, 39/2, July 1980, p. 139.
5. Graeme Davison, J.W. McCarty & Ailsa McLeary, *Australians 1888* (Sydney, 1987), pp. 8-10.
6. *Our Own Little Rebellion: The Story of the Eureka Stockade* (Melbourne, n.d. [1913]).
7. I first drew attention to this in 'Victoria – The Ideal State?', *Meanjin*, 37/3, October 1978, p. 279.
8. Marian Aveling, 'A History of the Australian Natives Association 1871-1900, Ph.D. thesis, Monash University, 1970, pp. 1-3, 36.
9. *Advance Australia*, 1 June 1897, p. 7. The blurb for the Association first appeared 1 July 1898.
10. *Advance Australia*, 1 July 1898; 7 April 1899, pp. 7-8.
11. *Op. cit.*, p. 300.
12. *Advance Australia*, 1 August 1898, p. 1 [?]; 1 July 1898, inside cover.
13. *A History of the Colony of Victoria* (London, 1904), vol.2, p. 323.
14. *Advance Australia*, 1 December 1897, p. 1. O'Dowd wrote under the pen name 'Ullmaroa'.
15. Deakin to Catherine Deakin, 24 March 1887, Deakin Papers, National Library of Australia, MS.1540/19/35.
16. J.A. LaNauze, *Alfred Deakin: A Biography* (Melbourne, 1965), p. 37.
17. Brookes to Deakin, 14 February 1905, Deakin Papers, MS.1540/19/185-6.
18. 'Testament prepared by Alfred Deakin in 1890 for the guidance of his daughters', printed copy, Deakin Papers, MS.1540/19/356.
19. Quoted by LaNauze, *op. cit.*, p. 646.
20. Quoted, Walter Murdoch, *Alfred Deakin: A Sketch* (London, 1923), p. 190.
21. Given in full by La Nauze in his edition of Deakin's *The Federal Story: The Inner History of the Federal Cause* (Melbourne, 1963 [1944]), pp. 177-9.
22. The prayers quoted from are CCXXXIII, 4 June 1898, and CCXXXVIII, December 1900, Deakin Papers, MS.1540/5.
23. Deakin to Brookes, 23 November 1899, MS.1540/19/82.
24. 4 December 1900 (London *Morning Post* 8 January 1901), Alfred Deakin, *Federate Australia: Selections from Letters to the Morning Post 1900-1910*, ed. J.A. LaNauze (Melbourne, 1968), p. 8.
25. Richard Jebb, *Studies in Colonial Nationalism* (London, 1905), pp. 191-2.

BRUCE BENNETT

Myths of Innocence and Experience

When I was a boy, in the 1950s, I would put on shoes and socks, grey serge shorts, a shirt and tie to catch the electric trolley bus into Perth. Having no car, we planned what we would do. My mother would wear her best shoes and dress, my father his Akubra hat, tie and sports jacket. We called it going to town ('city' was too pretentious a word), and it was an event. The suburb from which I came, Wembley, was neat and plain (pretension was frowned on). Our 1930s house overlooked a string of corrugated iron factories which produced pipes and stoves, where the hammering began at seven in the morning.

In our brick and orange-tiled house on the rise, my two brothers and I slept, dreamed, talked and fought on a back verandah converted to an asbestos-lined sleepout with louvred windows. To the east was town, seldom visited; to the west, twenty minutes by bike, was the beach. The choice between these two sites, the one offering commerce and culture, the other sea and surf, an innocent life in the open, was easy. The uncomplicated outdoors life was first choice every time. We were happy contributors to a West Coast myth of innocence.

Perth, the town which I occasionally visited from my suburban home in the 1950s, was still not quite a 'real' city. Still in the thrall of its primary--producing country areas, its principal ethos and sustaining mythology was a rurally-derived concept of innocence, in which many Perth-ites found it convenient to believe; the other side of this coin – a coin which many of us still choose to employ – is that too much knowledge is dangerous. These were the politically flatulent fifties, the undeniably Anglo-centric Menzies years. Those of us who dreamt of other cities, as I did, were drawn not to Sydney or Melbourne but to London and the great capitals of Europe. A few years later, in the early 1960s, when I found myself writing a university dissertation, I called it 'Images of the City in the Poetry of T.S. Eliot and Baudelaire' and was living high on my dreams of corruption and adventure in London and Paris, while I taught swimming classes on the Swan River: I was mentally and emotionally adrift from the community I otherwise inhabited.

As West Australians, we still felt cut off from the Eastern States and Europe; but Europe was the greater attraction and Asia had hardly as yet entered our calculations. Randolph Stow's novel *The Merry-go-round in the Sea*[1] has brilliantly revealed suburban West Australians in the 1940s as still

Fig. 1. Where the Swan meets the sea, H. Van Roalte, *Western Australian Giftbook*, 1916.

un-awakened to a wider world, in spite of the war; the fifties compounded this isolation mentality with an increasing belief in material 'progress' and development of natural resources, principally minerals. State politicians told us we were 'leading Australia' with our economic initiative and daring. Here were the seeds of the emblematic Poseidon boom of 1969-1970, and the Era of Experience whose fallout we are witnessing in the 1990s.

If growing up involves an understanding not just of economics but of the myths and counter-myths of the society which we inhabit, Perth offers an interesting set of problems. Since the 1950s, the moral discourses of the principal churches, Anglican, Protestant and Catholic, have receded in the public consciousness along with a wider secularisation of society. Public recognition of the arts has increased, but they have not filled the vacuum left by the retreat of the mainstream religions, nor would most people want them to do so in an age of plural discourses and general scepticism. Nevertheless, as synthesising discourses, the arts (and especially literature) may provide some understanding of the concealed logic of our times, the myths and counter-myths by which we live.

The late 1980s and early 90s have been marked by media events highlighting violence, racism and corruption in Western Australia's capital city. An orchestrated campaign of violence against Asian immigrants has led to the fire bombing of restaurants, assaults and murders; clashes between Aborigines, police and government over the redevelopment of the brewery site on the Swan River have received major television and newspaper coverage; sex crimes have increased geometrically; and the 'WA Inc.' saga of corruption by leading businessmen and officials has dominated popular culture, amounting at times to cliché. If the public culture once presumed innocence in the citizens of Perth, the climate of the 1990s is one of presumptive guilt.

In the light of such current circumstances, how then might we read the past of this city? What is its psycho-cultural archaeology? Have the people of Perth, in the space of one generation, fallen from a state of grace? Or have the seeds of corruption always been among us? Have we been duped as much by our myths as by our businessmen?

Some ore samples from previous times might be tested. What, for instance, do the decades of the 1920s and 30s reveal? Even here, perceptions and truth are difficult to pin down. Historians differ in their views of this period, reminding us that historical writings are themselves only 'readings' of a time and place.[2] Nevertheless, it is interesting to note G.C. Bolton's picture of Western Australia in the late 1920s and early 1930s as an isolated corner of the world with optimistic expectations and a strong sense of community.[3] The Depression certainly had its impact and there were marches of the unemployed, but Bolton observes that the Depression did little to damage the social fabric of Western Australia, largely because of the West's isolation and its citizens' capacity to

Fig. 2. Unemployed march in Perth, 1930. From C.T. Stannage, *The People of Perth.*

Fig. 3. Late afternoon in St George's Terrace, Perth, *Western Mail,* Christmas, 1938.

construct 'a myth of the hostile and unhelpful Eastern States'.[4] Bolton thus sees the secession movement of the early 1930s as a 'safety valve'; the dominant tradition in the 'overgrown country town' of Perth remained that of the pioneers - characterised by hard work, self-help, a capacity to put up with rough conditions, a belief in 'the superior goodness of primary production, to share fairly with those in need who were willing to help themselves'.[5] C.T. Stannage takes a more critical view of what he sees as the 'gentry' view of Western Australia and presents a more 'bottom-up' perspective on Perth.[6] While not disputing Bolton's view of Perth as 'the home of a happy and contented people' Stannage observes that – as Bolton himself had shown – 'behind the Western Australian looking glass, there was a less visible Perth – people suffering from stunted ambitions, inadequate housing, and inadequate employment'.[7] These different historical perspectives, and their accompanying ideologies, deserve further investigation in the light of the literary and visual arts, produced in the crucible of the interwar years.

One of the richest sources of literature and art of the 1920s and 30s is the *Western Mail* annual, published every Christmas from 1897 to 1955. In their introduction to a recent anthology of material from the *Western Mail* annuals, Ffion Murphy and Richard Nile summarise their view of its dominant ideology:

> The *Western Mail* Christmas annual celebrated the industry with which men brought the physical world under their control; it upheld the values of conquest, immigration and settlement which would turn a wilderness into a civil society; it apotheosized work and revelled in its rewards; it spoke the language of men and women who sought to make the world their own ... In the *Western Mail* annuals, the public and private spheres of human life merged and conformity to social norms presupposed personal happiness and material well-being.[8]

Respectability was maintained by an insistence on a moderate tone. Readers' views were welcome so long as they were 'restrained in ... discourse'.[9] May Gibbs's cover illustrations and cartoons for the *Western Mail* from 1905-1909 set an example of local imagery allied with a view of Western Australia as an outpost of Empire, a view which would scarcely alter through the years of the First World War and after. May Gibbs's successor, Ida S. Rentoul, offered 'an essentially optimistic, perhaps unrealistic or fairytale vision of Western Australia'.[10] In these ways, the *Western Mail* may be seen to have contributed to a Western myth of innocence.

The myth of innocence rooted in a rural Arcadia was remarkably persistent through the 1930s. Paul Hasluck's autobiography, *Mucking About*[11], reinforces this view, presenting Perth as a place where civilisation and nature could co-exist in a relatively happy balance. Alongside a Wordsworthian sense of the South-West bush environment went the 'civilizing mission' of Hasluck and his friends, whom he describes in retrospect as 'eager for the development of all sides of life – for art, music, plays and especially for books. In all this we wanted to find foundation for a pride in being Australians, and especially for being Western Australians'.[12]

The Perth milieu evidently provided these opportunities for Hasluck, who appears to have been a balanced, inquisitive, public-spirited journalist in the 1930s, concerned as a federalist for Western Australia's role in the Commonwealth during the campaigns for secession in 1933 and with social issues such as the injustice suffered by Aborigines. A visit to Asia in 1938 opened Hasluck's eyes to the cultures of Australia's near north, but, like most of his countrymen at this time, he returned with an enhanced sense of his Europeanness. In reviewing Hasluck's autobiography, Bolton comments that it reinforces the concept of Western Australia in the interwar years as 'essentially a secure, confident and tolerant society, accessible to those who wished to improve themselves and their community'.[13] He observes further that 'It may not have been like that entirely; but it is not a bad myth for a community to carry with it into the last quarter of the twentieth century'. Bolton wrote this in the 1970s. Is the myth still sustainable in the 1990s?

The myth of innocence in the Golden West depends heavily upon the influence of 'nature' – a physical environment from which the 'overgrown country town' of Perth is perceived in the interwar years as not yet having insulated itself, as certain other cities had. T.A.G. Hungerford's retrospective view of the decade of the 1930s in his *Stories from Suburban Road*[14] reinforces this view of Perth. In his autobiographical narrative, Hungerford reconstructs a semi-rural boyhood paradise on the banks of the Swan River in South Perth, a suburb which has been perceived quite differently by other writers such as Walter Murdoch, Peter Cowan and Dorothy Hewett. Hungerford's boyhood idyll is in part formed by its literary genre, autobiography; the innocent years of pleasurable adventure present themselves in terms of a *Bildungsroman,* as prelude to the autobiographical persona's initiation into manhood in the Pacific War. The single recurrent note is one of nostalgia for simpler times. In Hungerford's use of his autobiographical narratives, actions speak louder than words, nature than culture: the boy's sensuous relationship with his natural environment is central; the river, the Chinese market gardens, the birds, frogs and goannas are presented with vivid clarity as exempla of times lost, to be found again only in memory and contemplation. Like Randolph Stow in his autobiographical novel *The Merry-go-round in the Sea,* Hungerford presents his slice of Western Australia as a wonderful place in which to be young. Wars, and growing up, happen elsewhere. The note of nostalgia, as in my opening paragraphs in this essay, tends to simplify into the innocent, child's-eye vision. In the visual arts, as in literature, the rural idyll is a typical genre of the interwar years. C.T. Stannage has shown how two of the *Western Mail*'s principal artists, Amy Heap and Fred Flood, 'sought out and selected what was beautiful and bountiful in nature and joyous in human nature'.[15] But the 1930s do reveal another, more urban and potentially less innocent face. Some of the photographs of Fred Flood and the paintings of Portia Bennett indicate this other face. As David Bromfield has pointed out, Perth remained, in visual terms, 'a British country town which still thought of itself as such'.[16] Bennett's paintings, centred on the Perth Town Hall, somewhat qualify this view. In Bromfield's words, Bennett's work is 'a product of an anxious compromise between [her] desire to see the streets of Perth as the streets of a modern city and the fear that this would provoke in her most likely patrons [the middle-class business people]'.[17] Some photographs by Fred Flood also indicate, in Bromfield's opinion, a desire for a kind of modernism in architecture and styles of living in Perth. These include his photograph 'Perth Rises' in the *Western Mail* in 1938 and 'Late Afternoon in St George's Terrace, Perth'. In 'Perth Rises' we see the desire for a modern city-scape based on New York; in 'Late Afternoon' the figures with their long shadows cast behind them may suggest a heroism in modern city life.[18]

Along with such tentative shifts towards urban imagery, Perth's small intellectual élites were becoming more socially conscious. Innocence, it was becoming clear, could be exposed as a restrictive ignorance: doubleness, duplicity, was perhaps 'natural' for social beings. By 1930, the town could boast a seventeen-year-old university. Comparing the diffuse revolutionary feelings of himself and fellow university students in these years with 'Auden and Co.' in England, Norman Bartlett has recalled that 'Our enemies were not "our hunting fathers" but our working-class fathers who were more interested in immediate means of improving their material conditions than in literary fashions or revolutionary theory'.[19] A rhetoric was available, if not direct experience, as war approached: 'the more innocent among us continued to think that anti-Fascism, like anti-capitalism, was a propaganda conflict of intrigue and words'.[20] But the political culture of the Left was having some influence. In addition to Katharine Susannah Prichard's work for the Communist Party (more famous in retrospect, perhaps, than at the time), the Workers' Art Guild was active, producing plays by Clifford Odets, Irwin Shaw and others. And Oscar Walters was publishing some stirring socialist verse in the *Westralian Worker*:

Our foes have privilege and wealth,
  Their hirelings round them fawn,
They work by cunning and by stealth
  To hold the world in pawn.
Through schemes and guile they look to win
  Their long-sought victory.
The only strength we have is in

> Our solidarity.[21]

For Walters, the patriotism he knew as a Gallipoli veteran had been lost in the unemployment queues of the early 1930s.[22] He now lived in a divided society.

The most fully frontal assaults upon the idea of Perth as an innocent city in the 1930s occurred in the form of realist novels. Perhaps the most dramatic of these assaults was J.M. Harcourt's novel *Upsurge*.[23] This novel was officially banned because of its explicit use of sexual details, but Richard Nile has suggested that the real reason was its support for 'a radical political programme and its marxian analysis of the depression'.[24] The socialist realist flavour of *Upsurge* is epitomised in the reflections of one of Harcourt's characters who, after being forced to seek sustenance work, wearily looks down on the city from King's Park with a jaundice which has been strongly discouraged by the tourist industry:

> The brick and stone and concrete cliffs of the city reared themselves behind the gardens along the waterfront. Groom reflected that every building in the huddled mass meant money. He saw the city suddenly from a new point of view in terms of money. Millions and millions of pounds sterling were frozen there in the huddled mass of the city, and every penny of it belonged to somebody else. The riches of the antipodes were there beneath him, and not a penny of it could be touched ...

Harcourt's presentation of the city as a site of middle-class capitalist greed and exploitation is reinforced in Katharine Susannah Prichard's novel *Intimate Strangers*[25], which also recalls the demonstration marches by the unemployed victims of this time. But the city and its ubiquitous river are also presented as stimulants of Eros, a seldom uncomplicated drive. When Elodie, escaping temporarily from an ailing marriage, catches a bus to the city to buy a dress in which she imagines herself greeting her new lover, the prose sings with a buoyant lyricism:

> As the bus flew along it seemed a great jaunting car. Such an excursion this ordinary bumpy drive into the city became! And how lovely everything looked. The hills and the suburban gardens, larkspurs, marigolds, roses and sweet peas flaring about them: patches of blue and yellow wildflowers on blocks of scrubby vacant land. Crossing the long bridge over the river, she could see the pelicans and gulls feeding on the sandbanks, grey cranes fishing in muddy pools. The river stretched, shining and placid, red-roofed houses on its distant shores blooming beneath a clear blue sky. Elodie was as delighted and excited as if she were seeing them all for the first time. She admired the broad tree-planted thoroughfare the bus swung into, entering the city; told herself it was a boulevard, and stately old houses overlooking the river, as dignified and self-possessed as people of another generation, despite the scurry of gaudy buses, trucks, motor cars and a few slow-moving horse-drawn market carts passing them.
>
> Walking along the narrower crowded streets, she rejoiced in the little pictures of blue river and distant suburbs at the end of the streets.

A lover's mood is here shown to induce images of a city which still admits nature; and this mixes uneasily at times with the novel's social reformist polemics. In this lover's mood, however, the city thrills the senses while Elodie simultaneously dreams of a romantic escape with her lover to the magic-sounding cities of Asia – of Java, Siam, China. Her duplicity is an aspect of her vitality. In a prelude to the collapse of her romantic dreams and the recognition of duty to family and to the cause of socialism, she decides not to buy the expensive clothes after which she lusts in the city's shop-windows. As the evidence of betrayals in love, marriage and work mounts up around her, Elodie finds release (as Katharine Prichard also found a kind of release following the suicide of her husband Hugo Throssell) in 'the fire of a regenerating idea', a socialism which could give heroic stature to those who struggled with the ordinariness of city and suburban living. This is her form of transcendance, which emerges less from the circumstances of her experience at a certain time in this city than from a quasi-religious ideology of hope.[26]

While politics and eroticism are associated with Harcourt's and Prichard's fictional renderings of the emergent city of Perth in the 1930s, Philip Masel's little known novel *In a Glass Prison* brings crime and punishment to the fore. Masel's fictionalised Perth is deceptively calm; behind its daily rituals lurk dark secrets, betrayals and corruption. The isolation of this relatively small community is stressed, but not its innocence. Indeed, guilt is the defining feature of this community, which Masel explores in the trial for murder of a Perth shopkeeper and its aftermath. Masel's focus in his novel is not so much on the events themselves – drug smuggling and murder – as on the social and psychological consequences of these events upon the lives of the murderer's wife, son, and especially his daughter. Through the sufferings of the murderer's daughter, Jean Mottram, in particular, the author shows how a powerful and self-righteous élite of Perth society (lawyers and doctors in particular) visit vengeance upon those who stray, publicly, from the designated paths of righteousness. The imagery of the glass prison adroitly reveals Jean Mottram's fate in this enclosed society just as the lawyer Lamond's vanity is demonstrated in his frequent recourse to a mirror. Class distinctions are signified by the contrast between working-class Victoria Park and 'Beauty Bay' (Peppermint Grove, Claremont), where the leaders of Perth society entertain each other and intermarry. Once again, the river functions as a signifier of nature: a fruitful and restorative place, but also destructive, as in the sudden storm which drowns the Mottram son.

Masel presents a far more sinister image of Perth's high society than Lucy Walker's relatively mild Pepper Tree Bay series of prose romances in the post-war years. His 'low-life' scenes occur not in dance halls as in *Intimate Strangers* but in a boxing gymnasium where Tod Mottram tries to carry out his father's injunction, 'fight to win'. But the plausibly polite establishment figures in their mansions overlooking the river are also fighting, from more privileged positions, to win; and the odds are stacked in their favour. *In a Glass Prison* provides an exploration of the power of public opinion, rumour and moral retribution in a provincial town with pretensions to the status of a city. It is this sense of enclosure which Randolph Stow's Rick Maplestead was to rail against in *The Merry-go-round in the Sea* prior to his voluntary exile from Australia, and which Stow transferred from Perth to the East Anglian port of Harwich in his later novel *The Suburbs of Hell*.[27] In Masel's novel, the protagonist, and sentient centre, remains however in Perth. Bearing the stigmata of her father's crime she becomes a victim of the moralistic, judgmental business and professional classes but manages to retain a certain pride and independence. Looking out over the Swan River at the end, she knows its beauty but the sunshine gives her only a 'mocking assurance' of contentment.

The decade of the 1930s represents a critical phase in the literary history of Western Australia. One hundred years after British colonisation, here was a laboratory society inhabiting the banks of a paradisal river three thousand kilometres from the nearest similar settlement. Many wanted to cut themselves further adrift, as the majority vote for secession in 1933 shows. From one point of view, Perth was the very model of a peaceable small urban community, whose inhabitants could choose an appropriate mix of nature and culture; from another it was a society riven by internal divisions and secrets buried deep. An emergent urban literature reflected these changes, but showed little of the confidence which could make H.G. Wells's character Mr Polly say 'If the world does not please you, *you can change it*'.[28] Moreover, a powerful counter-myth of the outback persisted. Louis Kaye's novel *Tybal Men: A Struggle for Survival in the Outback*[29] exemplifies this still powerful tradition of rough-edged realism, a masculinist ethos, racism and battles for survival in 'the wild land'. The primitivism of this life still has more appeal than the city for many writers and readers.

A second major phase in urban literature in Western Australia may be seen to occur in the 1970s and 80s and is linked with the 1930s through the figure of Peter Cowan. The 1930s were Cowan's seed-time, a decade when, as an itinerant bush worker, he learnt to appreciate the harsh beauty of the Australian countryside. His writing contains a constant dialectical opposition between images of city and bush. Characters often escape from the confines of city or suburbs to the hills, bush or beaches. These are the places of authenticity, as they were for Hemingway or Faulkner, where the simple self may reassert itself in primal physical activities. Cowan's fiction suggests that the bush is the place to live, and to die. His suburbs represent the middle way between the extremes of bush and city and are often a living death. The city, on the other hand, is a place of mirages. From the all-male boarding-houses or hotels of the post-war years to the city apartments of the 1980s Cowan explores the tensions and complexities of urban living. In his recent story 'Apartment,'[30] for instance, Karen, an ex-addict and prostitute, enjoys the relative luxury of an apartment where she has been asked to live with a man on weekends and evenings and to satisfy his bizarre needs, apparently as a pay-off for some drugs arrangement. The segments of this fine story do not *tell* the reader what to think; rather, they hint at possibilities, drawing the reader into the intrigue as an active participant in the puzzle.

The disembodied voices of Cowan's actors of the modern city come to us without the usual costumery of 'character'. They speak, rather, from the depths of a communal subconscious, reminders of what Freud called the night-time side of the self. In stories such as 'Apartment', Perth becomes part of late twentieth century anonymity and anomie. Geographical location is deconstructed and we are placed in what some post-modernist writers have called 'the zone', an objective correlative for 'marginal, heterogeneous and outlaw' experience.[31] Yet the silences, and sense of distance between people in Cowan's fictions also act as a powerful statement of emotional need.

Other Western Australian authors of the 1980s have also registered shifts in an urban consciousness, which are somewhat more revealing than the recent expensive study which proved that city dwellers walk faster than country people.[32] Yet Perth remains a transitional city, harking back to rural and provincial ideals (and still contains some slow walkers), while it also embraces high-rise hopes. In 1969, Hal Colebatch used William McGonagall's verse form to ridicule the modernist aspirations:

> The city of Perth by the diminished Swan River,
> Is not really a place for a high-liver,
> And indeed when astronauts arrive and scan it,
> I am surprised they do not plant a flag, for to claim it
> as another planet.[33]

Dorothy Hewett's personal mythology required a 'real' City which she located in Sydney as a contrast to the 'Garden' of her pastoral childhood zone in the Great Southern region of Western Australia.[34] Perth would not do. Nicholas Hasluck, in poems such as 'Houdini' and 'Flats'[35] and the novel *Truant State*[36], presents the city as a zone of change, providing images of chicanery in business and psychological imprisonment in the offices of high-rise buildings, but also as an imaginative space in which to perceive alternatives within the frame of a tolerantly comic world-view. Marion Campbell[37], Terri-Ann White[38] and others have given a distinctively female and sometimes feminist set of perspectives on the city.

Perth has now grown to the extent that it stimulates and comprehends a large number of fragmentary possible worlds. It is now possible to call this Western city a literary, artistic and even to some extent a cinematic centre, traversed by many voices and styles, including those of the relatively dispossessed – especially Aborigines and immigrants. Colin Johnson's novels *Wild Cat Falling*[39] and *Long Live Sandawara*[40] and Archie Weller's *The Day of the Dog*[41] provide vivid representations of the metropolitan malaise of modern Aboriginal youth. The city which has been satirised for its racism and small-town commercialism, as in Robert Drewe's novels *The Savage Crows*[42] and *Fortune*[43], has also been memorialised as a place of survival by 'exiles' such as the Greek-born poet and short story writer Vasso Kalamaras[44], and Malaysian-born immigrant and poet Ee Tiang Hong:

> On *terra firma, Australis*
> don't ask me how I got out, Eddy,
> and, Bruce, this isn't a suicide note,
> Heaven forbid! No sailing
> to Byzantium, either. Indeed,
> thankful just to have survived then –
> around an edge of consciousness,
> new faces, fellow Australian.[45]

Perth is no fabled city, like Yeats's Byzantium, for Ee Tiang Hong's persona, but a place of respite; even, beside the fructifying river, a place to forget.

Perth has not yet occasioned an intensity of hellfire imagery from its writers and artists, yet it has proved its power to inflame social consciences as well as to enchant with its unique blend of natural and built environment. If Arcadia no longer seems the appropriate image for this fast-growing city which may double its population to two million in the next generation, nor yet do its writers or artists present it as an Inferno. Somewhere between these extremes, it offers shifting perspectives from lyric to satire. The river which runs beside this city and has provided a recurring symbolism seems an appropriate place to pause and contemplate, with returning Perth-ite Robert Drewe, the strange mix of innocence and experience which it prompted in the late 1970s:

> I walked along the length of the beach up to the Royal Perth Yacht Club with its massed wealth floating serenely in the shallows, and back to Mounts Bay Road. On my right the city skyline stood out sharply against the sky (especially the letters BOND, in dark blue, atop one building)... A magpie carolled in the distance, right on cue. It was quiet and still and as I strolled past where the old Crawley Bay tearooms once stood two butterflies flapped lightly into my face. They were copulating on the wing, fused gently together and just too languid to get out of my way.
>
> Talk about symbolism! I thought. 'I've got to get back here.' Seduced again![46]

Drewe's prose here is more lyrical than satiric: his seduction seems 'natural', though the imagery of conspicuous wealth links his perceptions with those in Philip Masel's novel *In a Glass Prison* and the work of other realists in the 1930s, who saw beyond the facades of innocence. All of that was of course before the Fall of the House of Bond and its associated mysteries and horrors. Can the river, and stray butterflies, still cast their old spell?

Fig. 4. Perth, 1988, 'Where to now?'.

Fig. 5. 'Perth in 2029', *Western Mail,* 1929.

NOTES

1. Randolph Stow, *The Merry-go-round in the Sea* (London: Macdonald, 1965).
2. See Hayden White, *The Content of the Form: Narrative Discourse and Historical Representation* (Baltimore: Johns Hopkins University Press, 1987).
3. G.C. Bolton, *A Fine Country to Starve In* (Nedlands: University of Western Australia Press, 1972).
4. *Ibid*., p. 267.
5. *Ibid*., p. 268.
6. C.T. Stannage, *The People of Perth* (Perth: Perth City Council, 1979).
7. *Ibid*., p. 337.
8. Ffion Murphy and Richard Nile (eds), *The Gate of Dreams: The 'Western Mail' Annuals, 1897-1955* (Fremantle: Fremantle Arts Centre Press, 1990), p. 11.
9. *Ibid*., p. 14.
10. *Ibid*., p. 19.
11. Paul Hasluck, *Mucking About: An Autobiography* (Melbourne: Melbourne University Press, 1977).
12. *Ibid*., p. 193.
13. G.C. Bolton, 'A Local Identity', *Westerly*, no.4 (December 1977), p. 77.
14. T.A.G. Hungerford, *Stories from Suburban Road: An Autobiographical Collection 1920-1939* (Fremantle: Fremantle Arts Centre Press, 1983).
15. See C.T. Stannage, *Embellishing the Landscape: The Images of Amy Heap and Fred Flood 1920-1940* (Fremantle: Fremantle Arts Centre Press, 1990), p. 12.
16. David Bromfield, 'Modernism's Back Alley – Perth Streets as Signs of the Times', *Westerly*, 31, 4, (1986), p. 96.
17. *Ibid*.
18. *Ibid*.
19. Norman Bartlett, 'Perth in the Turbulent Thirties', *Westerly*, 4 (December 1977), p. 62.
20. *Ibid*., p. 68.
21. The *Westralian Worker* (20 March 1931).
22. See '17' and '32' in the *Westralian Worker* (15 April 1932).
23. J.M. Harcourt, *Upsurge: A Novel*, (London: John Long, 1934); facsimile edition (University of Western Australia Press, 1986), introduced by Richard Nile.
24. *Ibid*., xxiii.
25. Katharine Susannah Prichard, *Intimate Strangers* (London: Jonathan Cape, 1937).
26. See Van Ikin, 'The Political Novels of Katharine Susannah Prichard', *Southerly*, XLIII, (1983), pp. 80-102.
27. Randolph Stow, *The Suburbs of Hell* (London: Secker and Warburg, 1984).
28. Quoted in Norman Bartlett, 'Science, Sex and Mr Wells', *Westerly*, 23, 2, (1978), pp. 66-67.
29. Louis Kaye, *Tybal Men: A Struggle for Survival in the Outback* (London: Wright and Brown, [1931]).
30. Peter Cowan, *Voices* (Fremantle: Fremantle Arts Centre Press, 1988), pp. 29-40.
31. Brian McHale, *Postmodernist Fiction* (New York: Methuen, 1987), Ch. 3.
32. The International Geographical Congress in 1988 was informed that a study in five Australian and five English towns and cities found that city dwellers walked about 7 percent faster than those in the country. *West Australian*, (27 August 1988), p. 5.
33. 'A Poetic Gem', first published in *Westerly*, 4, (December 1969).
34. Dorothy Hewett, 'The Garden and the City', *Westerly*, 4, (1982), pp. 99-104.

35. See *Wide Domain: Western Australian Themes and Images*, eds. Bruce Bennett and William Grono (Sydney: Angus and Robertson, 1979), p. 185, p. 227.
36. Nicholas Hasluck, *Truant State* (Ringwood: Penguin Books Australia, 1987).
37. Marion Campbell, *Not Being Miriam* (Fremantle: Fremantle Arts Centre Press, 1988).
38. Terri-Ann White et al. (eds), *No Substitute: Prose Poems Images* (Fremantle: Fremantle Arts Centre Press, 1990).
39. Colin Johnson, *Wild Cat Falling* (Sydney: Angus and Robertson, 1965).
40. Colin Johnson, *Long Live Sandawara* (Melbourne: Quartet Books, 1979).
41. Archie Weller, *The Day of the Dog* (Sydney: Allen and Unwin, 1981).
42. Robert Drewe, *The Savage Crows* (Sydney: Collins, 1976).
43. Robert Drewe, *Fortune* (Sydney: Picador, 1986).
44. See Vasso Kalamaras, *Twenty Two Poems* (Greek-English), The Author (Daglish, 1977); and *Other Earth: Four Greek-Australian Stories*, trans. Reg Durack (Fremantle: Fremantle Arts Centre Press, 1977).
45. Ee Tiang Hong, 'Coming To', *Westerly*, 31, 3, (1986), pp. 56-57.
46. Robert Drewe, *The Bulletin*, March 1977.

JUDITH L. KAPFERER

Rural Myths and Urban Ideologies

Thr argument of this paper is grounded in the centention that the traditional city/bush, urban/rural distinctions made of Australian society represent a false dichotomy. Rather, it is suggested that this distinction serves an ideological purpose in opposing, for example, rural and urban workers, rural and urban owners/managers etc. The rhetoric and the reality of Australian cultural mythologies is analysed with the aim of demonstrating the ways in which images of Australia and Australians are exemplified and enacted in the daily life of country towns. To this end, the paper offers an examination of (a) massmedia and (b) some 'urban' aspects of the rural economy, particularily the control of rural industries by urban and transnational interests.

(a) INTRODUCTION

It is an item of public knowledge that Australia is one of the most highly urbanised countries in the world, with the majority of its population clustering around (clinging to) the coastal belt, while only around one quarter of the population of New South Wales, for example, lives in and around settlements of fewer than 20,000 people.

But the question I want to address here is why and in what ways a minority of the population has such an impact upon 'Australians' understandings of themselves and their identity as separate and different from the citizens of other nations. That it does have such an impact is, I think, incontestable. In song and story, art and literature, history and international relations, the ruralism of what has been called 'the Australian identity' is emphasised. Ned Kelly and Ben Hall, Peter Lalor, Clancy of the Overflow, Jack Dunn, Les Darcy and hundreds of nameless diggers, sportsmen, pioneers, shearers, bullockies, selectors and swagmen constitute a host of battlers, underdogs whose skills and exploits are mythologised and celebrated as quintessentially Australian. And yet it must be noted that qualities and characteristics such as egalitarianism, individualism, independence, physical endurance, doggedness, taciturnity, loyalty, resistance to oppression, fortitude and a perhaps naive faith in humanity are not of themselves particularly *rural*. To take a contemporary example, there is at least as much of the Sentimental Bloke in *Crocodile Dundee* as there is in 'The Man from Snowy River'. Nor are these characteristics peculiarly Australian, though for cultural and ontological reasons, their configurations, interpretations and manifestations may well be.

My purpose in essaying an analysis of rural myths and urban ideologies – and in distinguishing elements of the two – is to achieve some purchase upon the ways in which Australian culture is generated and regenerated by the interplay of myth and ideology. Along with Geertz (1973), I take culture to be the humanly constructed 'webs of meaning' within which people are enmeshed, and within which they conduct their daily lives. Myths, as forms of communication, as *accounts* of the genesis and power of deeply held beliefs and values (see Barthes, 1973) I take to be among the fundamental building blocks of ideologies. Ideologies, on the other hand, as sets of beliefs which take the real relations and conditions of existence, achieve their power and legitimacy through the selective and systematic interpretation and organisation of widely held myths (see Kapferer, 1988, 80).

The argument presented here, then, is grounded in an approach which seeks to discover aspects of the mythology of the rural (for example, self-reliance, mateship) within widespread, urban-constructed and politically motivated ideologies of, for example egalitarianism, nationalism, class relations and so on (see, e.g. White 1981, 102, 131). Historians like White, and Hirst (1973, 1983), and political scientists (Jaensch, 1983; Aitkin, 1972) make much of a perceived cleavage between rural and urban styles of life and cultural orientations; but what I want to demonstrate here is not only that this cleavage is more perceived than real, but also that it has *ideological* significance, is itself, indeed, an ideological construction. That is to say that the characteristic figures and images of rural mythology, generated in specific historical and material conditions, find continued resonance in the contemporary circumstances of social and political action across the nation, in metropolises, suburbs, regional centres, country towns and isolated habitations. I have characterised these circumstances as ideological in that their organisation and orchestration is structured in and through the cultural institutions of Australian society and the ideological apparatuses of the Australian state, achieving a coherence which informs the social and political action of large and more or less identifiable groups. Such groups, often referred to as, for example, Business, Industry, the Economy, the Market, Labour, or, more generally, as the community, Youth, the aged, the party, the poor, women, 'ethnics' and so on, are influenced by, and in turn influence, the ongoing constructions of ideological thought which have significance in their daily lives. This is so whether these constructions are conscious and formalised (as in political manifestos, or in legislation, for example) or are taken-for-granted common sense and 'natural' understandings of lived experiences.

Moreover, these ideologies are to be conceived of as urban for two reasons. The first is simply that, in Australia, the greatest proportion of their construction is undertaken within the context of an *urban* environment. The majority of the Australian population lives and works in the cities and big towns where legislation is enacted, business is conducted and professionals are trained. But secondly, and more significantly, the major ideologies within which Australians are enmeshed are metropolitan in both their generation and application. Australia is bound within a world economy dominated by a capitalist ideology originating in the great *metropolitan* centres of the western world at a time, not only of imperialist expansion, but of accelerated urbanisation. Technological advances, neocolonialist economic policies and the emergence of huge transnational conglomerates (see Crough and Wheelwright, 1982) have locked Australians more securely than ever before into a 'global village' which is nothing other than a global *city*.

This is not to suggest that there are no differences between Australian ideologies and those of other nations – Australian egalitarian individualism, for example, bears a different meaning-load from the egalitarianism and/or individualism of, for example, U.S. or French formulations (see Kapferer, 1988.) It is, however, to suggest that the source of such distinctions as can be drawn lies in the refraction of Australian rural mythology through the construction of ideologies which are, in the end, urban and international.

I focus upon two New South Wales towns with populations of less than ten thousand: Bombala (1,500) in the southern Monaro, and Cootamundra (6,000) on the southwestern slopes of the Great Dividing Range. The data reported here represents the first fruits of a more comprehensive and ongoing investigation of the construction of Australian cultures. Bombala and Cootamundra were chosen as fieldwork sites in the initial phase (1987-8) of this research for a number of reasons. They are both towns and districts with which I had some familiarity, and although far enough from most major research centres to be considered virgin territory (especially in the field of youth studies) were still reasonably accessible. They are also small enough to enable the use of those qualitative research methods (observation, interview, documentary analysis, for example) demanded by cultural analysis. Furthermore, country towns form one of the fundamental popular images of 'Australian-ness', of community, and of social conservatism. Verrall *et al.* (1985) for example, build their analysis of rural conservatism around just such conceptions, referring to the power of specifically local elites, conformity to 'dominant community attitudes' and the force of 'parish pump politics'. Jaensch (1983) also stresses the influence of 'rural consciousness' and conservatism upon political culture: 'rural areas have a distinctive economic base. Rural people have a distinctive political culture (1983, 67)'.

Studies of Australian country towns (e.g. Oeser and Emery, 1954, Oxley 1973; Wild, 1974) have generally not addressed questions of the links and connections between country town and metropolis, conceiving of these towns as, in the tradition of community studies, more or less self-contained entities. Similarly, political scientists are mostly concerned, in their analyses of party politics, to stress the 'cleavage' between urban and rural interests: 'Country Party movements arose and were sustained...when and where there were sharp cleavages between rural producers and metropolitan economic and political interests (Costar and Woodward, 1985:6).'

While I make no claims for the 'typicality' of Bombala and Cootamundra as Australian country towns, beyond the fact of their representative size and distance from more populous centres, both towns unquestionably constitute fertile ground for a case study of the interaction of rural myth and urban ideology in the formation of 'national' culture and consciousness.

Both towns grew up as service and market centres for the surrounding pastoral industry, but in recent years have suffered a decline in population accompanying the rural crisis of the past decade. Both towns also, I think, generally conform to the visual image of the country towns which Australians hold, of wide streets, somnolent, dusty and dominated by the summer sound of 'locusts burnt in the pepper trees'. If visitors no longer see 'farmers bouncing on barrel mares' they are still struck by the practice of parking rear-to-kerb, and the absence of traffic lights and parking meters. The openness and easygoing ambience of the Australian country towns portrayed by Slessor contrasts with what I take to be the dominant image of the American small town as popularised by Sherwood Anderson and Sinclair Lewis. Bombala and Cootamundra are not like Winesburg, Ohio or Zenith, precisely because they are *Australian* country towns, reflecting and refracting peculiarly Australian ideas of who we are and what we are like as a people. Unlike the American towns portrayed by Vidich and Bensman (1960) for example or the English villages depicted by Bell (1971), Bombala and Cootamundra are, by virtue of a highly centralised system of government, administration and economic transactions, towns whose people are forced to take greater cognizance of national and international trends and events in both their working lives and in their political thought and action than are the inhabitants of more economically and politically self-sufficient communities.

I want to make the point at the outset that the image of Australia as the bush, and of Australians as embodying virtues mythologically conceived of as essentially 'rural', remains as fundamental to our understandings and mystifications of ourselves, in relation to each other and to outsiders, as it has ever been. The notion of rural virtue as opposed to urban vice has, of course, a long history in Western thought, reaching back into classical times, as Williams [1975] makes clear:

> On the country has gathered the idea of a natural way of life: of peace, innocence and simple virtue. On the city has gathered the idea of an achieved centre: of

> learning, communication, light. Powerful hostile associations have also developed: on the city as a place of noise, worldliness and ambition; on the country as a place of backwardness, ignorance, limitation (1975, 9; see also White, 1981).

And yet, Williams reminds us, in the conventional contrast of rural virtue and urban vice, the 'regular, necessary and functional links between the social and moral orders' of the two are not to be denied:

> The greed and calculation, so easily isolated and condemned in the city, run back, quite clearly, to the country houses, with the fields and their labourers around them. . .The exploitation of man and of nature which takes place in the country, is realised and concentrated in the city. But also the profits of other kinds of (urban) exploitation... come to penetrate the country (1975,64).

In Australia the rural-urban contrast has enormous ideological significance, underpinning such diverse manifestations of 'Australianness' as the solidarity of mateship (in the bush, in battle, in trade unions, in political manoeuvring); the free-booting and unemotional self-sufficiency of the individual (from the Drover's Wife and Crocodile Dundee to contemporary tycoons like John Elliott and Alan Bond; and the often brutal racism and ethnocentrism of relations between whites, Aborigines and Indo-Asians, and Anglo and non-Anglo ethnic groups. Our understandings of liberty, equality and fraternity are closely intertwined with our understanding of our history as a pioneering people battling against, on the one hand, the natural elements, and on the other, the social prejudices and injustices of the colonising power.

I begin, therefore, with the notion of rural and urban as opposed categories of human existence having particular relevance in Australian sociology and ideology. What I want to argue in this paper is that the rural-urban dichotomy is a false one, having its genesis in the industrialising and urbanising upheavals of eighteenth and nineteenth century Britain and Europe, and its development in the progression from laissez faire free enterprise capitalism to the transnational and corporate capitalism of the contemporary world. The enclosures, urban destitution and crime, the ills so graphically depicted by Mayhew and Rowntree along with the peasant and later tribal migrations in Europe and the colonial territories administered from Europe, as well as a long artistic and literary tradition, have all structured our perceptions of a radical difference between rural and urban styles of life.

From the time of Marx, Weber, Durkheim and the birth of sociology as a distinct discipline, urban and rural have been categories deeply ingrained in the sociological consciousness, structuring and directing much of the analysis of Western industrial and, more recently, other industrialising societies. Indeed the very distinguishing of rural sociology from urban (that is, all other) sociology makes this clear. These categories have influenced our understanding of an array of social phenomena – poverty, crime, economic and political development, cultural change, inequality and disadvantage. They have also influenced our understanding of, and preference for, the desirability and viability of certain 'solutions' to social problems – centralised, bureaucratised, materialist and, often, mean-spirited.

The Australian situation, however, historically presents a reversal of the European pattern of migration and urbanisation: the first rural workers and landowners were, by and large, urban people – convicts currency folk, military men and emancipists. It is significant too that one of the first (1886) and for a long time one of the most powerful trade unions (commonly thought of as a distinctively urban phenomenon) the Australian Workers' Union, was a combination of *rural* labourers ranged against large landowners. Australian country towns did not develop over long centuries of tribalism and feudalism, but rather sprang, fully armed as it were, from the industrial world of the nineteenth century.

The rural areas of Australia have taken their social form from the urban origins and continuing urbanisation of the Australian colonies and the Australian State. The country towns, especially those in the east (see Hirst, 1973), emerged as an extension, perhaps even a distillation, of the class structure of the cities. Large landowners, themselves often oriented to the city for commerce, finance, education, for example formed and continued to form the ruling elite of rural districts, dominating the petty bourgeoisie and the professionals of the country town, as well as the smaller landholders and share farmers of the area. Increasingly, they have been joined as rural power brokers by individuals and firms whose financial assets are city based: the television personality Mike Willesee in Cootamundra, and multi-national partnerships such as that of Harris-Daishowa in Bombala. In one sense, of course, this situation presents something of a reversal of the social structure of the city where the central business district dominates the suburbs, but this is so only in strictly geographical terms: capital, whether centrifugal or centripetal, still dominates labour, in the country town as in the city. Furthermore, that capital is more and more urban capital, circulating in an international arena.

The development of political parties is illustrative of this trend: the long standing (if shaky) coalition of the Liberal and National (formerly Country) Parties – that is, the parties of urban and rural capital – has not been uniformly successful as an anti-labour force in the rural areas, especially in New South Wales (see Costar and Woodward, 1985) for the very reason that the capital labour or boss/worker distinction is as clear in the bush as it is in the big smoke. The influence of so-called 'country-mindedness' also has a variable effect on the electorate successes of both conservative parties, while interest groups such as the National Farmers Federation pursue a pragmatic line which permits selective support of National Party, or Liberal Party, or even, on occasion, Labor Party. Marshall, (1985) for example notes a 'major ambiguity' in the position of agricultural producers: 'while committed to individual enterprise they yet claim as a right assistance from government and demand that those who will not cooperate with policies which will benefit the majority should be brought to heel (1985, 25)'.

The Federal member for Eden-Monaro (Bombala) is of the Australian Labor Party, while, until 1988, both Burrinjuck (Cootamundra) and Bega (Bombala) were represented in the New South Wales parliament by Labor members, both in Cabinet. The 1988 State election indeed saw the Labor Party lose government across the State, with both urban and rural constituencies changing sides. Both the new members for Bega and Burrinjuck are, significantly, of the Liberal rather than the National Party, as is the Federal member for Hume, the classically rural area in which Cootamundra is situated.

Verrall *et al.* (1985) make the point that National and Liberal (non-metropolitan) constituencies have very similar 'socio-economic profiles'. In Hume, for example, 31.1 per cent of the workforce is engaged in 'agriculture etc.' and 30.3 per cent in farming occupations, while in Eden-Monaro these figures are 12.7 per cent and 12.6 per cent respectively (1985, 11-12); 'In National seats a mean average of 58.8 per cent live in towns of 1,000 or more ... Whilst the comparative statistic for Liberal rural seats ... is 58.5 per cent (1985, 15).'

Thus the two parties do not vary significantly in terms of the kinds of voters they attract. And this is not altogether surprising, since both parties are conservative parties, building upon many of the same mythological foundations: rural conservatism is not as distinct from urban conservatism as many analysts claim (see, e.g. Costar and Woodward, 1985).

(b) THE URBAN IN THE RURAL

The worldwide transformations of capitalism have their effects as much in the country towns of Australia as in the great metropolitan centres. These transformations have produced social and environmental disruptions which exercise the minds and energies of policy makers and analysts across the land (see, e.g. Lawrence, 1987). The rise of agribusiness and the concomitant push towards the deregulation of industry, the augmented role of the State and of national and transnational corporations in moulding the everyday lives of the people, are all deeply implicated in the changing structures of employment and unemployment and the quality of life, in the country towns as in the cities.

The consolidation of large landholdings, often owned by city based companies, has not, contrary to popular understanding, substantially altered the population size of country towns. The 1986 census shows that in New South Wales, more country towns (63 per cent) had increased in size than had decreased since 1981 (see A.B.S., 1981).

Of the 46 new towns with populations of 200-1,000, seventeen, or almost 40 per cent, are unequivocally coastal, with names like Emerald Beach, Chain Valley Bay, Pacific Palms, Corindi Beach. Others, like Perisher Village and Kurrajong Heights, are inland resort towns, while others (Colo Vale, Murrumbateman) are centres catering to hobby farmers and city workers. Of the 53 towns in the 1,000 to 45,000 population group that have decreased in size, only seven (13 per cent) are to be found east of the Great Dividing Range. The attractions of the coast seem to be as great as ever, not only for annual holidays, but also for specialist and hobby farmers and those in search of a more relaxed style of life especially retired people: there is a plethora of newly established old people's homes in the coastal towns, a trend which would seem likely to continue, given the greying of the Australian population. All these figures suggest a movement between and among country towns, rather than a drift to the cities. As Williams notes, this sort of trend forms part of a long tradition:

> What is idealised is not the rural economy, past or present, but a purchased freehold house in the country, or a charming coastal retreat, or even a barren offshore island'. This is then not a rural but a suburban or dormitory dream. And it is in direct reaction to the internal corruption of the city: the rise of lawyer, merchant, general, pimp and procurer; the stink of place and of profit; the noise and danger of being crowded together (1975, 62.1).

At the same time, regional centres have increased in size, at the expense of surrounding smaller towns. The population of Wagga, for example, increased from 36,800 in 1981 to 37,500 in 1986; but nearby towns (Narrandera, Gundagai, Murrumburrah (Harden), Temora, Junee and Cootamundra all decreased in size. Similarly, the population of Armidale increased from 18,900 to 19,500, while surrounding towns like Inverell, Glen Innes, Tenterfield, Walcha, Barraba all suffered population decreases.

The regional centralisation of commercial facilities and government instrumentalities has affected this movement to regional centres, as has the decline in the number of smaller family farms west of the ranges. As farming in Australia becomes more capital intensive and less labour intensive, and as family farms are swallowed up by city-based corporate agricultural businesses, working people look to the towns to provide employment. This may often be provided by the State, though it is women who are most able to take up the clerical and sales jobs available, since professional and semi-professional positions are often the preserve of a kind of itinerant labour force – teachers, social workers, police, for example – whose career trajectories are often premised upon moves from one town to another.

As well, the full range of welfare facilities, and such amenities as a reasonably frequent public transport system, are only available in the larger country towns, as are opportunities for special, further or higher education. The closure of branch railway lines, and the 'rationalisation' of both privately owned and state owned industries, have also affected employment opportunities in country towns, especially those with populations of between 5,000 and 10,000.

The narrow economic base of a dominant primary industry and its associated services in smaller country towns is undergoing an enforced transformation as national and transnational firms streamline their operations. A case in point, and one of particular relevance to Cootamundra, is the meat industry.

(c) THE MEAT INDUSTRY

Metro Meat, a subsidiary of the South Australian Adelaide Steamship Company, has meatworking operations across the country. In 1972 it bought out a family-owned abattoir in Cootamundra, and presented an application to change its employees from a state to a federal wages award. The employees went on strike, and though the application was eventually refused, industrial relations remained sour. In 1987 Metro closed the abattoir, giving as its reason the over-capacity of its own and other abattoirs in New South Wales.

This affair has elements in common with the celebrated (or notorious) Mudginberri dispute of 1985, and indeed there is no reason to suppose that the outcome of the Mudginberri case did not strengthen the employer's arm in Cootamundra in 1987. Mudginberri has achieved fame largely because the issues involved were perceived by both Right and Left to threaten the trade union movement in Australia, and to enhance the power of individual employers vis-à-vis both the State and their employees. As Williams noted, 'Mudginberri is the medium for a concerted effort to crack union control of wages and conditions' (1986 18). The case involved civil action being taken in an industrial dispute under Section 45D of the Trade Practices Act; its outcome, with the Australasian Meat Industries Employees Union being fined $1.8 million has been hailed as a victory, albeit a costly one, for small business and free enterprise (Houlihan, 1986; Lander, 1986).

What is important to note here however is that the small (36 employees) Mudginberri abattoir, in an effort to alter unilaterally its payment practices, was supported by an array of big guns which included the Northern Territory and Queensland governments (both of the National Party); the National Farmers Federation; the Small Business Association; the Confederation of Australian Industry; and, most significantly, the Westpac Bank, the latter providing a two million dollar line of credit which was guaranteed by the Northern Territory government.

While the banks and big business have rarely been considered the champions of the rural, or indeed of the urban, labour force, in the case of Mudginberri the Australian Council of Trade Unions was reluctant to support a member union, and the Federal Labor government was similarly reluctant to intervene. Indeed, the Labor government's policy on several economic and industrial issues has been seen on numerous occasions as more supportive of the owners and managers of capital than it has been of the interests of labour. Such was clearly the case in the New South Wales elections of 1988, which saw the demise of the Labor government within that state. I want to turn now to a brief examination of one aspect of this political development.

(d) THE TIMBER INDUSTRY

Bombala is a timber town, typical of those many small country towns dependent on a single industry for their livelihood and welfare. Its biggest employers are Tablelands Sawmills (owned by a Victorian timber company) and the New South Wales Forestry Commission, upon both of which many private contractors, with large investments in felling and hauling rigs and equipment, depend. It is the State itself, the urban business interests which have the greatest economic power in the southern Monaro. The town and, indeed, the surrounding district, are bitterly divided over conservation issues, with teachers and some pastoralists supporting the 'greenies' to the chagrin of the local workers. The latter, traditionally Labor voters, voted for the Liberals in 1988, on the grounds that the Labor Party was threatening to turn more of the southern hardwood forests into national parks.

Like Cootamundra only more so, Bombala is dependent on government instrumentalities located at some distance from it, for example the State Forestry Commission at Orbost (in Victoria); the state Departments of Agriculture, Health and Tourism and Motor Registration at Cooma; Consumer Affairs, Youth and Community Services and the regional Education Office at Wollongong. Like Cootamundra also, Bombala loses its young people to the larger country towns, the regional centres and the city for tertiary education and training. As in Cootamundra too, there is little manufacturing industry to be found in Bombala: Tableland sawmills, for example, sends its woodchips to Victoria for paper manufacture, while Shepherd Woolskins in Cootamundra is confined to making items such as rugs, underlays, boots and steering wheel and car seat covers made from straight skins. Thus many educational and employment opportunities, as well as leisure facilities, are denied the local inhabitants, while the frustration of not being able to deal face to face with government officials, a frustration common to the powerless everywhere, is heightened by distance.

I have dwelt upon these two cases at some length, in order to make the point that the division between urban and rural, in both economic and political terms, is not only a false one, but also one that is constantly utilised, highlighted and exacerbated in a divide-and-rule attempt by dominant financial fractions, in the bush as in the city.

(e) RURALISM AND NATIONALIST IDEOLOGY

This false opposition of the interests of rural and urban workers is paralleled by a continuing mystification and ideologizing of life outside the metropolitan areas by the mass media. Box office successes like *Crocodile Dundee*, popular television soap operas like *A Country Practice* and *The Flying Doctors*, and television magazine programmes like *That's Australia* and *Countrywide* present an essentially urban fantasy of life beyond the city limits. *Countrywide*, for example, makes much of rural initiatives in the tourist industry, organic farming and successful small-scale, high-tech, export-oriented agricultural projects like yabby farming and the production of exotic fruits. In another genre, *A Country Practice*, like its perhaps better known, and urban, counterpart *Neighbours*, usually avoids tendentious economic and social questions, concentrating all the while on the interpersonal relations of the town's elite and/or respectable (doctors, vets, nurses, teachers, police) and emphasising the harmony and tranquillity of country life *vis-à-vis* the city. Such problems as there are (an invasion of punks, a retarded boy's relationship with a local girl) are usually tidily resolved in one of at most two episodes. *The Flying Doctors*, set in the outback, also presents an idealised portrait of country folk pulling together for the common weal, against natural disasters and despite occasional interpersonal animosities.

The flying doctors of Coopers Crossing, and other inhabitants of the little town, portray those rural virtues of resourcefulness, independence, energy, sincerity, mateship and good judgement which are characterised not only as belonging to country people, but indeed to all Australians. These are the values characteristic of 'country-mindedness' subscribed to as much by urban as rural folk. Verrall *et al.*, while admitting that 'country-mindedness' is 'a rather imprecise concept' suggest that it turns upon a defence of 'the family, Christian faith, Empire loyalism, sexual moralism, reward for effort, and so on' (1985, 21). It is worth noting, in this connection, that the tribulations that beset the inhabitants of Coopers Crossing, and those of Wandin Valley, site of *A Country Practice*, are either natural disasters (bushfire, snakebite – very rural) or problems arising from individual foolishness or wilfulness. They are problems amenable to the application, by ordinary, decent folk, of good will and common sense. They are not, it is important to note, the intractable problems caused by or involving governments and bureaucracies, the banks' demands and the law's delays. Such issues are not of course the usual fare of soap opera, nor indeed of the ideological state apparatuses in general. What is being promoted in these shows, and what finds resonance with their viewers, is an ideal of individual responsibility for both success and failure, an ideal that lies at the heart of Australian egalitarian individualism (see Kapferer, 1988).

It is for this reason that the images of the sunburnt stockman and the drover's wife will not go away. But nor will the counter-image of country people as simple, slow thinking, at one with nature, practical, conservative and gullible: easy marks, like the Man from Ironbark, for wily city slickers or the swagless swaggie. Each marks too, one might suggest, for the banks, the Pitt Street farmers and the multinational corporations. In this connection it might be noted that it was the (city-based) union which took on the Mudginberri management, not its local employees, who were reportedly happy with the deal offered them. Similarly, the strikers at Cootamundra were opposed by their wives and other women of the town, who set up a counter-picket pleading with them to return to work. The image of bucolic slow-wittedness and buffoonery, so beloved of city folk, is one that can be turned to good effect in dividing and ruling urban and rural workers who do not have the advantage of everyday contact with their counterparts, an advantage enjoyed by the owners and managers of capital. As well, the mass media, as an apparatus of the ruling group, work to ensure not only the force of conservative social thought in rural areas, but also to enhance a perceived contrast between such rural conservatism and the more 'liberal' and 'enlightened' views of urbanites.

An illustrative case is that of the leader of the New South Wales National Party, Wal Murray, a grazier from Moree and member for Barwon, described as 'as cunning as an outhouse rodent' – though this observation is unsupported by evidence – in an article that plays to urban dwellers' vision of rustic idiocy (*The Australian* 4 March 1988, p.l). The paper's report on the launching, in Cootamundra, of the National Party's 1988 election campaign refers, for example, to the lack of 'a modicum of intelligence' and a sense of timing on the part of a National Party official ('the chap in the red Wrangler shirt and moleskins'), to voodoo economics and the unspeakable boredom of it all: 'One woman in the audience either was asleep or found she concentrated better on Mr Murray's speech by closing her eyes and letting her head drop forward.'
The Australian notes also, in traditional journalistic style, that Murray 'did not want to answer questions about the case of his Deputy Leader Ian Armstrong's reported comments at an anti-gun rally that curbing gun sales wasn't the answer. "We've got to get rid of crime, drugs, hoons and coons", he is reported as saying'.

Country people can by these means be made to carry the can for an Australia-wide racism and intolerance that embarrasses the intellectuals of the city as imagined by the journalists. It also might embarrass thoughtful rural people, but in this darker side of rural mythology such people are thought not to exist. Country people may also be portrayed as the standard bearers of what they (and many city people too) would call conservative values, of rural purity, innocence and moral strength opposed to urban danger, viciousness and moral turpitude. Wal Murray is described by *The Adelaide Advertiser* as making the dictatorial Sir Henry Bolte 'seem a cream-puff' and as dwarfing 'Queensland's monumental Russ Hinze' at a conference in Dubbo at which he promised to 'tighten up' discipline in New South Wales schools by, for example, public corporal punishment ('six of the best across their backsides like they would if they misbehaved at good private schools') and sending repeat offenders to gaol.

Such statements are of course not unknown in conservative quarters across the land, even if they are more subtly phrased (see, for example journals like *ACES Review or Quadrant*). My point here is simply that rural districts and their inhabitants provide a convenient and non-threatening site and mouthpiece for the promulgation of those conservative and fundamentalist orientations which are gaining national ascendancy. Rural people are seen as standing four-square behind, and as embodying, those cherished egalitarian individualist ideologies which support:

the deregulation of industrial relations, and unfettered private enterprise (as at Mudginberri and as demonstrated by the Cootamundra women's picket);
private and personal responsibility (as demonstrated by the opposition to the control of guns);
the right to work (as demonstrated by the anti-conservationist stance of the timber and mining industries);
privately arranged contractual relations between employer and employee (as at Metro and Mudginberri); and
the Family (as represented by the Country Women's Association.)

Country people are not seen as bludgers and/or larrikins (long the picture of urban life, from Ginger Mick and the Woolloomooloo Lair to the current Federal Treasurer and unemployed youth.) Nor are they seen as, Jin Big Wal Murray's terms, the 'drug pushers, hoodlums, rapists, muggers, prostitutes and homosexuals' (*Australian*, 4 March 1988) who throng the city. In other words, country folk remain the ideal-typical Australians of urban mythology – clean-living, morally upright, egalitarian individuals, straightforward, uncomplicated, unpolluted and ultimately noble.

Even foreign travel writers are seduced by this myth. I quote from *The Jerusalem Post* of August 11, 1988, page 7:

> You can meet many an Australian living in the city, selling insurance or building homes, who likes to feel that there is a bit of the bucolic somewhere inside him. Instead of looking down his nose at the rural resident he admits he would prefer the farmer, the drover or the woodsman as his ideal. Many an Australian will tell you that the farming community is the backbone of the nation, even though it

> represents a minority, and that Australia depends on its farmers, be they 'squatters', or only 'cow-cockies'.

In reality, many Australians, and especially those of the urban working class, see rural dwellers as whingers, layabouts and bludgers off the taxpayer and the welfare state. The National Farmers Federation, for example, which is much attached to the Friedmanite economics of not only the right-wing H.R. Nicholls Society, but also increasingly of many Labor government members, is much at odds with the National Party and its supporters who are committed to the maintenance of government subsidies for agriculture. Many country people on the other hand see the National Farmers Federation as a rich squatters' lobby bolstered by and in partnership with urban corporate capital. (But see Lawrence, 1987, 79-80).

Life in the bush and in country towns is different from life in the cities. In the aptly titled *Life Has Never Been Easy* (1988), rural women complain, through the Country Women's Association, of poor or nonexistent transport, communications and education facilities, employment opportunities and health and community services. The largest areas of complaint concern isolation, loneliness or remoteness, and financial pressures on production and consumption (Dept. of the Prime Minister and Cabinet, 1988, 14). It might be noted, however, that these problems, with the exceptions of physical isolation and the high cost of agricultural production, are common to women across the country. Similarly it is observed that

> Other social problems ... include the problems of using a single mother, stress, lack of control over children, fear of vandalism and domestic violence drug and alcohol abuse, married women having to work to help the family survive, dashed expectations, unions, vagaries of the weather and nature.... and lack of opportunities to meet and socialise with unmarried men (1988, 15).

Again, with the exception of the vagaries of the weather, and perhaps of the marriage market, these problems are ubiquitous. What is one noteworthy in this survey is the conservative nature of rural women, who blame many of their problems upon government policies (1988, 16). The narrow economic base of country towns not only makes for less solidarity among workers, and between them and the rest of the community, as has been indicated for Cootamundra, it also underlies the potential for the pursuit of arbitrary management policies and unilateral management decisions, especially within industries operating on a national or international scale, as in the case of the closure of the Metro abattoir.

When the Metro abattoir closed, Cootamundra people were angry and disappointed, envisaging the demise of the town's economy. But less than a year later, most of the Metro employees had found work in two smaller privately and locally owned abattoirs in Cootamundra, and one in the nearby township of Murrumburrah. The officers of the Cootamundra Advancement Corporation – one the wife of a local pastoralist the other the wife of the newly elected Liberal member for Burrinjuck neither of whom might normally be expected, from their class and status positions, to identify strongly with the interests of workers – maintain that the Metro closure was actually the best thing ever to happen to the town, as it forced a diversification of independent entrepreneurial and industrial activity, stirring local commercial concerns out of their complacency, and urging a more 'rational' attitude towards industrial relations. Through Shepherd Woolskins, Metro is still the town's largest single non-government employer, with up to 129 workers on two shifts though the work is seasonal, peaking between October and April, and it is significant that the majority (about 100) of its 130 employees are non-unionised married women engaged in machining.

The confidence, indeed the boosterism, of the Cootamundra Advancement Corporation is matched by a widespread, if more wary optimism about a rural revival discernible among professional economists. Professor Richard Blandy, for example, director of the National Institute of Labour Studies, and well-known for his championship of a small-is-beautiful stance, maintains that the continuing revolution in communications technology, for instance, must be of economic benefit to country towns (particularly the larger ones) and their individual residents (*Sydney Morning Herald*, 6 June 1987, 2; *The Australian*, 8 June

In an economic situation which produces not only government emphasis on the earning of export income (an area in which Australia's rural regions have long been dominant) but also an increasing stress on the so-called 'service industries' as a source of such income, country towns are faced with an urgent need to re-tool their economic bases. As farms and stations come under urban and foreign ownership, as Australia's markets for primary produce are eroded by global capital transformations, and as governments concentrate resources in the manufacturing sector, the traditional rural economic problems of vast distance and sparse population reassert themselves.

Tourist brochures tend to make much of scenery, wildlife and sophisticated coastal resorts. The majority of country towns, however, have none of these to offer. While place names like Wollongong, Oodnadatta, Coonawarra, Wagga Wagga and Cunnamulla may stir some interest, the towns themselves, with the possible exception of Coonawarra, seem ill-equipped to seduce the tourists who are impressed by wild animals sun and surf or dazzling nightlife.

Nonetheless, Cootamundra and Bombala are as concerned as other towns to increase their attractiveness to tourists. The 'hospitality industry' is currently enjoying privileged though controversial status as an income earner for small and large communities alike. For example, Corowa on the New South Wales-Victorian border attracts gamblers from Victoria (referred to as 'Mexicans') and golf players from ever further afield, while coastal resorts such as Tweed Heads are cashing in on the increasingly fashionable 'convention market'. Farm holidays, especially those which do not require excessively strenuous activity, and those which accentuate the 'real' Australia of the tourist brochures (horse-riding, campfires under the stars) are also much in demand, but these are essentially private concerns which do not generate large incomes for their owner operators.

For a number of reasons neither Bombala nor Cootamundra is highly successful as a tourist centre. In the case of Bombala despite its situation in the beautiful country of the Monaro High Plains, it is, as a potential resort, in competition with the even more beautiful south coast of New South Wales, and the Snowy Mountains. These two areas offer more than just scenery, with fishing, surfing, swimming on the one hand, and skiing, mountain and lake fishing, bush-walking and climbing on the other. Bombala appears stuck between the two. Despite its centrality as a location for trout fishing and bird watching, tourist accommodation is virtually unavailable, and devotees of these activities are anyway not usually counted as high rollers, nor are they likely to be foreigners. Bombala is not located on a major interstate highway, so that the ubiquitous caravans of the Pacific, Princes and Hume Highways are rarely encountered on the Monaro. Nor does a convenient rail service pass through the town, which is equidistant from Sydney and Melbourne, two major ports of entry to the country.

Cootamundra, on the other hand, does have a daily rail connection to Sydney and Melbourne. But it too is not located on a major highway, and the countryside while pleasant, is not spectacular. Its one claim to fame in tourist terms is that it is the birthplace of Don Bradman. Nonetheless, its shire council is considered to be more 'go-ahead' than many others, and concentrates its efforts on attracting and maintaining light industries (helicopter repairs, cabinet-making, furniture component manufacture etc.), efforts which included, in 1988, an 'Expo' to bring further light industry to the town, on the grounds that it is central to Adelaide, Sydney and Melbourne.

In many ways, the Australian boom in the tourist industry has elements of a cargo cult, with state governments and the Federal Government vying for the dollars and yen of Pacific rim tourists. (The suggestion has been made in South Australia, for instance, that street signs and other directions should be produced in Japanese.) Of greater significance here, however, is the way in which tourist oriented development is considered by many conservationists to require a desecration of our natural heritage (in the demolition, rebuilding, refurbishing and glamorising of old buildings to conform to alien and mythologised notions of 'Australianness' for example.) Officials of the State castigate the conservationists as reactionary, while directing a spate of sometimes desperate homilies (in newspaper articles, letters to the editor, training courses) at those in the hotel and restaurant industries, and in municipal councils who seem to them to be obstructing the kinds of development which might bring in valuable export earnings.

The burden of these political and bureaucratic reprimands is that Australian notions of 'service' must be radically revised to cater to the demands of tourists with very different understandings of service and servility, hierarchy and equality, from our own. This is true also for those involved in commercial transactions and business dealings.

Australian egalitarian individualism, encapsulated in such phrases as 'Who do you think you are, mate?' is premised upon an understanding of equality as founded in sameness and identity. Such understandings provide an extremely shaky foundation for such cultural revisions. In country towns, as in the metropolis and the hinterland, it is just this understanding of self and society which gives the image of Australia as 'the bush', and Australians as free-spirited bushmen its force and deep-rooted ideological significance. This is so even, or perhaps especially, in an urban and global economic environment which is being daily pushed to become more homogeneous, cosmopolitan and internationalised.

(f) CONCLUSION: THE RURAL IN THE URBAN

I have tried in this paper to make one major point. This is that the separation of rural and urban interests, a taken-for-granted assumption not only in everyday life but also in political, economic and social analyses of Australian society (and indeed of other Western industrial social formations) is an idea which has hegemonic force. As such, it provides an unquestioning and unquestioned foundation for the mythologising of Australianness as the embodiment of rural virtue, a virtue which is none other than an ideology produced in, by and for an urban industrial world.

The social and political relations of the non-metropolitan world are varying manifestations of the central principles of a modern capitalist process; the relation of the country town to the city can be conceived of as iconic with the relation of Australia to the dominant economic powers of the capitalist world. The ideological rendering of these relations as *rural*, however, is not a false consciousness, as this term has conventionally come to be used. It is an ideological reality that country people in Australia live.

It is in such reality that the modern social and political relations of the countryside are formed and, in fact, become the real basis for conflict and opposition within country contexts, and between urban and rural situations. This rural ideology may be recognised elsewhere in the modern world as the Australian version of barbarism (the rejection of 'civilisation' as a repressive force). As elsewhere, however, this ideology can become as much a vital factor in the ideological opposition to forces of domination, as it is already the hegemonic principle for the reproduction of dominant power.

REFERENCES

D. Aitkin, *The Country Party in New South Wales* (Canberra: ANU Press, 1972).

Australian Bureau of Statistics (19811 Census 86 – Persons and Dwellings: New South Wales, Catalogue No. 2462.0 Canberra, Commonwealth Govt. Printer.

R. Barthes, *Mythologies* (London: Paladin, 1973).

C. Bell, Community studies: an introduction to the sociology of the local community, London, Allen & Unwin.

Country to National, edited by B. Costar and D. Woodward (Sydney: Allen & Unwin, 1985).

G. Crough and T. Wheelwright, *Australia: a client state* (Ringwood: Penguin, 1982).

C.W.A., *Life has never been easy* (Canberra: Office of the Prime Minister, 1988).

C. Geertz, *The interpretation of cultures* (New York: Basic Books, 1973).

J.B. Hirst, *Adelaide and the country* (Melbourne: University Press, 1973).

J.B. Hirst, *Convict society and its enemies* (Sydney: Allen & Unwin, 1983).

P. Houlihan, 'A brief history of Mutginberri and its implications for Australia's trade unions' in *Arbitration in contempt* (Proceedings of the Inaugural Seminar of the H.R. Nicholls Society, Melbourne, 1986.) Melbourne, H.R. Nicholls Society.

COLIN PATRICK

Does Urban Australia Need a New Bush Myth?

Myths are essential components of a nation's self-image, encapsulating the 'essential truths' about its history, culture and scales of values. They provide convenient and memorable summaries of 'what it means to be an Englishman/Australian/American ...', and perform important roles in maintaining national cohesion and common-purpose, especially in times of adversity. The essentially simplistic form of the National Myth produces unquestioning acceptance, inhibits rational re-evaluation and provides a firm support to the maintenance of the status quo. As a result myths play important political roles. Valid myths can be highly beneficial, but outdated ones can be dangerous as they purvey distorted and misleading national views. If myths are to play acceptable roles in society they must be continuously re-evaluated, with invalid ones being replaced by new versions better able to reflect changed national priorities.

Australian society has developed a wide range of myths, dominated by The Bush Myth and The Urban Myth. The Bush Myth derives from the problems of establishing a new society in an alien land. It became enshrined in literature and art and then played an important role in determining national consciousness for over 150 years. Although its roots were valid, and the struggle against the natural environment in the Outback genuine, The Bush Myth was never entirely representative of a country whose population has always been predominantly urban. In spite of this unreality The Bush Myth was politically convenient, firming up national resolve, and became enshrined in the nation's literature, art, history and other disciplines. The mismatch between myth and reality became progressively more acute after the Second World War as urbanisation was accentuated; over 80% of Australia's population now lives in towns and cities. The academic recognition of this situation came in the 1970s with a revision of the Australian Mythology; The Bush Myth was rejected and replaced by The Urban Myth. The Urban Myth is now considered to express more precisely the nature and spirit of modern Australia. It has not been codified formally, as was The Bush Myth, so that its principal characteristics must be inferred from more dispersed and diffuse comments, nuances and general attitudes now displayed towards Australian society in literature, art, television and other sources.

Although superficially attractive as a piece of essential 'conceptual modernisation' the replacement of The Bush Myth by The Urban Myth must not be accepted unquestioningly. If unquestioning acceptance of a Bush Myth, peddled with evangelical zeal, distorted the views of Australia held by five generations of its citizens, what damage could similar zealous peddling and unquestioning acceptance of its replacing Urban Myth achieve? The merits of the two myths must be evaluated to establish which serves Australia's interests best, and, if necessary, to develop a third myth from them.

The Bush Myth was dominated by the supremacy of the natural environment and its processes, their control over all aspects of individual and communal life and the consequent interference with the realisation of personal aspirations, limitation of the freedom of action possible and the need to operate on a communal rather than an individual basis. Failure to accommodate to the imposed demands led to disaster. Even though a robust and resourceful society developed under these restrictive conditions, within which the concept of 'mateship' was established, The Bush is now seen only in terms of impositions, restrictions and the need for constant vigilance. In contrast The Urban Myth sees cities as self-contained havens, even City Fortresses, in which careful design of the infrastructure has excluded the threats and limitations associated with environmental processes, rendering any consideration of the environment (except for the beach) unnecessary. In this setting individuals are free to pursue their own aspirations and to develop a society whose character is determined by social preferences rather than by environmental constraints.

The Urban Myth may succeed in reflecting accurately some characteristics of modern Australian life, but its view of the role played by the natural environment in urban society is deficient. It suffers from a too-ready rejection of all aspects of The Bush Myth, discrediting them by association rather than by rational analysis, without regard to their possible relevance to modern Australia. The Urban Myth thus fails to achieve its aims. This failure is of more than purely academic interest as it will affect, and possibly form, the attitudes towards Australia held by writers and commentators, determining the images then held by Australians of their country, and especially of the cities. The limited, and environmentally complacent, view which The Urban Myth engenders permits the development of urban conditions which can be dangerous to individuals in their everyday lives and could, in the long-term, threaten the survival of the cities.

Any reconsideration of the merits of The Urban Myth must focus on its three basic postulates. These are:

- that the character of the city owes nothing to the environment,

- that the essential functions of urban life are independent of natural processes, and

- that the city is isolated from the surrounding Bush.

The 'character' of Australian cities is composed of several distinct factors, all affected by the environment. Their locations are controlled primarily by the influence of climate, topography and geology, water, soils and vegetation. These determine the existence of acceptable living conditions, the availability of basic necessities and of raw materials for manufacture, and the feasibility of communications with other settlements. They account for both the gross, peripheral, distribution of the cities and many of the details. Port Jackson was preferred to Botany Bay for First Settlement on the grounds of better water supply and the quality of the harbour. Newcastle was founded, albeit as a penal settlement, after the discovery of coal in the area, and the discovery of gold determined the locations of many Victorian towns, which then persisted because of the agricultural opportunities.[1]

The detailed setting of cities is similarly affected, if not dominated, by natural features. Canberra's skylines are determined by mountains within the city, Mount Ainslie and Black Mountain, and the surrounding Brindabella Mountains. Perth derives its classic setting from its location on the Swan River estuary. Within Sydney the Harbour and the Heads, the locations of the Harbour Bridge and the Opera House, and the ability to build high rise developments in the city centre all stem from the presence and nature of the Hawkesbury Sandstone.[2] Similar factors are still controlling urban development, as can be seen in the proposals for the Sydney Western suburbs.[3]

Town layouts are strongly influenced by the scale of the environment, which permits the adoption of large blocks and wide streets, but may show local differences depending on the geology, as in Ballarat.[4] House designs, with wide verandahs and construction on stilts, and garden and street vegetation are similarly determined by the requirements of, or opportunities provided by, the natural environment. Beyond the urban areas natural areas such as mountains and forest, whose attractions and quality are determined by the natural environment, complement the recreational opportunities provided by the beach.

Essential functions of everyday urban life, such as the disposal of sewage and waste gases, and the concomitant avoidance of water and air pollution, also depend on the operation of environmental processes. Natural processes provide opportunities and impose limitations. Conventional sewage disposal relies on the ability of the environment to dilute and assimilate organic wastes, and to remove bacteria. In The Bush liquids from earth closets were generated in small quantities. These infiltrated into the ground and were accommodated readily by natural processes in the soil and groundwater. As settlements developed the increased numbers of earth closets and septic tanks increased the liquid discharge, and overloaded the natural purification processes. As a result partially-treated sewage effluents appeared in streams. These conditions were both unsavoury and insanitary, and were exacerbated by industrial discharges direct to surface waters. Concern about potential and actual ill-effects from this water pollution and the detrimental effects on recreational waters, led to the construction of trunk sewers. These collected domestic and industrial effluents and conveyed them to centralised sewage treatment works. Treated effluent was then discharged into rivers or the sea, in which it was intended that final purification would be achieved by natural processes.

The success of the improved arrangements depended on the abilities of the receiving waters to achieve the dilution and assimilation required. Under Australian conditions both sets of processes are limited by natural conditions. Dilution is impeded by the generally low river flows, and self-purification capacity is reduced due to the high water temperatures. As a result noxious conditions, excessive algal growths, fish kills and the generation of offensive smells, can develop relatively easily.[5,6] In inland areas, where sewage effluents are discharged into rivers, the need to avoid these problems has affected the design of sewage works. At Canberra the Lower Molonglo Water Quality Control Centre, whose effluent contributes 70% of the normal flow in the Molonglo River, had to incorporate sophisticated and costly Tertiary treatment processes to remove nutrients. This reduced the possibilities of unacceptable conditions developing in the Molonglo or Murrumbidgee Rivers, or in Burrinjuck Reservoir.[7] A similar approach has had to be adopted at Albury-Wodonga, where sewage effluent is discharged to the River Murray.

The effects of limited self-purification capabilities in streams on sewage disposal opportunities can be overcome to a large extent by adopting discharge through marine outfalls. Here the potential dilution and assimilation capacities of the sea are immense. Advantage has been taken of these abilities in the major coastal cities, with the discharge of partially--treated or untreated sewage direct to the sea or tidal waters. This approach significantly reduces the costs of sewage disposal. Increasing discharges from outfalls have led, however, to the contamination of beaches by sewage solids and bacteria.[4] This experience indicates again the need to adapt the design of a scheme to the nature and abilities of the environment. Improvement of the marine discharge procedures adopted at Sydney, to accord with the actual behaviour of tidal currents and waves, has involved the construction of longer sea outfalls and the introduction of prior sewage treatment facilities.

The replacement of septic tank systems by integrated sewage disposal facilities commenced in the main cities and towns in the 1960s. Subsequent urban expansion has, for financial reasons, not been tied into these facilities and domestic sewage disposal now depends heavily on the use of septic tanks. The large scales of the developments, and the consequent overloading of the self-purification capacity of the groundwater, have led to the recurrence of stream and groundwater pollution. In the Melbourne Metropolitan area 50,000 properties are not sewered, as are few of those in the outlying new commuter developments, with the result that the Yarra River is polluted. The severity of the situation was shown graphically in a Tandberg cartoon in the Melbourne 'Age', commenting on a Report from the Environment Protection Authority for Victoria. This consisted of two pictures. One showed 'Man searching for the source of the Nile' and passing a major waterfall, the other was of 'Man discovering the source of the Yarra' and dashing into the Dunny.[7] Similar extensive use of septic tanks in Perth, with 50% of the properties in the city area unsewered, has led to contamination of the groundwater.[5]

Waste gases and smoke from domestic and industrial combustion can be discharged most conveniently to the atmosphere. Initially the capacity of the atmosphere to accommodate them was of little interest as air pollution was restricted to areas of heavy industry. Unfortunately the implicit assumption that air movements would promote adequate dispersal and dilution, and not limit the number or nature of atmospheric discharges, was soon found to be erroneous. Greater concentration and intensity of industrial activity, and increased numbers of houses, in the late 1950s and early 1960s was accompanied by extreme atmospheric pollution. This resulted principally from excessive smoke, which restricted visibility and reduced sunlight, and produced conditions damaging to health, vegetation and materials. The causes of these conditions, particularly the industrial sources, were removed successfully by the introduction of Clean Air legislation.

Success was short-lived, however, as new air pollution problems developed during the 1970s. These resulted from the introduction of new pollutants, hydrocarbons from the increased use of petrol and diesel-powered vehicles, and smoke from increased backyard burning in the expanding suburbs. Local topographic and meteorological conditions restricted atmospheric dispersal, allowing pollutants to concentrate and become subject to chemical reactions under the strong sunlight. As a result photochemical smogs developed in the summer, and brown hazes in the winter. The smogs are unpleasant and damaging to health and vegetation, and the hazes cause reduced visibility and sunlight. These conditions developed in Newcastle, Sydney, Wollongong and Melbourne and persisted for periods of time ranging from a few days to a few weeks. The consequent air pollution made Melbourne and Sydney two of the most polluted cities in the world, with World Health Organisation maximum permissible concentrations for some contaminants being exceeded for large parts of the year. As the capabilities of the lower atmosphere around the cities to accommodate pollutants are finite the solution to these smog and haze problems has to be sought through modified behaviour. This involves reduced use of internal combustion engines, with modifications to the fuel and exhaust systems, and controls over backyard burning.[7,8]

The sequences of events in the development of acceptable procedures for the disposal of sewage and waste gases in the urban areas demonstrate clearly the dependence of the city on environmental processes, and the limitations then placed upon urban aspirations by their specific mode of operation and finite capacities. In both cases failure to recognise the roles played by the environmental processes as integral parts of the urban infrastructure, and to then make the accommodations required, has already produced unpleasant, and could produce disastrous, results.

If the dependence of the city on the environment for its setting and essential processes can be accepted it may still not be agreed that The Urban Myth has been falsified, as the environmental influences demonstrated are 'internal' to the city. The claim may still be made that the full environmental influences of The Bush have been excluded from the city area. The fallaciousness of this view is demonstrated clearly when the effects of natural disasters on the cities are recognised. Natural disasters are still characteristic, and very significant elements of urban life[9], as shown by the brief summary of incidents given in Table 1.

These examples demonstrate clearly that Australian cities are subject to natural disasters. It does not follow, however, that the urban areas must accept their effects passively. Most of them can be mitigated, or even prevented, by appropriate alterations in behaviour. In bushfireprone areas the incidence of fires can be reduced by the imposition of 'No Burn' days, when backyard burning is prohibited[13], and further control can be achieved by the use of greater care in all burning. If fires do develop within the urban area, or intrude from outside, their impact can be reduced by locating houses away from the edge of the Bush, constructing them to limit the risk of house ignition, and spacing them adequately to prevent the spread of fire. Cyclone damage can be reduced in a similar manner by strengthening houses in the areas known to be at risk.

Bushfire and cyclone events are largely uncontrollable, and it is only their impacts which can be reduced by appropriate preparation. In contrast flood incidence and magnitude, as well as impact, can be reduced to some extent. Removal of buildings from floodplains, or prevention of their construction would reduce flood impact to almost zero. In addition their partial or total removal would reduce flood levels, as buildings impede the passage of floodwaters and cause them to rise higher than necessary, and reduce the scale of the impact. The relationship between floodplain development and flood impact was recognised by Macquarie. His Order of 1819 had little success then, and subsequent attempts to control floodplain development have met with only limited success. In view of this lack of response it is salutary to note that the most flood-prone area of Australia, the coastal strip from Newcastle to Brisbane, is also the area of most rapid development.[12]

Table 1 Major Natural Disasters in Australia

Disaster Type/Location	Date	Deaths	Effects
Bushfire[10]			
Hobart	Feb. 1967	62	1085 houses destroyed, $ 40M damage
Princes Highway (Melbourne to Geelong)	Jan. 1969	17	
Dandenong Range (Melbourne)	Ash Wed. 1983	47	1719 houses destroyed, 8000 homeless, $ 195 M damage

(The areas most at risk from bushfires are the margins of Sydney, Melbourne, Adelaide and Hobart. Major fires can be expected, on average, once every 3 years in the coastal strip from Melbourne to Newcastle.)

Disaster Type/Location	Date	Deaths	Effects
Cyclone[11]			
Mackay	1958	32	
Townsville (Althea)	1971	3	$ 50 M damage
Darwin (Tracy)	1974	49	Insurance loss $ 500 M, actual loss probably > $ 1 Billion
Flooding[5,12]			
Gundagai, N.S.W.	1852	89	
Hunter Valley, N.S.W.	1955	25	$ 30 M damage
Woden Valley, Canberra	1971	7	$ 180 M damage
Brisbane	1974	3	13,000 properties affected

(Throughout Australia the total number of buildings considered to be at risk from flooding is of the order of 61,000. The greatest number of buildings at risk in one city is in Adelaide, and the greatest single potential financial loss is in the Brisbane/Ipswich area.)

The incidence of natural disasters in the city demonstrates that the City Fortress idea is, at best, questionable. Further examination of the City/Bush relationship demonstrates a dependence on the extra-urban areas for everyday necessities, such as water, electric power and food, showing conclusively that the City Fortress idea is completely invalid. The extra-urban areas involved can be seen as 'Areas of Concern'. For Sydney the 'Area of Concern' based on water supply, from the Hawkesbury, Georges River and Shoalhaven catchments, is nearly 32,000 sq. km[14]. When power generation is included, from the Lake Macquarie and Hunter catchments, this area increases to nearly 60,000 sq km. The total 'Area of Concern' to citizens of Sydney is thus roughly 150 times the actual area of the city. Similar relationships exist between other cities and their 'Areas of Concern'. Within the 'Area of Concern' water availability for supply, and for flood generation, can be affected by changes in the agricultural activities and the nature of the river channel. Grassed areas shed more water than forested areas, giving reduced water resources and more floods. Flood protection works affect the nature of flood episodes, as they determine the manner in which flood waves travel. These examples indicate clearly that the cities not only depend for their necessities on extended areas of The Bush, and their natural operation, but on the activities of those living there. The well-being of a city may depend upon the activities of the non-urban population, and their willingness to adapt their aspirations to accord with the best interests of the city population.

The City/Bush dependence developed so far in this discussion has been based on the physical implications of natural processes for the city. Their influence is not, however, restricted to this level as they also have considerable impacts on the social, financial and political aspects of life. The social implications follow directly from the intrusion of disasters and shortages into everyday life, the need for adaptations of lifestyles, and the consequent trauma and frustration. Financially the natural environment and its processes affect cities at all the three levels previously cited. At the townscape level climate and geology affect construction costs, as with the foundation problems experienced with the Victorian Arts Centre and the thermal expansion of steel during construction of the West Gate Bridge in Melbourne, which was a contributory factor in its eventual collapse[15]. In the disposal of effluents to water and the air, and the prevention of pollution, costs are incurred in the construction of sewer networks and treatment works, and in the implementation of preventative measures. The Lower Molonglo Water Quality Control Centre cost \$ 57 M (in 1980), and the costs of fully sewering Melbourne and Perth will be, respectively, \$ 250 M and up to \$ 1,000 M.[5]

Natural disasters impose similarly large costs directly, via reconstruction and compensation (as shown in Table 1), and indirectly through anticipation and control. In the Hunter Valley the accumulated flood loss over the period 1960-80 was nearly \$2 M. Since the 1955 floods total spending in the Hunter Valley on flood control measures has exceeded \$15 M. Similar works in the Paramatta and Toongabbie areas of Sydney would cost nearly \$ 2 M to give protection from potential losses of up to \$ 9 M. Throughout Australia the total investment required to reduce the flood hazard in urban areas to an 'acceptable level' is of the order of $ 300 M (flood costs are given in 1980 prices).[5]

Although the magnitudes of the financial interference produced by these natural disasters are considerable the greatest single environmental interference results from drought over the 'Areas of Concern', and beyond. In these areas drought affects water and power supplies, and agricultural productivity. In the 1982-83 drought agricultural production was reduced by 20% throughout Australia, with an estimated value of $ 3 Billion. This loss to national income was considered to have resulted in a reduction in the National Economic Growth by 1% to 1.5%, and must have had significant effects on the normal financial operations in the cities[16].

The total annual cost imposed on the economy, and thus on the cities, through the influence of environmental factors can be estimated crudely, using plausible assumptions about the incidence of events and the costs of preventive activities, to be of the order of $ 0.5 Billion. This is equivalent, on a pro-rata basis, to an annual reduction in National Economic Growth of the order of 0.5%. Regular diversion of these amounts of money from the Economy, which showed a Growth Rate of only 1.5% in 1990, must affect the options available for development.

The physical, social and financial consequences of the operation of natural environmental processes on the activities in Australian cities leads, inevitably, to their inclusion as an important element in Australian politics. This affects Local, State and Commonwealth Government activities. The problems of organisation, monitoring, control, financing and provision of authority involved in responding to natural processes must be resolved by legislation, and have required the commitment of considerable legislative time and expertise on a routine basis. They have led also to their involvement more specifically as items in State elections. A recent example is provided by the 1984 New South Wales election, when the Floodplain Mapping Programme, intended to form a basis for reducing flood hazard and damage, was seen to have implications for property values, became politically contentious, and was dropped[17].

This review of the roles played by environmental processes in the life of the Australian city demonstrates clearly that their apparent exclusion from consideration when The Bush Myth was revised to give way to The Urban Myth is unacceptable. It can even be argued that, far from being excluded from everyday urban life by the City, the environment actually intrudes into modern Australian life as much now as it ever did, although in different ways, and that the effects may even be more disruptive than before. Any realistic assessment of modern Australia, reflecting its urban nature, as is the aim of The Urban Myth, must therefore recognise:

- that the establishment and maintenance of the urban fabric depends upon the nature of the natural environment, and the benign operation of its processes,

- that this dependence extends well beyond the city area,
- that the effects of these limitations, the need to recognise their effects, and manage life accordingly must bring the environment into all aspects of social, financial and political life.

When adapted in this manner The Urban Myth will become more than a fashionable way of rejecting an apparently outdated concept. It will become, instead, a valid paradigm of modern Australia with significance not only within the natural and applied sciences but within the social sciences and humanities, and within society at large. The revised self-image which can then result must be beneficial to the rational development of the Nation as a whole.

NOTES

1. Observations on the origins of goldfield towns, and on the street pattern at Ballarat, are given in W. Bate, *Lucky City, The First Generation at Ballarat* (Melbourne: Melbourne University Press, 1978).
2. The significance of geology in the development of the Sydney area is discussed in P.J.N Pells, *Engineering Geology of the Sydney Region* (Rotterdam: A.A. Balkema, 1985).
3. Compare the *Investment Prospectus for Western Sydney* (Western Sydney Organisation of Councils, 1982) with the *Regional Environmental Study of the Sydney Region*, North West Sector. (New South Wales: Department of Environment and Planning, 1984).
4. See footnote 1.
5. See Water 2000. Consultant's Report No. 9, *In-Stream and Environmental Issues* (Canberra: Department of Resources and Energy, 1983); and State Pollution Control Commission, New South Wales, Annual Report for 1978-9.
6. See Water 2000. Consultant's Report No. 12, *Water Demand and Availability with Reference to Particular Regions*, (Canberra: Department of Resources and Energy, 1983).
7. See Water 2000. Consultant's Report No. 7, *Water Quality Issues* (Canberra: Department of Resources and Energy, 1983).
8. See *Report of the Environment Protection Authority*, Victoria, for the Year ended 30 June (Melbourne: Government Printer, 1984).
8. See *Annual Report of the State Pollution Control Commission*, New South Wales, for 1979-1980.
10. See R.L. Heathcote, B.G. Thom, *Natural Hazards in Australia* (Canberra: Australian Academy of Science, 1979); S. Leivesley, 'The Social Consequences of Australian Disasters', *Disasters*, vol. 4(1), pp. 30-37; and S. Leivesley, 'Natural Disasters in Australia', *Disasters*, vol. 8(2), pp. 83-88.
11. See Standing Committee on Environment and Conservation, *Bushfires and the Australian Environment* (Canberra: Australian Government Publishing Service, 1984) and N.P. Cheney, 'Bushfire disasters in Australia, 1945-1976', *Australian Forestry*, vol. 39(4) (1976), pp. 245-268.
12. See J.R.G. Butler, D.P. Doessel, 'Who bears the costs of natural disasters? - an Australian case study', *Disasters*, vol. 4(2) (1980), pp. 187-204.
13. See Water 2000, Consultant's Report No. 11. *Flooding in Australia*, (Canberra: Department of Resources and Energy, 1983); and D.I. Smith, J.W. Handmer, 'Urban Flooding in Australia: policy development and implementation', *Disasters*, vol. 8(2) (1984), pp.105-117.
14. See Bush Fire Council of New South Wales Leaflet, 'What does TOTAL FIRE BAN mean?'
15. See *Review of Australia's Water Resources 1975* (Australian Water Resources Council, 1976).
16. See *Report of Royal Commission into the Failure of West Gate Bridge* (Melbourne: Government Printer).
17. See *Water Resources Aspects of Drought in Australia* (Canberra: Department of Resources and Energy, 1983), Water 2000, Consultant's Report No. 13; and W.J. Gibbs, 'The great Australian drought', *Disasters*, vol. 8(2) (1982-83), pp. 89-104.
18. See J.W. Handmer, 'Flood policy reversal in New South Wales, Australia.' *Disasters*, vol. 9(4) (1985), pp. 279-285.

NOTES ON CONTRIBUTORS

STEPHEN ALOMES is the co-editor (with Catherine Jones) of *Australian Nationalism: A Documentary History* (Angus and Robertson, 1991) and with Dirk den Hartog of *Post-Pop: Popular Culture, Nationalism and Post-Modernism* (Footprint, VUT, 1991). He was the co-founder of the Australian Studies Association, co-edits its publication *Australian Studies* and is a Senior Lecturer in Australian Studies at Deakin University, Geelong, Victoria.

JOHN BARNES, reader in English at La Trobe University, is the Editor of *Meridian: The La Trobe University English Review*. He is the author of various studies in Australian literature, the most recent being *The Order of Things: A Life of Joseph Furphy*. His current research interests range from spiritualism in nineteenth-century Australia to recent Aboriginal writing in English.

BRUCE BENNETT is Professor of Australian literature at the Australian Defence Academy, Canberra. He is co-editor of *Westerly*, has written a biography on Peter Porter and is one of the foremost specialists in Australian Literature. His book, *Spirit in Exile* won the WA Premier's Historical and Critical Award.

CARL BRIDGE teaches at the history department at the University of New England, Armidale, NSW. He was previously deputy director at the Sir Robert Menzies Australian Studies Centre in London and his publications include *A Trunk Full of Books: The Official History of the State Library of South Australia* (Adelaide: Wakefield Press, 1986).

FRANK DAVIDSON teaches at the University of Sydney where he specialises in Australian literature.

TONY DENHOLM was born in England and educated at the Universities of Wales and London. He has taught at Manchester Polytechnic, the University of Hong Kong and for the past twenty-three years at Adelaide University where he is Associate Professor in History. He has written a history of the 1848 Revolution in France and a biography of Lord Ripon (1827-1909). In recent years he has published on aspects of British and South Australian urban history.

PETER FITZPATRICK is Senior Lecturer in English at Monash University, and Director of the University's centre for Dance and Theatre Studies. He is the author of *After 'The Doll': Australian Drama Since 1955* (1979) and critical books on the plays of David Williamson and Stephen Sewell, and is currently engaged on a biographical study of Louis Esson.

LIONEL FROST lectures in the Department of Economic History, School of Economics and Commerce, La Trobe University, Australia.

ROBIN GERSTER teaches Australian and Asian literature at Monash University, and has a special interest in urban fiction. He is the author of *Big-noting: The Heroic Theme in Australian War Writing* (winner of the *Age* 'Book of the Year' award for non-fiction in 1988), *Seizures of Youth: 'The Sixties and Australia* (1991), and numerous articles in books (including *Vietnam Days* and *The Penguin New Literary History of Australia*), journals and newspapers.

GARETH GRIFFITHS is Professor of English and Head of Department at the University of Western Australia. He has written on post-colonial literatures and on modern (especially Australian) theatre. He is currently writing a *History of African Literature in English* (East and West) and editing a collection of essays on the work of John Romeril.

RENATE HOWE is associate Professor in the School of Humanities at the Centre for Australian Studies at the Deakin University, Victoria. At present she is a Research scholar in the Urban Research Program at the Australian National University, Canberra.

JUDITH KAPFERER was born and schooled in rural New South Wales, before attending the Universities of Sydney, Zambia and Manchester. She lecturers in the sociology of education at Flinders University from where she obtained a Ph. D. in Sociology in the early 1980s. She has published widely on youth policy, the role of the State in education, and social inequality, and is currently writing a book on contemporary Australian cultural practice.

RODERICK J. LAWRENCE graduated in architecture from the University of Adelaide, South Australia in 1972. After two years work in professional practice, in Sydney, he accepted a postgraduate research fellowship at St. John's College, Cambridge, England. From 1978 to 1984 he worked at the Ecole Polytechnique Federale de Lausanne, in Switzerland. Since then he has been a Consultant to the Committee for Housing, Building and Planning of the Economic Commission for Europe, and a Visiting Lecturer and Researcher at the School of Architecture at the University of Geneva. He is currently appointed to the Centre for Human Ecology and Environmental Sciences at the University of Geneva. He has published numerous articles and chapters of monographs in both English and French concerning,the reciprocal relations between architectural and behaviourial parameters in housing, building and planning from cross-cultural, societal and psychological perspectives that address historical processes. He is also the author of two books: *Le Seuil franchi: logement populaire et vie quotidienne en Suisse romande, 1860-1960* (Georg Editeur, Geneva, 1986) and *Housing, Dwellings and Homes: Design Theory, Research and Practice* (John Wiley, Chichester, 1987).

COLIN PATRICK lectures in the Institute of Environmental and Biological Sciences at the University of Lancaster.

HELEN PROUDFOOT is an Urban History Consultant and Planner based in Sydney. She has done much research and consultancy work on the early foundations of Sydney.

PETER PROUDFOOT is Associate Professor in the School of Architecture at the University of New South Wales.

PETER QUARTERMAINE is associate Professor of the Centre for American and Commonwealth Arts and Studies at the University of Exeter. He is editor of *Diversity Itself* and has done much research on Australian art and literature.

ANNA RUTHERFORD is a graduate of the University of Newcastle, NSW and has taught for many years at Aarhus University, Denmark. She is editor of the international arts magazine *Kunapipi* and director of Dangaroo Press. She was born and grew up in the suburb of Mayfield, Newcastle and lived at 67 Scholey Street, Mayfield.

ARNIS SIKSNA is a Senior Lecturer in urban design at the Department of Geographical Sciences and Planning, The University of Queensland. He has worked both in architecture and town planning, and between 1973 and 1978 was chief planner at the National Capital Development Commission in Canberra. His teaching and research interests concern the urban form of cities – their layout, their design, their urban spaces, and their evolution in response to cultural factors.

JENNIFER STRAUSS teaches in the English Department of Monash University. Author of a number of reviews, critical articles and of *Boundary Conditions: the Poetry of Gwen Harwood* (due in 1992 from University of Queensland Press), she is also a widely published poet, with three collections: *Children and Other Strangers* (1975), *Winter Driving* (1981), and *Labour Ward* (1988).

SHURLEE SWAIN lectures in the Humanities Department, Deakin University, Victoria.

HELEN THOMSON is a Senior Lecturer in the English Department of Monash University. She has edited three volumes of Catherine Helen Spence's writing, and published in the area of Australian women's writing. Her teaching interests include 18th century feminism and she has been theatre critic for *The Australian* and The *Sunday Herald* newspapers for many years.